STRESS TEST

STRESS TEST

Reflections on Financial Crises

TIMOTHY F. GEITHNER

BUSINESS
BOOKS

1 3 5 7 9 10 8 6 4 2

Random House Business Books
20 Vauxhall Bridge Road
London SW1V 2SA

Random House Business Books is part of the Penguin Random House group of
companies whose addresses can be found at global.penguinrandomhouse.com.

Penguin
Random House
UK

First published in Great Britain by Random House Business Books in 2014

www.randomhouse.co.uk

A CIP catalogue record for this book is available from the British Library.

ISBN 9781847941244

Printed and bound in Great Britain by
CPI Group (UK) Ltd, Croydon, CR0 4YY

For the intrepid public servants at the Treasury and the
Federal Reserve who worked with great skill and devotion
to help guide their country through the crisis

CONTENTS

STRESS TEST

INTRODUCTION

The Bombs

On the morning of January 27, 2009, my first full day as secretary of the Treasury, I met with President Barack Obama in the Oval Office. The worst financial crisis since the Great Depression was still raging, and he wanted to put out the fire for good. The banking system was broken. The broader economy was contracting at a Depression-level rate. Consumer confidence had sunk to an all-time low, and millions more Americans were in danger of losing their jobs, their savings, even their homes. The President looked calm and reasonably comfortable after a week in the White House, despite all the bad news he was getting.

I was about to give him some more.

First, I thanked him for coming to my swearing-in the night before, a nice gesture of personal confidence in me. We had met just three months earlier, and I was in many ways an unorthodox choice to lead Treasury. I wasn't a banker, an economist, a politician, or even a Democrat. I was a registered independent without much of a public profile—and the profile I had didn't exactly signal Obama-style hope and change. As head of the Federal Reserve Bank of New York,

I had spent the past year working with a Republican Fed chairman, Ben Bernanke, and a Republican Treasury secretary, Henry Paulson, Jr., to design a series of spectacularly unpopular rescues of financial firms. I didn't look like a Treasury secretary, either. I was forty-seven. I lacked gray-haired gravitas. Barney Frank, one of my closest allies in Congress, later observed that when I spoke in public, I looked like I was at my own bar mitzvah.

And I was already politically damaged goods. I had been portrayed throughout my confirmation hearings as a tax cheat, a tool of Wall Street, an enemy of Main Street. Even though I had spent the previous two decades in public service, I was routinely described as a venal investment banker. Some thought I might be the first Treasury nominee rejected since before the Civil War, and I had considered withdrawing before the vote. I was eventually confirmed, by the narrowest margin since World War II; I already felt crushing guilt about the humiliation I was forcing on my family, and the political capital the President had to spend on me.

But now it was time to get to work. I took a seat on a sofa facing away from the Rose Garden, the seat I would take hundreds of times over the next four years. The President sat in his official chair to my right. On the couch across from me was the renowned economist Larry Summers, a former Treasury secretary who had met me when I was a junior civil servant in the department and had helped promote me up the ranks. Now Larry was running the President's National Economic Council, so we would fight the crisis together. It should have been an exciting moment for me—a career technocrat entering the epicenter of power, alongside a brilliant former boss and an inspiring new president.

It didn't feel exciting. It felt dark and daunting.

I had spent much of my career dealing with financial crises— in Mexico, Thailand, Indonesia, Korea, and beyond—but this was the big one, the hundred-year storm. Bernanke, Paulson, and I had already engineered a series of emergency interventions for a variety of financial giants, culminating in the Troubled Asset Relief Program (TARP), a $700 billion intervention for the entire financial system. But we hadn't ended the crisis. The index measuring the risk of corporate defaults was even higher than it had been after the chaotic collapse of the Lehman Brothers investment bank in September 2008, when stock markets crashed, bond markets went haywire, and even supposedly safe money market funds were overwhelmed. Foreclosures were at an all-time high. The economy was shedding more than 750,000 jobs a month.

We had slowed the post-Lehman panic, but the financial system was still frozen. Banks that had overextended themselves during the boom were now in defensive retreats, hoarding cash, depriving businesses of financial oxygen. There was virtually no private credit available for ordinary borrowers who wanted to finance a new car or a college education, much less a new home. We had slipped into a vicious cycle, as the financial earthquake began to ripple through the broader economy. As laid-off workers and other nervous consumers spent less, businesses were laying off more workers and investing less, prompting families and businesses to cut back even more. The crippled financial system was making the recession worse, while the deepening recession was making the financial system worse. Wall Street and Main Street were going down together. I had recently started reading Liaquat Ahamed's *Lords of Finance,* a history of the policymakers whose mistakes helped create and prolong the Great Depression, but I had put it down after a few chapters. It was too scary.

The President knew he couldn't fix the broader economy without fixing the financial system. Banks are like the economy's circulatory system, as vital to its everyday functioning as the power grid. No economy can grow without a financial system that works, safeguarding the savings of individuals, moving money where it's needed, helping families and businesses invest in their futures. And ours was still a mess.

"Now that I'm official, I can tell you how bad it really is," I said.

• • •

FOR STARTERS, I told the President, we still had five "financial bombs" to defuse.

By bombs, I meant huge, far-flung, overleveraged institutions whose failure could spark the kind of global panic the Lehman bankruptcy had sparked in the fall. I listed them: Fannie Mae, Freddie Mac, AIG, Citigroup, and Bank of America. They all were much larger than Lehman. All five had received major infusions of government cash to save them from failure; AIG had been rescued three times in four months. But they all were in trouble again, and we needed to make sure they didn't explode—not to protect them from the consequences of their mistakes, but to prevent another messy failure from ravaging the rest of the economy. The politics would be awful. People hated the idea of government bailouts for mismanaged financial behemoths. But if their creditors or the markets in general lost confidence that any of them could meet their obligations, we'd be looking at a worldwide financial meltdown, and a much deeper economic crisis.

Fannie and Freddie, the Washington-based housing giants that backed most U.S. mortgages, needed the most help. They were quickly burning through nearly $200 billion in taxpayer aid, and without another $200 billion or so—the equivalent of more than three years' worth of federal education department spending—they risked catastrophic defaults. Even a modest increase in that risk would push mortgage rates higher and home prices lower, intensifying the recession.

AIG was the closest to exploding, and the most egregious financial basket case. But while the century-old insurer had become a three-letter symbol of excessive risk, AIG also had tens of millions of innocent policyholders and pensioners who depended on it, plus tens of thousands of derivatives contracts with businesses around the world. A default on its debts or even a downgrade of its credit rating would reignite the panic.

Citi and Bank of America were the biggest of the bombs, Exhibits

A and B for the outrage over "too big to fail" banks; my aides called them the Financial Death Stars. But the world was so fragile, and they really were so big, that if we didn't want a reprise of the Depression— an obliterated banking sector, 25 percent unemployment, thousands of businesses shuttered—we had to make sure they didn't drag down the system, even if it looked like we were rewarding the reckless.

That was a lot to dump on a new president's plate. But the problem was bigger than the bombs.

We weren't just dealing with five severely undercapitalized firms that could blow up the financial system. We were dealing with a severely undercapitalized system. Even after the TARP investments and our other emergency assistance, it did not have enough capital to cover its potential losses, much less finance an economic recovery. And Larry and I were concerned that our new administration didn't have enough cash—or enough authority—to repair it.

My former New York Fed colleagues had privately calculated that the banking sector alone might need another $290 billion to survive a bad recession, and as much as $684 billion to survive an "extreme stress scenario." Those numbers didn't include the potential cost of stabilizing "nonbank" financial institutions such as AIG. They didn't include the potential cost of rescuing General Motors and Chrysler, which were also on the verge of bankruptcy. And we had only about $300 billion left in uncommitted TARP funds.

Larry and I told the President we might have to ask for another TARP, at a time when Congress had zero interest in more bailouts.

I couldn't claim I knew exactly what would work. There hadn't been a crisis this severe in seventy-five years, and never in a financial system this complex. Repairing our banks and other financial institutions, while necessary, would not be sufficient to fix the economy. That's why the President was already pushing a massive fiscal stimulus bill—$800 billion in government spending and tax cuts—to offset lost income and wealth, revive demand, and create jobs. The Fed was also expanding the frontiers of stimulus through monetary policy.

Financial rescue, fiscal stimulus, and monetary stimulus—along with the President's efforts to prop up the beleaguered auto and housing sectors—would all have to work together, if they were to work at all.

But stabilizing the financial system was our most immediate problem. A renewed banking panic would quickly overwhelm any fiscal and monetary support we could provide. Larry and I were convinced we had to try to get ahead of the crisis, instead of continuing to chase it from behind. We told the President we had to err on the side of doing too much, even though the public thought we were already doing too much. In an emergency, temporizing half-measures would be riskier than overwhelming force, and ultimately more expensive for taxpayers—not only in dollars, but in lost jobs, failed businesses, and foreclosed homes.

The President took all this in quietly, patiently, seemingly unfazed. His instinct was to move quickly to repair and restructure the entire financial system, not to let it limp along or sweep its problems under the rug. He wanted to be aggressive and comprehensive.

"We need to rip the Band-Aid off," he said. "I want to do this right, and get it over with."

I agreed, but with a qualification. There was intense pressure on us to punish the Wall Street gamblers who had gotten us into this mess—to nationalize or liquidate floundering firms, or force bondholders to accept "haircuts" rather than the face value of their bonds. Those get-tough actions would feel resolute and righteous, but in a time of uncertainty, they would damage confidence and accelerate the downward spiral. As we had seen in the panic of the fall, that would hurt Main Street, not just Wall Street. We wanted to avoid the long, sideways drift that Japan had experienced after its crisis in the 1990s, but also the trauma of another Great Depression.

"We do have to rip the Band-Aid off," I said. "But we have to make sure we don't break the financial system."

The President wasn't sure what I meant, so Larry translated: "What Tim means is, we can't afford a plan that shatters a fragile system, destroys confidence, and causes the stock market to crash."

The President's charge was direct and forceful: Come back soon with a plan to clean up this mess. He wanted to do the hard stuff early, take the pain quickly. "Leave the politics to me," he said. Just focus on the substance, what will work best, how to restore confidence. He understood the inherent uncertainty we faced, the real possibility that reasonable decisions would produce horrible results, the absence of a perfect or even an attractive option. He made it clear he was willing to take serious risks to try to get this nightmare behind us.

I was impressed. But I didn't feel very confident.

EVERY FINANCIAL crisis is a crisis of confidence.

Financial systems, after all, are built on belief. That's why the word *credit* is derived from the Latin for *believe,* why we say we can "bank" on things we believe true, why financial institutions often call themselves "trusts." Think about how a traditional bank worked. Depositors entrusted it with their money, confident it could repay them with interest at any time. The bank then lent out their money at a higher interest rate, confident that everyone wouldn't want their money back at the same time. But when people lost confidence in a bank—sometimes because of rational concerns about its lending or leadership, sometimes not—they *would* all want their money back at the same time. The result was a run on the bank, like the famous scene in *It's a Wonderful Life* when depositors rush to pull their money out of a Depression-era savings and loan. Confidence is a fragile thing. When it evaporates, it usually evaporates quickly. And it's hard to get back once it's lost.

A financial crisis is a bank run writ large, a run on an entire financial system. People lose confidence that their money is safe—whether they're stockholders or bondholders, institutional investors or elderly widows—so they rush to pull it out of the system, which makes the money remaining in the system even less safe, which makes everyone even less confident. This has happened a lot throughout history, in rich countries and poor ones, in sophisticated systems and simple ones. Human beings are prone to panics, just as we are prone to the kind of irrational confidence (in real estate, or stocks, or seventeenth-century Dutch tulips) that produces the booms that precede panics. And once the stampede begins, it becomes rational for individuals to join it to avoid getting trampled, even though their collective actions are irrational for society as a whole. These panics almost always have brutal consequences—for teachers and construction workers, not just investors and bankers—and policymakers almost always make them worse.

The question facing us in early 2009 was: How can the government restore confidence during a crisis? Part of the answer, while distasteful, was simple. The government can stand behind faltering firms, removing the incentives that turn fear into panic. Banks under siege used to stack money in their windows to reassure depositors there was no need to run; when governments put enough "money in the window," they can reduce the danger they'll have to use it. The classic example is deposit insurance, Franklin Delano Roosevelt's response to Depression-era bank runs. Since 1934, the government has guaranteed deposits at banks, so insured depositors who get worried that their bank has problems no longer have an incentive to yank out their money and make the problems worse.

Of course, the banking system that FDR inherited didn't have "collateralized debt obligations," "asset-backed commercial paper," or other complexities of twenty-first-century finance. In the panic of 2008, insured bank deposits didn't run on any significant scale, but all kinds of other frightened money did—and in the digital age, a run doesn't require any physical running, just a phone call or a click of a mouse. By early 2009, the government had put a lot of money in the window through TARP and other emergency measures. We had backstopped tens of trillions of dollars' worth of financial liabilities. But the financial system was still paralyzed. The markets could see the five bombs. And our crisis response had seemed so inconsistent, with so many policy zigzags and unexpected lurches, that investors and creditors were uncertain we had the capacity and the will to finish the job. Uncertainty is also at the heart of all financial crises. They simply don't end without governments assuming risks that private investors won't, taking catastrophe off the table.

The obvious objection to government help for troubled firms was that it rewarded the arsonists who set the system on fire. This objection took two forms. One was a moral argument about justice, what I called the "Old Testament view." The venal should be punished. The irresponsible shouldn't be bailed out. The other was an economic argument about incentives, the "moral hazard" critique. If you protect risk-takers from losses today, they'll take too many risks tomorrow, creating new crises in the future. If you rescue pyromaniacs, you'll end up with more fires.

Those are valid concerns. And in most states of the world, they're sensible guides for action. During a typical recession or even a limited crisis, firms should face the consequences of their mistakes, and so should the investors who lend them money. But trying to mete out punishment to perpetrators during a genuinely systemic crisis—by letting major firms fail or forcing senior creditors to accept haircuts—can pour gasoline on the fire. It can signal that more failures and haircuts are coming, encouraging creditors to take their money and run. It can endanger strong as well as weak institutions, because in a stampede, the herd can't tell the difference; that's basically the definition of a financial crisis. Old Testament vengeance appeals to the populist fury of the moment, but the truly moral thing to do during a raging financial inferno is to put it out. The goal should be to protect the innocent, even if some of the arsonists escape their full measure of justice.

Our approach did create some moral hazard, although the critics I came to call "moral hazard fundamentalists" tended to overstate our generosity to failed risk-takers. Shareholders in the five bombs had already absorbed huge losses; the leaders of Fannie, Freddie, and AIG had been pushed out; Lehman had ceased to exist. But the larger point, as President Obama later said, was that you shouldn't refuse to deploy fire engines to a burning neighborhood in order to highlight the dangers of smoking in bed. The President told me to focus on firefighting.

• • •

ON FEBRUARY 9, the President pitched his fiscal stimulus bill in Elkhart, Indiana, where unemployment had soared from 5.2 percent to 19.1 percent in just a year. But that night, at his first press conference as president, he emphasized that stimulus was only part of the solution. Credit needed to start flowing again, and confidence in the financial system needed to come back.

"Tomorrow, my Treasury secretary, Tim Geithner, will be announcing some very clear and specific plans," he said. A reporter asked him to elaborate, but he said to wait a day. He could not have been more generous, or raised expectations any higher: "I don't want to preempt my secretary of the Treasury. He's going to be laying out these principles in great detail tomorrow. . . . I want to make sure that Tim gets his moment in the sun."

A small team of advisers had been working around the clock with me on a financial stability strategy, but so far we had only a general framework in place. We weren't actually planning to announce the specifics of our plan. My team had anticipated this problem in an internal memo: "Many details will remain opaque at initial launch. This could create great uncertainty and volatility in markets." And we had another problem: few of our other colleagues thought highly of our strategy, not even Larry.

But the President went out of his way to express confidence about my debut, even urging the White House press corps to come see me speak.

"He's going to be terrific!" the President said.

I DOUBTED that.

Treasury secretaries are supposed to inspire confidence. Our signatures go on dollar bills. And I knew that good theater—being clear and calm, conveying an impression of competence and credibility—could be as important to confidence as good substance. But I had always been a backstage guy. I had spent my career behind the scenes. Ever since high school, I had dreaded public speaking. Now I had to perform for the world for the first time, using a teleprompter for the first time. And I didn't feel great about my message. I had lived through enough crises to know that they're always unpredictable and blanketed with fog. Americans desperately wanted assurances that things would get better soon, and I wasn't sure how to project an air of confidence I didn't feel.

Theater aside, it seemed unlikely that an angry public would embrace anything I had to say after my ugly confirmation fight. And what I had to say seemed unlikely to ease the anger no matter who said it. I would be pledging more government support for financial firms, which was not what a bailout-weary nation wanted to hear. The fact that my framework was so contentious inside our administration suggested it probably wouldn't inspire wild enthusiasm outside the administration.

Our strategy was also rather novel, which would make it an even harder sell. We didn't intend to preemptively nationalize major banks, and we didn't intend to let them fail; both of those familiar strategies would have accelerated the panic, but they would have been a lot easier to explain. The centerpiece of our approach was a "stress test," which sounded more like analysis than action. Regulators would delve into the books of major financial firms to calculate how much additional capital they would need to survive a truly catastrophic downturn, just as doctors stress-test patients to see how their bodies would respond to strenuous conditions. The firms would then be required to raise enough capital to fill the gap. And if an unhealthy firm couldn't raise enough from private investors, government would forcibly inject the missing capital.

This was key. The stress test would be more than a rigorous test. It would be a mechanism to recapitalize the financial system so that banks would have the resources to promote rather than prevent growth. We'd give them a chance to prove they could attract the cash they would need to survive a depression without our help.

If they couldn't, we wouldn't stand by and let their failure trigger a meltdown. We'd rely on private capital whenever possible, but we'd turn to public financing when necessary. The stress test would provide a form of triage, separating the fundamentally healthy from the terminally ill. And by ensuring the system could sustain depression-like losses, we thought we could make a depression less likely.

But I wasn't ready to provide much detail yet. We hadn't figured out how the stress test would work. And the rest of my speech was just as vague. I would announce a new program to buy some of the distressed assets that were weighing down banks, while acknowledging that it wasn't ready. I would promise "a comprehensive plan to address the housing crisis," with little further explanation. And I would signal that we would not allow any more Lehman-style failures, a crucial commitment designed to prevent an even more chaotic run, but that line was hedged and buried in my twenty-sixth paragraph.

As the President had promised, this would be my moment in the sun. The world wanted to see American leadership. The markets wanted to see a credible plan. The public wanted to see change it could believe in, the "Yes We Can" audacity that had fueled the President's journey to the White House. And everyone wanted to see if his embattled new Treasury secretary was up to the job. As I took the stage in Treasury's ornate Cash Room, in front of a profusion of giant flags that made me look like a politician at a campaign event, I knew my reputation was at stake.

It's fair to say the speech did not go well.

I swayed back and forth, like an unhappy passenger on an unsteady ship. I kept peering around the teleprompter to look directly at the audience, which apparently made me look shifty; one commentator said I looked like a shoplifter. My voice wavered. I tried to sound forceful, but I just sounded like someone trying to sound forceful. Early on, I caught a glimpse of *Wall Street Journal* financial columnist David Wessel, and I could tell from his pained expression that I was in trouble. The President had raised expectations. I was deflating them.

Stocks plummeted more than 3 percent before I even finished talking and nearly 5 percent by the end of the day—not quite a crash, but not good. Financial stocks would drop 11 percent for the day. After I finished, I sat down with the NBC anchor Brian Williams—my first television interview ever—and saw a graphic on the screen: "Is Geithner's Neck on the Line?" Williams began by invoking a prominent financial commentator.

"I heard Larry Kudlow say: 'Geithner was really kind of a disaster,'" he said. "Mr. Secretary, that was among the nicer comments I heard from Larry Kudlow."

Kudlow was not an outlier. I didn't read the reviews at the time, but the phrase "deer in the headlights" appeared in a lot of them. An actor playing me opened *Saturday Night Live* by announcing that my solution to the crisis was to give $420 billion to the first caller with a solution to the crisis. The substantive critiques were just as withering. "Someone should have told Treasury Secretary Timothy Geithner that the one thing to avoid at a time of uncertainty is raising more questions," the *New York Times* editorial board declared. The widely respected *Financial Times* columnist Martin Wolf actually began his analysis: "Has Barack Obama's presidency already failed?"

It was a bad speech, badly delivered, rattling confidence at a bad time. I somehow managed to convince the public we'd be overly generous to Wall Street while convincing the markets we wouldn't be generous enough. Our populist critics concluded we were more eager than ever to shovel cash to arsonists; former World Bank chief economist Joseph Stiglitz described our plan as "banks win, investors win—and taxpayers lose." But banks and investors were mostly confused.

"Investors want clarity, simplicity and resolution," one financial executive told Reuters. "This plan is seen as convoluted, obfuscating and clouded."

After my speech, a friend emailed me Teddy Roosevelt's "Man in the Arena" quote about how it's not the critic who counts, but the man "who comes up short again and again . . . who at the worst, if he fails, at least fails while daring greatly." I thought it was a nice hang-in-there sentiment, until my inbox began filling up with variations on the Man in the Arena. Another friend called to say that what didn't kill me would make me stronger, which I didn't find all that reassuring, either. I knew I'd have to resign if our strategy didn't work—and more important, the economy was hanging in the balance. At his daily economics briefing the morning after my speech, the President was not happy.

"How the hell did this happen?" he asked.

He wasn't trying to put it all on me, but I knew it was all on me. And there wasn't much I could do or say to reassure him or anyone else. We just had to start laying out details of our plan, and hope we could convince people it was a good plan. I figured that if we did what we said we would do, and it worked, confidence would eventually come back. And if it didn't work, the quality of our theater wouldn't matter much.

HISTORY SHOWS that even modest financial crises cause horrific pain.

One study of fourteen severe twentieth-century crises found that, on average, the unemployment rates in the affected countries jumped 7.7 percentage points. Many of them ended up nationalizing most or all of their banking systems. Financial crises have also been exorbitantly costly for taxpayers. The direct fiscal costs—just the money that governments have spent stabilizing their financial systems—have averaged more than 10 percent of GDP. For the United States, that would have amounted to about $1.5 trillion.

There was nothing modest about our crisis. It began with a colossal financial shock, a loss of household wealth five times worse than the shock that precipitated the Depression. Bond spreads rose about twice as sharply in the Lehman panic as in the panic of 1929. Serious investors were buying gold in bulk and talking about burying it in their yards. Stock markets dropped to more than 50 percent below their 2007 highs.

Naturally, most analysts expected that U.S. taxpayers would pay an astronomical price to repair our financial system, too. Simon Johnson, a former chief economist of the International Monetary Fund, warned that the government's price tag could be $1 trillion to $2 trillion, "in line with the experience" of other nations. An IMF study estimated the final tab at nearly $2 trillion. "If we spent a million dollars a day every day since the birth of Christ, we wouldn't get to $1 trillion," said Congressman Darrell Issa, the top Republican on the House government oversight committee. "And we're likely to lose far more than that."

But we didn't.

Our outcomes were not in line with the experience of other nations, in past crises or this crisis. They were much better. By that summer, we had not only averted a depression, our economy had started growing again. House prices stabilized. Credit markets thawed. And our emergency investments would literally pay off for taxpayers.

Most Americans still believe we threw away billions or even trillions of their hard-earned dollars to bail out greedy banks. In fact, the financial system repaid all our assistance, and U.S. taxpayers have turned a profit from our crisis response, including our investments in all five of those financial bombs. We had been so worried about our limited resources that the President's first budget included a $750 billion placeholder for a second TARP, but in the end, we didn't have to ask Congress for another dime.

Of course, our goal wasn't to earn money for taxpayers. Our goal was to save the families and businesses of America from the calamitous pain of a failing financial system. I hoped we wouldn't have to spend 10 percent of GDP to fix that system, but everyone I know would have gladly paid that fiscal price to avoid reliving the 1930s. As one of my close advisers, Meg McConnell, blurted out during a tense moment in the crisis, we were not far from a rebirth of Depression-era shantytowns. And no one I know—neither critics who thought we were foolish nor supporters who thought we might know what we were doing—imagined that we would put out the financial fire so quickly and actually make money on our investments.

The recession of 2007 to 2009 was still the most painful since the Depression. At its depths, $15 trillion in household wealth had disappeared, ravaging the pensions and college funds of Americans who had thought their money was in good hands. Nearly 9 million workers lost jobs; 9 million people slipped below the poverty line; 5 million homeowners lost homes. Behind those numbers lies real suffering by real people who didn't put banks in danger with reckless bets they didn't understand. I had relatives and friends and relatives of friends who lost jobs and much of their savings, who saw their businesses devastated. Even when they were gracious to me, I could see in their eyes and hear in their voices a sense of: Why couldn't you protect me from this? Pointing out that the downturn could have been much worse won't help pay their rent or feed their kids.

But it's true.

Our unemployment rate rose to 10 percent, but not to 25 percent as in the Depression. By the end of 2013, it was below 7 percent. Our recovery began much faster than was typical in previous crises, and it's been much stronger than the recoveries of other major advanced nations. Our output returned to pre-crisis levels in 2011; output in Japan, Great Britain, and the eurozone had yet to do so by 2014. We've had private-sector job growth every month for the past four years, restoring almost all of the 8.8 million jobs lost in the Great Recession. The stock market has exceeded its pre-crisis peak, so retirement funds that lost $5 trillion during the crisis have gained it back. Many Americans are still suffering, but a lot more suffering has been averted.

And yes, the financial system is alive and flourishing again. That's partly because of the strategy I helped design and execute, which is why I'm often described as a "Wall Street ally." The *New York Times* once did an amusing story about my unearned reputation as a "Wall Street insider." People still seem to think I cut my teeth at Goldman Sachs. But nothing we did during the financial crisis was motivated by sympathy for the banks or the bankers. Our only priority was limiting the damage to ordinary Americans and people around the world.

During the crisis, we did a lot of things that would be unthinkable in normal times in a capitalist economy. But we kept our promises that our interventions would be as limited as possible. By the end of 2010, the U.S. government no longer owned a piece of any major bank. By contrast, the federal government's 1984 takeover of Continental Illinois—the seventh largest U.S. bank at the time, a tiny fraction of the size of some of the troubled banks in our crisis—lasted seven years before the bank returned to private control.

Our economy is still reeling from the worst financial crisis in generations. Our jobless rate is too high and income growth is too low. But the U.S. recovery has outperformed expectations, history, and most of the developed world. So far, the prophets of doom who have predicted runaway inflation, runaway interest rates, a double-dip recession, a collapse in demand for U.S. government securities, and other horrors for America have been false prophets. I remember half-joking to the President that we had two types of critics attacking us for failing to produce a stronger recovery—people who were blocking our proposals to produce a stronger recovery, and people who believed in unicorns.

Still, plenty of Americans who don't believe in unicorns do believe we bungled the crisis. The public despised our financial rescues, to the extent that the President joked at a Washington dinner in mid-2009 that he needed to house-train his dog, Bo, "because the last thing Tim Geithner needs is someone else treating him like a fire hydrant." And the outrage has endured. Conventional wisdom still holds that we abandoned Main Street to protect Wall Street—except on Wall Street, where conventional wisdom holds that President Obama is a radical socialist consumed with hatred for moneymakers. The financial reform law that we wrote and pushed through a bitterly divided Congress after the crisis, the most sweeping overhaul of financial rules since the Depression, is widely viewed as too weak, except in the financial world, where it is described as an existential threat.

Those perceptions are partly my fault, failures of communication and persuasion.

I'm proud of most of the decisions we made to try to save the economy. And I'm under no illusions that better marketing or better speechmaking could have made those decisions popular. That said, I never found an effective way to explain to the public what we were doing and why. We did save the economy, but we lost the country doing it. As the crisis was winding down, I suggested to my adviser Jake Siewert that Treasury ought to put out a long white paper explaining the rationale behind all our controversial decisions. He grinned and said: "Sounds great. Why don't you give it a shot?" I remember when I met Barbra Streisand at a White House state dinner in 2011, she told me: "Mr. Secretary, when I see you on TV, I get the feeling you're not telling us everything."

I laughed and replied: "You have no idea."

I can try to remedy that now.

Our response to the global financial crisis is still wrapped in myth and haze and misperception. And I was in the middle of it from start to finish, from boom to bust to rescue to recovery, leading the New York Fed from 2003 to 2008 and the Treasury from 2009 until I left public service in January 2013. Ben Bernanke, my closest colleague when I served at the Fed and then as Treasury secretary, was the only other principal combatant who fought the entire war. This gives me a particular perspective on how we got into the mess, how we got out of the mess, and how we tried to make future messes less frequent and damaging.

This book is the story of the choices we made before, during, and after the crisis. Not every choice was right, but this won't be an if-only-they-had-listened-to-me memoir, because I supported almost every choice at the time. I couldn't force our opponents in Congress or our counterparts in Europe to embrace our proposals, but I didn't lose many policy battles inside the Fed or the Obama White House. We almost always did what I thought was right and necessary, within the very real limits of our authority at the time.

The financial crisis really was a stress test for the men and women in the middle of it. The usual rhythm at central banks and finance ministries evokes the old line about life as a fighter pilot: months of boredom punctuated by moments of terror. We lived through months of terror. We endured seemingly endless stretches when global finance was on the edge of collapse, when we had to make monumental decisions in a fog of uncertainty, when our options all looked dismal but we still had to choose. If I had learned one thing from previous crises, it was the importance of humility—about our ability to figure out exactly what was going on, and our ability to parachute in with a simple solution. Those were useful thoughts to keep in mind during the cataclysm, but not uplifting thoughts.

The pressures we faced as first responders obviously paled in comparison to the sacrifices of many public servants, like real first responders or our troops overseas. We didn't expect medals or combat pay. But we felt an enormous burden of responsibility. And as my daughter Elise once reminded me, Americans at least understood our troops in Afghanistan were fighting for them. They weren't so sure about us.

The financial crisis was also a stress test of the American political system, an extreme real-time challenge of a democracy's ability to lead the world when the world needed creative, decisive, politically unpalatable action. That's not typically regarded as one of our great strengths, at least not in recent years, when the political news is usually about gridlock and dysfunction. And our interventions certainly didn't improve the public's opinion of government or politics.

Politics is not my life's work, but it left me with some scars, and I have some things to say about the soul-crushing pathologies of Washington. I witnessed some appalling behavior in the political arena—selfishness and grandstanding, shameless hypocrisy and mindless partisanship. At times, the failures of our political system imposed tragic constraints on our ability to make the crisis less damaging and the recovery stronger. And yet, at the moments of most extreme peril, the system worked. Two administrations—one Republican, one Democratic—managed to do what was necessary to end the crisis, start a recovery, and reform the system, attracting just enough bipartisan support to get a polarized Congress to do its part. A fractious group of policymakers worked together surprisingly well—arguing, agonizing, sometimes agreeing to disagree, but mostly trying to get the right answer, minimizing the time wasted on bureaucratic conflict.

Today, much of the public is skeptical that government is capable of managing a two-car funeral. Young Americans are reluctant to enter public service, and it's hard to blame them. But our system passed its stress test.

I hope this book will help answer some of the questions that still linger about the crisis. Why did it happen, and how did we let it happen? How did we decide who got bailed out? Why didn't we nationalize the banks, or let more banks fail? How did we convince the left we were Wall Street's wingmen while convincing Wall Street we were Che Guevaras in suits? Why didn't we do more (or less) about the housing market? Why didn't we get more (or less) fiscal stimulus? Why isn't the economy booming again? And what really happened with Lehman, anyway? Couldn't we have put out the fire back then?

This book is not intended to be a comprehensive minute-by-minute narrative of the financial crisis. Others have done that, although their accounts usually end in 2008. And this is certainly not a definitive history of economic policy in President Obama's first term. It's a history from one policymaker's perspective of the events leading to the crisis, the key choices we made during the crisis, the aftershocks of the crisis, and the fight to reform the system. I hope this book can add to the historical record, help correct some misperceptions that have been entered into that record, and give a sense of what it was like in the fire.

There is another reason I'm writing this book. Financial crises are perilous, and this won't be the last one. Yet the United States has no standing army for fighting financial wars, no Joint Chiefs of Staff, no

War College. It also has no playbook. All financial crises are different, but they have a lot in common, and there are lessons to learn from this extreme one that can help policymakers and the public during the next one. I hope this story can help illuminate them.

I start with my own education in financial crises during my first stint at Treasury, as I helped former secretaries Robert Rubin and Larry Summers confront a series of emerging-market messes. Many lessons of those crises would guide my approach to this crisis. I then describe my time as a financial regulator at the New York Fed before the boom went bust, discussing what I saw, what I did, and what I missed. I made mistakes during that period, though they weren't the mistakes most people think I made.

The heart of the story will be my perspective on the most harrowing crisis since the Great Depression, from its outbreak in 2007 through its resolution in 2009—not only the intense financial engineering that began during my time at the New York Fed, but our debates over the stimulus, the housing market, and the larger economy in the Obama era.

By the end of 2009, the worst of the crisis was over in the United States, but I still had a few challenges ahead of me. We were deep in the fight for Wall Street reform, our effort to set financial rules of the road that could make crises less frequent and less damaging in the future. Then Europe began to crumble, and I spent much of my remaining tenure urging the Europeans to tackle their crisis more aggressively. We also began a series of budget negotiations over the nation's fiscal path that nearly ended in catastrophe; our congressional Republican counterparts were threatening to force the U.S. government to default on our financial obligations, a true doomsday scenario.

These struggles were all echoes of the great crisis. But before I describe all this history, I ought to explain how I ended up in the thick of it. I wasn't an academic like Ben Bernanke or Larry Summers. I wasn't a Wall Street titan like Hank Paulson or Bob Rubin. I had more of an accidental path to history.

ONE

An American Abroad

I had an extraordinary childhood, but I was an ordinary kid.

I was a good student, never a great student. I was a decent athlete, nothing special. I wasn't particularly ambitious or hardworking. By the time I went to college, I had lived in Africa, India, and Thailand, through wars and coups, but I had little interest in politics, economics, or even current events. I had all kinds of amazing experiences—trips to Kashmir and Kenya, Beirut and Bali—but I rarely stopped to think about them.

My exotic upbringing didn't feel exotic at the time. It felt like life. Mostly, it felt like fun. I was lucky to grow up in a big, close, raucous family, with a lot of love and laughter, without a lot of drama. My sister, Sarah, is two years younger; my twin brothers, Jonathan and David, are four years younger. We were too busy playing and exploring to do much reflecting. My early memories are pleasant memories: trekking in Nepal, driving a small Boston Whaler off Cape Cod, dumping colored powder on my siblings during the Indian holiday of Holi. We weren't rich by American standards, but we were very privileged.

As unremarkable as my childhood seemed to me at the time, it exposed me to the world, to extreme poverty and vicious inequality, to diverse customs and cultures. My parents, Peter Franz Geithner and Deborah Moore Geithner, gave me this amazing gift of a global education. Even more important, they gave me a constant, generous, unconditional love. They taught me—by example, not by lecture— how to take life seriously without taking myself too seriously. They showed me how helping others can give work meaning. They modeled humility. They never pressured me to do this or do that, other than to be kind and curious, but they always seemed to have confidence in me, and that created confidence within me.

MY MOTHER is a musician, a teacher, a bleeding-heart liberal bursting with empathy and optimism. She says she has "up genes"; she got a tattoo of a horseshoe crab to keep her breast cancer scars company. She studied Hindi, Thai, and Chinese while living abroad. She's an enthusiast who shares her enthusiasm with everyone she meets, who makes lifelong friends everywhere she travels. My father is quieter, more reserved, more skeptical, more conservative in every way. He's an understated child of the fifties, a nice complement to my mother's exuberant spirit of the sixties. He's also a lifelong Republican, although he came of age in the Eisenhower era, before much of his party veered to the far right. He devoted his professional life to global development, not a typically conservative cause, and he voted for President Obama in 2008. But he supported Mitt Romney in 2012, even though I was still working for the President.

My mother is from a New England family dating back to the *Mayflower*, with relatives including the architect Buckminster Fuller, the journalist Margaret Fuller, and the novelist John Marquand. Her father, Charles F. Moore, Jr., was, among other things, a newspaperman, vice president of Ford Motor Company, and an adviser to President Eisenhower. Later in life, he served as a town selectman in Orleans, the small town on the Cape where my parents now live. My mother's older brother, Jonathan, spent his whole career in public service, helping to preserve the Cape Cod National Seashore as a Republican congressional aide, holding influential jobs at the U.S. Departments of State, Defense, and Justice, serving as the foreign policy adviser to Mitt's father George Romney's presidential campaign. I remember visiting him during the Watergate summer of 1973, just before President Nixon fired his boss, Attorney General Elliot Richardson, in the Saturday Night Massacre, and he resigned in protest. He was always busy, on the phone, doing consequential things. It made an impression on me.

My father's family didn't come to America on the *Mayflower* or work inside the American establishment. His father was a German immigrant who settled in north Philadelphia and ran a small business as a cabinetmaker. My father went to a public high school, mostly African American, where he was a star athlete, an excellent student, and his class president, a serious young man with a serious crew cut. The U.S. military paid his way through Dartmouth, where he made Phi Beta Kappa and—even though he was just five-foot-nine—captained the basketball team. He then spent four years as a Navy pilot, flying FJ-3 Furies and other fighter jets off carriers after the Korean War.

My parents met at Uncle Jonathan's wedding in 1957; my father, a friend of Jonathan's from Dartmouth, was the best man. He was also dating the sister of the bride. But my mother, then a freshman at Smith College, was drawn to him. When she heard he had moved to New York a few years later to work for a chemical manufacturing company, she sent him a Valentine from her dorm room. Nine months later, they were married. And they stayed married.

I was born in a Manhattan hospital on August 18, 1961. My mother says I was a wild and energetic baby, chasing her around our apartment before I could even walk. (To this day, I have a hard time sitting still.) My father soon joined the U.S. Agency for International Development and moved us to southern Rhodesia, which is now Zimbabwe, then to Northern Rhodesia, now Zambia. He took a job back at USAID headquarters when I was four, so we moved again to the Washington suburbs.

My mother tells stories about my close encounters with cobras, and a cloth diaper stuffed with coins that I used as a security blanket—my first interest in finance, she says—but I don't remember anything about Africa. I was apparently a mischievous kid. When our dachshund bit me, I tearfully admitted that I had bitten the dachshund first. Somewhat later in my youth, my mother tried washing out my mouth with soap when I cursed, but as my friends and colleagues know, that did not have a lasting effect. One of them suggested the title of this book should be *Bonfire of the Profanities*.

When I was six, the Ford Foundation asked my father to help run its programs in New Delhi. I still remember that first shock of India, driving in from the airport, overwhelmed by the heat and the smell, the strange and the awful. We drove to school seeing Brahman bulls wandering the roads, malnourished children—some crippled by adults to make them look more sympathetic—begging at every intersection.

I went to the American International School, which had an American curriculum, and I did American-kid things like join the swim team and play baseball. But unlike Foreign Service families, who were usually stationed at the embassy compound, we lived with other expats in an Indian neighborhood called Friends Colony. It was a quasi-colonial existence, with drivers, maids, gardeners, and night watchmen, but my parents' friends were Indian artists, activists, and intellectuals, as well as expats who worked at interesting places such as Oxfam, CARE, and the World Bank. My siblings and I played cricket with our cook's kids in our yard. We studied Hindi. My mother wore saris and *salwar kameez,* and sometimes dressed us in Nehru jackets and *churidar* pajamas. Our swim meets were sometimes held at the national stadium, in a pool full of dark green water, with frogs in the deep end and biting ants all over the deck.

Still, the contrast between how we lived and how most Indians lived was a constant presence in our lives. We always knew we were separated by fortune from hideous deprivation. I remember once after David had recovered from a broken leg, he handed his crutch out the car window to a disabled street kid. And since the Ford Foundation let us return to the United States every summer, we were always reminded of the wealth gap between America and much of the rest of the world. At a local supermarket in suburban Virginia one summer, I was stunned to see an entire aisle stocked with pet food. It seemed bizarre in a world full of starving people.

We returned to the United States after I finished sixth grade, when the Ford Foundation asked my father to run its developing-country programs from its headquarters in Manhattan. We settled into a traditional suburban lifestyle in Pelham, New York, a classic bedroom community north of the city. My father took the 5:36 p.m. train home from Grand Central almost every night when he wasn't traveling, so we could eat dinner together as a family. We attended an Episcopal church on Sundays, although we weren't very religious. I went to the public junior high school.

Initially, I felt like a visitor from another planet. I was tiny and scrawny, twenty pounds too light to qualify for Pop Warner football. I didn't make the basketball team, which was disappointing; my father once got an offer to try out for the Celtics. I had longish hair when that wasn't cool. I suffered a bit of junior high torture, kids dumping my school binders on the floor, papers flying everywhere. The culture was all new to me. I had never seen *All in the Family* or *Hawaii Five-0*. I didn't know what Pink Floyd was until a friend played me an album. The whole concept of going out with a girl seemed bizarre. Where were you supposed to go?

But I adapted. I played street hockey and touch football and stickball after school with a great group of kids on my block. I had a paper route. And toward the end of ninth grade, just as I was feeling comfortable in my own country, my parents announced that we were moving to Thailand, where my father was going to run the Ford

Foundation's programs in Southeast Asia. He wanted to be back in the field, not behind a desk in New York.

There's some trauma in moving a lot and having to find your place in new environments, but there's also the thrill of discovery. Bangkok was an incredibly appealing city, full of warm, tolerant, open people. My parents let me explore it on my own, by bus and taxi and three-wheel tuk-tuks. The end of our street was a typical crush of massage parlors and prostitution. Drugs were everywhere, and there was no apparent drinking age. That erased a lot of the allure.

I went to another American school in Bangkok. I got good grades without much effort. I liked the simple clarity of physics and math, much more than the messy complexity of government and history. I played baseball and tennis with modest distinction, but got cut from the basketball team twice; I served as manager for two seasons, taping my friends' sprained ankles, until I finally made the team. Somehow, I got elected president of my junior and senior classes; my main memory of that initial experience in leadership was how much I loathed public speaking. I've always gotten along pretty well with others, but I've never been a great communicator. When I left Treasury for the first time a couple decades later, a colleague would say in her farewell tribute that I spoke "a version of English so stripped down to the essentials that, like modern art, it can be incomprehensible." I guess I always have.

For a teenager, I was relatively free of angst, pretty comfortable in my skin. But I had no idea what I wanted to do in life. I remember taking one of those *What Color Is Your Parachute?* assessments, which concluded that I'd be good at a career in business. I thought: Well, maybe, but it doesn't sound that compelling. Other than an uncle who worked as a community banker, I had no real commercial influences in my life. I worked during our summers back in the States in Orleans—cleaning up a store on Main Street, then selling clothes at the store—but that didn't spark any entrepreneurial enthusiasm. I didn't think much about how I would earn a living.

I was still generally clueless about the world. My father rarely talked about his development work, even when he took us on trips to visit orphanages in India and hill tribes in northern Thailand, and I rarely asked about it. India and Pakistan had a brief war while we were living in New Delhi, so we had curfews and early lights-out, but I didn't really understand what they were fighting about. There was a coup in Thailand while we were there, but I wasn't aware of the cause; my brother Jonathan remembers me consoling him because the coup forced us to cancel a beach vacation.

Still, it was impossible to live in Southeast Asia in the wake of the Vietnam War without becoming conscious of the world's ambivalence toward America. In many ways, being abroad made me more aware of the exceptional things about America, but it took the edge off the more triumphal forms of American exceptionalism. I read *The Ugly American* and *The Quiet American,* books about our arrogance and ignorance of the world around us. I had an early exposure to the capacity of America to affect the world, in many ways for the better, in some ways not.

My parents didn't preach to us about these things. They believed in show, not tell. They exposed us to an incredible diversity of cultures and religions and customs, always without judgment. We learned to draw our own conclusions, to be curious about the world yet humble about our ability to understand it.

My first real adult decision was where to go to college. I had no idea what I really wanted, but I got into Dartmouth and Carleton; I got wait-listed at Williams and Wesleyan. My father and several other relatives had gone to Dartmouth, and I initially resisted the idea of going there—partly because I wanted to carve out my own path, partly because I felt guilty about the advantages I had applying as a legacy. I decided those were weak reasons not to go to a good school.

Dartmouth and the small college town of Hanover, New Hampshire, offered extreme culture shock when I arrived from Bangkok in 1979. It was cold, and I showed up without a winter coat. Academically, Dartmouth was much harder than my high school. And socially, I felt similar to the way I had felt after moving from India to Westchester for junior high: unfamiliar with and uncomfortable in the dominant culture. Most of my classmates seemed like they had been born at Exeter or Andover, and already knew exactly where their lives were headed. I had no idea.

I did have a moment of serendipity on my way to register for classes, when I overheard a professor swearing in Thai. It turned out that he had attended the same schools I had in India and Thailand. He suggested I sign up for Chinese, which I did and came to love, with the guidance of a great professor, Susan Blader. Otherwise, I was an unexceptional and mostly uninspired student. I had a few government classes I liked, but I took just one economics class and found it especially dreary. I had good friends, but I was not part of the fraternity mainstream on campus. I worked part-time throughout college to help cover the cost—washing dishes in the dining hall, taking photos for the college news service, working as a drill instructor for other students taking Chinese. I also did internships at Mobil Oil's corporate communications office and the Sawyer Miller political consulting firm. They were good experiences, I guess, but mostly in demonstrating that those lines of work were not for me.

I was a registered Republican then, but without much conviction. I had no passion for politics. I took pictures of the 1980 primary campaign for the college newspaper, but I don't remember if I even voted that year. I did develop a strong aversion to the strident conservative Republican political movement that was spreading across college campuses at the time. After the *Dartmouth Review,* the intellectual center of the movement, published a McCarthy-style list of gay students on campus, I ran into a *Review* writer named Dinesh D'Souza at a coffee shop and asked him how it felt to be such a dick. D'Souza would later become a celebrated right-wing intellectual and author of conspiracy-minded best sellers about President Obama, so I guess I didn't sway him. Several other *Review* founders would join the *Wall Street Journal* editorial page; they would not be big fans of my later work.

Some of my most important experiences during college happened off campus. The first was over Christmas break of my freshman year, when I got to photograph refugees in two massive camps along the Thai-Cambodian border for the Associated Press. These camps extended as far as the eye could see, with a horrifying level of deprivation and filth. They were filled with Khmer Rouge in black pajamas, fleeing the Vietnamese invasion of Cambodia. These victimizers turned victims cast a morally confusing shadow on the tragedy, but even after my experiences in India, the suffering left me numb. I took a lot of pictures, but there wasn't much satisfaction in depicting misery well. I loved the craft of photography, but I started to realize I did not want to spend my life as an observer. I wanted to do things, not just see things, even though I didn't know what it was I wanted to do.

I spent that summer as a low-level chef at a restaurant in Chatham on the Cape. I loved the manic energy the job required, the thrill of having to do six things at once, the unbridled profanity of the kitchen. But my next two summers were even more memorable, because I got to study in Beijing very early in China's opening to the West. Most of the foreign students there were from the Soviet Union or its satellites in Africa and North Korea; Americans lived in a special dorm, isolated from the others. On the walls of the showers, beneath a thin coat of white paint, we could make out Cultural Revolution slogans about evil American imperialists. The government read our mail. We were objects of fascination, surrounded by curious Chinese everywhere we went. We biked all over the city. I played Frisbee in Tiananmen Square. I remember one man at a market telling me he liked Americans, because we were optimistic and open like the Chinese—so different, he said, from the Japanese.

I was starting to wonder whether I wanted to live as a permanent expatriate, outside my own country yet never quite part of my host country, or whether I should become more of an American, with a community I could be part of. I took an unintentional leap toward door number two in the fall of my senior year, when I signed up to live in a run-down off-campus group house. I would join three house-mates, all of them women. One of them was Carole Sonnenfeld.

Plenty of men live with their wives before marrying them. How many men live with their wives before dating them? We fell in love quickly. Carole is an unbelievably appealing woman: strong, smart, beautiful, off-the-charts empathetic. She was a policy studies major, with a minor in economics—back then, she knew way more about the stuff I'd devote my career to than I did—but she was destined to be a social worker. She had already worked at a group home for emotionally disturbed teenagers and a legal office representing abused children. Anyway, we hit it off, and living together obviously acceler-ated things. As Carole's grandmother archly described our situation, it was *convenient*. We spent that wonderful first year living and study-ing together, cooking for our housemates, following recipes from her *Moosewood Cookbook* that still sits—heavily taped but intact—in our kitchen today.

CAROLE AND I graduated in the spring of 1983. Dartmouth's com-mencement speaker that year was the chairman of the Federal Reserve, Paul Volcker, the gruff giant who was braving intense public outrage in his quest to tame inflation by raising interest rates. Volcker would later become an adviser when I headed the Federal Reserve Bank of New York—and even later an Obama administration colleague who didn't always approve of my work—but at the time I don't think I even knew what the Fed was. I'd like to say that his speech inspired me to pursue a career as a truth-telling central banker and public servant, but, hon-estly, the sound system was so garbled I couldn't hear a word.

I had been considering the Foreign Service. Carole had intended to join the Peace Corps. But we abandoned those plans so we could stay together after we graduated in 1983. I still didn't know what I wanted to do when I grew up, except be with her. Our classmates were flocking to corporate and financial jobs, but I wasn't interested in those paths. Maybe it was just because I was fortunate enough to grow up without economic anxiety, but money wasn't on my radar screen, and it didn't occur to me that it might make sense to make some. I did endure one job interview with a management consultant, whose first question was about how I would turn around a small failing beer company. I had no idea.

Eventually, I decided to go straight to graduate school, if only to get it out of the way. I applied to a bunch of master's programs in public policy, and eventually chose the School of Advanced International Studies at Johns Hopkins, which, again, happened to be the school my father attended after the Navy. I never planned to follow in my father's footsteps, and he never put any pressure on any of us to take any particular path. But Sarah and David also went to Dartmouth, and Jonathan also went to SAIS. Sarah also followed our father into a career in global development, and is now a World Bank consultant, while Jon is a military analyst at a Washington think tank. David spent twenty years as an executive at Time, Inc., the only one of us to work in business. For me, at least, the richness and excitement of my father's career of service—and Uncle Jonathan's, too—dimmed the appeal of a lot of alternative paths. My parents would later head off on a new adventure in Beijing, where my father opened up the Ford Foundation's first office in China. He funded postgraduate education programs in the United States for a generation of Chinese officials, many of whom I would later meet during my own time in government.

I spent that summer after college shucking oysters and tending bar on the Cape. Then Carole and I moved to Washington to start our new life together. She supported us financially while I was in graduate school, first working at an economic consulting firm in Washington, then researching tax policy for Common Cause. But what she loved—what steered her into a career as a clinical social worker and therapist—was volunteering at night at a crisis hotline. Carole has always been an amazing listener, so in tune with the pain and sadness and frustration of others. She would later take a job teaching medical students how to better listen to their patients. I tend to try to analyze or problem-solve when I ought to just offer a sympathetic ear; later in my public life, Carole would often remind me about the importance of displaying more empathy.

At the time, I was finally getting motivated about school. SAIS had a practical, technocratic, problem-solving ethic that I found attractive. I became increasingly interested in Japan, which was getting a lot of attention back then as a potential threat to U.S. economic supremacy, and I started to study the Japanese language, while continuing Chinese. I got into Japanese films and literature, too. I loved learning something entirely new, as I had done in new countries while I was growing up.

I also slowly warmed up to economics. It wasn't particularly advanced or math-intensive economics, but I liked the focus on how to make choices, how the world works, what determines how well economies perform. I did reasonably well, though I was in no danger of getting drafted into academia. I played a lot of pool. During my orals, when one professor asked which economics journals I read, I replied that I had never read any. Seriously? Yes, seriously. The professor seemed incredulous. He decided my clear lack of interest in economics disqualified me from an honors grade.

By the time I got my master's degree in East Asian studies and international economics in 1985, I knew I wanted to try policy work with a global dimension. I had worked over the summer for the Overseas Private Investment Corporation, the U.S. government's development finance arm—the successor to the USAID office where my father once worked—and I figured I'd try government work. But I turned down entry-level civil service jobs at the Commerce Department and a few other executive branch agencies. I applied for the Presidential Management Intern Program, a favored path to top executive branch civil service jobs, but I didn't get it—perhaps because I botched the part of the interview that required role-playing in a fake government meeting, which seemed ridiculously forced and artificial to me. So I was still unemployed when Carole and I got married that summer at my family's house in Orleans.

But not long after we returned from our honeymoon in France, Henry Kissinger's international consulting firm hired me as an Asia analyst; my dean at SAIS had recommended me to Brent Scowcroft, one of Kissinger's partners. I went to work for Dr. Kissinger knowing that he was a controversial and complicated figure, but I thought of him mainly as the preeminent strategic thinker of his era, the architect of our opening to China. My basic foreign policy views were the establishment views of the realist tradition: a focus on national interests rather than idealistic moral goals, general support for market economies and free trade, an overarching sense that the world is a messy and dangerous place. Kissinger was the foreign policy establishment personified, and I was drawn to that ultimate insider world, perhaps more so because I had grown up as an outsider. His partners, Scowcroft and Lawrence Eagleburger, were also establishment internationalists who later served the first President Bush as national security adviser and secretary of state, respectively. They were imposing but smart, and Kissinger Associates seemed like an interesting place to start paying off my student loans.

I was now supposed to be something of an Asia specialist. For a time, I ran a Washington group of Japan policy analysts called the Kabanmochikai, "the briefcase carriers club." But I was daunted by how little I knew about my supposed topic of expertise. I mean, Asia was a vast and complex place. I'd seen more of it than most twenty-five-year-old Americans, but not a lot of it. I was writing memos that were supposed to help Henry Kissinger and his partners stay abreast of the politics and economics of the entire continent, and flying to New York once a month to brief them in person. But I knew virtually nothing about finance or business. And I had never worked in government, never stood in the shoes of the people making the policy choices I was reading and writing about.

Kissinger Associates was a great three-year postgraduate education, but one thing it taught me was that I didn't want to spend my life writing about what others were doing in government. I thought I should try doing it myself. I applied to the international division of the Treasury, which was at the center of what I thought were the most interesting policy issues of that time, and had a reputation for solid nonpartisan work. In August 1988, I accepted a civil service job in the International Trade Office of the Treasury Department. I was still a Republican—I voted for President Reagan in 1984 and George H. W. Bush in 1988—but I joined Treasury as a nonpolitical "career" civil servant, not a Reagan administration appointee. I was now a junior government official, a "GS-13," a Washington bureaucrat.

A few days after I started in my cubicle at the Treasury, Kissinger called me, one of the few times he ever did that. He was working on a book and had asked me to write two long essays on Chinese and Japanese foreign policy. He complimented my work, probably the first time he ever did that, and told me he needed additional research on Japan. When I explained that I worked for the government now, and couldn't continue to work for him on the side, he didn't sound happy and didn't prolong our conversation. We didn't have any contact for another fifteen years or so, until I was chosen to run the New York Fed, when he invited Carole and me to a private dinner. He joked that he had played an important role in my education in economics—he was proudly indifferent about economics—and would later take a lot of pleasure in claiming he had always known I would rise to great heights.

If so, he might have been the only one. I was a seriously late bloomer. When I arrived at Treasury, I felt as underprepared as I had felt at Dartmouth. I still had no long-term career plan, either inside or outside the department. I just wanted to do interesting, hopefully consequential work. And after spending so much of my life apart from America, I wanted to work for my country.

TWO

An Education in Crisis

The Constitution didn't grant the executive branch much direct power over the domestic economy. But the Treasury has more influence in foreign economic affairs, and its international division, a group of about two hundred civil servants when I joined, was known as a great place to work on issues that mattered. My first assignment was to write an analysis of what European financial integration could mean for the United States, a topic I knew nothing about at the time, though I would grapple with its consequences two decades later. It was interesting stuff for a twenty-seven-year-old kid.

My boss in the International Trade Office, a career civil servant named Bill Barreda, was my first really inspiring professional role model, a leader who made us feel connected to a mission larger than ourselves. He was smart and funny, without pretension. He rode his bike to work. He gave us economics tutorials on a blackboard in his office overlooking the East Wing of the White House. He was a talented manager, too. Whenever we produced briefing books for Secretary Nicholas Brady, Barreda brought our entire team together over beers to do the hole punching as well as the proofreading, administrative staff alongside PhD economists.

Barreda had an unstated technocratic code that I tried to adopt as my own: Focus on what's right. Tell your bosses what you really think. Understand the politics, but don't let it get in the way of figuring out the best policy on the merits. And never forget that our work affects the world. I worked for Barreda for only a year, but his get-the-right-answer ethic had a deep influence on me.

My next job at Treasury was working for the U.S. negotiator in the first international trade talks on financial services, flying to Geneva once a month to help design a new set of rules for global markets. This felt like the next frontier in economic policy, as more powerful rivers of capital were starting to flow across borders, and unlikely countries were opening their markets to foreign investment. And I was the guy with the "pen," keeping the drafts of the agreement on my IBM PC. I liked the feel of creating something new, starting from a blank slate. I also enjoyed the dance of diplomacy, the consensus building with foreign negotiators as well as the U.S. financial regulators whose support we would need for a deal.

In June 1990, Carole and I moved to Tokyo, and I started an even more interesting job as the assistant U.S. financial attaché in Japan. We stopped in Hawaii for a few days on our way to Tokyo, and a Salomon Brothers economist later told me I had looked like a kid who had just gotten off a surfboard when I arrived. In Japan, the Ministry of Finance is the most powerful and venerated government agency, and civil servants spend decades climbing its hierarchy. I was twenty-nine, definitely not what they expected from the U.S. Treasury. Although I had covered Japan for Kissinger, and I could read a newspaper in Japanese with some difficulty, I knew enough to know that I didn't know that much about Japan. And only a month after we arrived in Tokyo, the attaché unexpectedly left for a new job in Washington, leaving me in charge with almost no help at a fraught moment in U.S.-Japanese economic relations.

I felt like a foreign correspondent, trying to figure out another new place, sending dispatches home to a distant Washington. Japan was a challenge for any outsider to grasp, and much of the economic substance of my job was new to me. One of my tasks was producing Treasury's quarterly forecast for the Japanese economy. This was a useful education, mostly in making me skeptical of forecasting. I talked to economists and executives. I studied the data. But how on earth were we supposed to predict Japan's growth rate over the next two years? Even the best forecasts, I learned, were just educated guesses. They could tell a story about how the economy might evolve, but they couldn't predict the future.

Washington seemed to appreciate my work anyway. I remember when we were trying to get the Japanese to help defray the costs of the first Gulf War, I rode in a motorcade from the Tokyo airport with a senior delegation from Washington. Hollis McLoughlin, Secretary Brady's chief of staff, asked me what the Japanese police officers were yelling into their megaphones as they cleared our path. I didn't know the direct translation, but I replied: "They're saying: 'Get the fuck out of the way!'" I don't know if it was my limited Japanese or my fluent profanity that impressed him, but he told that story around the department to mark me as a young man to watch.

ONE OF my main responsibilities in Tokyo was helping to open up Japanese markets to U.S. firms, especially U.S. financial firms. The George H. W. Bush administration, like its predecessors, was concerned about Japanese trade barriers. It was also concerned about the anti-Japanese protectionist fever growing on Capitol Hill. The hope was that if we could get Japan to provide a more level playing field, Congress might be less inclined to enact legislation that would restrict Japanese access to U.S. markets. The dominant view of the time—and I shared this view—was that freer trade would benefit both countries.

In those days, the Japanese were seen as our main economic threat, making our camcorders and VCRs, buying Rockefeller Center. In the four years before I arrived, the Nikkei stock index tripled and Japanese real estate values tripled; Japan's land, an area the size of California, was worth nearly four times as much as the land in the entire United States. Publishers churned out books predicting that Japanese capitalism, with its cozy relations between government bureaucrats and huge corporations, would bury the American model. Politicians vowed to stop Japan, Inc., from stealing American jobs. Hollywood movies featured Japanese corporate villains.

But shortly before I moved to Tokyo, Japan's stock bubble burst, followed by its real estate bubble. The tide began to recede, and as Warren Buffett says, that's when you see who's swimming naked. Japan, Inc., no longer looked unbeatable. I got to watch the early stages of Japan's response to its financial crisis, which began deftly, as some failing banks were merged into stronger ones, but later became a case study in what not to do, as the government propped up weak banks and left them undercapitalized, helping to usher in a "lost decade" of stagnant growth. Inside the U.S. government, the pendulum swung back toward triumphalist demands for Japan to be more like us. I had never understood the hype about Japan's supposedly superior economic model, but I wasn't wild about the strains of arrogance in our reaction, either.

I mostly agreed with the substance of our push for open access. Many of Japan's trade practices were unproductive and unfair. Wal-Mart couldn't build stores in Japan, and U.S. financial firms were effectively shut out of Japan's mutual fund and pension fund markets. The specter of U.S. retaliation was also a legitimate fear. Even if it didn't spark an all-out trade war, it would have hurt American consumers as well as American manufacturers who depended on imports of Japanese parts. And our external pressure—the Japanese call it *gai-atsu*—strengthened the hand of Japan's reformers in their domestic debates, giving them an excuse (the danger of protectionist fervor on Capitol Hill) to open doors they wanted to open anyway.

I still felt uneasy about our paternalism. I had inherited some of my father's skepticism about Americans telling foreigners how to run their own countries, and I thought we were risking comparisons to General MacArthur ruling postwar Japan by decree. I was glad to advocate a level playing field, but the difficulties of American firms didn't always stem from Japanese discrimination against foreign goods and services. The Japanese system was rough on any firm, foreign or domestic, that wasn't part of its establishment. Some would say this model served Japan poorly and ultimately contributed to its lost decade, but that wasn't really our problem to solve. There was something ridiculous about the dance of American officials pressuring Japan to restructure its economy in our image, threatening that congressional protectionists might otherwise block its access to the U.S. market.

I played my modest part in all this. I was a civil servant responsible for executing the policies of the United States, including the ones I had mixed feelings about. And those policies ended up doing some good. We helped persuade Japan to relax some restraints on trade and investment. Congress refrained from enacting new ones in the United States. While our work didn't make big news at home—the only major story that broke on my watch was President Bush vomiting on the Japanese prime minister—I felt like we were making a difference.

My most enduring memory of Japan is becoming a father, although even that wonderful experience supplied a reminder that my work was taking over my life. I had promised Carole that I would learn some childbirth-related Japanese, in case there was no English-speaking obstetrician on duty when we had to go to the hospital. But I was preoccupied with work, so I started the lessons late, and had only three sessions with an embarrassed tutor before Carole's water broke at an embassy reception three weeks before her due date. I can't say I understood much of what the doctors and nurses said that night before they put my daughter, Elise, in my arms. Carole and I can laugh about my lousy ob-gyn Japanese now, but that wouldn't be the last time my work got in the way of my family obligations.

• • •

TREASURY ASKED me to return to Washington in 1992, and we moved into a small house in the same Wood Acres neighborhood of Bethesda where I had attended first grade. I took a front-office job for the assistant secretary of international affairs, reviewing and overseeing the flow of paper, trying to make the trains run on time. My boss's secretary, the venerable Zula Peperis, told me I'd be Treasury secretary someday. That made me laugh. I was still a junior official. No career employee had ever risen to lead the department. All the senior jobs were political appointments, serving at the pleasure of the president, typically recruited from outside the government. But I was fortunate to be in that D.C. staff job after Bill Clinton defeated President Bush, because one day I was assigned to brief Larry Summers, Clinton's nominee for undersecretary for international affairs. Larry would see more in me than I saw in myself.

Even more than graduate school and my early Treasury years, Larry opened my eyes to the possibilities of economics as a lens for thinking about the world and a tool for improving people's lives. Before that first meeting—which was at the World Bank, where he was chief economist—I read a paper he had written examining the appalling fact that infant mortality was higher in New York City than in Shanghai. It got me thinking in new ways about what determines whether countries are rich or poor, what governments can and can't do. That article stuck with me. After I became secretary, when speaking about our own national debates about the safety net for the poor, I would occasionally mention that an infant in St. Louis was more likely to die before her first birthday than an infant in Sri Lanka.

Larry had been tenured at Harvard at twenty-eight, and he had earned a reputation for brilliance, if not for concealing it. He was a former college debate star who would tell you why you were wrong, how you should have made your argument, and why your improved argument still would have been wrong. But he didn't mind being challenged, as long as you didn't mind being challenged back with-out excessive courtesy. He had an inspiring sense of possibility when it came to public policy, an assumption that evidence-based analysis could always produce a better way. We hit it off, and he made me his special assistant. He seemed to like that I wasn't afraid to speak my mind with him. Years later, when the chairman of the New York Fed asked him if I was tough enough to run the place, Larry said I was always willing to tell him he was full of shit. I remember thinking that was not a particularly impressive credential. It was just what you were supposed to do when you thought your boss was wrong.

Larry seemed to recognize that while I didn't pretend to offer him much in the way of economics insight, I knew some things he didn't, like how Treasury worked, how diplomacy was conducted, and how to get things done. I remember at Dulles International Airport before his first meeting with his fellow Group of Seven deputies, Larry reviewed all the positions he was going to take, and all the impeccable arguments he had on his side. I tried to explain that it's not enough to say what you're for, that you have to know how to achieve it. You've got to move others to your side, and you can't just convince them with your superior logic; you've got to figure out where you have leverage over them—something they need from you or fear from you. Larry teased me sometimes—after I made a substantive comment while tak-ing notes for him at a later G-7 deputies meeting, he dubbed me "the noisy scribe"—but he listened to me, at least occasionally. Larry once said he could envision me as the managing partner of a law firm, or running some big institution, if only my credentials weren't so thin.

"I just don't know how you'd get hired in the first place," he said.

I planned to help Larry for only a few months; before we met I had accepted a new job elsewhere in the Treasury. But Larry wouldn't let me leave. A year later, he decided to promote me from noisy scribe all the way to deputy assistant secretary, one of the top career jobs in the department. It was an honor, but it was a big jump for me, and I knew it would take a toll on my family. I was already working fourteen-hour days, not including late-night calls from Larry, and Carole was pregnant again. We were on a short beach vacation when I got a congratulatory fax from Larry saying Secretary Lloyd Bentsen had approved the promotion. I sent back a fax saying I had decided to stay on the beach and teach tennis instead.

In my new job, I would help oversee our dealings with the G-7 and the International Monetary Fund, as well as any other global financial issue that arose. Once again, I felt underprepared. I was replacing a well-respected official who was retiring after working at Treasury since before I was born. I was not confident that I could live up to Larry's expectations; there was too much about the job that was unfamiliar to me. I remember once after Haitian protesters created an international stir by turning back an American ship, Secretary Bentsen called me to ask what he should advise the President. I had no idea. I didn't know anything about Haiti, and this wasn't about economic policy. I wanted to ask: Why are you calling me?

At least one of my responsibilities was familiar: managing yet another negotiation over Japan's trade barriers in financial services. I still thought helping U.S. firms compete abroad was a legitimate objective. After one Larry-being-Larry session where he challenged a group of Wall Street CEOs seeking greater access to Japanese markets to explain what they were doing to create jobs in the United States, I told him there was no need to be so contrarian. The reforms we were pushing were sensible. Japan's financial sector was still primarily a closed market, and the Japanese finance ministry seemed pretty captured by its financial establishment.

But Washington could be a bit captured, too. When Hank Greenberg, the feisty chief executive of American International Group (AIG), threatened to go to war against the Clinton administration and the World Trade Organization if we didn't extract some insurance concession, I told the Japanese we needed the concession or we would block the entire global agreement—and they conceded. I remember telling Larry that we were spending way too much time and energy on this kind of financial mercantilism, opening markets for Wall Street. I used to joke that our agenda should be more ambitious than making the world safe for hedge funds.

I didn't have a purist's faith in the genius of the free market; I was seeing in Japan what could happen when financial systems fail, and when governments are too captured by the financial sector to clean up the mess. But overall, I believed in our efforts to open foreign markets to competition. And I was comfortable with the broad thrust of U.S. economic policy under President Clinton, who combined a strong commitment to fiscal responsibility and free trade with public investments in areas such as education and scientific research.

I hadn't planned to stay in government for more than a few years, and I felt terribly guilty about neglecting my family. That winter, I was traveling in China when our furnace failed during a blizzard in Washington; Carole, six months pregnant and alone with our two-year-old, had to climb up a ladder to our attic and lug down an electric heater. Our son, Ben, was born in April 1994, and we got to experience again all the anxiety and amazement of parenthood. I loved that stage of life, watching your kids experience the world, but I was missing a lot of it. I put too much of a burden on Carole, and too much of their lives happened without me.

I hated being away so much, never available, always on call, but I was completely engaged by my work. I liked the constant intellectual challenge of working for Larry, who could figure out the flaw in any idea but continued to push for perfection. When the head of President Clinton's National Economic Council, Robert Rubin, replaced Secretary Bentsen in January 1995, I liked working for him, too.

Rubin was the former head of Goldman Sachs, but he was self-deprecating and funny, demanding without Larry's rough edges. He believed in good process. He wanted input from all his advisers no matter where we were in the hierarchy, even if we disagreed with him—especially if we disagreed with him. He was calm, dispassionate, and almost comically deliberate, analyzing problems from every possible angle, scribbling down risks and probabilities on his yellow legal pad, gathering information and "preserving optionality" until he absolutely had to decide. He often reminded us that you can't judge a decision by how it turns out, only by whether it made sense given the information available at the time. His decisions generally did.

Secretary Rubin would guide the department through a series of financial crises, valuable training for the larger crisis still to come.

• • •

ONE MEMORIAL Day weekend during college, I was driving my family's old Boston Whaler off the Cape when I saw a sailboat capsized in the surf, with a man and a woman hanging on for dear life. I didn't know how long the couple had been in the icy water. I anchored my boat, swam to their boat, and convinced them to swim back to my boat with me. Hypothermia seemed like a greater risk than drowning.

Big mistake. I never should have told them to move. The current was too powerful, and they weren't strong enough swimmers. They thrashed in the waves for a few minutes before giving up and heading back to their boat. Fortunately, they made it, and I made it to my boat, too. Eventually, the waves pushed them toward shore, and the beach patrol picked them up, so my bad advice didn't have tragic consequences. It was a scary but relatively painless way to learn about making judgments under the pressure of a crisis, about weighing the relative merits of various choices with potentially catastrophic outcomes.

JUST OVER a decade later, I was sitting next to Secretary Rubin in the back of his government car, returning from Capitol Hill during a different kind of crisis.

The secretary had just testified before the House Banking Committee about the Mexican peso crisis, often described as the first financial crisis of the twenty-first century. Mexico was on the brink of defaulting on its obligations, and Rubin had made the case for a $40 billion emergency loan. The reaction was withering. With public opinion running 80–20 against a U.S. government rescue, Republicans and Democrats accused the secretary of plotting to waste tax dollars on foreigners, bail out his Wall Street pals who had speculated in Mexico, and even line his own pockets. Federal Reserve Chairman Alan Greenspan, who was usually treated like the Oracle at Delphi on the Hill, received almost as rough a reception.

It was a troubling spectacle, and I guess it showed on my face.

"What's wrong?" Rubin asked.

"I'm just worried," I said.

There was a lot to worry about. Congressional leaders had initially promised President Clinton that they would back his loan request, but they were clearly running for the hills. We were developing an alternative plan to help Mexico unilaterally if Congress wouldn't back us, but it was starting to look like Congress might try to block us. And if we did manage to get money to Mexico, none of us were sure we'd ever get it back. Not only would that be a political disaster for Clinton and Rubin; it could cripple America's ability to intervene in future crises.

These worries were Rubin's worries, too. He always wanted us to think five moves ahead, to question our assumptions, to imagine worst-case scenarios.

"It's good that you're worried," he told me.

Over the next few years, I would be reminded again and again that during a financial crisis, if you're not worried, you're not thinking carefully enough. I like to say that concern is not a strategy, but it's a prerequisite for good strategy.

MEXICO HAD been hailed as a model for emerging markets, a fast-growing destination for foreign capital, the first new country invited to join the Organization for Economic Cooperation and Development in more than two decades. But during the country's boom, the Mexican government became far too dependent on short-term borrowing—the kind of money that can easily run when confidence is shaken. Mexico also had a fixed exchange rate, pegging its peso to the dollar—a recipe for instability when confidence goes.

Sure enough, when insurgents assassinated Mexico's leading presidential candidate early in 1994, investors and bondholders and other creditors started to fear the country wasn't as stable—and their money wasn't as safe—as they had believed. Runnable capital began to run. Confidence in the peso began to evaporate. The government tried to buy pesos to prop up their value and defend the peg. But that just drained its dollar reserves and heightened fears that it would default on its debts, especially a pile of short-term bonds called *tesobonos* that were linked to the dollar. After taking office in December, Mexico's new president, a Yale-trained economist named Ernesto Zedillo, faced reality and abandoned the unsustainable fixed exchange rate. But as the peso plummeted in value, so did confidence in the country.

By the end of 1994, Mexico had clearly lost control of its finances. The government had only $6 billion left in reserves, with $30 billion worth of *tesobonos* coming due over the next year. And markets no longer considered it creditworthy, so it couldn't raise money to pay its bills. I remember Jeff Shafer, an assistant Treasury secretary, suddenly announcing he had figured out Mexico's problem: "It's a sovereign liquidity crisis!" In other words, it was a run on the country, a national version of the rush to George Bailey's bank in *It's a Wonderful Life*. Mexico had a modest long-term debt burden and the power to tax, so in theory, it should have been able to pay what it owed over time. It did not have a fundamental *solvency* problem; it was by no means a hopeless case. But it had an immediate *liquidity* problem. Without cash on hand, it couldn't meet its obligations. Like George Bailey, it needed help in a hurry.

Default would have been a nightmare for ninety million Mexicans, a potential prelude to hyperinflation and mass unemployment. It also would have been a problem for us. Mexico was our third largest trading partner, and the Fed staff calculated that a messy crisis could affect hundreds of thousands of American jobs, reduce U.S. growth by an entire percentage point, and increase illegal immigration 30 percent. We also feared that investors unnerved by Mexico might abandon other emerging economies that seemed to have similar vulnerabilities. Brazil and Argentina were already experiencing this "Tequila Effect," as their markets slumped in sympathy with Mexico's. Finally, we knew that if Mexico cratered a year after the North American Free Trade Agreement eased its barriers to foreign capital, protectionists at home and abroad would claim a propaganda victory. It would build momentum for trade restrictions in Congress, while encouraging developing nations to wall themselves off from the world.

Larry recognized that a typical International Monetary Fund loan, which would be limited to Mexico's "quota" of $2.6 billion, would be woefully inadequate to stop the run. It would be up to the United States to fill the gap. He suggested that Colin Powell's doctrine for U.S. military intervention—deploy overwhelming force, but only when American interests were at stake, and only with a clear exit strategy—should also apply to U.S. financial intervention. At an early meeting to discuss options, Greenspan suggested that $20 billion would be a "wall of money" large enough to overwhelm the *tesobonos* and reassure the markets, a figure we ultimately decided to double. The chairman was a free enterprise Republican, reluctant to meddle in markets, concerned that rescuing Mexico (and its bondholders) would embolden future Mexicos (and future creditors) to take similarly irresponsible risks. But we all agreed the potential moral hazard cost of a bailout paled in comparison to the actual cost of default. It was, as Greenspan said, "the least-worst option."

We called that plan Mexico One. But after the politics soured in Congress, we needed a Mexico Two. That's when we turned to the Exchange Stabilization Fund, a pot of money that Treasury was authorized to use to reduce volatility in currency markets and promote financial stability. It had never been used on a scale like this, and I thought it would be imprudent to commit the bulk of our foreign exchange reserves to this cause. But Ted Truman, who ran the international part of the Fed in Washington, figured out a way for the Fed to help us make $20 billion available for loans to Mexico and still preserve some firepower for other contingencies. It wasn't the $40 billion we had requested from Congress, but it was the only way we could act without legislation. And IMF director Michel Camdessus pledged $18 billion, by far the largest package in the fund's history. So we were pretty close to Larry's Powell Doctrine goal.

Several of our European allies, especially the Germans, were furious with the IMF's commitment—partly because of moral hazard fears, partly because they felt inadequately consulted. Members of Congress were also furious about our use of the ESF—again, partly because of substantive concerns about putting taxpayer money at risk to save Wall Street speculators and a reckless neighbor, partly because we had just authorized the largest U.S. aid package since the Marshall Plan without their approval. And we were still negotiating terms with the Mexican government, so Mexico Two was not a done deal.

We thought the deal had to include some tough conditions, including credible government commitments to get its finances under control and to raise interest rates high enough to keep private money from fleeing the country. Ultimately, the rescue wouldn't work unless Mexico's leaders proved they were worthy of investor confidence, and as Larry liked to say, we couldn't want reform more than they did. But we didn't want to impose conditions so punitive that they would weigh down the Mexican economy and depress confidence even further—or force Mexican leaders to resist to prove they weren't helpless suppliants to the United States.

It was a delicate tightrope, and investors—uncertain about the Mexican government's appetite for reform, and rattled by the political opposition in the United States—were skeptical that we'd make it across. Capitol Hill leaders were pushing to block us from using the ESF, or at least tie our hands with restrictions governing everything from Mexican labor standards to Florida tomato exports. Internally, even after we signed the deal in late February, Rubin kept playing devil's advocate, asking us to persuade him we weren't dumping tax dollars into a lost cause. News of those discussions seeped out of the Treasury building, fueling rumors that we were reconsidering the loans, which further unnerved the markets.

Rubin liked to say that nothing in life was certain, and none of us felt highly confident of success. Every blip of bad news—a rebel advance in Chiapas, a drop in the peso's value—made us fear for the program. But we went ahead with our rescue plan. And President Zedillo and his team of technocrats kept their promises to raise interest rates while imposing tax hikes and budget cuts, which helped persuade investors they were committed to getting Mexico's finances under control. After a few months of lurches, markets stopped running.

By the end of 1995, capital was trickling back into the country. By 1997, Mexico's economic output had returned to pre-crisis levels, and its government had repaid all its loans early, netting U.S. taxpayers $1.4 billion in interest. Markets in South America, Asia, and eastern Europe that had suffered from Mexico comparisons all rallied after Mexico stabilized. The rescue worked. By that time, though, Mexico had fallen out of the news, and neither the success of the rescue nor the fact that we recovered our investments plus a profit got much attention—certainly not enough to offset the political hit that Clinton and Rubin took around the initial decision.

Mexico was a bracing lesson in the terrible politics of crisis response. I had never worked on something so controversial before, and it was searing to watch the abuse showered on Rubin and Greenspan—then near the peak of their public credibility—for taking a risk that seemed so compelling to me. It was instructive to contrast Clinton, whose support for the Mexican rescue never wavered even though his aides warned it could make him a one-term president, with congressional leaders who were with us until the public was against us. Senate Banking Committee Chairman Al D'Amato, a Republican from New York, actually urged us to expand the Mexico package before becoming one of its most vehement critics. That kind of congressional opportunism made it harder to restore confidence in Mexico, because it damaged confidence in our ability to keep our commitments.

In fact, once the crisis was over, Senator D'Amato pushed legislation through Congress that temporarily restricted our ability to use the ESF to fight future crises. And we knew there would be future crises. Globalization had unleashed enormous sums of "hot money" that could instantaneously flow across borders, while the aspects of human psychology that had helped produce financial booms and crises for centuries remained unchanged.

WE DIDN'T think the global community was ready to navigate this perilous new world of mobile capital. My colleagues at Treasury and the Fed believed the IMF needed more money for when the next Mexico exploded, plus the capability to deploy the money quickly and forcefully enough to contain a run. It had to be able to provide countries in crisis with sufficient cash to overwhelm the crisis as well as tough conditions to restore confidence in the markets.

But while the United States was the most powerful force at the IMF, we weren't a controlling force. The U.S. founded the IMF, and it was still based in Washington, but we provided only about a quarter of its total funding. As Camdessus once observed, we could block things, but we couldn't make things happen unless we persuaded our partners that they made sense. Even before Mexico was resolved, we began a major international effort to create a stronger global architecture for dealing with future financial crises.

Part of our work was promoting preventive medicine to help countries avoid becoming the next Mexico. We helped forge consensus in international communiqués for what we saw as best practices, urging countries to avoid excessive short-term debt in foreign currencies, to let their own currencies float freely, and to make sure their banks had plenty of capital to cushion against sudden losses. But those recommendations were purely voluntary. We couldn't force sovereign nations to follow them, and our ideas didn't get a lot of traction in those days.

Alongside our crisis prevention efforts, we also worked to improve our crisis response options for the next Mexico. I came up with the idea of a new $50 billion IMF reserve fund, which seemed like a lot of money at the time. We wanted to make sure that in future crises, the world wouldn't be dependent on the United States as the dominant funding source, especially now that the D'Amato restrictions limited our ability to offer bilateral loans. We also proposed an interesting design for the new fund. Instead of raising the money exclusively from the traditional group of advanced economies, we proposed that emerging markets should help finance it and help govern it. This was partly to reflect the new global balance of power; the rising Asian and South American economies deserved a more influential presence alongside rich establishment nations at the IMF. But it was partly to dilute the power of more conservative European countries; we didn't want their occasional parochialism and moral hazard fundamentalism to paralyze future crisis responses.

I flew around the world to make the case and negotiate the arcane details, often with Ted Truman from the Fed. I liked the challenge of the substance and the diplomacy—long flights to long meetings in windowless rooms, sometimes back and forth across the Atlantic without spending the night. I once did five countries in Asia in five days. I built relationships with a new generation of finance ministry and central bank officials. It was interesting, sometimes even exciting.

Many foreign officials were initially skeptical of our proposal for a new crisis fund, thinking we were just trying to find a way to deploy other people's money to finance our own interests. Some of my European counterparts called me "the smiling hegemon." And it's true that I tried to maximize U.S. influence. I remember asking Truman and another Fed economist, Lew Alexander, if we could somehow structure the fund to give the United States the power to force action as well as veto action. They laughed and said they didn't know any math that would give us all the power for just 25 percent of the funding. We settled for a veto. And our counterparts eventually realized the fund made sense for everyone.

By 1997, we had the framework of a deal. But before Congress would authorize this new arsenal for attacking the next crisis, the next crisis had arrived.

* * *

THAILAND HAD ignored the IMF's warnings about the dangers of fixed exchange rates and short-term borrowing in foreign currency. So had many of its fellow "Asian tigers." That didn't matter until their economies stopped growing rapidly. Then it mattered a lot.

Throughout the nineties, Thailand's banks enjoyed easy access to dollars and yen, which they used to finance an investment boom, much of it in real estate. But a lot of the investment was not productive. When the bubble popped in 1997, the banks were overloaded with nonperforming long-term loans, and their creditors cut back their short-term access to dollars and yen. Confidence in the Thai baht flagged. Instead of letting it adjust, Thai leaders followed Mexico's bad example, draining their foreign exchange reserves to defend an indefensible peg to the dollar, hoping the storm would blow over. It didn't. In July 1997, they gave up and devalued the baht. Panic ensued. Thailand was less connected to the United States than Mexico, but we knew there was a chance its crisis could drag down other Asian economies. And Asia was an increasingly vital part of the world economy.

Thailand was also less prepared for financial shocks than Mexico, which had experienced repeated crises in the past, and had attracted a lot of financial talent to serve in government. I remember calling a senior Thai finance ministry official from my parents' house on the Cape early in the crisis to ask what was going on. He didn't seem to know much, and didn't seem to want to share what he did know. The Thais were so reticent it was hard to get a sense of what they were thinking, and none of us really understood their country. My colleagues sometimes assumed I'd have a feel for the place after spending my high school years there; Larry teasingly called me "Mr. Asia." But my time in Thailand gave me no relevant insight into the country's crisis—empathy, maybe, but no additional knowledge that could help us help the Thais.

Our inclination at Treasury—and the IMF's inclination, too—was to try to replicate what had worked in Mexico. We hoped to put a lot of "money in the window," enough to look big compared to the liabilities that could run. We would loan the money at a fairly expensive rate, to make sure it would be repaid as soon as possible once the crisis passed. And we would attach other conditions designed to prevent Thailand from repeating mistakes that had led to the crisis, with the goal of re-storing investor confidence in the country.

But in the Thai crisis, unlike the Mexico crisis, the United States couldn't take the financial lead, so we wouldn't be calling the shots. Senator D'Amato's restrictions on the ESF blocked us from provid-ing the large long-term loans we thought were needed. That left the IMF as the only large-scale source of finance. At a meeting of finance officials in Tokyo that August, after Japan pledged to lend $4 billion to the Thais, I had to explain that the United States could not make a direct commitment, even though our economy was in stronger finan-cial shape than Japan's. "How does it feel to be a superpower?" I said to my Japanese counterpart. It was a deeply uncomfortable situation for me—and, I thought, for the United States.

Despite resistance on its board, the IMF leadership commit-ted about $4 billion and cobbled together another $13 billion worth of other commitments. But the package didn't look as generous as Mexico's, and the Thais felt betrayed that none of it came directly from us. Other Asian countries were offended, too, and the Japanese tried to exploit our perceived weakness, quietly floating the idea of an Asian Monetary Fund that would supplant the IMF's role in Asia. We thought this was a bad idea for the global financial system and for Asia; a regional fund model would be more susceptible to being overwhelmed by a regional crisis. I warned Bob and Larry that we were suffering huge damage to our credibility in Asia. Even with one hundred thousand troops stationed on the continent, our influence was waning.

We risked making the problem worse with a fight about transparency. The Thais were publicly claiming they still had $20 billion in foreign exchange reserves, but we knew the real number was closer to zero; the Thai central bank had sold its dollars in the forward markets to conceal the depth of its problems. Chairman Greenspan felt strongly that as a condition of any IMF assistance, Thailand should have to reveal the truth. Bob and Larry agreed. I expressed doubts. I thought full disclosure could shatter confidence and accelerate the run.

I was wrong. Allowing the Thai government to withhold information might have avoided some near-term pain, but it would have risked a lot of damage to their credibility and the IMF's when the truth came out. In a financial crisis, uncertainty is the enemy of confidence. The markets didn't trust the Thai numbers anyway, and the absence of reliable information already encouraged investors to assume the worst. At the time, though, it looked like my fears were coming true, like America was messing up an intervention it wasn't even funding. After the IMF announced the loan in late August—and revealed Thailand's lack of reserves—the baht resumed its swan dive and capital continued to flee.

That fall, I was promoted to assistant Treasury secretary for international affairs, my first political appointment after a decade as a civil servant. At Larry's suggestion, I had switched my party registration from Republican to unaffiliated, to make it easier to get the White House on board. I had voted for President Clinton twice, anyway. But I was too busy worrying about Asia to savor my promotion; Rubin had to administer my oath of office in a hotel in Hong Kong. There was a lot of excitement in those days, but what I mostly remember was a constant feeling of dread. The crisis was spreading to Indonesia, Malaysia, and Korea, as pressure built on their fixed exchange rates. Markets in Brazil, Argentina, and Mexico were falling in sympathy with Asia's, as investors tried to get ahead of the spreading contagion. The United States was enjoying strong growth, wages were rising, and the federal budget was on the verge of its first surpluses in decades, but the Asian crisis still hit home in late October, when the New York Stock Exchange had to suspend trading after a sudden 7 percent drop in the Dow.

I was getting a remarkable education from talented colleagues—such as Rubin and Greenspan, celebrated in those days as the magicians behind the U.S. economic boom; Larry, who was our leading international economic strategist and now deputy secretary; David Lipton, a former IMF economist and experienced "country doctor" who had Larry's old undersecretary job; and Truman, the veteran Fed crisis-fighter who traveled with me around Asia. President Clinton supported our strategy, and we didn't feel constrained by politics. If anything, we took a perverse pride in the unpopularity of our work. We just focused on finding the best option among a mix of bad choices, debating and arguing and brainstorming at rolling meetings that never seemed to end. I dubbed them "clusterfucks," which became standard Treasury lingo, to the point that Larry would announce we needed a CF on Thailand.

We were feeling our way, refining and relitigating our strategy, painfully aware of our inadequate information and the limits of the tools at hand. We always felt a few steps behind the crisis. We kept rushing to catch up, hoping that each moment of calm we purchased would mark the turning point, the end of the cascade of interconnected problems. Those hopes were usually betrayed.

INDONESIA WAS the next domino to fall.

Its currency was collapsing, its banks were overextended, and its corrupt government—led by the aging dictator Suharto—seemed helpless to respond. By early November, Suharto had reluctantly signed a $23 billion IMF loan agreement, but it wasn't clear that he was committed to the program or that his government would be able to restore confidence. The day after the IMF board approved the loan,

Truman and I met with Indonesia's top economic officials in Jakarta. The finance minister entered the room and asked the central bank governor what was happening with interest rates. The central banker cheerfully said they were up. The finance minister responded: "I thought you told me the program would bring them down!"

Truman and I shot each other looks that said: *This isn't going to work.*

Indonesian execution was a problem, but the IMF made mistakes, too. The most damaging may have been forcing Suharto to shut down troubled banks—including one owned by his son—with a very limited deposit insurance system in place. That triggered a run on deposits in the rest of the banking system, as depositors feared these bank closures were the first of many and understandably concluded that if their money wasn't safe with favored insiders, it wasn't safe anywhere. And Suharto's son simply bought a new bank a few weeks later, shifted many of the same assets into it, put it in the same location, and gave it a new name—a stunning signal to potential investors that reform hadn't arrived in Indonesia.

In any financial rescue, many of the toughest decisions involve how to set conditions, the policy changes required in exchange for financial support: what kind of medicine will help, what's the right dose, what might kill the patient. In Thailand, for example, the IMF demanded sharp increases in interest rates, to try to stop the fall of the currency and keep capital in the country, as well as some modest budget cuts to cover the costs of the repair of the banking system. That was a standard IMF prescription for an economy caught in a mess like Thailand's, designed to assure investors that the country was creditworthy and wouldn't simply squander its financial aid. But Thailand's fiscal deficits were already low, and painful measures such as tax hikes and spending cuts would further weaken its economy during a downturn. The IMF later reversed course on fiscal austerity in Thailand after new data showed that the economy was in recession, the first of many revisions to the program.

The IMF imposed more sweeping conditions on Indonesia—not only the conventional fiscal austerity and interest rate increases, but a comprehensive dismantling of the economic privileges that Suharto had granted to favored elites. We didn't design these conditions—they mostly came from the IMF, the World Bank, and reformers within the Indonesian government—but we had some sympathy for them. It would have been hard to justify risking billions of dollars to support the kleptocratic status quo, and we thought foreigners would be reluctant to invest in Indonesia as long as Suharto and his inner circle controlled major industries.

But these conditions went too far. It wasn't clear how ending the cashew and clove monopolies would be vital to restoring confidence. Corruption wasn't the root cause of the crisis, and there was no way we could plausibly eliminate it while the crisis was still raging. Expressing concern about the scope of the conditions during our internal debates, I joked that Lipton was playing General MacArthur, trying to reshape the Indonesian economy. But I didn't present a credible alternative. My concern was not a strategy.

In any case, the program was a mess. The rupiah lost over 80 percent of its value in a couple months. Suharto repeatedly committed to reforms he had no intention of implementing, and probably no ability to implement. The crisis broke the political system that had held Indonesia together for decades, and the IMF's money couldn't repair the damage.

THE FIRE spread next to South Korea, a significant economic power and a vital geopolitical ally. We feared that if South Korea burned, investors would conclude that no emerging-market investments were safe. We didn't even want to imagine how totalitarian North Korea might try to exploit a collapse of its democratic neighbor.

Like the other Asian tigers, Korea had enjoyed years of impressive growth. Like Mexico, it had recently joined the Organization for Economic Cooperation and Development. But its banks had taken out big short-term loans in foreign currency, while making big long-term loans in Korean won to sprawling, state-subsidized conglomerates called *chaebols*. Now *chaebols* were in trouble, banks were facing runs, and the government was draining its foreign exchange reserves to prop up the won. When Truman and I arrived in Seoul in mid-November, Korea's lame-duck president had replaced his finance minister merely for proposing to seek IMF help, exhibiting the same kind of denial we had seen in Thailand and Indonesia. And Korea's central bank governor told us the situation was again even worse than it seemed; almost all the country's reserves were gone. I asked him why the new finance minister had even agreed to take the job.

"Because he hasn't seen the books," the central banker told us.

A few days later, Korea agreed to seek IMF help.

This time, we were determined to put enough money in the window to stop a run. We wanted to contain the contagion before it infected the world; I remember telling Rubin we simply couldn't stand by and let Korea burn. He didn't respond well to assertions of imperative or appeals to necessity. If we couldn't devise a plan with a plausible chance of success, he said, then standing by and letting Korea burn would be a perfectly appropriate response. He liked to remind us that just because there was a problem didn't mean there was a solution. But as I liked to point out, the absence of a perfect solution didn't mean there wasn't a problem. Korea had a bigger economy than Thailand and Indonesia combined. The stakes were getting higher. Korean banks had creditors banging on their doors, and Korean businesses and individuals had substantial savings in the banks that could rush for the exits at any time.

"Everything can run," I said to Rubin.

With the crisis escalating, and the D'Amato restrictions expired, we took a much more direct role in shaping the international response to Korea. We helped the IMF put together an unprecedented $55 billion rescue package, including a $20 billion "second line of defense" from the U.S. Treasury and other countries in case the IMF's portion was fully drawn down. Mexico had received almost seven times its IMF quota, uncharted territory at the time. Korea got nineteen times its quota. This was Larry's inspiration. He basically changed the rules in the middle of the game, convincing the IMF to lend much more and much faster. In the early months of the Asian crisis, the United States had been unable to commit our own resources and deferential to the preferences of the IMF. In Korea, Larry put the Powell Doctrine into action.

But even this commitment of what we thought was overwhelming force didn't stop the run. The markets weren't sure the commitment was credible, or large enough to cover all the bad debts that South Korean banks were hiding. The IMF's initial payments quickly flowed out of the country as the foreign creditors of Korea's banks rushed for the exits. The won depreciated 40 percent in three weeks, and the government essentially ran out of foreign currency. We were starting to doubt that we could save the country; we seemed to have no good options. Frustrated and exhausted during one late-night conference call, I suggested we could buy some time by simply accelerating payments to Korea from the next tranche of the IMF loan. Larry scoffed that I was suggesting a Vietnam War strategy, a recipe for defeat.

"Gradual escalation isn't going to work," he said.

Part of Korea's challenge was a collective action problem. Creditors were refusing to renew short-term loans to Korean banks they thought were at risk of default. But by demanding repayment as these loans matured, they were making default more likely. Because Korea's government had plenty of resources and its economy was very productive, the best outcome for the creditors would be if they all kept financing the Korean banks to avoid a more chaotic collapse. But they all worried that if they didn't take their money and run, other creditors would, so they were all trying to beat one another out the door. This is a common dynamic in crises, where rational individual decisions can create disastrous collective outcomes. We had to break the cycle if the broader package was to have any chance to work.

Truman and I came up with a relatively simple idea to address this critical part of the run. We proposed to try to persuade Korea's major private creditors—a group of American, Japanese, and European financial institutions—to extend the maturity of their loans to Korea's banks. We couldn't force the creditors to agree, but we thought we could convince them that a voluntary "standstill" would be in their mutual interest, since we could credibly say the likely alternative was a government default that would produce deep losses. We convened all the CEOs of the major global banks on a series of conference calls with their finance ministers, where they were all given the same message: If you all agree to convert short-term loans into longer-term loans, we will accelerate the IMF's payments to Korea, and you'll all have a good chance of getting paid back in full. But if you won't come together to stabilize the situation, we can't be sure the IMF will continue to lend, and you'll all face much greater losses.

The banks were a bit stunned at first, but Rubin made a compelling case, and they came around, agreeing first to a temporary standstill, and later to a broader debt refinancing. The panic subsided. And South Korea's new president, a lifelong democracy activist named Kim Dae-jung, made it clear that he was committed, as President Zedillo had been in Mexico, to doing whatever was necessary to restore confidence in his country. Korea's economy contracted severely over the next year, but by 1999 it was growing again at an impressive 11 percent rate.

It took Thailand longer to reverse its slide, but after a new prime minister showed a real commitment to reform, its economy rebounded as well. Indonesia was a harder case. Its gross domestic product fell 13 percent in 1998, one of the worst drops anywhere since the Great Depression. There were riots over rapid price increases, and physical attacks on ethnic Chinese businessmen blamed for Indonesian hardships. Suharto was forced to resign after thirty years in power, creating new uncertainty without ending his country's battles with the IMF. Indonesia's loan had to be renegotiated twenty-three times. Eventually, though, the economy began a slow recovery. Indonesia's government has had several peaceful democratic transitions, and the country has enjoyed a long run of healthy growth.

The IMF, despite its weaknesses, was a vital institution, designed to be as detached as possible from the politics of its member nations. And while we didn't control it, as some claimed, we cared a lot about its ability to defuse crises around the world. So even in the midst of the financial firefighting, I encouraged opposition to the Japanese proposal for an Asian Monetary Fund. This wasn't a difficult feat of diplomacy, given the ambivalence in China and other Asian nations about a more assertive Japan. We made the case that a regional fund would leave Asia worse off, because the rest of the world would have less of an incentive to respond to a future crisis on the continent, and the regional political influence over loan conditions would make the Asian fund's programs less credible in the eyes of investors. Of course, we didn't want the United States to be excluded from future crisis responses, and neither did many Asian countries that still viewed the U.S. security presence as an important part of regional stability.

We thought these were pretty compelling arguments. But ultimately, Japan's weakening economy doomed its plan for the Asian fund, forcing its finance ministry officials to withdraw their proposal. It was a humiliating episode for them. We took no pleasure in Japan's economic struggles, which hurt the United States and the global economy by reducing growth in Asia and exacerbating the crisis. But we were pleased to protect the IMF's role as the sole international lender of last resort.

When I left Treasury at the end of the Clinton administration, my colleagues put together tongue-in-cheek recommendations for my next job; for instance, Rubin suggested I could be Larry's biographer. Greenspan proposed "first assistant to the deputy to the managing director of the Asian Monetary Fund," his wry way of celebrating its nonexistence.

• • •

THERE WAS a lull in the crisis in the spring of 1998. After almost a year of running on adrenaline, I started getting migraines; I began competing in triathlons to compensate for the sharp decline in stress. But financial crises can have an unpredictable rhythm. The Asian crisis was slowly spreading beyond Asia. By the summer, Russia, Ukraine, Brazil, and Turkey were all at risk of default.

Russia was in the most dire straits, and its leaders were threatening not to pay back the IMF or their other creditors. I had little involvement in our earlier efforts to support reforms in Russia, but Rubin did ask what I thought of a rescue plan that Larry and David Lipton were discussing with the IMF as a last-ditch effort to prevent default. I was usually on the aggressive side of our team when it came to intervention—and the permissive side when it came to conditionality—but I thought it would be crazy to throw good money after bad. Russia looked hopeless then, financially and politically. Rubin agreed. As hard as the United States had worked to encourage Russia's transition to a market economy, and as worried as we were about instability in a nuclear-armed state, default seemed inevitable, and additional loans felt like they would be a waste of cash and credibility.

But when the financial world is in a fragile place, defaults can have damaging and unanticipated consequences. The shock waves from Russia's default prompted investors to pull back from risk, triggering declines in the prices of financial securities around the world. And these dynamics helped bring the overleveraged U.S. hedge fund Long-Term Capital Management to the brink of failure, raising fears of broader damage to its Wall Street creditors and other institutions with similar risks. Bill McDonough, the head of the New York Fed, helped arrange a private-sector solution even neater than the one we had arranged in Korea. The major Wall Street institutions—with the notable exception of the investment bank Bear Stearns—agreed to inject cash into LTCM until its trades could be safely unwound. We would revisit the LTCM solution when a much more severe crisis hit the United States a decade later.

The collapse of a giant hedge fund with a risk management strategy engineered by two Nobel laureate economists illustrated the dangers of finance in the interconnected modern era. We got yet another reminder in the fall, when the aftershocks from Russia drove Brazil into crisis. After an initial program withered, we helped the IMF assemble another huge wall of money. And once an initial attempt to maintain the real's peg to the dollar was abandoned, superb economic leadership from Brazil helped turn things around within months.

By 1999, the global financial system had calmed down enough that *Time* magazine featured Rubin, Summers, and Greenspan on its cover as "The Committee to Save the World." I was now undersecretary for international affairs, Larry's original job at Treasury, and I was part of a group featured inside the magazine as "The Subcommittee to Save the World." It was a welcome affirmation of our work, but it was over-the-top. We had made lots of mistakes. Our interventions didn't always work wonders. Even Mexico, Korea, and Brazil, the clearest successes, had suffered devastating economic contractions, because deleveraging after a credit bubble is always painful. And I knew the triumphalist tone would offend our colleagues around the world. The money we helped deploy to countries in crisis was critical, but money can't compensate for the absence of political will. The choices we made in Washington were important, but they worked only when we dealt with competent and credible leaders in the affected countries. Brazil's central banker, Arminio Fraga, who also has U.S. citizenship, was so impressive that I later mentioned him to President Obama as a potential Fed chair.

As the "Committee to Save the World" article pointed out, the "astonishingly robust U.S. economy" was making all of us look smart. Even though I had nothing to do with our domestic successes, I saw how our economic strength at home enhanced our influence abroad. When other countries thought we were managing our economy well, they were more inclined to listen to us.

But my main recollection from that era was how scary it was, how little we knew, how we struggled to figure out what mix of money and conditions could restore confidence in a particular country. The economic damage was brutal, even when our interventions worked. It was scarring to see how quickly markets could overwhelm even an aggressive rescue program, how debilitating one wrong move could be during a panic, how indiscriminately contagion could spread, how reluctant most politicians were to approve the unpopular actions needed to contain it. The most important thing I learned about financial crises is that they're awful.

So what caused the Asian contagion? Some of our partners in Europe—and some conservative critics at home—believed that we did, by creating moral hazard. In their view, we were arsonists pretending to be firemen. By bailing out Mexico, we supposedly sent a message to government leaders—and the creditors who financed their risky bets—that they would be bailed out again if their bets went bad again. To the moral hazard fundamentalists, that's why governments continued to make risky bets and creditors continued to finance them.

That story had a lot of power over a lot of people, but it wasn't a very credible explanation. Throughout history, financial crises have always caused tremendous economic and political carnage. A politician might be tempted to borrow too much and leave the consequences to his successor, although the emerging-market crises cost the leaders of Mexico, Thailand, Indonesia, and Korea their jobs. But what foreign bank or investor would finance a weak government or a weak bank in an emerging economy on the belief that the IMF would step in quickly to protect them from losses? Before Mexico, the IMF had lent only relatively small amounts of money to countries in trouble, and the economic and financial damage from their crises was typically extensive. Even in Mexico, there was a lot of pain and losses for ordinary families and investors before and after our rescue began to work. It should have been a cautionary tale, not an attractive model to emulate.

It is true that the overall losses to banks and investors were lower than they might have been without the IMF's rescues, but still they had little reason to feel confident they would be protected again. Before Mexico, plenty of banks around the world had been nationalized or liquidated, often wiping out shareholders and bondholders in the process. Even after Mexico, there was no reasonable expectation of a safety net, no way to know which investments would or wouldn't remain at risk even if the IMF did get involved. When Russia was teetering on the brink of default, some investors did buy its bonds as a "moral hazard play," but their assumption that a rescue was inevitable turned out to be wrong and expensive.

It is possible that at the margin, the success of the Mexico program made investors somewhat more confident about financing the Asian boom, not because they thought it marked the end of crises or they expected protection from losses, but because we had demonstrated a way to reduce the depth of the crisis—the extent and duration of the decline in economic activity. But there's no way to solve a financial crisis without creating some moral hazard, without protecting investors and institutions from some of the consequences of excessive risk taking. They were, in Ted Truman's phrase, collateral beneficiaries of an effective emergency program. It was impossible to design an effective rescue for the intended beneficiaries—the people who lived and worked in those countries—without some collateral beneficiaries.

But the success in Mexico did not produce Asia's boom or the willingness of investors to help finance it. During one meeting in Manila early in the Asian crisis, when some of Europe's finance bureaucrats were invoking Mexico and moral hazard to argue against a generous financial response, Stan Fischer, the excellent American economist who was the IMF's deputy director—I would later recommend him to Obama as a potential Fed chair as well—passed me a note pointing out that condoms don't cause sex. Stan's point was that the IMF loan program didn't cause financial crises. It's hard to believe that the existence of firehouses causes fires.

I thought a better explanation of the core problem was a set of beliefs, a general overconfidence that a long stretch of calm and stability foreshadowed more calm and stability. Less charitably, you could call this a *mania*. Years of dramatic growth convinced investors that the Asian tigers and other emerging markets would keep recording dramatic growth, that past was prologue. While we were firefighting in Asia, I read Charles Kindleberger's classic history of financial crises, *Manias, Panics, and Crashes,* and his explanation of the recurrence of crises over centuries was the most consistent with what I had observed. In Asia, credit nearly doubled in the three years before the crisis. The sustained period of rapid economic growth caused investors to ignore the vulnerability of fixed exchange rates and forget that capital inflows could become outflows in a hurry. They assumed that past performance would indicate future results. As the American economist Hyman Minsky explained in work I would read a decade later, stability can produce excessive confidence, which produces the seeds of future instability.

This penchant for self-delusion is inherently human, but it does not inevitably lead to financial and economic crises. At the time, a similar dynamic was fueling the U.S. dot-com bubble, as investors enthralled by winners like eBay threw cash at losers like Pets.com. But the bursting of that bubble didn't cause a major crisis, because it was financed mostly with equity rather than bank debt. Investors lost their money when their Internet stocks tanked, but the broader economy suffered only a modest slowdown.

To cause a severe crisis, a mania must be financed by concentrated *leverage,* by excessive debt. When financial institutions or governments get overextended, they become vulnerable to creditors demanding their money back. This is especially dangerous when their borrowing is in the form of short-term debt that can run when the mania ends. The classic example is a bank that borrows short from its depositors, who can demand their money back at any time, and lends long to businesses and homeowners. This kind of "maturity mismatch"—the use of short-term funding to finance long-term investments—is how George Bailey got into trouble in *It's a Wonderful Life,* and it's why we now have deposit insurance to avoid bank runs. But a lot of short-term loans to financial institutions can look a lot like uninsured bank deposits, and they can run when confidence goes. When creditors call in the loans and the institutions can't recover the money they had lent to finance longer-term investments, they can fail in a hurry. This is unfortunate if it happens to a single bank, but devastating if it happens to the banking system as a whole.

That was the combustible combination in Asia: mania plus leverage in runnable forms. The overconfidence that fuels bubbles can become panic when bubbles pop, as investors who thought certain types of investments were perfectly safe suddenly decide that nothing that even resembles those investments is safe. Markets stop discriminating among loans, among banks, among countries. They become as blind to strengths as they had been blind to weaknesses. The more money runs, the more pressure mounts on other money to run. That's how financial fires spread. And that's when you need a good fire department, with strong leaders and modern equipment.

We eventually managed to set up the IMF's new firefighting fund, which wasn't easy. We had to negotiate for months with congressional Republicans, who held up the U.S. contribution by attaching completely unrelated abortion restrictions on U.S. foreign aid to our funding bill. I also helped lead a push to create the Group of Twenty, an expanded international forum for financial cooperation, including emerging economies such as China, India, and Brazil alongside the more advanced economies. In the Obama administration, we would go a step further and make the G-20 the main arena for global economic issues, eclipsing the outdated G-7.

Just about every debate we had during the Asian crisis would recur in the global crises a decade later: tough love versus unconditional love, Old Testament justice for arsonists versus pragmatic concern for innocents, transparency versus reassurance, austerity versus stimulus, liquidity versus solvency. In every country, we debated how long to let the fire burn before we should intervene aggressively, what the likelihood was that it would spread, and whether the people we wanted to save could be trusted to do what they promised. We learned it could be costlier to offer too little money than too much; as President Zedillo put it, when markets overreact, policy should overreact, too. We also learned that while no one wants to hand out money without strings attached, too many strings could strangle.

There was no foolproof formula for crisis response. It was more art than science, more shades of gray than black and white. It required flexibility and creativity and humility, not unswerving principle. I liked to paraphrase the boxer and philosopher Mike Tyson: *Everyone's got a strategy until they get punched in the face.*

I DIDN'T go into government to be a reforming crusader. I just wanted to do interesting and consequential work. I wanted to be part of something larger than myself. At Treasury, I had the great privilege to help craft policies that would shape the fortunes of nations and improve millions of lives. And when the emerging-market crises were over, I got to turn my attention to a new set of challenges that didn't involve rescuing investors or enraging the public, the kind of challenges that had first drawn me to public service.

As the end of the millennium approached, Pope John Paul II and other religious leaders were calling for rich nations to forgive the debts of poor nations, where nearly three billion people were living on $2 a day or less. This "Jubilee" movement had a powerful moral case, and I had seen the evidence growing up abroad. Globally, one in three kids was malnourished, and their leaders routinely mortgaged their futures to finance wars and villas and Swiss bank accounts. In many countries, interest payments exceeded health and education budgets. I believed—as did Larry, who became Treasury secretary after Rubin stepped down in 1999—that there were also economic and strategic reasons to help poor countries escape crushing debts that hurt their people and destabilized their regions. So we proposed to substantially reduce the loans of the IMF and the World Bank to the poorest countries, and to write off the U.S. government loans entirely over time. We also proposed some creative conditions. To qualify for debt relief, governments would have to divert the money they saved on interest payments into health care and other services for their people.

There was strong resistance among some Treasury staff and from finance ministries around the world, where forgiving debt was seen as an expensive gesture and a moral hazard–inducing precedent. The IMF had never forgiven debts; it raised money from member countries by assuring them its loans would always be senior and paid back in full. The same was true of the World Bank. And some Europeans argued that relief would only encourage irresponsibility in developing countries.

But we didn't think the rich countries that had provided the corrupt dictators of those developing countries with money and weapons had the moral or economic high ground. When I met the U2 rock star and debt relief activist Bono, he did a funny impression of moral hazard fundamentalists lecturing the poor. I told him it was weird to hear a Scottish guy speak in a German accent. Bono, of course, is Irish, but he apparently forgave my faux pas; when I left Treasury, his suggestion for my next job was drummer for his band.

I handled most of the global negotiations over debt relief. I also did much of the political negotiating on Capitol Hill, which I thought would be even harder. Republicans had just impeached the president over an extramarital affair. They had held up a routine increase in the U.S. debt ceiling to try to get President Clinton to slash domestic spending, and when Secretary Rubin had taken a series of creative financial measures to avoid a catastrophic government default, they had threatened to impeach him, too. Republicans tended to view the IMF as a U.S.-funded welfare program for the world. And many liberal Democrats were just as hostile to the IMF, seeing it as a tool for imposing laissez-faire economics and austerity in the name of "structural reform." I hired an excellent Oxfam activist, Lydia Williams, to help design our

strategy and reach out to the left. But after the trauma of impeach-
ment, the partisanship on the Hill seemed too nasty to overcome.

Implausibly, though, the cause of global debt relief brought together an extraordinary coalition of evangelical Republicans and liberal Democrats who wanted to do the right thing for people in need.
We worked successfully with southern conservatives such as Dick
Armey of Texas as well as northeastern liberals such as Barney Frank of
Massachusetts. On November 6, 2000, the day before an election that
would inspire a month of partisan litigation, I was part of a bipartisan
group that watched President Clinton sign legislation forgiving loans
to twenty-two poor countries.

"I believe this will put our country squarely on the side of human-
ity for a very, very long time to come," he said that day in the East
Room of the White House.

It was a cool thing to celebrate. In my twelve-year initial stint
at Treasury, I caught many glimpses of Washington's pettiness and
dysfunction, but I also got a somewhat unrealistic view of the positive
impact that public servants could have on the world. That debt relief
legislation, for example, included a $50 million U.S. contribution to
a global vaccination fund that Sheryl Sandberg, Larry's chief of staff,
and I had championed. These were good causes, and we were able to
do something valuable for countless people we would never meet.

I HAD started at Treasury as a civil servant, but I was now an appointee in a Democratic administration. So when President Bush took
office, it was time for me to leave. The Council on Foreign Relations
graciously offered me a position at my government salary while I tried
to figure out what to do with the rest of my life.

I talked to a few financial firms, but I still felt no attraction to
that work. One friend who had left Treasury for an investment bank
advised me that if I wanted a finance job, I should decide where to go
solely according to which firm would pay me the most, because that
would be the best measure of how much they valued me. It sounded

like a bizarre way to think about work. I never considered trying to get rich, and it never really occurred to me to choose a job based on what I would make rather than what I would do. We lived very comfortably, and even as a public servant, my salary was higher than the vast majority of American paychecks. Carole never put pressure on me to earn more. She just wanted me around more.

I ended up right back in the world of financial crises. When my friend Stan Fischer stepped down as the IMF's number two, a job traditionally held by an American, Horst Koehler, the German head of the fund, proposed me for the job. But John Taylor, a Stanford economist who had replaced me at Treasury, blocked my appointment. I was now considered part of the Clinton crowd; Taylor thought we had created too much moral hazard in the emerging-market crises, and the Bush administration wanted to signal a departure in policy. They proposed a Republican from Stanford, Anne Krueger, instead. Koehler then asked me to take another senior job, as head of policy and review. I accepted. Larry and some of my other friends thought it was a step down in prestige, but the job came with real responsibility. My department was the arbiter of policy, and had to sign off on every commitment of financial resources. I was pleased to have the chance to keep doing compelling work.

The IMF was a more formal and less fun place to work than Treasury. The meetings were endless, with crushing bureaucracy, an intrusive and fractious executive board, an appalling amount of paper, and a lot of factional conflict among various fiefdoms. The salaries were exceptionally generous for the public sector, which was awkward given the public mission of the institution and our interventions in poverty-ridden and crisis-stricken countries. The pace was much slower than I was used to. And I was not that good at sitting still.

The IMF was full of smart and dedicated people, but not many had experienced the burden of making policy decisions as government officials. There was a lot of paper and bureaucracy and talking. I once asked my colleague Ken Rogoff, the IMF's excellent chief economist, how he made it through all the long meetings with senior officials. Rogoff, who had been a chess prodigy as a kid, told me he survived by playing a dozen games simultaneously in his head.

Still, I got to work on some consequential issues. I helped design a set of principles to guide lending decisions in future financial crises, to better distinguish when we should force countries to restructure their debts and when we should help them meet those obligations. I helped define a set of limits for IMF assistance, an effort to mitigate moral hazard while preserving room for aggressive actions in truly systemic crises. I helped call more attention to the vulnerabilities that come from risky forms of financing, alongside the IMF's traditional focus on large fiscal deficits and inflation. And while the Bush team liked to criticize the bailouts of the Clinton era, they ultimately supported large IMF rescue packages for Brazil, Uruguay, and Turkey with the familiar wall-of-money strategy. That was what the IMF was for.

Years later, Mervyn King, the governor of the Bank of England, joked at a farewell dinner that I was a textbook proof of the difference between correlation and causation. "Tim was present at all the crises," he said. "But he didn't cause the crises. The crises caused him." Again and again, I got to see how indulgent capital financed booms, how cracks in confidence turned boom to bust to panic, how crisis managers could help contain panics with decisiveness and overwhelming force, and how the kind of actions needed to defuse crises were inherently unpopular and fraught with risk.

That turned out to be valuable experience.

THREE

Leaning Against the Wind

In early September 2003, I was in London on IMF business when I got a call from Pete Peterson, the billionaire cofounder of the Blackstone Group private equity firm. Peterson was the chairman of the board of the Federal Reserve Bank of New York, and he asked if I'd be interested in talking to the board about running it.

My first reaction was to laugh, and ask: "How much do you know about me?" I gently pointed out that it seemed a bit early in my career for that job.

The New York Fed, the government's main outpost in America's financial center, is the largest and most influential of the Federal Reserve's twelve regional banks. Its president serves as vice chair of the Fed committee that sets monetary policy; its staff buys and sells government securities to implement monetary policy; it shares responsibility for supervising some of America's biggest banks, including Citigroup, JPMorgan Chase, and Bank of New York Mellon. At the time, it was mostly unknown to the public—except for the seven thousand tons of gold in its basement, the stash Jeremy Irons tried to steal in the film *Die Hard: With a Vengeance*—but it was a venerable institution, and traditionally its leaders had been financial giants.

Its first president, Benjamin Strong, Jr., a member of J. P. Morgan's powerful inner circle, had been the dominant force at the Federal Reserve in its early years. Its recent presidents were also prominent financial statesmen: Bill McDonough, a former banker who had held the job for the previous decade and helped defuse the LTCM crisis; Jerry Corrigan, a gravelly-voiced, blunt-spoken economist who was a Goldman Sachs managing director; and the legendary Paul Volcker, my Dartmouth graduation speaker, a six-foot-seven former Chase Manhattan banker who had gone on to the Fed chairmanship and was considered the conscience of Wall Street. I was only forty-two, and I had never worked in the finance industry.

Peterson's first choice to lead the New York Fed, the former IMF deputy Stan Fischer—at the time a top Citigroup executive—had turned him down. Other potential candidates, including John Taylor, my replacement at Treasury, hadn't found enough support on the board. So Larry Summers, who had become president of Harvard University, and Bob Rubin, who had also joined Citigroup, suggested Peterson reach out to me. Chairman Greenspan also supported my candidacy, although he told me he hadn't realized during my time at Treasury that I wasn't a PhD economist.

Peterson was still worried that I looked too young to command a room, as he put it. But with his characteristic humility, Larry told Peterson I had been strong enough to stand up to him, which meant I was strong enough to run the New York Fed. He apparently found that persuasive. Some of his board members were concerned about the social aspects of the job; they even asked to interview Carole to gauge her suitability as a first lady, a request I politely declined. Previous presidents had joined all kinds of civic groups and attended frequent Manhattan receptions. I told the board I preferred spending evenings at home with Carole and the kids, but I'd show up around town when necessary.

I guess the board was OK with that, because they asked me to take the job. My family was less OK. Our twelve-year-old, Elise, burst into tears when I told her we were moving to New York; she said I was ruining her life and her mother's career. Nine-year-old Ben didn't seem as troubled, but he was generally less vocal than his sister. Carole was supportive but not thrilled. She would have to close her therapy practice and leave the George Washington University Medical School, where she was teaching listening skills to future doctors. And she had understandable reservations about the disruptions to all our lives. I had reservations, too. I would have to commute between Washington and New York until the end of the school year, and I knew Carole would bear most of the burden of the transition. But she was willing to make the sacrifice—"if you really want to do it," she said—so I was able to accept the job.

Once again, I felt intimidated by how much I had to learn. The Fed played a central role in responding to financial crises, and although I may have already been "baptized by fire," as one of Peterson's advisers for the search process told the *New York Times,* this job came with a much greater level of responsibility. And I didn't have much experience with the rest of the Fed's work. I had never supervised or regulated banks or markets. I hadn't thought much about monetary policy, either; I doubted I could offer much help on that front to Greenspan, who was regarded at the time as a monetary maestro.

I also understood why people questioned my gravitas; another one of those gag suggestions for my post-Treasury job had been star of a sequel about the teen doctor Doogie Howser. The night before I started at the New York Fed, I stopped at a convenience store to pick up yogurt, milk, beer, and other basics for my one-bedroom apartment on the Upper East Side.

I got carded.

• • •

I CAME to the New York Fed as an outsider, and I didn't bring any of my own people with me to try to change it. I wanted to show respect for the institution, figure out how it worked, learn its strengths and weaknesses. It already had a solid reputation for being knowledgeable and sophisticated about financial markets, though some considered it a bit too close to those markets.

The Fed's twenty-two-story building at 33 Liberty Street, a sandstone-and-limestone throwback to the banking houses of the Italian Renaissance, sits just a few blocks from Wall Street, in the shadows of the modern skyscrapers of the world's major financial firms. My initial impression was that it was a bit musty with tradition and heavy on hierarchy. The walls were thick, the atmosphere dark, the daily rhythm slow and comfortable. The top ten senior officials all had spacious offices on a wood-paneled executive floor, separated from their teams on lower floors and across the street. It was exceedingly quiet up there. Oil paintings of my predecessors hung on the walls of an ornate boardroom named for Paul Volcker. And there were some weird formalities. During the day, coffee was brought to my desk on a silver tray. The first time I hosted a dinner at the New York Fed, I was served first while my guests watched. A buzzer was placed in front of me in case I needed to summon the staff. I would eventually change or eliminate many of these staid traditions, starting with the buzzer.

My initial briefings were awkwardly formal, too. Typically, a senior executive would spend almost the entire time presenting a deck of PowerPoint slides, leaving only a few minutes for me to ask questions. Junior staffers seemed hesitant to speak. I met plenty of smart and competent people, but the meetings were not designed to promote debate or discussion, much less decisions by a new president with no history at the institution or experience in the field.

I developed a lot of respect for the bank's senior leaders, but I also began to reach out to talented staffers I found lower on the organizational chart. I asked that every memo submitted to me include the phone numbers of the staffers who drafted it, so I could call them directly with questions. And I began to change the expectations around meetings, asking everyone to read the slides and papers in advance so we could spend our time debating substance. I made it clear I expected everyone to say what they thought, regardless of how junior they were, regardless of the prevailing view in the upper hierarchy of the Fed in New York or Washington.

This was a time when things seemed to be going pretty well in the American financial system. The U.S. economy was recovering from a mild recession, after weathering a series of financial disturbances with relative ease—the global crises of the 1990s, the demise of LTCM, the dot-com bust, the September 11 attacks, and a rash of accounting scandals that took down Enron and Arthur Andersen. Growth and confidence were getting stronger. Inflation was low. Credit was cheap and widely available. The banks under New York Fed supervision showed no signs of distress; on the contrary, they were enjoying their biggest profits in decades. They had high levels of capital, so they seemed well-positioned in case the good times stopped rolling.

At the Fed in Washington, at the time, there was little apparent concern about the stability of the financial system. In New York, with some exceptions, there was also a general sense that things were under control. The bank supervisors had a pretty good record, although you could argue that with the banks thriving, they were like the old Maytag repairmen who didn't have much to fix. When I started, there was a lot of understandable focus on fighting the last war, prioritizing post–September 11 issues such as hardening market infrastructure to survive terror attacks. Bank supervisors were consumed with compliance issues, making sure rogue states didn't park cash in American institutions and lenders didn't violate antidiscrimination laws. One former New York Fed board member, Bob Wilmers of M&T Bank, once told me that 70 percent of his bank's examination process involved anti-money-laundering and consumer protection.

Those were important issues, but they seemed to be eclipsing more subjective and challenging systemic questions, such as whether banks were adequately managing their risks and retaining enough capital and liquidity to survive a crisis. In those days, systemic risk—the vulnerability of the financial system to a severe crisis—wasn't prominent on the national radar screen. In fact, economists were starting to debate whether America's long stretch of stability constituted a new normal, a Great Moderation, a quasi-permanent era of resilience to shocks. There was growing confidence that derivatives and other financial innovations designed to hedge and distribute risk—along with better monetary policy to respond to downturns and better technology to smooth out inventory cycles—had made devastating crises a thing of the past.

I did not share that confidence. I had no particular knowledge or insight into whether the new financial innovations were stabilizing or destabilizing, but I was reflexively skeptical of excess conviction in any form, especially excess optimism. My dominant professional experiences had involved financial failures. I had seen during the emerging-market crises of the previous decade how long periods of stability and growth could breed instability and disaster. Confidence had always been an evanescent thing, and in this new age of mobile capital, trauma in one part of the world or one corner of the financial system could spread quickly. I didn't see how a few years of calm or some clever financial innovations would cure the basic human tendency toward mania and self-delusion. History suggests that financial crises are usually preceded by proclamations that crises are a thing of the past.

In my very first public speech at the New York Fed in March 2004, I tried to push back against complacency, telling a room full of bankers that the wonders of the new financial world would not necessarily prevent catastrophic failures of major institutions, and should not inspire delusions of safety on Wall Street. I even cited my favorite theorist on financial irrationality, the leading promoter of the idea that periodic financial crises are practically inevitable.

"These improvements are unlikely to have brought an end to what Charles Kindleberger called 'manias and panics,'" I said. "It is

important that those of you who run financial institutions build in a
sufficient cushion against adversity."

So I started my new job with some generalized concern about the
inherent vulnerability of financial systems to periodic crises. And I
was troubled from the beginning by a more specific vulnerability of
the U.S. system. The Fed was seen as America's financial stability regulator, and the New York Fed was Washington's best window into
Wall Street, touching the markets every day. But our power to con-
strain risk in the financial system did not extend to the entire financial
system. Our authority was disturbingly limited.

The Fed shared responsibility for supervising commercial banks
with insured deposits. And if one of those banks ran into liquidity
problems, it could go to the Fed's discount window for emergency
loans that could help prevent a run. But as I started thinking about
a potential crisis on my watch, one glaring danger stood out. Huge
swaths of the financial system—investment banks, Fannie Mae and
Freddie Mac, and many other large firms that behaved like banks
without having to obey bank safety and soundness rules—were outside the Fed's jurisdiction as well as the Fed's safety net. These "nonbanks," or "shadow banks," were borrowing short and lending long,
just like George Bailey's bank or any other bank. But they were not
subject to the capital requirements and other safeguards imposed on
banks to limit risk, they did not have deposit insurance to prevent
runs, and they would not be able to access the discount window if
they faced runs. In that initial March 2004 speech, I suggested that
financial innovation was driving risk and leverage into corners of the
financial system with weaker supervision, and that our tools for monitoring systemic risk weren't keeping up.

Overall, more than half of America's financial liabilities had migrated outside of banks and beyond the Fed's direct purview. There's
nothing inherently dangerous about risk outside the traditional banking sector, unless the risk is concentrated in large bank-like entities

The Rise of "Shadow Banking"
Financial Sector Liabilities

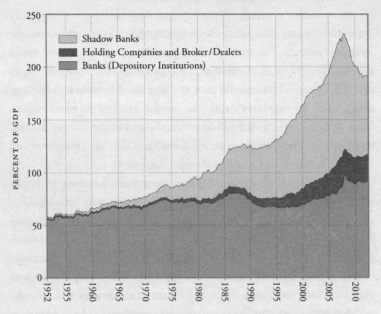

The tremendous growth in financial sector credit from the 1980s through 2007 was almost entirely outside the traditional banking system. Risk consistently migrated to institutions that had fewer constraints than banks and did not have access to the government safety net.

Source: Federal Reserve Board.

with heavy leverage and short-term funding without bank-like regulations. But that's exactly what had happened in the United States. This evolution in the structure of our financial system—the proliferation of risk in nonbank institutions that borrowed short and lent long just like banks—struck me as an overwhelmingly consequential problem for us as a financial stability regulator and a lender of last resort. I can't say I had any idea what to do about it during my early days at the Fed. But as I had told Bob Rubin in another context, just because a problem didn't have an obvious solution didn't mean it wasn't a problem.

I knew that any financial crisis would end up at the New York Fed's doorstep, whether it began in our jurisdiction or not.

In those early months, I often joked that being president of the New York Fed was like being the Wizard of Oz; my friend and former Treasury colleague Sheryl Sandberg, who had become a vice president at Google, used to call me the man behind the curtain. There was a widespread perception that we had awesome powers to fight financial fires, but when I studied our actual firefighting equipment—cataloged in a New York Fed binder known internally as "the Doomsday Book"—I was not particularly impressed.

In addition to its monetary policy instruments, the Fed could lend to institutions that needed cash in a crisis—but only if they were commercial banks with insured deposits, and only if we thought they were fundamentally solvent, with their assets worth more than their liabilities. We did have additional authority in "unusual and exigent circumstances" through Section 13(3) of the Federal Reserve Act, but the Fed hadn't invoked it since the Great Depression, and even that break-the-glass, only-in-extremis power was severely constrained. Under 13(3), the Fed could conceivably lend to a nonbank we deemed solvent, but only if it was in such deep trouble that no one else would lend to it, and even then only if we could secure collateral that could plausibly cover our exposure. So we wouldn't be able to take much risk, and we wouldn't have much preemptive power to help firms before they were past the point of no return, even if we thought the financial system depended on it. That struck me as a problem, too.

Over the next few years, while financial markets and home prices and nationwide borrowing soared, my colleagues and I spent much of our time and energy trying to make the system more resilient, better prepared to withstand a crisis. Ultimately, of course, our efforts were insufficient. We failed to prevent the worst financial crisis and the deepest recession in generations. I had the dubious distinction of being in charge of the New York Fed when Wall Street imploded.

The crisis later inspired a lot of commentary suggesting that the Fed was a reluctant regulator—and that I was too close to Wall Street, too confident in the competence and integrity of bankers, too devoted to the free-market fundamentalism I supposedly inherited from Rubin, Summers, and Greenspan. I was routinely described as a tool of the industry, bent by the banks. Even critics who didn't suggest I was corrupt assumed I was captured by the establishment's finance-friendly view of the world. So before I explain what we did at the New York Fed and why, as well as what we missed and why, I want to describe my attitudes toward the financial world when I started the job.

I HAD never thought of finance as a particularly special or prestigious profession.

My classmates who headed to Wall Street weren't disproportionately smart or distinguished, though they weren't especially dim or ethically challenged, either. Reading *Liar's Poker,* Michael Lewis's scathing portrait of life in the bond markets, reinforced my view of finance as a business I wouldn't be good at and couldn't imagine being part of. I remember after the death of Carole's mother in 1987, a trauma that inspired her to write a young-adult novel about life after losing a parent, her Merrill Lynch broker called to urge us to shift her modest inheritance into some new securities. He was obviously motivated by what his firm wanted to sell, not by what made sense for us, leaving me with a distaste that I never forgot.

At Treasury in the 1990s, I witnessed repeated episodes of finance at its worst. In Japan, I saw a banking system that had gotten wrapped up with crime syndicates known as *yakuza*s while financing a real estate boom. And the relationships between the bureaucrats of the Japanese finance ministry and the institutions they were supposed to supervise were so close it was hard to tell who was running whom. I then watched more financial booms blow up in Latin America, Asia, and Russia. I learned how vulnerable markets could be to herd behavior, to uninformed, indiscriminate shifts in sentiments. Many financiers who lent money in Asia did not seem to know much about the risks they were taking or the countries they were playing in.

But I did not view Wall Street as a cabal of idiots or crooks. My jobs mostly exposed me to talented senior bankers, and selection bias probably gave me an impression that the U.S. financial sector was more capable and ethical than it really was. I spent more time with smart executives such as Deryck Maughan, a Salomon Brothers banker I knew in Japan who later became CEO, and smart investors such as Stan Druckenmiller, a hedge fund billionaire I sometimes consulted about markets, than I spent with the sordid elements of the financial industry. And working for Secretary Rubin surely affected my view of Wall Street competence, because he was as competent as anyone I knew.

I did come of age professionally at a time when financial innovation and the freer flow of capital across borders were widely seen as good things. As a young international negotiator, I pushed for open markets for the U.S. financial industry, even though I sometimes had misgivings that we were pushing too hard. I greatly admired Rubin, Summers, and Greenspan, and I shared their general approval of markets and financial innovation. But the common broad-brush caricature of that trio as unswerving free-market ideologues is unfair. For example, during the Clinton years, they all pushed for stricter regulation of the mortgage giants Fannie Mae and Freddie Mac, the "government-sponsored enterprises" (GSEs) that were exploiting their implicit federal backstop to load up on low-priced leverage. Fannie and Freddie had immense bipartisan influence in Congress, so reform didn't happen, but it should have.

Greenspan did have an almost theological belief that markets were rational and efficient, as well as a deep skepticism that government supervision and regulation could make them safer. But he was a strong supporter of our financial rescues in the emerging-market crises. Rubin, the only member of the trio who had made a living in the markets, had much less faith in their inherent wisdom and rationality.

He consistently expressed concern about excessive leverage, although he was also skeptical of government's ability to do much about it. Larry's view of the world fell somewhere in between, probably closer to Greenspan's at the time. I didn't have the strength of any of their convictions, but by disposition, my view was closer to Rubin's. My formative exposure to finance was the emerging-market crises, which were not attractive advertisements for free-market fundamentalism.

My responsibilities at Treasury in the 1990s covered international issues, so I was mostly a bystander during the Clinton administration's debates over financial regulation, and I didn't have strong views about them at the time. I played no role in the noble but futile efforts to rein in Fannie and Freddie. I also had no involvement in the central battle of the time, the bipartisan effort to formally end the Depression-era "Glass-Steagall" legal boundaries between commercial banking and other financial activities, boundaries that had already been substantially eroded by changes in regulation and financial innovations. But I did play a peripheral role—and not a very distinguished one—in the debate over derivatives, the financial instruments such as swaps, options, and other contracts that derive their value from some underlying price or rate.

In 1998, Brooksley Born, the chairwoman of the Commodity Futures Trading Commission, floated the idea of regulating privately traded "over-the-counter" derivatives, customized deals that were not posted on public exchanges. She didn't unveil any specific plans, but she did suggest that swaps—including foreign exchange swaps, which cut across my international portfolio—ought to be regulated as futures contracts by the CFTC. I didn't know much about the issue, but all the other U.S. regulators and my Treasury colleagues were deeply concerned that her plan could create dangerous legal uncertainties about trillions of dollars of existing derivatives contracts. The air was thick with warnings that Born's ideas would create financial chaos.

The popular narrative of Born's crusade has been boiled down to a morality play, pitting a heroic Born against nefarious financial

Goliaths. But the reality was less black-and-white. In many ways, the battle was more about turf and interests than substance or ideology. The Fed and other regulators fought the CFTC; the New York banks that dominated the derivatives business fought the Chicago exchanges that hoped to expand their market share; and the lobbies for the various business interests fought one another on Capitol Hill. Even Born was not proposing to ban derivatives. She just thought they should be regulated as futures by the CFTC and traded on the Chicago exchanges. My biases were with the Fed, mostly because of the quality of the Fed officials I had worked with during the earlier crises. The CFTC did not have a sterling reputation for market sophistication, and was widely perceived as captured by Chicago.

But Born's motives were noble, and her concerns about the lack of regulatory oversight of the derivatives market were prescient. She just didn't have a concrete or plausible plan. I remember she began one meeting at the CFTC by pulling out a yellow pad and reading from dozens of pages of handwritten notes about our messy securities laws. She clearly felt strongly about the cause of reform, but her proposals for reform were mostly impenetrable.

With limited knowledge, I found myself sympathetic to the substantive case that Larry, Greenspan, and the New York faction of the derivatives industry were making against Born's proposals. They saw derivatives as valuable tools for hedging and distributing risks—airlines, for example, use derivatives to protect themselves from future increases in fuel prices—and more specialized over-the-counter derivatives as particularly valuable for specific businesses facing specific risks. They argued that firms already had good incentives to manage derivatives carefully, and that government interference in private transactions could stifle innovation in a dynamic industry. During one discussion in Rubin's small conference room, I invoked the lazy argument that regulating the over-the-counter market might drive derivatives offshore. I must have sounded like a bank lobbyist, and Rubin shot me a derisive look.

"That's the weakest argument you can ever make against reform," he said.

Rubin had run a financial institution with a large business in derivatives, and while he recognized their benefits, he thought their complexity combined with their tendency to increase leverage could make them extremely dangerous. He was nervous about institutions taking on derivatives risks they didn't understand. But he didn't think much of Born's proposals, either. Her credibility suffered from the weakness of the CFTC's credibility. And the fears about legal uncertainty, while surely exaggerated by the CFTC's turf-conscious rivals as well as bankers who reflexively oppose new regulations, were real. When Born released a concept paper, Treasury, the Securities and Exchange Commission, and the Fed all opposed her approach to reform.

Born's ideas had no chance in an anti-regulatory Republican Congress anyway. Still, her instinct that derivatives were falling through the regulatory cracks absolutely had merit. We shouldn't have been so dismissive of the general concern about derivatives just because we had issues with her remedies. Treasury did favor mandatory "clearing" of futures contracts, but Greenspan objected, and the idea went nowhere at the time. Overall, the bipartisan legislation that President Clinton eventually signed was an unfortunate missed opportunity, and in some respects, it weakened the already limited oversight of derivatives. By the time I got to the New York Fed in late 2003, the derivatives business would be much bigger, much more complex, and near the top of any sensible list of concerns about the financial system.

IT'S FAIR to say that I had not been a vocal critic of the financial system before I started my new job. I wasn't a staunch defender of the financial system, either, and I had seen how its failures could cause significant pain. But the New York Fed president is often viewed as a servant of the financial establishment, in part because the optics of the institution's governance are awful.

Like the Fed's other eleven reserve banks, the New York Fed is technically "owned" by the banks in its region. By law, three of the nine directors on the New York Fed board must be representatives of those banks; they also elect three of the other directors, ostensibly to represent the public, with the Federal Reserve Board in Washington appointing the final three directors. But the directors have no involvement in regulation or supervision or emergency lending, and only an advisory role on monetary policy; unlike the shareholders of a normal corporation, the New York Fed's bank shareholders do not control its operations. However, the board does select the president and set the president's compensation, subject to the approval of Washington. So the New York Fed has always been vulnerable to perceptions of capture by the big banks. And I made some changes to the board that unfortunately made those bad optics even worse.

The board that I inherited had an interesting mix of talent, but it was a bit weak on financial experience. I thought we needed a stronger board with more leaders of the major New York companies, to better reflect the composition of our changing financial system. So I recruited some prominent financiers to join it, including Lehman Brothers CEO Dick Fuld; JPMorgan Chase CEO Jamie Dimon, former Goldman Sachs Chairman Steve Friedman, who was still on the firm's board of directors; and General Electric CEO Jeff Immelt, who also oversaw his company's financing arm, GE Capital. I basically restored the New York Fed board to its historic roots as an elite roster of the local financial establishment. But Paul Volcker, whom I consulted often for advice, presciently warned me that I was exposing the Fed to too much "reputational risk." I would end up having to ask Fuld to resign from the board on the eve of Lehman's collapse. Friedman later resigned after public disclosures that he had bought Goldman stock during the crisis; though he had complied with Fed rules, his actions caused an uproar.

Volcker was a towering figure in the financial community and a thundering critic of modern Wall Street, especially investment banks such as Lehman and Goldman. He didn't like the conflicts of interest, the mind-boggling compensation, the elevation of risky trading of newfangled products over careful and conservative banking. He would later quip that there hadn't been a useful financial innovation since the ATM. I took his discomfort seriously, but I didn't have the strength of his convictions. I had never worked in banking, so I had no basis for comparison to the past. I didn't see the financial sector as either irretrievably broken or inherently wise. I saw it as an inherently risky business, a collection of profit-maximizing individuals with profit-maximizing shareholders, providing generally valuable economic services. I was rarely shocked by reports of rapacious behavior. I took it as a given.

I rarely socialized with Wall Street executives—I did run into Volcker once at a lavish celebration of Peterson's Blackstone Group, and he whispered, only half-jokingly: "You shouldn't be here!"—but I talked to them regularly to get their perspectives on the markets and the economy. That was an important part of my job. I thought some of them seemed very capable, others less so. I also thought they had pretty good incentives to try to keep their firms from self-destructing, but I knew we couldn't leave the stability of the system in their hands.

At one early meeting, several senior bankers complained to me that new capital rules would hinder their ability to take on leverage. I said I understood why they might find that a problem, but they didn't get to set the rules that determined how much risk they could take.

"That's our job," I told them.

Obviously, we didn't do that job well enough.

MY FIRST inclination and my most important decision at the New York Fed was to increase the attention we paid to systemic risk.

We had many other responsibilities competing for our time and resources, and we were careful to give them the attention they required. We managed the nation's large-value payments system, the Treasury auction process that financed the government, and a substantial portion of the Fed's cash distribution business. And we shared responsibility for enforcing consumer protection and anti-money-laundering laws. Seven months after I arrived, we slapped a hefty fine on Citigroup after an affiliate took advantage of unsophisticated borrowers and then misled the Fed during the subsequent investigation; Volcker called to say he was pleasantly surprised.

I did not get very involved with the emerging concerns about the subprime mortgage market. Ned Gramlich, a Fed governor in Washington, was already leading a process to examine excesses and abuses in the mortgage business serving lower-income Americans. I was impressed by Gramlich's work, and those issues seemed to be getting a fair amount of attention from the Fed in Washington. I didn't want us to be like kid soccer players, all swarming around the ball. I wanted us to focus on the systemic vulnerabilities that were getting less attention—starting with our own banks, but looking outside them as well.

Inside the New York Fed, I convened a series of "risk breakfasts" to bring together staff from the organization's disconnected silos— supervision, markets, payment systems, international, research, and more—to share information about potential dangers to the system. We set up a more formal Financial Risk Committee that reviewed detailed analyses of systemic threats. We also conducted "horizontal risk reviews" of all the institutions we supervised directly, to get a sense of how the different banks managed different risks, and to try to promote more conservative approaches across the industry. The idea was to identify best practices, highlight them, and push banks to imitate their most forward-thinking competitors.

I spent much of my time trying to understand whether banks under our supervision had enough capital—the cushion that could help them absorb losses, retain confidence, and remain solvent in a crisis. Generally, capital represents the money a bank would have left over if it sold all its assets and paid all its liabilities, the liquidation value of the company. It's a measure of conservatism, the flip side of leverage; the heavier an institution's reliance on borrowing to finance its operations, the lower its capital levels. In a crisis, capital serves as a shock absorber, a first line of defense against losses. A well-capitalized bank can take hits without creditors questioning its ability to meet its obligations. It's like a down payment for a homeowner with a mortgage, a life jacket keeping the borrower above water even if the home loses value.

So in those early months at the Fed, I began asking questions about capital: Do our banks really have enough? How can we be sure? Our banks were holding capital equivalent to 13 percent of their "risk-weighted assets," well above the required 8 percent. But I kept pestering my staff: Are we confident we know how to measure the risk in those assets? Why was the requirement only 8 percent? Would those capital levels still be adequate if the world looked darker? What if the world looked darker than it has looked in recent history?

The banks themselves were confident they had more than enough capital. As part of our horizontal risk reviews, we asked them to conduct internal "stress tests" to model the impact of losses from recessions and other potential shocks; not one bank produced a scenario that significantly dented its capital. The worst outcome considered in their internal tests didn't even eat through a quarter's worth of earnings. Their overconfidence was perhaps understandable at the time. Default rates were low, the economy was growing, and they were making a lot of money. In that environment, prudence would have been an expensive strategy. And leverage was the great multiplier, a source of greater potential profits, but also greater risk.

For example, if you were a shareholder in a bank or an investment bank that had $100 worth of assets financed by $10 of shareholder capital, a 10:1 leverage ratio, you'd double your money if the assets rose in value to $110. But if your bank had that same $100 in assets with only $5 in capital, a 20:1 leverage ratio, the same $10 increase in value would triple your investment. Of course, if the asset value instead decreased $6, from $100 to $94, the bank with only $5 in capital would be insolvent; leverage dramatically increases "wipeout risk." But in those days, the financial community didn't expect asset values to decrease. A financial CEO who was unusually cautious about leverage during the boom probably would have been fired before the bust. Many bank executives didn't even want to think about truly extreme events.

But even when the Fed's own bank supervisors and economists analyzed the system, they thought there was plenty of capital in the banks to absorb a substantial increase in losses. These public servants had good incentives to be tough, because a crisis would fall to us to clean up, and they were a talented, experienced, thoughtful group. Even so, they had a hard time coming up with economic scenarios that would generate losses large enough to seriously impair bank capital. One internal Fed analysis calculated that losses in consumer portfolios would have to be four times as large as in any recent downturn—essentially Great Depression levels—to deplete bank capital to dangerous levels. By existing regulatory standards, the banks under the Fed umbrella seemed well capitalized. Compared to the more leveraged investment banks as well as Fannie Mae and Freddie Mac, they seemed very well capitalized. At the time, trying to force our commercial banks to raise more capital (and dilute the holdings of their existing shareholders) so that they could survive a Great Depression would have seemed arbitrary and unnecessary, like imposing a thirty-mile-an-hour speed limit on an expressway. And it would have driven more risk into nonbanks.

Still, since we had no way of knowing what the future would bring, and I had vivid memories of the crises of the previous decade, I wanted us to examine the darkest possible scenarios, the seemingly implausible "tail risks." In meeting after meeting, I argued that regulators and risk managers alike needed to set aside assumptions about the implausibility of a major shock and study the impact of that shock if it somehow happened. This provoked a fair amount of skepticism internally, and derision outside the Fed. In that apparently benign state of the world, many bank executives thought it was totally unreasonable to expect them to prepare for a deep recession, much less a depression.

I tried to lean against the prevailing winds of complacency—not only behind closed doors, but in public. In one speech to a group of bankers two years after I arrived in New York, I emphasized "the need to improve stress testing and scenario analyses," citing a half dozen analytical problems we were seeing "even at the most sophisticated institutions." In another speech, I noted that banks seemed reluctant to address "the effects of the failure of a major counterparty," as well as "the risk of a major shock to market liquidity." That was unsettling, I suggested in my typically impenetrable prose, in part because the banks and their counterparties had gotten much bigger: "The greater concentration in the financial system means the systemic consequences of the failure of a major firm could be more acute."

We would find out that was true the hard way.

I DIDN'T enjoy public speaking, and I wasn't good at it, so I wasn't inclined to do much of it. But I couldn't be invisible in my new job. I rarely discussed monetary policy or the broader economic outlook, continuing a New York Fed tradition of public deference to the chairman on those issues. But I did talk a lot about risks to the stability of the financial system, usually to financial audiences. I didn't consider my speeches a particularly powerful way to influence behavior. I didn't seek media coverage, and I didn't get any. But I did try to convey what I was learning about the strengths and weaknesses of the system, and to outline my hierarchy of concerns. In my careful, qualified, occasionally tortured way, I tried to lean against the wind.

"We need to maintain a degree of humility and caution about our capacity to anticipate the nature and dynamics of future stresses to the financial system," I said in May 2004. I gave an entire speech that October about strengthening our regime for addressing systemic risk: "If you want peace or stability, it's better to prepare for war or instability." In February 2005, I said the financial community's main challenge was a challenge of imagination: "How do we generate the will today to build a greater degree of insurance against a more uncertain future, particularly if the risk of adversity seems remote and the immediate future looks strong?"

And so on. Even though the financial sector seemed healthy, I talked about systemic risks in almost every speech I delivered as New York Fed president.

These speeches weren't designed to be warnings. I didn't try to be Chicken Little. I expressed my concerns in the on-the-one-hand-on-the-other-hand tone of a central banker, as if I were suggesting that the recent history of celestial stability did not necessarily rule out the possibility of some portion of the sky falling at some point in the future. In my first speech, "Change and Challenges Facing the U.S. Financial System," I didn't address the challenges until my sixteenth paragraph; the first fifteen were mostly about positive developments. I thought audiences might be more willing to think about our vulnerabilities if I acknowledged our strengths, but I probably made it easy for people who just wanted to hear good news to block out the caveats. And while I didn't have Greenspan's flair for eloquent fog, my speeches were never a model of clarity or hair-on-fire force. I was careful to express my concerns in understated, nuanced, deliberately dull language that wouldn't move markets or depress confidence. I had once seen an offhand comment about the yen by Secretary Bentsen trigger a damaging run on the dollar, and I had no intention of making a similar mistake.

Still, there was an undertone of anxiety to all my speeches. And the main source of my anxiety was the rapidly growing, heavily leveraged, lightly regulated nonbank financial system. Here's some typical Fed-speak from my October 2004 talk about systemic risk: "There are a larger number of nonbank financial intermediaries operating outside the supervisory safety and soundness framework that are sufficiently large or integral to the financial system that their failure or anticipated failure could have major implications for the functioning of the markets in which they operate and their financial institution counterparties."

In other words, a big nonbank could cause big problems.

• • •

I WASN'T confident that our rules would ensure that Fed-supervised banks had enough capital to survive a severe crisis. But I knew many nonbanks had much less capital, even though they didn't have the safeguard of insured deposits and wouldn't have access to Fed loans in an emergency. For example, by the end of 2007, capital levels at the five SEC-regulated Wall Street investment banks—Bear Stearns, Lehman Brothers, Merrill Lynch, Morgan Stanley, and Goldman Sachs—were just 3 percent of assets. At the mortgage giants Fannie Mae and Freddie Mac, they would drop to barely 1 percent of the assets they owned and guaranteed.

The question was what to do about it. The Fed didn't have the legal authority to force Bear Stearns, Lehman Brothers, or other investment banks to raise more capital. We couldn't even generate stress scenarios bleak enough to force the banks we regulated to raise more capital. Perhaps our capital buffers were too thin, but they were already thick enough to drive trillions of dollars of assets—more than there were in the entire commercial banking system—outside our direct supervision. In a time of seemingly unbounded optimism about the trajectory of housing prices and the stock market, investors were willing to finance substantial increases in leverage, and that money tended to flow where the regulatory constraints were weakest.

A big part of the problem was America's balkanized regulatory system. It was riddled with gaps and turf battles. It was full of real and perceived sources of capture. And nobody was accountable for the stability of the entire system.

Even the traditional banking sector was a byzantine mess, with responsibilities for supervising thousands of commercial banks divided among the Fed, the Federal Deposit Insurance Corporation (FDIC), and the Office of the Comptroller of the Currency (OCC), as well as state banking regulators working from fifty different sets of rules. The Office of Thrift Supervision (OTS) regulated "thrifts," which were essentially banks focused on mortgage markets; their deposit-taking subsidiaries were subject to capital requirements and eligible for the Fed's discount window, but the riskier affiliates and parent companies generally operated without adult supervision. There were also geographic divisions within the Fed. The New York Fed oversaw Citigroup and JPMorgan Chase, while the Richmond Fed supervised Bank of America and Wachovia, and the San Francisco Fed handled Wells Fargo.

Often, multiple agencies oversaw a single institution. For example, the Fed supervised the "holding companies" of Citigroup and JPMorgan Chase, the umbrella entities sitting atop hundreds of bank and nonbank subsidiaries, but not their actual commercial or investment banks. We were supposed to keep tabs on the institutions as a whole, but by law we had to defer to the primary supervisor, in those cases the OCC for their commercial banks and the Securities and Exchange Commission for their investment banks. The Fed also shared responsibility for the U.S. affiliates of foreign banks with state regulators, as well as home-country supervisors in London, Zurich, Frankfurt, and around the world. These divisions of labor evoked the parable of the blind men and the elephant, with nobody accountable for seeing the full picture of a corporation, much less the interconnections of the entire system.

This glut of watchdogs with overlapping jurisdictions encouraged regulatory arbitrage. Banks often reorganized as thrifts to get the notoriously weak OTS as their supervisor, or shopped for another regulator they thought would give them favorable treatment. The OTS and OCC were both funded by fees they collected from their member banks, which gave them an incentive to try to woo banks into their orbit by offering lighter enforcement. At the time, Republicans controlled Congress as well as the White House, and the prevailing mood in Washington was averse to regulation; the FDIC's 2003 annual report featured a photo of bank representatives helping regulators slash "red tape" with a chain saw.

But if the scrutiny of commercial banking was problematic, the rest of the financial system was under even less scrutiny, with none of the constraints of bank regulations and virtually no safety and soundness oversight. Investment banks were monitored by the SEC, which was much better equipped to focus on investor protection issues than on the financial health of the investment banks, and imposed few constraints on leverage. Money market funds, which functioned much like traditional banks, offering deposit-like instruments to their customers, were also under the SEC umbrella, but without the capital requirements or constraints on risk taking faced by banks. Hedge funds were growing fast without any meaningful oversight or leverage limits. The same was true of large finance companies such as GE Capital and the General Motors Acceptance Corporation (GMAC). Fannie and Freddie had their own compliant Washington regulator, which allowed them to build up a huge portfolio of mortgage assets without requiring them to hold much capital. The CFTC was supposed to monitor futures traders. State insurance departments were largely responsible for insurance companies, even though AIG and other insurance firms had evolved into multinational financial conglomerates.

Again, none of those firms were subject to strong supervision or capital rules, and none of them would have access to the Fed's safety net in case of a run. Unless we wanted to be like the proverbial drunk searching for his keys under a streetlight because it was dark everywhere else, we couldn't just worry about risk within the banks we supervised. We had seen during the LTCM crisis in 1998 how quickly the potential failure of a financial firm could infect the overall financial system—and there was now much more risk outside the banking system in institutions with much more leverage.

But the Fed had no legal authority to impose limitations on risk outside the banks we supervised. We could use private and even public pressure to try to persuade nonbank institutions and their supervisors to address problems, but I wasn't impressed with the power of those tools. I asked my colleagues at the New York Fed to analyze the capital buffers at Fannie Mae and Freddie Mac, and they concluded quite reasonably that the buffers were thin. I noted in a speech that Fannie and Freddie's "regulatory framework, capital regime, and . . . internal risk management framework need to be upgraded to a standard more commensurate with their risk profile and the risks they present to the system." But it was Congress that set and defended their low capital requirements, and Fannie and Freddie had a lot of friends in Congress. They ended up with $75 worth of leverage for every $1 in capital, the corporate equivalent of a $4,000 down payment on a $300,000 home.

We were even more concerned about the big investment banks, which New York Fed Vice President Mike Silva described to me in an email as "the 800-pound gorilla" of our financial stability efforts. It was obvious that the SEC was poorly equipped to judge how safe they were, or what would happen if one of them ran into trouble, but we couldn't do much more than politely raise awareness and urge vigilance. "Since [our] relationship with the SEC is chilly at best, a very subtle approach is probably the only one that has any chance of actually achieving results," Silva wrote.

Since simply expressing concern was not a strategy, I tried to figure out a way to get more traction across the entire financial system. In late 2004, I asked Jerry Corrigan, the former New York Fed president, to lead a new Counterparty Risk Management Policy Group of industry officials. I thought of Corrigan as a kind of John Madden of finance—big, gruff, old-school, a well-respected student of the game, with a similarly animated rhythm to his commentary. Corrigan had co-chaired the original counterparty risk group after LTCM imploded in 1998, and had produced recommendations to help firms prepare for the failure of a major financial player. The new group examined the state of risk management across investment banks, foreign banks, hedge funds, and commercial banks. Incidentally, despite his anti-regulatory instincts, Greenspan was fully supportive of this work. When I asked for his blessing before launching, his response was: "That's what you're supposed to do."

The Corrigan group provided a venue for risk managers and risk takers from all the relevant parts of our financial system to sit around a table and talk about vulnerabilities. In 2005, it issued a 273-page report that included dozens of sensible recommendations to reduce risk. It was leaning against the wind, too, promoting caution at an incautious moment. We encouraged banks to adopt its recommendations, and shared them across the regulatory community.

Over the next two years, we used these findings to initiate a new round of horizontal risk reviews, applied not just to banks but to investment banks and foreign banks that were large players in our markets. We brought foreign agencies and our colleagues at the SEC into the process, hoping to improve coordination and help the firms in our various jurisdictions prepare for a severe recession or financial crisis. We were trying to create a kind of race to the top, pushing state-of-the-art stress testing and more conservative risk management throughout the system, encouraging peer pressure that might offset the competitive pressure to take on as much risk as possible. We also tried to rein in nonbanks a bit through our supervision of the banks that lent them money, which we called the "indirect channel" of supervision. We had some success limiting leverage by unregulated hedge funds by pressuring the banks that funded them, but we never launched an all-out effort to starve the most dangerous parts of the nonbank sector of financial oxygen.

Our efforts weren't much of a countervailing force against the vast sums of money looking for opportunity in an expanding global economy. Credit was exploding worldwide, while default rates were low and trending lower, making borrowers look unusually safe. Institutions outside the Fed system that could take on more leverage found it easy to do so; private markets enthusiastically financed the massive migration of risk and capital toward nonbanks. In retrospect, these rosy assumptions about the future look delusional, but the triumph of hope over fear was highly profitable until it wasn't.

We tried to push back against the frenzy, but our impact was modest. We sought improvements in risk management, but we couldn't compel change beyond the banks we regulated, and we missed major weaknesses in some of those banks, too. One of the best examples of our accomplishments, but also of the limits of our accomplishments, was in the realm of derivatives.

By 2005, the market in over-the-counter derivatives had quadrupled since Brooksley Born had started warning about them seven years earlier. Investors were gobbling up an array of new products, from "credit default swaps" to "synthetic CDOs." But there was still no single authority over derivatives, or over the banks and securities firms that manufactured and sold them. All this worried me.

In some ways, derivatives were just another form of risk taking, like simple bank loans or any other financial transactions. They could be useful tools for companies that needed to hedge risks, helping importers and exporters protect themselves against changes in exchange rates, or helping banks protect themselves against the bankruptcy of a counterparty. On balance, they seemed likely to add to the stability of the financial system, dispersing, diversifying, and balancing risks across individual firms and across broader markets. After all, there had been financial crises for centuries before derivatives even existed. Simple banking had proven to be pretty dangerous, and the hedging benefits of derivatives could reduce some of that risk.

But derivatives did create new dangers. If you were making a loan, and you were confident you could hedge some of the credit risk of that loan, you might be tempted to make a larger and riskier loan. And the instruments themselves often had leverage embedded in them, so investors could be exposed to greater losses than they realized. Firms weren't required by law to post any collateral (or "margin") to make derivatives trades, and the market wasn't requiring them to post much, either. This meant fewer shock absorbers for the system if those trades went bad. That's why Warren Buffett had called derivatives "financial weapons of mass destruction."

One of my concerns was that much of the derivatives market was untested by crisis. Nobody knew how the new products, particularly credit derivatives, would perform in a bad state of the world. They had been launched in a period of stability, and I feared their short history of relatively favorable performance could breed overconfidence and instability. Firms that considered themselves well hedged might discover that their insurance wasn't as solid as they thought. There were millions of contracts among tens of thousands of individual counterparties, and little capacity to monitor trends and vulnerabilities in the overall market. Idiosyncratic corporate difficulties that wouldn't have had larger implications before the explosion of credit derivatives—such as a downgrade of General Motors bonds, or the bankruptcy of the auto parts supplier Delphi—were already taking on what the *Wall Street Journal* called "a hold-your-breath air" as markets sorted out billions of dollars' worth of side bets in real time.

In general, derivatives made it tougher for firms to figure out what was going on—what exposures they had, which counterparties might be in trouble—and anything that added to uncertainty during a crisis could accelerate a panic. I said in my speeches that while derivatives might help prevent financial crises from erupting as frequently, they might also make the crises that do erupt more damaging and harder to contain.

To make matters worse, the infrastructure behind the derivatives markets was a mess. My friend and former colleague Lee Sachs, a Bear Stearns veteran from the 1980s and early '90s who had worked at Treasury and was now back in the financial industry, explained to me shortly after I arrived in New York that the plumbing of the derivatives business was hopelessly obsolete. Greenspan later called it a twenty-first-century industry reliant on nineteenth-century practices. Complex orders were scribbled down in pen and faxed to unattended machines. Trades remained unconfirmed for months, and dealers often reassigned them without notifying counterparties. So investors didn't know who was on the other side of their trades—again, a significant source of uncertainty. In a crisis, nobody would have any idea who owed what to whom, or whether whoever owed it would be able to pay—a recipe for a panicky sell-off and a deeper crisis. As Corrigan told me, it would be like trying to untangle a vat of cooked spaghetti.

This was not a problem the market could solve on its own. Financial infrastructure is a public good much like transportation infrastructure, benefiting businesses that are nevertheless unlikely to build it on their own. It wouldn't make sense for one firm to upgrade its back-office operations, address its backlogs of unconfirmed trades, and invest in electronic trading unless all the major derivatives dealers did the same. We decided to try to induce all of them to do it together. The fourteen top dealers handled 95 percent of the derivatives market, and even though the New York Fed supervised only two of them, Citi and JPMorgan, we invited all of them to one of our more imposing conference rooms in September 2005. We invited their regulators, too, including British and German authorities. Lloyd Blankfein of Goldman Sachs dubbed the group "the Fourteen Families," as if they were warring Mafia bosses meeting in a back room to discuss their common interests.

We put together an extensive list of quantitative targets and deadlines, and within three weeks, all fourteen firms had signed a letter with solid commitments, such as a 30 percent reduction of their backlogs within four months. We made the targets more ambitious over time. By 2008, after a lot of pressure and attention, the backlog of unconfirmed credit derivatives had been reduced by 92 percent, even though the volume had tripled. Electronic processing of equity derivatives had increased from 34 percent to 94 percent. All kinds of bad surprises would emerge during the financial crisis, but a malfunctioning back-office derivatives infrastructure wouldn't be one of them. As Lee Sachs said, it was one dog that didn't bark.

I don't want to overstate the importance of these reforms. The Wild West with better plumbing was still the Wild West. Large banks and nonbanks had a mutual interest in upgrading their derivatives infrastructure, so we managed to persuade them to upgrade it. But we couldn't persuade enough of them to reduce their leverage or manage their risks more carefully, because they didn't think that was in their interest. That was the real danger to the system.

OTHER THAN my anxieties about the future of finance, I felt comfortable in New York. My family and I moved to the small bedroom community of Larchmont, near where I had lived during junior high, and we built a nice life there together.

Carole took on a fulfilling job as a grief counselor for the Bereavement Center of Westchester, working with kids and adults who had experienced a major loss. Elise and Ben seemed to thrive in the local public schools. I woke up every morning at 5:15 to work out, finishing in time for breakfast with Carole and the kids. That early workout—a triathlon rotation of running in my neighborhood or on a treadmill, swimming at the YMCA or the middle school pool, or riding my stationary bike in front of a training video—was really the start of my .workday, my time alone to think. It also helped keep me centered at the office, more focused, less frustrated. I've always been calmer in motion than in repose.

The Fed's security officers drove me to and from work, which was an amazing luxury, an extra two or three hours a day to read five newspapers, catch up on my Fed paperwork, and talk on the phone in privacy. At first, the drivers sometimes used their sirens to get me around traffic, even on my way home at night, but I ended that New York Fed tradition, too.

Before long, the Fed started to feel less strange and I felt less like an interloper. I resumed my old habits of walking around the office in my socks, popping into colleagues' offices to talk instead of summoning them to my executive suite. I was gradually discovering more young talent, while trying not to alienate the old guard. I found close advisers such as Meg McConnell, a wonderfully smart and impertinent economist in our research department, and Mike Silva, the excellent attorney and manager who became my chief of staff. I also got to hire a new head of our markets group, Bill Dudley, an economist and Goldman Sachs managing director who would later succeed me as president. I liked my colleagues. They were talented, dedicated, and good company. I even played some basketball in the bank's rec league, which was a lot of fun, though a bit awkward for my staff. I came home after my first game and told Carole, with some pride, that I had shot three for four. She scoffed: They're not going to play defense against their boss.

As I had warned the board, Carole and I did the minimal amount of Manhattan socializing I thought necessary to do my job properly, including a few awkward birthday celebrations for our modern-day tycoons at various museums in Manhattan. I ate at home most nights, watched the previous evening's *Daily Show*, and went to bed by 10 p.m. All in all, it was a comfortable way to live, apart from the dread and burden of responsibility for a financial system that was defying gravity.

• • •

IN EARLY 2007, I had a meeting in Beijing with one of China's top financial regulators. I was generally treated with a fair amount of respect and deference in China, in part because of my father's connections to its government elite. But I had not met this official, and he was unusually arrogant and derisive of America.

"Nin de xitong hen luan," he remarked.

"Your system is somewhat complex," his translator repeated.

My Mandarin was rusty, but I knew *luan* did not mean "somewhat complex."

"No," I told the translator. "He said, 'Your system is wild, chaotic.'"

He had a point. Our system was kind of chaotic. We had a dizzying array of regulators, and a political climate in which some of them could pose for official photos with regulation-slashing chain saws. We also had all sorts of regulatory gaps, with nobody responsible for the entire system. And Wall Street, as President Bush later said, had gotten drunk. Financial firms were chasing higher returns through increasingly leveraged and risky trades even though they knew they were racing to the bottom; as Citigroup CEO Charles Prince memorably explained, "as long as the music is playing, you've got to get up and dance."

When a top Morgan Stanley executive named Vikram Pandit left the firm in 2005, we had lunch and he passed along the not-so-novel wisdom that the shift from private partnerships to public companies had poisoned the culture of Wall Street, encouraging executives to focus on quarterly profits and the exorbitant stock options that came with them. He thought our financial system had gotten too risky, and it was hard to disagree. Hank Paulson, the head of Goldman Sachs, also shared his concerns with me before he became President Bush's Treasury secretary, especially his view that excessive leverage was building up in the financial system.

That was the crux of the chaos. The entire system—really, the entire nation—was in the midst of a borrowing frenzy. In 2005, Lee Sachs and Stan Druckenmiller both began bringing me charts tracking the growth of credit in the U.S. economy. The rise was so sharp that Lee and I began calling them the Mount Fuji charts. I remember in August 2006, when I snuck out of the Fed's annual economic summit in Jackson Hole, Wyoming, to go fly-fishing, my guide was a mortgage broker; his horror stories of sketchy loans to homeowners with sketchy credit were a stark real-world supplement to the academic debates at the central banking summit.

Borrowing frenzies are prerequisites for financial crises, and too many Americans were using credit to finance lifestyles their salaries couldn't support. From 2001 to 2007, the average mortgage debt per household increased 63 percent, while wages remained flat in real terms. The financial system provided this credit with enthusiasm, even to individuals with low or undisclosed incomes, then packaged the loans into securities that were also bought on credit. The financial

"Mount Fuji"
Ratio of Household Debt to GDP

Lee Sachs and Stan Druckenmiller both periodically brought me versions of this chart while I was at the New York Fed, to warn me about the rapid growth of borrowing in the U.S. economy. Lee and I called it the "Mount Fuji" chart, and its steep slope tracked the credit boom.

Source: Federal Reserve Board (represents household and nonprofit credit market instruments).

sector now held $36 trillion worth of debt, a twelvefold increase over three decades. The federal government was also in the red; the unfunded Bush tax cuts, Medicare expansion, and wars in Iraq and Afghanistan had turned the large Clinton budget surpluses into larger budget deficits. And our trade deficit was at a record high, as we borrowed foreign capital to finance our consumption of imports.

"These imbalances—fiscal and external—cannot be sustained indefinitely," I said in a speech to the Economic Club of Washington.

A credit boom can't happen without plenty of money sloshing

around the economy, and monetary policy was historically accommo-
dative when I joined the Fed. As vice chairman of the Federal Open
Market Committee, I worked closely on interest rates and other monetary issues with the Fed chairman—Greenspan until January 2006,
then Ben Bernanke, a former economics professor from Princeton.
We would discuss strategy and review draft decisions and statements
before every FOMC meeting, along with the wise Fed vice chairman
Don Kohn, and we would meet in the chairman's office during breaks
to discuss last-minute adjustments. I supported every monetary policy
decision during my time at the Fed, so let me explain what we were
thinking.

The Fed has a dual mandate to keep unemployment low and inflation stable, which it executes by adjusting the "federal funds rate," the
short-term interest rate that banks use to lend to one another. In general, lowering rates (or loosening policy) is how the Fed steps on the
gas when it believes the economy needs help, expanding the money
supply to try to lower unemployment. Raising rates (or tightening
policy) is how the Fed steps on the brakes when the economy seems
overheated, contracting the money supply to try to keep inflation in
check. The heads of the twelve reserve banks all sit at the table during FOMC meetings, but they have only five votes that rotate among
them; New York is the only reserve bank with a permanent vote. The
seven presidential appointees on the Fed's board of governors also have
votes. In practice, decisions are made by consensus, with the chairman the dominant voice, and committee members dissenting only if
they feel strongly.

When I started at the Fed, the federal funds rate was just 1 percent, the lowest it had been since the fifties. Greenspan had responded
to the LTCM crisis, the dot-com bust, and September 11 with aggressive blasts of liquidity, prompting criticism that his predictable interventions to refuel markets whenever they sputtered were creating a
bad moral hazard precedent. The argument was that the "Greenspan
Put"—a put is a contract that pays off when an asset's value declines,

providing insurance against bad outcomes—encouraged investors to take too many risks, because they figured the Fed would create a soft landing for them if they encountered turbulence. With the Fed's rates so low, and spreads—the difference between interest rates on riskier securities and super-safe Treasuries—so narrow, investors were certainly "reaching for yield," taking on more risk and leverage in search of better returns.

The Fed stayed the monetary course during my first six months on the job. But in June 2004, we felt the economy was strong enough to start tightening policy, so we started raising rates a quarter point at every Fed meeting. Greenspan once called me to say he was nervous we were being too predictable in our tightening, encouraging too much confidence about the path of policy. I shared his concern that telegraphing the pace of our tightening in advance might be making the markets too comfortable with high levels of leverage and risk, but we didn't have a better alternative. We didn't think it made sense to create more uncertainty about the path of monetary policy just to keep investors guessing and induce more volatility.

That concern grew when our gradual increases in the short-term federal funds rate failed to boost long-term interest rates, a situation Greenspan dubbed "the conundrum." Bernanke, then a member of the Fed board of governors, called this the consequence of a "global savings glut," explaining that a flood of money from newly opened markets with lots of savings, such as China, was holding down borrowing costs, offsetting our efforts to shrink our own money supply. That seemed right to me. The Fed wasn't fueling the credit boom with loose policy anymore—we raised rates to 5.25 percent by 2006, well above the underlying inflation rate—but there was still an awful lot of money sloshing around. In many other countries, interest rates were below zero when adjusted for inflation, so the United States, and particularly its high-flying housing market, seemed like a relatively attractive place to invest extra cash.

We spent a lot of time back then trying to figure out how far the credit and housing booms were going to go and how they might end. A lot of internal Fed work and academic studies suggested that the run-up in home prices was justified by economic fundamentals, and that in any case sharp nationwide price drops had little historical precedent. In December 2004, the New York Fed's research division produced a paper titled "Are Home Prices the Next Bubble?" that concluded they weren't. It conceded the possibility of corrections along the coasts, but noted "regional price declines in the past have not had devastating effects on the broader economy." Six months later, in a presentation to the FOMC, Fed economists projected that even if there were a 20 percent nationwide decline in housing prices, it would cause only about half the economic damage of the bursting of the dot-com bubble.

Everyone could see there was "froth" in some housing markets, as Greenspan put it. We all knew lax lending standards were helping families buy more expensive homes with less money down. Other families were staying put, then using their existing homes as ATMs by borrowing against their soaring home values. I had seen in Japan and Thailand how lavishly financed real estate booms can end in tears. But I took too much comfort in analyses downplaying the risk of large nationwide declines, which hadn't happened in the United States since the Depression. We didn't even think the direct financial effects of a large decline would be that scary.

"We believe that, absent some large, negative shock to perceptions . . . the effects of the expected cooling in housing prices are going to be modest," I said during a rate-setting meeting in 2006.

With a hint of mischief, Bernanke then asked me for a report on crazy Manhattan co-op prices, and the committee laughed.

"I guess some people say that you can see a little of the froth dissipating," I replied. "But I don't think the adjustment is acute." At the time, it wasn't.

The conventional wisdom in central banks was that the blunt instrument of monetary policy was an inappropriate tool for trying to deflate credit bubbles or asset price bubbles. I shared that view and still do. In January 2006, I said in a speech that it would be irresponsible and ineffective to try to use monetary policy to pop bubbles. By that time, the Fed had been tightening steadily for a year and a half. But the idea of slowing down the entire economy faster than we otherwise thought necessary just to try to push down home prices or stock prices seemed like amputating an arm to fix a wrist injury. I didn't think we could be sure when prices were truly unsustainable, or even that tighter monetary policy would dent real estate prices.

Central bankers did not have a good record of identifying bubbles in advance, and neither did bank supervisors. In my early years at the Fed, I looked back at past episodes when U.S. bank examiners had issued cautionary guidance to try to tame excesses in credit growth and lending practices. The record was not encouraging. Typically, the guidance was issued at the peak of the boom or later. In 2006, the Fed conducted a review of commercial real estate lending across the banking system, which showed we were once again late to the party. Community banks had already built up huge concentrations of loans to developers, several times larger than their capital buffers. The bank supervisors issued some sensible guidance, and the bank examiners worked to limit additional lending. But the damage was already done.

AROUND THE time I was getting my stern *luan* lecture in Beijing, the subprime mortgage market, one of the wildest sections of our system, began to lurch downward.

New York was not the epicenter of subprime lending—that honor belonged to California, Florida, and other so-called sand states—but it was the epicenter of the business of packaging subprime loans into securities for sale to investors. In a March 2007 speech in Charlotte, I gave several reasons why everyone involved with subprime mortgages, as well as securities backed by subprime mortgages, ought to be concerned about "what we might call the adverse tail, or the negative extreme."

I noted that subprime lenders, who by definition targeted borrowers with less than stellar credit, were often rewarded according to the volume rather than the quality of the mortgages they generated. They had little financial exposure to the consequences of a default, which had ominous implications for lending and underwriting standards. I also warned that the firms that ended up with subprime exposure would find it even harder than usual to assess their risks, because of the complexity and the newness of the financial instruments into which the mortgages were sliced and diced. And I explained that the drift of risk from simple loans in traditional banks to structured products in leveraged nonbanks increased the danger of a " 'positive feedback' dynamic," a vicious cycle that could amplify a crisis. If asset prices fell, firms and investors would need money to meet margin calls, prompting fire sales that would drive asset prices even lower, and so on.

But March 2007 was pretty late in the game to be warning about subprime. And my view was that the only effective way to reduce the risks ahead was for supervisors to make sure significant financial firms had enough capital and liquidity to survive a crisis. "The most productive focus of policy attention has to be on improving the shock absorbers in the core of the financial system," I said. My conclusions about the tremors in subprime, while valid at the time, were too reassuring: "As of now, though, there are few signs that the disruptions in this one sector of the credit markets will have a lasting impact on credit markets as a whole."

Those signs would be everywhere in a few months. But the Fed staff's analytic work didn't flag subprime as a major systemic risk, which is why Ben suggested later in March that its impact "seems likely to be contained," a quote his critics have recycled ever since. Hank Paulson, the former Goldman Sachs head who became President Bush's Treasury secretary, made similarly optimistic statements even later that spring. Subprime was only about one-seventh of the mortgage market, barely $1 trillion out of the nation's $55 trillion in financial assets, and it didn't appear to be infecting the rest of the credit boom. "In fact, delinquencies and loan losses on consumer lending continue to run at quite low rates," my staff reported that March. "Signs of strain in the subprime area have continued to increase, but appear to remain contained to this sector." On April 18, 2007, my Financial Risk Committee presented an analysis concluding that if the entire subprime industry suffered losses of 14 percent, only two major banks, Wells Fargo and HSBC, would lose more than 10 percent of their high-quality capital.

The eventual losses in subprime went higher than 14 percent, especially in structured products that concentrated the riskiest loans. And mortgage losses spread further than subprime. The prevailing assumption that housing prices would not slump nationwide, though widely shared and backed by seven decades of history, also turned out to be wrong. This is often seen as our worst misjudgment, since so many subsequent problems in the financial system would involve mortgages and mortgage-backed securities. But it was not our most important miss.

Even though we did not expect a nationwide real estate bust, we did analyze scenarios where house prices fell sharply across the country. Unfortunately, we concluded that the impact on the financial system and the broader economy would be relatively modest. We didn't foresee that falling housing prices alone would trigger widespread mortgage defaults that could cause significant problems in the banking system, because we didn't examine the possibility that the initial fears associated with subprime mortgages and the general fall in house prices could trigger a classic financial panic, followed by a crash in household wealth and a collapse of the broader economy. This was the arc of crisis described in Kindleberger's book: manias, followed by panics, ending in crashes. And this was the death spiral I had seen so often at Treasury during the emerging-market crises of the 1990s.

We knew the long boom in credit in general and mortgage credit in particular exhibited all the classic signs of mania, including the widespread belief that housing prices would never fall to earth. And we were keenly aware that dangerous levels of leverage were building up throughout the financial system, especially in less closely supervised corners of the system. But we didn't appreciate the extent to which nonbanks were funding themselves in runnable short-term ways, or how vulnerable the banking system would be to distress in the nonbanks. We knew we were vulnerable to a panic, and I spent years concerned about our vulnerabilities, but ultimately we were even more vulnerable than we realized.

We also failed to anticipate the savage depth of the Great Recession, or the debilitating feedback loop between problems in the financial system and problems in the broader economy. A mere drop in housing prices could not have triggered mass mortgage defaults or depression-level losses in the banking system, but as unemployment increased and jobless homeowners missed payments, actual and expected mortgage losses increased as well, triggering margin calls and selloffs of mortgage-related assets, making the economy, unemployment, and the housing market worse. We weren't prepared for that kind of doom loop.

You could say our failures of foresight were primarily failures of imagination, like the failure to foresee terrorists flying planes into buildings before September 11. But severe financial crises had happened for centuries in multiple countries, in many shapes and forms, always with pretty bad outcomes. For all my talk about tail risk, negative extremes, and stress scenarios, our visions of darkness still weren't dark enough. When models told us that only a depression-level shock could cause severe distress to banks, we should have done more to consider what would happen in the event of a depression, no matter how unlikely it seemed. And when our analyses told us the financial system was well positioned to shrug off housing losses, we should have thought harder about the possibility that they could trigger panic.

It's not as if we were twiddling our thumbs during the gathering storm. The New York Fed was the leading source of initiative in the regulatory community in trying to reduce the financial system's vulnerability to a crisis. Even at the height of the boom in credit and leverage in mortgage-related markets, we tried to lean against the winds of confidence, to encourage major banks and nonbanks to prepare for the worst. We recognized there was a lot of dry tinder in the system, even if we were late to see how subprime losses could be the spark that ignited it.

None of this was enough. In the end, we still ended up with a raging inferno. We certainly could have been more prescient, more forceful, more imaginative. But we were human. And our limited authority left us with limited options. For decades, the U.S. government had allowed the financial system to outgrow and outflank its regulatory system. Financial stability cannot depend on omniscient supervisors identifying and preemptively defusing any potential source of crisis; it requires safeguards that can help the system withstand the force of a severe storm, and tools the government can use to limit the damage.

Even while our storm was gathering, we could see that the safeguards in our financial system were terribly inadequate and needed fundamental reform.

BY THE summer of 2007, the subprime market was imploding.

Borrowers with "no-doc loans" (without proof of income) and "liar loans" (with inflated claims about income) and "NINJA loans" (No Income, No Job, No Assets) were defaulting in droves. The second largest subprime lender, New Century Financial, went bankrupt, while the largest, Countrywide Financial, revealed that it was running short on cash. Meanwhile, the price of insuring bonds backed by subprime mortgages against default soared, prompting the rating agency Standard & Poor's to warn that hundreds of those bonds could be downgraded. And two big hedge funds financed by Bear Stearns—including one called, incredibly, the Enhanced Leverage Fund—collapsed after their subprime investments tanked.

I didn't find any of this shocking, or even necessarily unfortunate. The overheated subprime market was overdue for a cooling, and the investors who had bought securities expecting the boom to continue were generally consenting adults. The risk premiums that were now rising across the system had been too low for too long, encouraging too much reaching for yield. It was an absurd sign of the times that "enhanced leverage" had become a selling point for an investment vehicle, instead of a warning; it was like naming a new car model after its faulty brakes. At the Fed's rate-setting meeting on August 7, 2007, I described the turmoil in subprime as "a necessary adjustment, a generally healthy development."

But I also warned the committee that the turmoil had "the potential to cause substantial damage"—through a contraction in credit, through a liquidity crunch, "through the potential failure of more consequential financial institutions; and through a general erosion of confidence among businesses and households." I noted that investors were losing confidence in their ability to assess risk in mortgage markets, in the market's ability to value complex mortgage securities, and in the rating agencies that had assured them for years that those securities were safe. I also said we were entering a new realm of uncertainty and risk, and "a lot of that risk has gone to leveraged funds that have much less capacity to absorb this kind of shock."

I was more worried than many of my colleagues, but I was not nearly worried enough. Our debate that day was not about whether to cut rates. Unemployment was only 4.7 percent, so the economy didn't seem to need immediate help. Our debate was about whether we should hint that we might cut rates in the future, and most of the committee preferred to wait for more evidence that market disruptions were damaging the economy first. "If we took that approach," I warned, "we'd inevitably be too late." But the group wasn't ready to signal that a future rate cut was likely. In our official statement, the committee noted that "downside risks to growth have increased somewhat," but maintained that increased inflation was still a larger concern than an economic downturn.

I was uneasy. I urged caution. But I didn't clamor for action. I even conceded it would be tricky to temper our public optimism without "feeding the concern . . . about underlying strength in the fundamentals of the economy as a whole or in the financial system." I didn't want to sound too dark too soon.

I didn't have to wait long.

On August 8, I left to see my family on Cape Cod, the same place I had been a decade earlier when the Thai crisis hit. The next day, my staff called to tell me that French bank BNP Paribas, one of the world's largest financial institutions, was suspending withdrawals from three of its investment funds with heavy exposure to the U.S. subprime meltdown. BNP had announced that it couldn't even put a fair price on its subprime-backed securities, citing "the complete evaporation of liquidity" in those markets. Saying the bank had no idea what its subprime assets were worth was much worse than saying the values had declined by 20 or 30 percent. It intensified uncertainty about subprime, as well as other U.S. mortgage-backed securities, and helped to create the larger liquidity crunch I had warned my Fed colleagues about much too gently two days earlier.

But if the BNP Paribas announcement troubled me, the force of the European Central Bank response really got my attention. Under the leadership of Jean-Claude Trichet, a former French finance official I had known during my time at Treasury, the ECB was considered a solid and conservative central bank, generally reluctant to intervene to support the economy or the financial system. It wasn't being conservative now. First it announced that it would lend unlimited amounts at a discounted rate to any bank that requested it, an unprecedented effort to pump liquidity into the system. Then it announced that it was fulfilling 95 billion euros in requests for cash, about $130 billion.

Wow. My first response to the news was a string of expletives. I knew Trichet wouldn't put up a wall of money like that on a whim. This wasn't just a little problem on the fringes of the U.S. mortgage market.

I had a sick feeling in my stomach. I knew what financial crises felt like, and they felt like this.

FOUR

Letting It Burn

Central bankers are supposed to be the brakes on the boom, taking away the punch bowl just as the party gets going. But when there's panic in the air, and liquidity starts to evaporate, central bankers are supposed to be the accelerator.

In his 1873 book *Lombard Street,* the bible of central banking, Walter Bagehot explained that the way to stop a run is to show the world there's no need to run, to put money in your window, to "lend freely, boldly, and so that the public may feel you mean to go on lending." The loans should be expensive—Bagehot recommended charging "a penalty rate"—so it would be economically unattractive to borrow from the central bank once the panic subsided. And like any central bank loan, they should be secured by solid collateral. But the goal is to keep the financial system functioning by providing liquidity to solvent institutions when private markets freeze. That's what the ECB did on August 9, 2007. Creditors were pulling back from European banks, frightened by their heavy exposures to U.S. mortgages, and many of those banks were bleeding liquidity. The ECB told them: We've got cash. If you need it, come and get it.

Chairman Bernanke believed in Bagehot, and he believed that central bankers who fail to act in a crisis could make it exponentially worse. In his academic life, Bernanke had been a leading scholar of the Great Depression. His research at Princeton had demonstrated how the central bankers of the 1930s were too timid, too reluctant to provide liquidity, too faithful to the tight-money orthodoxies of their day, allowing widespread bank failures and clogged credit channels to turn a financial crisis into an economic disaster. Ben is a low-key guy, not prone to hysteria or exaggeration—I called him the Buddha of central banking—but he was determined not to repeat their mistakes. While our personalities and our backgrounds are quite different, we complemented each other. His strengths were my weaknesses, with his patience balancing my impatience. We would work in almost perfect harmony throughout the crisis. We trusted each other.

On a call that morning, Ben, Don Kohn, and I agreed we needed to make it clear the Fed was willing to inject liquidity into our markets, too. Fear was building across the financial system, especially in the corners that touched housing. Securities backed by "nonconforming" mortgages—the ones that weren't guaranteed by Fannie or Freddie—were becoming pariah paper; no one knew how much they were worth anymore, so almost everyone was running away from them. That had dangerous implications for financial institutions that were using them as collateral for short-term loans or had calculated how much capital to hold based on optimistic assumptions about their value. Countrywide Financial cited "unprecedented disruptions" to mortgage finance in an SEC filing that day. The bursting of the housing bubble had felt like the end of a mania, and the backlash against housing-related investments now felt like the start of a panic.

At the start of any crisis, there's an inevitable fog of diagnosis. You can recognize the kind of vulnerabilities that tend to precede severe crises, such as substantial increases in asset prices and dramatic expansions of leverage, but you can't be sure whether the initial market turmoil is a healthy adjustment or the start of a systemic meltdown, a precursor to a modest economic slowdown or something much worse. An orderly deleveraging of an overheated market can be a good thing, even if some big companies fail. That's how capitalism is supposed to work: weak, bloated, and mismanaged firms make way for more dynamic competitors. Creative destruction instills discipline in the survivors. But a healthy correction can spiral out of control if fear and uncertainty gain too much momentum. You don't want a central bank to underreact, allowing runs by depositors and creditors to unleash a cascade of fire sales, where firms desperate for cash have to sell assets into a depressed market, further depressing asset prices, inducing more cash shortages and more desperate selling. Once this dynamic of runs and fire sales gets started, it can be incredibly hard to contain, with enormous costs to the economy.

That said, if a central bank treats every disturbance as a potential catastrophe, riding to the rescue at the first sign of trouble, it can create real moral hazard—encouraging reckless risk taking, propping up nonviable "zombie" banks, re-inflating bubbles, and setting up the economy for a fall from an even higher cliff, ultimately magnifying the size of the next crisis. A central bank overreaction can even back-fire right away, feeding instead of easing concern. Markets sometimes conclude a situation must be dire if policymakers act like it's dire. Often it's better to stand back, as we had done in September 2006, when bad bets on natural gas futures sank a giant hedge fund called Amaranth Advisors. That looked like a one-off, an idiosyncratic casu-alty of bad risk management, unlikely to light the rest of the financial system on fire. And it was.

The situation in August 2007 seemed more dangerous and more systemic. We quickly pumped $62 billion into the U.S. financial system—not as much as the ECB poured into Europe, but enough to send a message that we were on the case. It was a fairly modest and completely conventional early-stage escalation by a central bank, injecting some liquidity into markets. Yet some of our colleagues on the FOMC already thought we were being too aggressive, prompting a debate reminiscent of the discussions we used to have about moral hazard during the Asian crises. On a conference call the morning of the 10th, Dallas Fed President Richard Fisher suggested we were helping banks without getting anything in return, "putting our finger in the dike" without extracting promises of more lending now or more responsible behavior in the future. He said he wanted to make sure "we don't send any signal that we're just going to be . . . indiscriminate."

"I don't think that's the way to think about it," I said. We needed to signal that cash was available, to help thaw what Ben called "a general freeze-up" in mortgage markets, so that liquidity shortages didn't create a vicious spiral of forced asset sales and falling asset prices. That meant committing to provide the liquidity that markets needed to function, without conditions, even if it did make us look indiscriminate. "You can't condition that statement without undermining its basic power," I said.

Fisher's discomfort foreshadowed what we were up against. Even inside the Fed, we were susceptible to Old Testament and moral hazard critiques. One day into the crisis, some already thought we were coddling the perpetrators. That's the way it always is in a crisis. And I felt that familiar nausea of foreboding.

I headed back to New York to a familiar blizzard of strategy meetings. I remember Carole calling in the middle of one tense conference call to tell me that bats were flying around our cottage on the Cape, scaring the kids. She had a debilitating case of calcific tendinitis, which made her hand feel like a truck had run over it, an ailment that was not conducive to bat removal or single parenting. I was absent again, just as I had been so often when our kids were babies. I would rarely be fully present over the next several years. I would be the guy coming home late and walking through the door holding cell phones on both ears. My brother Jonathan once said he could always tell from the moment he saw me at family gatherings whether I was really there or not; after August 2007, I usually was not.

I felt overwhelmed by dread about what lay ahead, worse than I had ever felt while fighting crises at Treasury. I knew our financial system was heavily leveraged and vulnerable to a sudden shift in psychology. I wasn't confident we had the tools to deal with a panic. And I knew there was a lot we didn't yet know.

FOR EXAMPLE, the California lender Countrywide wasn't on our radar screen until shortly before the night of August 15, when it nearly paralyzed the entire system.

Countrywide was not only the largest subprime mortgage lender, it was the largest mortgage lender, period, originating nearly half a trillion dollars in loans in 2006. *Fortune* had dubbed it "the 23,000% Stock," a tribute to two decades of spectacular growth. It owned a midsize bank with insured deposits, which it had reorganized as a thrift in order to get the lenient OTS as its regulator, but most of its action was in largely unsupervised nonbank affiliates on the wild frontier of the mortgage markets. It was a case study in regulatory balkanization: big enough to matter, but without a regulator responsible for overseeing the institution as a whole, or its potential risks to the system. The New York Fed did not supervise any part of Countrywide, but it was about to become our problem.

At a time when mortgages were becoming radioactive, Countrywide's business model was all about mortgages: originating them, servicing them, selling them, packaging them into securities, trading those securities, and using those securities as collateral for borrowing that financed the rest of the operation. And Countrywide had helped lead the erosion in lending standards across the country, selling exotic mortgages to families with dubious credit. In late July, it revealed that its delinquency rates in subprime had doubled in three months; CEO Angelo Mozilo told investors the housing market was the worst since the Great Depression. When investors saw those unexpected losses, Countrywide became an obvious target for a run.

In my Charlotte speech in March 2007, I had expressed concern about subprime mortgage lenders who sold all their loans and didn't face the financial consequences of default. Some critics later blamed the crisis on this "originate-to-distribute" model—on lenders with limited incentives to worry about the long-term creditworthiness of borrowers because they had no "skin in the game." This was a problem, but Countrywide had plenty of skin in the game. It hadn't distributed *enough* of the risks it originated. It was like a drug dealer who got high on his own supply. Its main problem was not bad incentives, but bad beliefs—the widespread delusion, profitable for so long, that home prices would defy gravity indefinitely.

That problem only became an existential crisis because of Countrywide's reliance on unstable, runnable short-term funding. The firm raised much of its operating cash by issuing "commercial paper," corporate IOUs that matured in nine months or less. Typically, lenders "rolled over" commercial paper at maturity, renewing the IOUs, but there were no guarantees. Countrywide also financed itself through a complex market known as "tri-party repo," selling securities while agreeing to repurchase them at a specified time, often as soon as the next day—essentially, borrowing overnight with the securities as collateral. Much of the firm functioned like a thinly capitalized bank without deposit insurance, dependent on the confidence of its funders. They could decide to stop funding at any time.

In early August, some of Countrywide's lenders refused to roll over its commercial paper, forcing it to sell assets to pay them back. Those were the "unprecedented disruptions" Countrywide disclosed on the 9th. The next day, I was forwarded a rosy email from Countrywide's supervisor, OTS Director John Reich, suggesting the firm was not only safe, but poised to benefit from the upheaval in its industry. "The longer term looks positive, as their competition has greatly decreased," he wrote. Reich added that Washington Mutual, another obviously troubled thrift, was in "very good shape to weather the current conditions."

On the 15th, with the price of insuring Countrywide's debt against default up eightfold in just a month, a previously bullish Merrill Lynch analyst issued a report titled "Liquidity Is the Achilles' Heel," warning that cash pressures could force Countrywide into bankruptcy. Mozilo insisted his firm was fine, accusing the analyst of shouting fire in a crowded theater. But when confidence goes, it's hard to recapture. As Bagehot wrote, "every banker knows that if he has to *prove* he is worthy of credit, however good may be his arguments, in fact his credit is gone."

That evening, I had my second traumatic surprise in a week. My general counsel, Tom Baxter, walked into my office to tell me that Bank of New York Mellon, Countrywide's tri-party repo clearing bank, was threatening not to "unwind" the firm's $45 billion repo book the next morning. That had never happened before, and it would have had devastating implications.

BoNY's role in tri-party repo was mostly operational—shifting cash and securities back and forth between borrowers and lenders, pricing collateral—but it also provided borrowers with several hours of daytime (or "intraday") credit while arranging their transactions. Now it was about to tell the world it couldn't take the risk of Countrywide failing during those hours. Instead of returning the cash that money market funds and other investors had lent to Countrywide overnight, BoNY was threatening to give those lenders the securities that Countrywide had put up as collateral. Countrywide would get tarred with a potentially fatal vote of no confidence. And the money market funds and other investors that had lent the firm short-term cash would get stuck with securities they didn't want, including some mortgage securities that were already plunging in value. They might start pulling away from other firms that looked similar to Countrywide, triggering a run on the entire $2.3 trillion tri-party-repo market.

My colleagues and I at the New York Fed made a flurry of calls that night, trying to persuade BoNY to unwind, trying to figure out how markets would react if it didn't. I participated in thirty-seven calls, the last one at 2:32 a.m., including multiple conversations with Ben, Don, Mozilo, BoNY CEO Gerald Hassell, and Countrywide's bankers.

We were all worried about fire-sale dynamics. Money market funds need to remain liquid, and they're not allowed to hold risky long-term assets. If they got stuck with Countrywide's securities, they'd have to sell them right away into a falling market, which would exert more downward pressure on prices, produce more problems for firms with mortgage exposures, and exacerbate concerns about the solvency of the financial system. That was scary. But three-fourths of Countrywide's collateral was in ultra-safe Treasury securities or almost-as-safe Fannie- or Freddie-sponsored "agency" securities with an implicit federal backstop. That made the situation even scarier. One banker observed to me that night that BoNY's concern over a portfolio dominated by Treasuries was the classic definition of a panic. Nobody questioned the value of Treasuries, but fear was displacing greed, and perception was becoming more important than reality. Institutions didn't want exposure to Countrywide or even the appearance of exposure to Countrywide, regardless of the quality of its collateral.

BoNY and Countrywide both urged the Fed to intervene to assume the risk and protect the system, which would become a recurring theme throughout the crisis. BoNY executives said they'd roll over Countrywide's book if the Fed guaranteed the resulting intraday credit exposure to the firm, indemnifying them against losses if Countrywide failed while they were on the hook. They were basically asking us to stand behind the entire tri-party repo market, because if we backstopped one firm we'd have to backstop them all. At the same time, Countrywide was requesting emergency help from the Fed. Its thrift was eligible for our discount window, but its cash crunch was in its nonbank affiliates. We couldn't help them unless we allowed them to shift assets out of their troubled nonbanks and into their thrift, or unless we agreed to lend directly to those affiliates, which would have required invoking Section 13(3) of the Federal Reserve Act, the "unusual and exigent circumstances" clause.

We thought about it, conferred with Washington, and said no. We hadn't lent to a nonbank since the Depression, and it was too soon for such extraordinary measures. We were still feeling our way, trying to figure out how bad things were. Financial crisis response is, after all, an exercise in triage. The goal is not to save every major firm regardless of its viability; that's a recipe for the kind of moral hazard that can sustain bloat in the system and increase the risk and intensity of future crises. The goal is to make sure contagion doesn't get out of control, killing the healthy along with the terminally ill. And the Fed was the lender of *last* resort; Countrywide wasn't even at the point where it had exhausted all its other options. It still had access to an $11.5 billion credit line from a consortium of banks. Mozilo was understandably afraid that drawing down the cash would signal weakness, but the point of a credit line is to provide liquidity in a pinch. How could the Fed justify invoking emergency powers to help a nonbank that wouldn't even help itself?

I talked to Mozilo for the first time that night, and the call reminded me of my first chat with Thailand's bewildered finance minister early in the Asian crisis a decade earlier. Mozilo seemed overwhelmed and unclear about what was happening. Like many of the more desperate CEOs I would deal with during the crisis, his main focus was what the government could do to help his firm, and what we could say to get markets to stop fretting about it. He seemed more concerned about the critics pointing out Countrywide's weaknesses than about those actual weaknesses.

By midnight, though, we had the outline of a possible solution. BoNY was one of only two clearing banks in tri-party repo—the other was JPMorgan Chase—and we made it clear to BoNY's executives that refusing to unwind would harm their own interests as well as the system. If money market funds started reevaluating their assumptions about the safety of tri-party repo and pulling out their cash, it would threaten one of BoNY's core businesses, and could potentially leave BoNY with crippling exposures to other borrowers. Ultimately, BoNY agreed to unwind if Countrywide upgraded its collateral. And Countrywide agreed to draw down its credit line to do so. When the markets opened, Countrywide's stock price continued to plummet, but a $2 billion investment by Bank of America soon eased fears of a collapse. In January, Bank of America would buy the rest of the firm for another $4 billion.

The Countrywide episode foreshadowed much of what came later in the crisis. It was a bracing reminder of the limits of our ability to fix problems outside the traditional banking system—problems that could unleash shocks with the power to harm banks as well as non-banks. It also revealed just how dependent the entire financial system had become on fragile short-term funding arrangements, a central vulnerability in every financial crisis. And it showed that this fragility extended even to the secured funding markets—where lending decisions, in principle at least, were based on the borrower's collateral rather than just its underlying creditworthiness.

At the New York Fed, we had spent a lot of time worrying about the risks in tri-party repo, which had expanded tenfold in a decade, but we hadn't made progress on its worst vulnerabilities. BoNY had operational problems after the September 11 attacks, and we had spent a lot of time trying to make sure the market would be able to function if something physical or financial happened to one of the two clearing banks. But we had never devised a way to make tri-party repo less vulnerable to a run in the event a major borrower lost the confidence of the markets, even though some firms ended up financing more than $400 billion worth of securities at a time.

We had paid even less attention to the asset-backed commercial paper market, which had nearly doubled during my Fed tenure to $1.2 trillion. In general, we had tended to view secured funding markets as relatively stable, but the collateral that had made them seem stable was now a source of instability. Since many of the assets backing the commercial paper were linked to housing, the entire market was now under pressure. In one week, the spreads between yields on Treasuries and asset-backed commercial paper had soared from 35 to 280 basis points.

I had also spent very little time familiarizing myself with the risks posed by money market funds, which had accumulated more than $3 trillion in assets, and in many ways functioned like banks. They offered deposit-like accounts to investors, with the ability to withdraw from the accounts at any time at a stable price, and invested that money in securities that weren't risk-free or perfectly liquid. They did this without the deposit insurance or discount window access enjoyed by banks—and without the supervision and capital requirements that banks must face in return for those benefits. But money market funds were under the regulatory purview of the SEC, and I don't remember considering them much of a danger to the system before the crisis, even though Paul Volcker and others did. There seemed to be so many other greater dangers, like the investment banks. But money market funds had provided much of the financing for those other sources of systemic risk.

Now we saw that these funds could be a threat. On an FOMC videoconference the evening after the Countrywide drama, the new head of my markets division, Bill Dudley, warned that mortgage-related losses "could conceivably cause some funds to 'break the buck,'" meaning they wouldn't be able to redeem deposits at the fixed one-dollar-per-share value their investors took for granted. "In the worst case, this could even result in a run from these funds," Dudley said.

Even in those early days of the crisis, the financial system looked much more vulnerable to runs than we had appreciated. Markets were fleeing to safety, looking for cash or cash-like instruments with minimal credit risk, shunning illiquid securities tainted by links to mortgages in general and subprime mortgages in particular. Many of the instruments that were being unloaded had been highly rated and perceived as safe—and once these perceptions of safety changed, investors wanted out. Not everything was runnable, but enough was runnable to make the system extremely fragile.

I KNEW from the crises of the past that financial turbulence was likely to damage the broader economy. Credit was already getting tighter for families and businesses. In talks with Ben Bernanke and Don Kohn, we all agreed we would need to ease monetary policy soon; the question was whether to cut rates right away or wait until the next FOMC meeting. With unemployment still just 4.6 percent, and most private forecasters expecting continued growth, an immediate rate cut between meetings seemed premature, and might be perceived as panicky. Ben was also concerned that it would be condemned as a bailout for risk-seeking investors, a "put" offsetting their recent losses and signaling a desire to protect them from future losses.

At the time, our more pressing concern was the rapid erosion of liquidity within the financial system. We decided to try something unusual right away: to reduce the penalty rate that banks paid to borrow from the Fed's discount window. That "discount rate" was usually set well above the federal funds rate, to limit its use to emergencies. We proposed to cut the discount rate by half a percentage point, to reduce the stigma for banks who feared that using the window would signal distress, while also extending the terms of the loans. We wanted our banks to remain as liquid as possible, so they'd be in a better position to lend. And we wanted the markets to see that the Fed was taking action.

Ben and Don proposed the changes during that FOMC videoconference on August 16. These still felt like extremely modest responses, but some of our colleagues bristled. At one point, Richmond Fed President Jeffrey Lacker asked a question about how we expected the banks to respond, then turned to me. "Vice Chairman Geithner, did you say that they're unaware of what we're considering or what we might be doing with the discount rate?" he asked.

Yes, I replied.

"Vice Chairman Geithner, I spoke with Ken Lewis, president and CEO of Bank of America, this afternoon, and he said he appreciated what Tim Geithner was arranging by way of changes in the discount facility."

Lacker was basically accusing me of leaking our discount-rate plan. I hadn't done that, but I had held a series of conversations with bankers and market participants over the previous few days. Some had suggested that we find some way to use the discount window, and I had asked how those ideas might be received in the market. I never would have disclosed an action in advance, but Lacker was understandably irked that he had first heard rumblings about possible use of the discount window from the CEO of a bank in the Richmond Fed district.

This kind of tension and resentment within the FOMC would be another recurring theme, reminiscent of the emerging-market crises of the 1990s, when many European officials bristled at being presented with rescue plans the United States had shaped with the IMF management. Ben, Don, and I—along with Fed Governor Kevin Warsh, a former Morgan Stanley investment banker who often joined our strategy sessions—sometimes spent weeks developing ideas that we only shared with the rest of the FOMC on the verge of an announcement. That was often unavoidable and probably desirable given the circumstances, but our lack of consultation would add to the divisiveness of our policy debates.

Lacker also had substantive objections to our approach, an early reflection of a real divide within the FOMC. The divide was partly a disagreement about the extent of the risk that the financial trauma in New York would pose for the overall economy, and partly a difference over whether the benefits of trying to mitigate liquidity problems in markets were worth the moral hazard risks. At that meeting, Lacker was disturbed that our proposed statement, which warned that the risk of an economic slowdown had risen "appreciably," did not mention the risk of inflation. "Did I miss something?" he asked derisively.

Ben drily replied: "No."

Lacker was part of a group of hawkish regional Fed presidents—including Fisher of Dallas, Thomas Hoenig of Kansas City, and Charles Plosser of Philadelphia—whose main concerns were preserving the Fed's inflation-fighting credibility and avoiding moral hazard. They did not expect a downturn, so they generally did not believe the upheaval in mortgages and capital markets justified lower interest rates. And they frequently deployed populist arguments against our lender-of-last-resort initiatives, starting with our plan to cut the discount rate.

"To some extent, this looks to me like a sort of sham," Lacker said.

"We could easily be portrayed as helping banks make a lot of money on this."

Lacker noted that bankers often go running to Fed officials when markets wobble, but he urged us to ignore them. "I recognize that this turbulence in financial markets makes everyone apprehensive," he said. "I realize the urge to act—to do something or at least be seen as doing something—can be irresistible. But I think we need to avoid the urge to play Mr. Fix It."

I don't think I'm hawkish or dovish by nature. I've always been pretty pragmatic, suspicious of ideology in any form, and I took both halves of the Fed's dual mandate seriously. But I found the more hawkish obsessions with moral hazard and inflation during a credit crunch bizarre and frustrating. Recession seemed like a more plausible threat than inflation. The notion that a slight tweak in the discount rate was too aggressive during an incipient panic just baffled me; in fact, it ended up being largely ineffectual at overcoming the stigma of the window, since only a handful of banks actually came and borrowed. I often joked privately during the crisis that the hawks on the FOMC thought they lived in Dubai at the peak of an oil boom. Sure, Kansas City and Dallas were still relatively calm, so perhaps from those vantage points— far from Wall Street and the global markets, less directly damaged by the housing collapse than the coasts—the risk of recession seemed remote. The inflation hawks seemed confident that the "real economy" could operate just fine no matter what happened in the markets, but given the scale of the credit and housing booms, it seemed more likely that financial fragility would lead to serious economic weakness.

So this seemed like a perfectly appropriate time for the central bank to do something. Ben was not a creature of Wall Street; he had literally grown up on Main Street in a small South Carolina town. When I had hosted dinners for him at the New York Fed, he had mingled awkwardly with Wall Street's tycoons. They worried he was too academic, too short of experience in markets. But while Ben was the understated opposite of a classic financial CEO, he was not afraid to act to protect the financial system. He understood the danger that trauma in the markets could cause for ordinary Americans, that, as he put it, "the grass gets trampled when elephants fall."

I shared his fear, if not his quiet way of expressing it. A full-blown financial crisis would threaten jobs, homes, retirement savings, car loans, student loans, small business loans, and international trade, not just exorbitant Wall Street bonuses. Perhaps I had a bias toward action, but the Mr. Fix It criticisms felt like excuses for inaction. In the emerging-market crises, I had attended countless international meetings where similar arguments about moral hazard, inflation risk, and central bank credibility had been invoked to justify delay. Well, delay could be risky, too. Mervyn King, governor of the Bank of England, had criticized the ECB and the Fed for overreacting after we pumped liquidity into the markets in early August, warning that we were creating dangerous moral hazard. He was less critical after September 14, when he had to provide similar assistance to Northern Rock, a mortgage lender that had become the target of England's first bank run in nearly 150 years.

On September 18, we cut the federal funds rate target by a half point, and the markets rallied. Financial tensions in Europe and the United States eased a bit. We cut another quarter point in October, and the markets continued to show signs of calm. I was still worried we faced a long war, so I assigned my staff to investigate new ways to inject liquidity in times of stress, including potential aid to nonbanks. I also tried to bring more force to our broader efforts to enhance the resilience of the financial system. We convened an international "Senior Supervisors Group," bringing together U.S. and foreign regulators of the largest commercial banks as well as investment banks to encourage more prudence in risk management. Using the model of our horizontal risk reviews, we wanted to push major institutions to improve their stress testing and prepare for a severe crisis.

By October 17, things seemed calm enough that I referred to the crisis in the past tense in private remarks at a seminar with international financial officials in Washington. "In important respects, the system worked," I said. "The capital cushions at the largest banks proved strong enough to withstand the shock."

I did point out that the events of August had exposed significant fragility in the system. Market assumptions about limitless liquidity had been proven wrong. Leverage had piled up outside the traditional banking sector. "The very substantial improvements in risk management since the last crisis did not capture some risks that inevitably look more obvious in retrospect than they did left of the boom," I said.

Left of the boom was a phrase I had picked up from analysts studying improvised explosive devices at the RAND Corporation think tank, where I served on the advisory board. The phrase referred to the time before an IED explodes. In October 2007, I thought we had survived a major financial explosion.

In fact, we were still left of the boom.

A WEEK later, the investment bank Merrill Lynch announced $7.9 billion in mortgage-related losses, the largest write-down in Wall Street history. That was almost twice as large a write-down as Merrill had predicted three weeks earlier, leaving the impression that losses were exploding and more unpleasant surprises lay ahead. Merrill CEO Stan O'Neal was forced out, although he did receive a $161.5 million severance to ease the blow.

The bulk of Merrill's losses came from "collateralized debt obligations," piles of mortgage-backed securities where the income streams had been sliced up and repackaged into smaller streams known as "tranches." Merrill was a leading manufacturer of CDOs, and it had made billions selling them to investors around the world. But the investors, reaching for yield, had shown little interest in the safest tranches, the "super-senior" CDOs that would pay out in full unless mortgage losses were so severe that investors in every tranche below them were wiped out. That seemed highly unlikely, so Merrill usually kept the super-seniors on its balance sheet. Their modest returns were still more than the cost of financing them, and they seemed almost bulletproof. Standard & Poor's estimated a mere 0.12 percent chance that one of its AAA-rated CDOs would fail to pay out over five years—and super-seniors were considered safer than typical AAAs.

But as Nate Silver noted in *The Signal and the Noise,* his excellent book about why many predictions fail, the actual default rate for AAA-rated tranches of CDOs would be 28 percent, more than two hundred times higher than S&P had predicted. Their perceived safety rested on all kinds of flawed assumptions, starting with the notion that housing prices would never fall simultaneously across the country. CDOs were often spliced together from geographically diverse piles of subprime mortgages, which was supposed to mitigate the effects of a housing slump in any one region. But geographic diversity didn't help much when borrowers started defaulting nationwide.

The forecasts also failed to anticipate the financial-death-spiral effects of the panic, the danger that market psychology could amplify problems in the real estate market. Regardless of the actual safety of the super-seniors, once it became clear that the AAA-rated pieces of CDOs were less safe than previously believed, investors who had bought them (or accepted them as collateral) without examining what was in them began to sell them (or reject them as collateral) with just as little thought. Panic is the flip side of overconfidence; once markets start racing to safety, investors rarely bother to try to distinguish truly overvalued assets from assets that seem similar but might be getting a bad rap. Once a stampede begins, everyone wants to get out the door, and hesitation can be deadly.

The mortgage contagion soon infected one of the world's biggest banks, one of the New York Fed's banks. On November 4, Citigroup broke Merrill's new record, warning that it might take as much as $11 billion in write-downs, seven times what it had projected on an earnings call three weeks earlier. Citi also revealed it had $55 billion worth of subprime exposure, four times what it had said on that mid-October call. Citi's last piece of news was that Chuck Prince, the

CEO who had said banks needed to keep dancing while the music kept playing, was out of a job.

Clearly, the music had stopped.

WE NEVER thought of Citigroup as a model of caution. It had been at the center of the Latin American debt crisis of the 1980s. The New York Fed had cracked down on it for shenanigans related to the Enron scandal shortly before I arrived, and we hit it with the subprime lending fine that pleased Paul Volcker shortly after I arrived. In 2005, after Citi was forced to shut down its private banking operations in Japan because of illegal activity, we banned the company from major acquisitions until it fixed its internal controls and other overseas governance issues. The British banker Deryck Maughan, whom I knew from his days running Salomon Brothers in Japan, came to see me after he was forced out of his job as chairman of Citigroup's international operations. His message was that Citi was out of control.

Citi had more than three hundred thousand employees in more than one hundred countries, and frequent drama in its executive suites. Our supervisors always considered it a laggard in risk management, unwilling to imagine ugly states of the world, unsure how to evaluate exposures across its far-flung businesses. These weaknesses were troubling, but the firm did not appear nearly as vulnerable as many other institutions, certainly not compared to the investment banks, the GSEs, or other nonbanks that didn't have insured deposits and didn't have to hold as much capital. Bob Rubin's presence at Citi surely tempered my skepticism as well. Even though he had no management responsibility or authority, he sat on the board, and he probably gave Citi an undeserved aura of competence in my mind.

Citi wasn't as well capitalized as we thought—partly because a very small share of its capital was common equity, the strongest bulwark against future losses, partly because we vastly underestimated the riskiness of its AAA-rated mortgage assets. Like Merrill, Citi was a leading manufacturer of CDOs, and like Merrill, it kept many of its super-senior tranches. The AAA label ended up being very misleading. The rating agencies were not exceedingly competent. Their ratings typically lagged cycles in finance, staying too optimistic too long. Since the issuers rather than the purchasers of securities paid them, they had some incentive to give generous ratings that kept issuers happy. Moody's revenue from rating structured products such as CDOs had risen 800 percent in a decade.

By 2007, Citi's $2 trillion balance sheet was much riskier than it looked. And Citi had stashed another $1.2 trillion in assets off its balance sheet in ways that allowed it to hold virtually no capital against losses in those assets. Citi didn't expect funding for these off-balance-sheet vehicles to dry up, because of the same delusions that made risky securities seem safe to investors and rating agencies. They didn't understand how quickly losses could boomerang back onto its balance sheet, and neither did we.

For example, Citi financed some of its off-balance-sheet securities by issuing asset-backed commercial paper, while providing assurances that it would buy the paper if no one else wanted it. When markets ran from asset-backed commercial paper—the market shrank 30 percent in the second half of 2007—Citi had to shell out $25 billion to make good on its assurances. Citi also had exposure to securities in off-balance-sheet "structured investment vehicles," a popular financing mechanism that swiftly became unpopular after a few SIVs stocked with subprime mortgages failed. Markets began to flee other SIVs, even those with less subprime mortgage exposure, forcing them to liquidate assets in a hostile market. Some SIVs were wiped out, while Citi and other sponsors had to bring assets from SIVs back onto their balance sheets. That's how the company's perceived exposure to subprime quadrupled in four weeks.

The international Senior Supervisors Group concluded in November that Citi's managers had no idea how close they were flying to the sun, that the company "did not have an adequate, firm-wide consolidated understanding of its risk factor sensitivities," that its stress tests "were not designed for this type of extreme market event." Citi wasn't as weak as many other banks—not to mention the thrifts, Fannie and Freddie, AIG, and several investment banks—but its unexpected losses were very damaging to overall confidence. As Citi's supervisors and regulators, the New York Fed, the OCC, and the SEC had missed what Citi's leadership, creditors, and shareholders also missed: its dramatic exposure to an increase in mortgage defaults and even more dramatic declines in the price of mortgage securities. We weren't expecting default levels high enough to destabilize the entire financial system. We didn't realize how panic-induced fire sales and radically diminished expectations could cause the kind of losses we thought would happen only in a full-blown economic depression.

A few days after Prince stepped down, Sandy Weill, the former CEO who had built Citi into a mega-firm in the 1990s, told me he was going to propose to its board that I should succeed Prince as CEO. I thought this was a crazy idea, for Citi and for me. Carole was appalled by the thought. She thought it sounded unseemly, and would put me in a hornet's nest. I didn't yearn for an eight-figure income. And I couldn't imagine abandoning a job I loved, particularly in the middle of a crisis. I asked Weill not to put my name forward.

"I'm not the right choice," I told him.

A week later, after we met for lunch, Rubin made it clear he didn't think Weill's idea made sense, either. He asked me: Would you really want to spend your days arbitrating fights over compensation? He thought my challenges at the Fed were more interesting and meaningful, and so did I. Citi's board gave the CEO job to Vikram Pandit, the former Morgan Stanley executive who had once warned me that Wall Street was broken.

WE HADN'T pushed our banks to raise more capital in good times, because they were comfortably above the required regulatory ratios. As their losses mounted, we did push the weaker banks to raise more capital, but by now it was harder for them to raise money on a major scale. We considered forcing banks as a group to stop paying dividends in order to conserve capital, but we were concerned, perhaps mistakenly, that doing so might do more harm than good. It would be unfair to the relatively strong, and it would make investments in financial firms less attractive, which could make it harder for the entire system to raise more capital if conditions deteriorated.

However, we did force Citi to reduce its dividend, which it had pledged not to do, and we told it to raise new capital. The bank managed to raise $20 billion over the next few months, mostly from sovereign wealth funds in the Middle East and Asia. Those funds, the last big sources of liquidity left in the markets, also injected capital into other struggling firms, including Merrill and Morgan Stanley.

I believed then and still believe now that forcing banks to hold enough capital and liquidity to absorb significant losses is the best defense against future crises, the ultimate shock absorber. My financial reform mantra after the crisis would be "capital, capital, capital." The question, of course, is how much is enough. At the Fed, we hadn't required Citi to hold enough capital because we hadn't fully understood the extent of the risks it was taking. We also let banks, including Citi, count lower-quality capital, such as preferred stock and certain forms of subordinated debt, that technically complied with the rules but didn't absorb losses as well as common equity. And I hadn't pushed the Federal Reserve in Washington to change the rules to raise regulatory capital requirements, because those rules were then mired in protracted international negotiations. The United States could have toughened the existing rules on our banks unilaterally; I didn't think there was much hope of swift and meaningful reform, but knowing what we know today, we should have tried to do more. Even though banks were better capitalized than much of the rest of the financial system, they were not strong enough to absorb the damage that was still to come.

As the crisis escalated, markets continued to run from mortgage assets that looked toxic, and as investors shunned them, they became toxic, adding to concerns that the financial system had inadequate capital to absorb losses. Firms with too many toxic assets began to lose their ability to borrow to finance the assets, leading to fire sales that further depressed the prices of the assets and forced the firms to take additional losses, intensifying the vicious cycle and exacerbating the concerns about inadequate capital. In that August videoconference, one Fed governor described the toxic assets as "dreck." Fisher called them "flotsam and jetsam." By any name, they were poisoning the system.

One analogy for the flight from toxic assets, from the economist Gary Gorton, would be the kind of understandable hysteria that breaks out after *E. coli* turns up in someone's hamburger. The problem might be poorly inspected ground beef from a single factory, but individual consumers have no way of knowing if the burger or even the steak they want is bacteria free. They just know that meat advertised to be safe turned out not to be, so they respond by distrusting advertisements trumpeting meat's safety and avoiding meat altogether. But the financial version of an *E. coli* hysteria was even worse, because once consumers started to avoid certain financial products, they dropped in value regardless of their level of contamination, which made them even more dangerous to consumers and ramped up the hysteria. It was as if avoiding meat actually caused *E. coli* to spread.

In a climate this tense, uncertainty about the quality of mortgage-related assets mattered more than the actual quality of the assets. Rationally, not every mortgage was going to end up in default, and even mortgages that did go into default would ultimately recover some value as the foreclosed homes were sold. But uncertainty overwhelmed that kind of analysis, so irrational valuations became rational for investors. Nobody knew when more bad earnings news could cause another paroxysm of asset selling, which could cause more margin calls and collateral demands, followed by more write-downs and capital shortfalls, followed by yet another paroxysm of asset selling. In theory, the mortgage securities would all be worth something someday, but in reality, no one wanted to buy them because everyone was trying to get rid of them, which meant their real-time "distressed" price was next to nothing. As Keynes supposedly said, the market can stay irrational longer than you can stay solvent.

This dynamic would recur throughout the crisis, raising tough questions about what assets were really worth. If a security sold at its $100 "par" value a month ago, and you couldn't sell it for $30 today, but it might be worth $80 in five years, what was its true value? And what kind of write-down should you take? Those kinds of questions would help determine whether banks were insolvent or merely illiquid, and how to remove toxic assets from their balance sheets.

My colleagues and I talked a lot about whether and how government could help provide a backstop for those assets to avoid fire sales. At that point, Treasury had no such authority, and we didn't see a strong case for a Fed role. Treasury Secretary Hank Paulson wanted to support a private-sector solution, a massive "Super SIV" financed by big banks that would issue commercial paper to buy toxic assets from existing SIVs. The banks initially pledged to participate, but the effort quickly fizzled, because they needed their cash to absorb losses from their own toxic assets. Without government backing, the case for the Super SIV relied on what felt like circular reasoning; it required the private sector to do what the private sector was already refusing to do.

So most toxic assets remained on the balance sheets of banks, burning holes in their capital, unsettling investors. In four months, Citi lost half its market capitalization. And plenty of institutions were in worse shape than Citi.

By December 2007, market conditions were deteriorating again. Credit spreads were widening, and liquidity was draining away. Real estate was still in a tailspin, with foreclosures nearly double from the previous year. The credit crunch and the housing mess were also leaking into the larger economy, with unemployment rising to 5 percent; the National Bureau of Economic Research would later peg the start of the Great Recession to that month.

Ben, Don, and I decided to move on two fronts: another interest rate reduction and a new liquidity program. We hoped the combination of the two tools would increase their power.

Ben's inclination was to cut rates another half point. But Thomas Hoenig of Kansas City had dissented from the last quarter-point cut, and the FOMC's tight-money wing still thought inflation was a serious risk. Unlike Greenspan, who expected the Fed to follow his lead, Ben's instincts ran toward deference and consensus building. He wanted to chart a course acceptable to the hawks as well as doves such as Janet Yellen of San Francisco and Eric Rosengren of Boston. So we compromised on another quarter-point rate cut. This time, Rosengren dissented, saying the cut should have been bigger, and apparently many investors agreed. Stocks fell sharply.

The next day, we announced the Term Auction Facility, the first of many novel efforts by the Fed to unclog the pipes of the credit system. The TAF made four-week Fed loans available to the thousands of banks with discount window access, through an auction process designed to avoid the stigma of the window. We also put in place large foreign exchange swap lines with the ECB and other central banks, so they could make dollars available to their own banks, a dramatic expansion of a traditional central bank instrument. Within a year, we would be lending five times as much through the TAF as the discount window. And we would have over half a trillion dollars in outstanding swaps, a lifeline for overextended foreign banks that had borrowed in dollars to buy U.S. mortgage assets. The Fed would become the world's lender of last resort.

At the time, though, our initiatives did not provide the reassurance we had hoped. We had separated our announcements of the rate cut and the liquidity programs by a day, because our European counterparts didn't want to get caught up in a U.S. monetary policy action, but markets were so disappointed by the rate cut that the liquidity programs seemed anticlimactic. Rubin told me that markets thought that the Fed was behind the curve, that we didn't realize how bad it was out there. Larry needled me about our Vietnam approach, mocking our incremental efforts to whittle away the crisis with underwhelming force.

We were still feeling our way, taking tentative steps. The TAF was innovative and the swap lines were helpful, especially for European banks that needed dollars, but they weren't going to reduce the losses on mortgages, fill the capital holes of troubled firms, or provide liquidity to the investment banks and other U.S. nonbanks that needed it most. It would have been nice if our commercial banks had used funds from the TAF to lend to more troubled institutions or buy up their toxic assets, but the psychology of the markets had shifted toward caution, and few bankers were in a lending or buying mood.

The day after we announced the TAF, I delivered welcoming remarks at the second annual New York Fed–Princeton University conference on, coincidentally, liquidity. "Your timing is good," I told the group. "Perhaps too good."

In my usual stilted Fed-speak, I painted a dark picture of investors fleeing to safety, banks hoarding liquidity, and creditors mistrusting counterparties. "The danger this poses," I said, "is the risk of an adverse, self-reinforcing dynamic"—in other words, a vicious cycle, a doom loop. Really, we had already fallen into that dynamic, and we hadn't figured out a way to reverse it, or even to slow it down.

BY CHRISTMAS, I felt bone tired and numb. My family and I used airline miles to visit Bali, but even Bali didn't offer much of an escape. It was the rainy season. We all got sick. And the island was a much busier place than the rustic paradise I had visited in high school. I read *War and Peace,* which was therapeutic, but its tragic themes of human failure were not uplifting. I spent most of our days in Indonesia worrying that our rate cuts and our liquidity tools weren't getting much traction.

Chairman Bernanke was usually a calm and conciliatory presence, but on a call in early January 2008, he sounded worried, too, and frustrated by the constraints of consensus on the FOMC. Ben told me he no longer intended to be so deferential to the FOMC's hawks. If they wanted the Fed to stand around inert as the crisis intensified, they could dissent. He wouldn't meet them halfway anymore.

"If I'm going to be hung, I want to be hung for my own judgments," he said. "Not theirs."

I was delighted to hear that. If we wanted to do the right thing for the economy, we couldn't keep placating the hawks for the sake of consensus.

Unfortunately, our first move after Ben's shift into assertive mode didn't go as well as we hoped. Ben had signaled in a speech that a rate cut was coming at our next meeting, but on Martin Luther King, Jr., Day, when a sell-off shook global markets while U.S. exchanges were closed, we decided not to wait. We reduced rates by three-quarters of a point, the largest cut since 1982 and the first cut between meetings since the September 11 attacks. We only learned the next day that the sell-off was mostly driven by a French bank trying to unwind the positions of a rogue trader, not a new wave of concerns about global growth. We were accused of being clueless and trigger-happy, of trying to boost asset prices and rescue speculators instead of focusing on macroeconomic fundamentals. We cut rates another half point at our next formal meeting, to 3 percent, prompting more howls of protest that we were reinstating the Greenspan Put. Fisher dissented, saying we shouldn't have cut rates at all, continuing to see inflation around every corner.

It looked like we were lurching. When it came to the expectations game of monetary policy, I often talked about how important it was to get the theater right as well as the substance. The general view was that we had botched the theater, undermining our substance. At the annual economic forum in Davos, Switzerland, in January, the buzz in the hallways was that the Fed had overreacted and made things look worse than they were, undermining confidence.

I thought our critics were too complacent. At one roundtable, I made the case to a group of central bankers that included the ECB's Jean-Claude Trichet and his future successor, Mario Draghi, that the balance of risks had shifted dramatically toward economic weakness and financial distress.

"In these circumstances, you don't have perfect foresight," I said. "You're going to make mistakes, and you've got to decide which kind of mistakes are less damaging."

It would be easier to correct the mistake of doing too much, I argued, than to escalate too slowly, let the situation burn out of control, and have to correct the mistake of doing too little. It made more sense to err on the side of averting a financial meltdown, to buy insurance against a macroeconomic disaster.

Much of the Davos crowd thought we were feckless. First we had rattled the markets by underreacting, then we had rattled the markets by overreacting. But a panic tends to make everyone look feckless, in the same way a mania makes everyone look brilliant. I remember arguing with Larry in the lobby of the Belvédère hotel about some harsh words he'd said and written about Ben and Hank. I was probably overprotective of my colleagues in the foxhole—and overly defensive about my own role—but I told Larry that it was bad form for a former Treasury secretary to second-guess a successor in public, and that not even he could imagine the constraints Ben and Hank faced.

"You have no idea how hard this is," I said.

• • •

I TRAVELED with my family to California in February to look at colleges for my daughter, Elise, but again, I wasn't really with them. We stayed with my former Treasury colleague Sheryl Sandberg, who was especially close with Elise, but I spent most of the time on my cell phone. We also spent a few days at Big Sur, staying at a hotel that had yurts overlooking the ocean. This time, I spent most of the time on a satellite phone; I had to drive to the edge of a cliff just to get a signal, and spent hours in a light rain on call after call. I remember hearing two of my board members, Dick Fuld of Lehman Brothers and the developer Jerry Speyer, describe the carnage in the real estate markets with a new level of concern in their voices. There was more fear, more urgency, more direct appeals for the Fed to do more.

Every morning, the New York Fed's market room sent around a dashboard of about fifty economic and financial indicators. Most were heading the wrong way. Mortgage-backed securities were still bleeding. Rating agencies were belatedly downgrading them, leading to margin calls, forced asset sales, and more bleeding. Prices for credit default swaps—derivative contracts insuring against the failure of a firm or default of a security—were rising. Ambac, MBIA, and other large monoline insurers that stood behind many mortgage securities faced downgrades as well; even the dull municipal bonds they backed were starting to wobble. The New York state insurance commissioner, Eric Dinallo, had tracked me down in Davos, frantically informing me that the monolines were in trouble and that Charlie Gasparino was criticizing him on CNBC for not doing something about it. I didn't know who Gasparino was—I didn't watch much TV—but in any case I told Dinallo the Fed couldn't help mortgage insurers.

I would later be criticized as a walking source of moral hazard, too willing to provide financial assistance, but to many firms and investors caught up in the early phase of the crisis, we were not nearly generous enough. I routinely rejected requests for public support of private institutions. John Snow, Hank's predecessor at Treasury, once came to see me with the CEO of the private equity firm Cerberus. The CEO explained they were patriots who had tried to help America by investing in Chrysler and GMAC, the troubled financing arm of General Motors; now they wanted the Fed to help them. My staff and I were darkly amused by the idea that these investments had been acts of patriotism. But we got many similar requests for assistance, though I don't remember anyone else invoking the patriot defense.

In fact, there's nothing wrong with letting a crisis burn for a while, as long as you have the ability to contain it before it rages out of control. Just as a modest wildfire can get rid of some underbrush and improve the health of a forest, a modest crisis can clear out dry tinder in the system and make the financial system more resilient. But I was growing increasingly pessimistic that we had the authority or the fire-fighting tools to contain this one. The fire wasn't responding to some pretty aggressive monetary easing and a pretty forceful provision of liquidity to banks. The markets were looking to us for more powerful solutions, but I didn't think our options were that powerful. That feeling of responsibility combined with helplessness, the inability to alter the path of events, ate away at me.

The most flammable parts of the system were the institutions reliant on tri-party repo and other short-term financing markets, where some creditors were flatly refusing to accept mortgage securities that didn't have Fannie or Freddie behind them, while the rest were demanding more collateral. Institutions loaded with these "non-agency" securities now struggled to finance them. For example, the investment bank Bear Stearns had to ratchet up its reliance on tri-party repo in 2007 after creditors stopped rolling over its commercial paper; now a sizable chunk of the collateral behind its repo book was in illiquid assets, and it wasn't clear how long its lenders would accept them. In early March, margin calls led to fire-sale liquidations of several major investment funds, including one owned by the vaunted Carlyle Group, and the cost of insuring against a default by Bear nearly doubled in a week. We were slipping into a more dangerous phase of the deleveraging spiral.

My staff had been working for months on an innovative new program, the Term Securities Lending Facility, designed to provide some relief where it would do the most good. The TSLF would allow the twenty "primary dealers," including the five large stand-alone investment banks, to borrow Treasuries from the Fed against an unprecedented range of collateral, including the AAA-rated non-agency securities that the private sector would no longer finance. We hoped to thaw the frozen markets for those securities, since they would now be exchangeable for Treasuries. We also hoped to ease liquidity pressures throughout the system, reaching beyond commercial banks for the first time to the most troubled part of the markets.

This required us to invoke the Fed's emergency powers, the "unusual and exigent" language of Section 13(3). Kevin Warsh, a well-connected Republican who advised Ben about politics as well as finance, suggested that accepting collateral nobody else wanted could expose the Fed to potential criticism as well as losses. But Ben didn't flinch. On Sunday, March 9, 2008, he emailed the members of the Fed board to rally their support for this bold step.

"This is unusual, but so are market conditions," he wrote. "I strongly recommend that we proceed with this plan."

On Monday, the Fed approved the TSLF. Unfortunately, the $200 billion program wouldn't be ready for two weeks. By then, the circumstances would be even more unusual and exigent.

• • •

"I THINK I've been around long enough to know a serious problem, and this seems like one."

It was Wednesday night, March 12, and Rodgin Cohen was on the phone. Rodge was the lawyer to see for financial institutions with problems, a legendary fixer known as "Wall Street's trauma surgeon." I spoke to him all the time, because he seemed to represent everyone in town—including Lehman Brothers, Fannie Mae, AIG, and just about every other firm that got in trouble during the crisis—and he always had something thoughtful to convey about what was going on. This time, he was calling on behalf of Bear Stearns and its CEO, Alan Schwartz. "They're really worried," Rodge said. After Moody's downgraded some mortgage securities Bear had issued, markets had started running from the eighty-four-year-old investment bank. Rodge wondered if we could speed up the TSLF launch so that Bear could swap some illiquid assets for Treasuries. Then its skittish repo lenders might be more willing to extend it credit.

"If Alan is worried, he should call me," I said. I didn't think we could help, but I wanted to hear his voice, and get a better feel for how bad things really were.

Bear had survived the crash of 1929 without shedding a single employee, but ever since subprime mortgages sank its memorably named Enhanced Leverage Fund in the summer of 2007, markets had viewed it with suspicion bordering on disdain. It was the smallest and most leveraged of the five major investment banks, with $400 billion in assets and $33 in borrowing for every dollar of capital. It was seen as Wall Street's weakest link, badly managed, disproportionately exposed to mortgages. For months, its lenders had been demanding more collateral. Bear's previous CEO, Jimmy Cayne, had been forced out in January as its losses piled up.

The SEC, Bear's regulator, had never expressed much concern about its condition, at least not to us. The SEC's core mandate was to go after market manipulation, fraud, and insider trading; they didn't focus much on financial stability. As late as that Wednesday, SEC staffers were still assuring us Bear had plenty of liquidity. And SEC Chairman Christopher Cox told reporters his agency had "a good deal of comfort" with Bear's capital cushion.

Schwartz had gone on CNBC at 9 a.m. to try to beat back rumors that Wall Street no longer wanted to do business with his firm. "None of those speculations are true," he said. But as Bagehot knew, a banker forced to defend his credit has already lost it—and the speculations were in fact true. Hedge funds were closing out brokerage accounts with Bear. Derivatives counterparties were "stepping out" of existing trades and rejecting new ones to avoid exposure to Bear. CNBC interrupted the interview with the news that New York Governor Eliot Spitzer was resigning amid a prostitution scandal, but that bizarre interlude didn't stop Schwartz from complaining, accurately if not wisely, that investors were choosing to "sell first and ask questions later . . . which creates its own momentum." Bear's liquid reserves had dropped from $18 billion to $12 billion in two days. This felt much darker than the Countrywide scare, because Bear seemed more systemic, and the broader financial world was in a much more fragile place.

The run became a sprint on Thursday, leaving Bear with just $2 billion in cash at the end of the day. The markets had lost all confidence in Bear. Some of its repo lenders were preparing to stop rolling over its loans on Friday, including loans with safe Treasuries as collateral. Around 7:30 p.m., when I had just gotten home, Schwartz called to let me know that Bear planned to file for bankruptcy in the morning. Yikes! I convened a call with the Fed and the SEC. The SEC officials said they saw no way to avert a filing, then outlined the limited steps they expected to take to protect the brokerage accounts of Bear's customers.

"OK, we're going home," the senior SEC official on the call finally concluded. "We'll talk in the morning."

Really? With a $400 billion investment bank about to default on its obligations, it seemed a bit early to call it a night. Nothing is more dangerous during a panic than the sudden liquidation of a major institution, so I asked my chief of staff to call our people back into the office. Even if we couldn't prevent an ugly crash, I wanted to explore ways to put "foam on the runway"—anything to mitigate the damage.

The New York Fed's executive floor was being renovated, so most of our team huddled in windowless conference rooms in our temporary offices on the thirteenth floor, trying to assess how bad things would get if Bear Stearns defaulted. We also sent a group to Bear to examine its books. So did JPMorgan Chase, which was interested not only as Bear's tri-party repo clearing bank, but as a potential buyer for some or all of its businesses.

The initial news was all bad. Bear's books were full of ugly surprises, and JPMorgan was unwilling to buy anything without more time for due diligence. At 2 a.m., I trudged off to a nearby hotel with a horrible pit in my stomach, hoping to get some rest ahead of the market open. Friday was going to be brutal. Our only obvious option was the standard announcement that the Fed stood ready to provide liquidity to the markets. That wouldn't be much foam on the runway.

At 4 a.m., my staff woke me up with a phone call and said I should come back to the office. The news, for the most part, had gotten even worse.

The closer Fed officials looked at Bear's connections with the broader financial system, the more they feared its sudden failure would unleash utter chaos. Bear was not that big—only the seventeenth largest U.S. financial institution at the time—but it was completely enmeshed in the fabric of the system. It had nearly four hundred subsidiaries. It had trading positions with five thousand counterparties around the world. And it had borrowed about $80 billion in the tri-party repo market, presenting even greater risks of runs on money markets and investment banks than we had confronted the previous August with Countrywide.

About a third of Bear's repo collateral was in the form of mortgage securities. So if Bear went down, its repo lenders would have to unload its collateral, which would depress the price of those securities and the value of everyone else's collateral, intensifying the downward spiral. Repo borrowers would face margin calls or lose access to credit, as lenders would stop rolling over loans. And as clearing banks, JPMorgan and Bank of New York Mellon faced catastrophic losses if they kept providing intraday credit to borrowers who could easily become the next Bear. Just about everyone would want to limit exposure to just about everyone else.

Bear also had 750,000 open derivatives contracts. While our work with the Fourteen Families on derivatives infrastructure had made it easier for firms to determine their direct exposure to Bear, they had no idea how much exposure their counterparties had. During a panic, they would be inclined to assume the worst and pull back from everyone potentially exposed to a Bear default. As the British statesman David Lloyd George once said, "Financiers in a fright do not make a heroic picture." While the direct impact of Bear's failure would be bad, the real danger was that it would spark runs or margin calls on other firms perceived to have similar vulnerabilities or exposure to counterparties with similar vulnerabilities, triggering a chain reaction of fear and uncertainty that could imperil the entire system.

"Too big to fail" has become the catchphrase of the crisis, but that night, our fear was that Bear was "too interconnected to fail" without causing catastrophic damage. And it was impossible to guess the magnitude of that damage. There were too many other firms that looked like Bear in terms of their leverage, their dependence on short-term funding, and their exposure to devastating losses as the housing market dropped and recession fears mounted.

But there was one piece of better news. Tom Baxter, our general counsel, taking a page from the Doomsday Book, the binder full of information about the New York Fed's emergency powers that he had helped write years earlier, proposed an idea that could keep Bear alive through the weekend, a "back-to-back" loan involving JPMorgan. Rather than lending directly to Bear, Tom said, we could make a short-term loan to JPMorgan that it would "on-lend" to Bear, while pledging some of Bear's securities as collateral. That would give Bear enough liquidity to survive the weekend, so we would have a couple of days to seek a more permanent solution. Many lawyers look for reasons to say no; Baxter was creative and intrepid about finding ways we could act.

We knew we would be crossing a line the Fed had not crossed since the Great Depression, indirectly lending to a brokerage house that was supposed to function outside the bank safety net. We would insist on enough collateral to secure the loan to our satisfaction—meeting the legal test that we have a reasonable expectation that we wouldn't lose money even if Bear defaulted—but, in reality, we'd be taking some risk. The moral hazard risk was real, too. We didn't want investment banks, or any nonbanks, to think they could rely on our safety net, and several of my senior colleagues in New York—including Bill Dudley, who ran the Fed's markets function, and Meg McConnell, my close adviser—thought the loan was a bad idea.

On a 5 a.m. conference call with Washington, I walked through the arguments for and against the loan, urging the dissenters to make their case. With limited time and limited sleep, we would be making a momentous decision, and I wanted everyone fully aware of the objections and possible repercussions. But I thought the loan was the right thing to do; we had to buy time to at least try to avert disaster. Ben and Don asked all the right questions, but they agreed we should do whatever we could to prevent the chaos we thought would accompany the failure of a major investment bank. If Bear collapsed, any institution that looked anything like Bear could be the next domino to fall.

Lehman Brothers, for example, had nearly one-third of its repo collateral in mortgage securities, just like Bear, and was widely considered the next weakest of the large investment banks. The end of Bear could easily mark the start of a run on Lehman, with Merrill Lynch next in line. In fact, all five of the large investment banks, and many other nonbanks, shared a common vulnerability, borrowing short and lending long without the stability of insured deposits or access to the discount window. Among the defining features of a panic is the fact that markets become less discriminating—more likely to run from everyone rather than try to figure out whose fundamentals seem strong. At a time when creditors were pulling back loans, counterparties were demanding more margin, and investors were fleeing for safety, not even the relatively strong institutions were safe.

After two hours of discussion and angst, I reminded everyone that we had to make a decision before the markets opened, and I recommended we go ahead.

"Let's do it," Ben said.

THE RUN on Bear continued on Friday, March 14. The rating agencies, with characteristically late and lousy timing, downgraded Bear's debt to near-junk status. By the closing bell, its stock price, which had peaked at $168 a year earlier, dropped below $30. Gold soared to an all-time high, a classic sign of market phobia.

Bear was history. Schwartz thought he had some time to find a buyer, because he mistakenly thought that our loan would mature in four weeks, but that was wishful thinking. Hank and I told Schwartz he had to make a deal before markets opened in Asia on Sunday night. He was not pleased.

On Saturday morning on the way into the office, I stopped to see Volcker at his Manhattan apartment. He greeted me with a mischievous reference to the Dutch boy with his finger in the dike. "How's your finger?" he asked.

I had come to explain to Volcker what we were doing, not just because I valued his advice, but because I wanted to marinate him in our terrible choices. Volcker had a sterling reputation as the wise man of public policy—the brave Fed chairman who tamed runaway inflation in the 1980s—and no opinion in the world of finance carried more weight. I made it clear that I did not think the Fed could keep Bear afloat, and I was not prepared to lend into the run while Bear sought a path to redemption. I said our plan was to see if we could find someone strong enough to buy them and guarantee their obligations before Asia opened. Failing that, we were searching for ways to try to cushion the impact of a major default.

Volcker was pretty sympathetic. He recognized that the situation was awful and could easily get much worse. Central banks exist to try to reduce the damage in situations like this. It wouldn't be easy to find a buyer with the desire and the balance sheet to take on Bear's risk during a major financial crisis, but Volcker understood that we didn't have any good options.

Although several firms took a look at Bear, it wasn't much of an auction. It quickly became clear that Bear's options were JPMorgan or bankruptcy. I stayed in touch with JPMorgan Chase CEO Jamie Dimon all day Saturday while his team combed through Bear's books. By nightfall, Dimon said he was prepared to pay $8 to $12 a share— less than the current $30 price, but more than the $0 the stock would be worth Monday after a bankruptcy filing.

It seemed too good to be true, and it was. On Sunday morning,

Dimon called back to say the deal was off. The problem, he said, was not the price. It was the potential losses in Bear's mortgage book. Nearly three-fourths of the assets were subprime or only slightly safer, and he wasn't prepared to take those on at any price.

"There's just too much risk," he said.

Dimon had served on the board of the New York Fed for three years, and he came across as smart, tough, and good at his job. I had heard him give an impressive presentation at a New York Fed conference about the challenges of risk management, and why bankers tend to underestimate risk. I didn't think he was bluffing about his reluctance to take on more mortgage risk and stand behind Bear's trading book at a time when mortgages were in crisis, traders were panicked, and a recession loomed. His reservations sounded rational and credible. Still, Jamie knew he was the only likely bidder for Bear—and he had warned us that if Bear failed, the four other investment banks might fail as well, which wouldn't be good for anyone. I got the sense he might be willing to do a deal with some government assistance.

I called Ben and then Hank with the news. Hank was a bullet-headed former Goldman investment banker and CEO, as imposing and action-oriented as Ben was deferential and measured. He used to say his general approach to life was that if you see a problem, run at it, not away from it. He was open and direct, giving the impression that he laid it all out there, but he was also an insightful reader of people and their needs, which helped make him a formidable deal-maker. We worked really well together, even though we were from completely different worlds. He had asked me to be his deputy when he became Treasury secretary. Our working relationship became so close that some of Hank's aides complained he spent too much time on the phone with me. I know they sometimes felt I pushed him toward interventions that their conservative Republican administration hoped to avoid.

Hank and I spent the rest of Sunday morning on the phone with Dimon, separately and together. Dimon argued that buying Bear would weaken his bank. I argued that a disorderly collapse of Bear would be rough on JPMorgan, too.

"Jamie, what makes you think you'll be unaffected by this failure?" I asked. "You've got the biggest derivatives book out there. You're the clearing bank. You've got all this exposure. I don't get why you think you'd be OK."

Eventually, Dimon proposed that we take some of Bear's risk off his hands. U.S. law severely limits the risks the Fed can take, and in general, central banks shouldn't design one-off interventions to prevent the failure of individual firms. So I asked Hank if Treasury could tap the Exchange Stabilization Fund, the pot of money Treasury had used to rescue Mexico in 1995, to assume some of the risk in a Bear deal. His lawyers said no, the Treasury could not do that.

I talked to Ben and Don, and suggested that the New York Fed take on some of Bear's assets. Given the risks to the system, they were willing. I still thought it would be better for the Fed if we had some financial protection from Treasury, so I told Hank we'd do it only if the Treasury indemnified us from any losses. He said he'd try. I then told Dimon we were willing to take on some of Bear's risk. And I called Larry Fink, the CEO of the investment firm BlackRock, the only firm without potential conflicts of interest that had the expertise to advise us quickly, and asked him to send a team to evaluate the portfolio of Bear's assets that Dimon wanted to leave behind.

By the early afternoon, we had hashed out a deal. We would help JPMorgan buy Bear Stearns. Hank pressured Dimon to keep the price low, to avoid the perception that we were subsidizing a windfall for Bear's shareholders. So the offer was just $2 a share, or $236 million for a firm that had been valued at $20 billion the previous year. And at our insistence, JPMorgan agreed to stand behind Bear's obligations immediately, even though the deal wouldn't close immediately. That was a huge risk to take during a panic, a risk someone had to take to prevent Bear's remaining customers and creditors from fleeing, a risk we believed we couldn't take ourselves. All the

Fed could do was lend against collateral, not provide an open-ended guarantee.

The New York Fed agreed to lend JPMorgan $30 billion to facilitate the merger, backed by $30 billion worth of Bear's investment-grade assets. Larry Fink of BlackRock assured me that if we held on to the assets for a few years, we would probably break even, with at most a few billion dollars in losses; I made him repeat that on a call with Ben and Hank. I told Ben I thought that met the legal test under 13(3) that we be "secured to our satisfaction," and he agreed.

But late in the afternoon, Hank's lawyers told him Treasury couldn't indemnify the Fed without congressional approval. I was incredulous, and we both yelled at his lawyers for a while, but they were unyielding, and I decided they were probably right. Hank felt bad he couldn't deliver, and it was pretty remarkable to discover how little authority the secretary of the Treasury had to try to avert a major financial crisis in the United States. His attitude was: Just tell me what I can do, and I'll do it. So I proposed he write me a letter, publicly supporting the loan and noting that if the Fed incurred losses, they would reduce the profits we return to the Treasury each year. Hank called it his "all money is green letter," and while it merely stated fiscal facts, I thought it gave us some cover, implicating Treasury in the risks we were taking.

While we were scrambling to prevent a disorderly bankruptcy of Bear, we were also trying to put foam on the runway in case we couldn't. That weekend, a team at the New York Fed was designing a new credit facility intended to provide liquidity to the investment banks and the broader markets in case Bear collapsed. But once we found a deal for Bear, we still decided to go ahead with the foam-on-the-runway plan. That Sunday night, at roughly the same time as the Bear announcement, we launched the Primary Dealer Credit Facility, which provided a lending facility like the Fed's discount window to the big four surviving investment banks.

That night, we convened a call to explain these actions to the CEOs of the major financial institutions, and to ask them not to make a fragile situation worse. We had Jamie start by announcing that all their trading positions with Bear were now with JPMorgan, a relief to all of them. Hank and I then urged them to act responsibly. We didn't want them to pull back further and accelerate a spiral that could end up destroying all their firms. Our message was: You have a collective interest in making this work. How you respond will help determine whether the system holds. And we will be watching.

Vikram Pandit pointed out that the system would remain in limbo until Bear's shareholders approved an extremely unattractive deal. He asked: What if this falls apart? Then what do we get for acting responsibly? Dimon shot back a question of his own: "What happens to Citigroup if this institution goes down?"

DIMON HAD a point, but so did Pandit. Bear's shareholders were furious that their firm was being valued at less than Alex Rodriguez's contract with the Yankees. And Bear's clients and counterparties continued to run out of fear the merger wouldn't close. This uncertainty was a serious problem for Dimon. He told Hank and me he would raise his offer if he could be assured the merger would go through.

That was fine with me. I didn't much care what JPMorgan paid for Bear, as long as the deal got done and the system calmed down. Reopening the deal would also give us leverage to improve the terms for the government. We ended up getting JPMorgan to agree to take the first $1 billion of any losses from Bear's mortgage assets, which we agreed to hold in a new special purpose vehicle. (We named it Maiden Lane, after a street next to our building.) Meg warned in an email that it would look like we were launching a subprime SIV, which "seems like a PR thing we'll need to manage very aggressively from the start to keep it from becoming a big joke." But it was good to have a larger margin of safety.

Hank had his own concerns. He was still uncomfortable allowing the shareholders of a failed firm to benefit from a government rescue. But Ben and I helped persuade him that allowing JPMorgan to offer a somewhat better deal to the shareholders of Bear Stearns mattered less than the stability of the financial system. Dimon upped his offer to $10 a share, and the deal was done.

• • •

WELL, ALMOST done.

The New York Fed and JPMorgan spent the next three months locked in brutal behind-the-scenes negotiations, arguing over which Bear Stearns assets the Fed would take and how much they were worth, fighting over every security and every mark. Dimon wanted to leave as much risk with us as possible, especially now that he had given us a $1 billion cushion against losses. Tensions were running high. Everyone was on edge. On one occasion, well after midnight, Dimon unleashed a tirade at Tom Baxter so heated that Tom hung up on him; Tom then called me to say that the New York Fed could no longer negotiate with Dimon. I let him vent for a while, but eventually I interceded, Jamie apologized to Tom, and we were able to resume the negotiations.

Still, Dimon was relentless, and he put tremendous pressure on his team to be equally relentless. Near the end of the talks, I remember, I got on a call with Steve Black, one of Dimon's top lieutenants, to explain our final offer.

"Are you telling us as president of the New York Fed that this is the way it's going to be?" Black asked.

I hesitated. I didn't want JPMorgan to claim I used my power as its regulator to force a deal, or that the Fed had unilaterally changed the terms of the deal.

"We'd just like to know," Black repeated a bit more slowly. "Are you telling us as president of the New York Fed that this is the way it's going to be?"

Now I got it. Black just wanted to be able to tell Dimon that he had fought as hard as he could.

"Yeah," I said. "I am telling you as president of the New York Fed that this is as far as we will go. We are done."

And so we were. But the agony of papering the Bear deal made a lasting impression on me. It showed how hard it was to value assets that markets wouldn't touch during a crisis, and how vulnerable the government was to getting stuck with the worst. "Let's hope the BlackRock people have our backs," Meg emailed me at one point. "We don't have a clue what we're doing." Meg has a flair for darkness, but she was right to worry that we knew very little about the securities, except that Jamie and his team didn't want them. Ultimately, though, BlackRock and the small internal Fed team did a great job evaluating them; by the end of 2013, the Fed would be projected to earn a profit on Bear. But my skepticism about government purchases of complex illiquid assets would become important later in the crisis.

The entire Bear episode was a turning point for the Fed, erasing our long-standing lines between commercial banks we considered "inside the safety net" and the many firms operating outside that net. We had used our power to help prevent the disorderly collapse of a private firm, protecting creditors and counterparties from losses. We didn't want to do any of those things; we saw them as the least-bad options. But I thought we were pretty creative, considering the exceptional pressure and the constraints on our authority, in persuading a private financial institution to guarantee Bear's obligations and devising a way to lend against distressed assets with underlying value. Trichet called me to say we had done a masterful job containing the panic.

Larry called with a decidedly different take: "You're going to get killed over this!" He said the Bear merger would look like a corrupt bailout, a sweetheart deal for one of my board members. He said he didn't agree with those critiques, although as always he had an endless list of things we could have done better. I told him he sounded like the author William Greider, who savaged the Greenspan Fed in his populist critique *Secrets of the Temple.*

"It's going to be like Greider, but much worse," Larry replied.

I had learned about the lousy politics of crisis response during my time at Treasury, but it was still jarring to be a target myself, with critics questioning not just my choices but my motives. "That is socialism!" Republican Senator Jim Bunning of Kentucky thundered when Ben and I testified before Congress about Bear. Our Fed colleague Jeff Lacker publicly accused us of encouraging recklessness and laying the groundwork for the next crisis. Even Volcker declared the Fed had gone to "the very edge of its lawful and implied powers." He didn't say we went over the edge, but it was open season on the Fed, sometimes even from within the Fed. Richard Fisher, no fan of what we had done, sent me a gracious email with the message *"Illegitimi non carborundum,"* a slogan my grandfather had kept on his kitchen wall. It means: "Don't let the bastards get you down."

I thought the moral hazard fundamentalists were missing the point. Bear's shareholders absorbed huge losses; the final deal was 94 percent below the stock's peak. Bear's senior executives lost their jobs and much of their wealth. The firm itself disappeared. It was hard to imagine that other firms would take much comfort from Bear's plight or have any desire to follow Bear's path. And JPMorgan took extraordinary risks to guarantee Bear's obligations, even though its competitors would clamor for "Jamie deals" later in the crisis. We did create some moral hazard by protecting creditors and counterparties from the consequences of a Bear default, but that was unavoidable. We wanted to avoid what we saw during the systemic panics of the nineties, when the fear of cascading defaults and haircuts for bondholders and other creditors greatly amplified the damage. Once a run is under way, anything that increases the uncertainty of creditors about if and when they'll get paid will exacerbate the run. Crisis responders who get obsessed with moral hazard and Old Testament justice make crises worse.

I was equally unmoved by suggestions that Bear was a case study in the dangers of size, an illustration of the too-big-to-fail syndrome. Bear was only a midsize financial institution, with only one-fourth the assets of JPMorgan, illustrating that when the system is fragile, even relatively small institutions can threaten enormous damage. It also showed that size had some virtues, as JPMorgan was large enough and strong enough to take on Bear's liabilities.

Finally, while our critics saw Bear as a cautionary tale about complex new derivatives, I saw it as a familiar story about a failure to manage risk. Bear had borrowed too much and too short. In a time of mania, it used its financing to buy stuff that lost much more value than it had thought possible. Then its lenders got nervous and demanded their money back, money that it no longer had on hand. The real lesson of Bear was that in a world of extreme leverage and short-term financing, confidence can vanish in a heartbeat, and liquidity along with it.

This was not an uplifting lesson, because all those vulnerabilities were still present in the financial system, especially outside the commercial banks. But I was comfortable with what we had done. That spring, at the Microsoft CEO summit in Seattle, Warren Buffett came to the session where I made a presentation. He said he believed our interventions had saved the system from an unspeakable calamity.

"I was sort of hoping you wouldn't do it, because then everything would have crashed and I would have been first in line to buy," he said with a grin. "It would have been terrible for the country, but I would've made a lot more money."

I still felt incredibly dark about the state of the system. It doesn't bolster investor confidence to see a financial stock plunge from $57 to $2 a share over three days, no matter how aggressive the government response. I was worried about the potential risk that Lehman and other firms posed to the system, worried about repo, worried about the land mines we didn't know about yet. But in some ways, the low point for me was 2 a.m. that Friday morning, March 14, 2008, when I lay down in that hotel room thinking we had no way to prevent Bear from filing and the markets from collapsing. When I returned to the office a few hours later, the world still looked horribly dark, but at least I felt like we were trying to do something about it. It wasn't exactly a comforting feeling, but I liked it better than helplessness.

FIVE

The Fall

Now that the Fed had started lending to investment banks, and had even helped prevent the collapse of an investment bank, I told my team we needed to climb inside the investment banks. If they were going to enjoy access to Fed liquidity, we needed to understand and limit the risks they were taking. We couldn't rely on the SEC anymore. For the first time, the New York Fed sent a small team of full-time monitors into the surviving large investment banks: Lehman Brothers, Merrill Lynch, Morgan Stanley, and Goldman Sachs. Unlike the commercial banks, none of them had a stable funding base of insured deposits. All four were highly leveraged and vulnerable to runs, especially Lehman and Merrill; Goldman and Morgan Stanley seemed less precarious. But we pressured all of them to raise capital, increase their liquidity, and lengthen the maturity of their financing—basically, to batten down their hatches before the next storm.

The four investment banks did manage to raise $40 billion in capital in the spring of 2008, a reflection of the lull in the crisis after we helped salvage Bear and announced our new lending programs.

The stress in the broader markets eased a bit. There were even internal Fed debates about whether the system had stabilized enough to let our "unusual and exigent" programs expire.

But I told my colleagues: "Just because it feels calm doesn't mean it is calm." This felt like another false dawn, not a return to normalcy. Markets that overshoot on the way up tend to overshoot on the way back down, and I thought backing off our commitments to provide liquidity would further damage confidence.

"If we add to uncertainty in the markets about the duration of support, and raise concern about premature withdrawal in an environment where macro/financial uncertainty is still acute, we probably reduce our ability to bring about more repair/robustness to the markets," I wrote in an internal email.

The macro picture looked grim. Washington was so nervous about an election-year downturn that Hank had united Republicans and Democrats behind a $150 billion fiscal stimulus package, a rare bipartisan effort to jump-start consumer spending by sending Americans tax rebate checks. But the deterioration in the economy was overwhelming this stimulus. Unemployment rose a half point to 5.5 percent in May, the largest monthly increase in two decades. One in every eleven mortgages was past due or in foreclosure. Auto sales were plunging. And gasoline was soaring past $4 a gallon, stripping consumers of disposable income, significantly reducing the benefit of their tax rebates. Not only did record oil prices damage the economy, they triggered another round of inflation paranoia, which was discouraging the Fed from cutting interest rates to boost the economy. The ECB actually raised rates, which I found stunning and inexplicable. We wouldn't make the same mistake, but Ben did ask if there was anything else the Fed could do to lean against oil prices. I thought the few modest tools available were within the control of the executive branch.

"This mess is primarily for the Administration," I replied in an email.

My focus was the financial system, and how to make it more

resilient to additional shocks. We were especially worried about the risks in tri-party repo, so we persuaded the clearing banks, BoNY and JPMorgan, to push the market toward less short-term financing of less risky securities. We hoped that would reduce the danger of an uncontrolled run. We were also concerned that the spaghetti-like tangle of overlapping positions in derivatives markets could create uncertainty if another major firm failed. To shrink the plate and untangle some of the spaghetti, we encouraged the Fourteen Families to "tear up" offsetting trades of credit default swaps, getting dealers who had bought and sold the same insurance contract to step out of the offsetting trades and match up the counterparties. That way, if the dealer in the middle failed, the other firms wouldn't be exposed. We ended up eliminating about one-third of the outstanding contracts.

I was still painfully aware of our limited ability to contain the crisis. The ad hoc Bear intervention had worked out, because JPMorgan was willing and able to take on risks the Fed couldn't. But the government needed more formal powers to wind down failing large financial institutions and guarantee their obligations, like the FDIC already had for commercial banks. Hank and Ben took this "resolution authority" idea to the Hill, but Barney Frank, the Democratic chairman of the House Financial Services Committee, told them it had no chance. Hank and Ben and I also talked about seeking the ability to inject capital into struggling institutions or buy their toxic assets. Those ideas also went nowhere at the time, though they would become crucial down the road. It turned out that things had to get a lot worse before Congress would even consider expanding our authority to make things better, a common problem in crisis response.

Anyway, things would soon get a lot worse.

IF BEAR had looked like an outlier, I might not have felt such a deep sense of foreboding that spring. But Lehman had 75 percent more assets than Bear, much more real estate exposure, an even larger thicket of derivatives deals, and nearly $200 billion worth of repo financing that could evaporate quickly. In May, the hedge fund manager David Einhorn, who had bet heavily against Lehman, publicly accused the firm of overly optimistic accounting, and in June, Lehman announced a $2.8 billion second-quarter loss, prompting Dick Fuld to oust his longtime deputy and demote his chief financial officer. Lehman's stock price dropped nearly 75 percent below its peak. Fuld urged Hank and me to push the SEC to ban short selling, but that seemed like a shoot-the-messenger solution. The markets could see that Lehman was carrying assets at 80 or 90 cents on the dollar that other firms had written way down. And they were justifiably worried about what they couldn't see.

One thing we saw when our monitors dug into Lehman and the other investment banks was that their internal stress tests had not been very stressful. Most of them had never imagined that their repo funding could be vulnerable to a run, obviously a faulty assumption after Bear. We forced them to study much darker scenarios to see how vulnerable they would be to a sudden loss of funding. In May, the New York Fed staff calculated that Lehman would need $84 billion in additional liquidity to survive a severe run, a scenario we dubbed "Bear Stearns," and $15 billion to survive a somewhat less severe run we called "Bear Stearns Light." In a June 25 memo, our team concluded that Lehman had borrowed too much, too short, against too many illiquid assets, resulting in a "weak liquidity position"—a pretty mild way to put it.

But when Lehman's risk managers ran their own less conservative version of Bear Stearns Light, they concluded they would weather the storm with $13 billion in cash to spare. Merrill Lynch seemed almost as vulnerable as Lehman, and almost as deep in denial. "Merrill needs to embrace conservatism in its liquidity analysis and acknowledge that it needs to improve its liquidity position," our team wrote in another dry understatement. Throughout my time at the Fed, we found that the firms with cultures that valued risk management and risk managers tended to be stronger and more conservatively financed. When

Merrill CEO John Thain brought his team to see me that spring, there was an awkward moment when it became clear he didn't know the name of his chief risk officer, who was sitting right next to him.

Some would later argue that the moral hazard of the Bear Stearns rescue made this kind of complacency inevitable, that investment banks and other major institutions now had reason to believe they would be bailed out of their mistakes. I didn't think there was much evidence to support that. Investors had financed a huge increase in leverage at investment banks long before the Fed had intervened with Bear. And Bear's fate was not an appealing outcome for others to follow. The firm lost its independence, and its shareholders lost most of their money. We did get JPMorgan to protect Bear's creditors, but the markets didn't seem to think we would necessarily be willing or able to do that again. The remaining investment banks were larger and much harder for another firm to absorb; what bank would be strong enough to do what JPMorgan had done with Bear? Even after our extraordinary actions in March, counterparties gradually reduced their exposures to Lehman, and the cost of insuring against its default began to rise again over the summer.

One institution that did overestimate Lehman's ability to survive was Lehman. Hank and I repeatedly pressured Fuld to sell his firm or at least raise much more capital, but he was late to act and deeply unrealistic about the strength of his position. At one point we persuaded him to ask Warren Buffett to invest in Lehman, but Fuld demanded a much higher price than Buffett was willing to pay. Fuld often called me to complain that his competitors were spreading rumors, or to suggest it was our responsibility to help his firm get out of its worst investments. Like many of those atop the more vulnerable financial institutions in the summer of 2008, Fuld seemed to think that he was a victim and our job was to save him from an unfair world.

By contrast, the leaders of the stronger firms seemed more realistic, more willing to face the darkness. Around that time, a team of the best economists at the New York Fed gave a presentation to our board on the potential losses ahead for banks, based in part on outcomes from recent recessions. Jamie Dimon laughed at them. He told them to throw out their historically based estimates and triple their projected losses.

Fuld didn't seem to understand that Lehman faced a crisis of confidence that the Fed couldn't fix. He once came to see me with the omnipresent crisis attorney Rodge Cohen to ask if we could let Lehman become a bank holding company like JPMorgan or Citi. That would have provided the impression of Fed protection, but on its own it wouldn't have done much to expand Lehman's access to Fed financing, which it was already receiving through the Primary Dealer Credit Facility (PDCF) we had launched over Bear weekend. I told Fuld it would only reinforce the perception of desperation, without addressing Lehman's deeper capital and liquidity problems. Fuld and his executives were also full of ideas for the government to buy their real estate assets at generous prices, or to help them spin off "bad Lehman" into a vehicle called SpinCo while leaving "good Lehman" to prosper. They didn't seem too eager to sell those assets themselves, because the losses likely would have eaten up their capital reserves.

Of course, our successful intervention to prevent Bear's collapse might have influenced Fuld's refusal to believe we would ever let Lehman collapse. There may have been people whispering in his ear that the Fed had vast secret powers to rescue anyone. But his reluctance to act probably had less to do with moral hazard than self-delusion. After nearly forty years at the firm and fifteen years as CEO, Fuld felt like Lehman was his baby, and he couldn't help but believe the firm was worth way more than the market did. He also owned millions of shares.

I used to joke that there would be less moral hazard in the Fed liquidity facilities if financial executives had to put up their own homes as collateral, ahead of the assets of their firms. That would be real skin in the game. When I was visiting my former Treasury colleague Lee Sachs on Martha's Vineyard that summer, we saw a graceful oceanfront mansion during a walk along the beach. Lee, who had worked at Bear Stearns in happier times, told me it belonged to the firm's former president.

"That one right there should've been the first loss," I said.

ON FRIDAY, July 11, Americans saw an actual bank run—not a metaphorical run, like the digital withdrawals that had crushed Bear, but a physical run on a physical bank, as in *It's a Wonderful Life.* That afternoon, the Office of Thrift Supervision and the FDIC shut down and seized IndyMac, a California thrift that was once part of Angelo Mozilo's Countrywide empire. IndyMac had flourished during the bubble by providing exotic mortgages to buyers without much in the way of income or assets. Its balance sheet was loaded with option adjustable-rate mortgages (ARMs), an almost comically irresponsible product that let borrowers choose their monthly payments, adding to their future obligations if they wanted to pay less at the moment. When the housing bubble popped, IndyMac popped with it, the largest U.S. bank to fail since the savings-and-loan crisis of the 1980s, though not even one-tenth the size of Bear Stearns. In Pasadena, TV cameras filmed tearful depositors lining up outside its locked doors, screaming for their money back.

The FDIC guaranteed deposits up to $100,000 at thrifts, so most of those panicked account holders had nothing to worry about. But depositors with more than $100,000 in their accounts were legitimately desperate to retrieve their cash. The FDIC paid uninsured depositors only half of what they were owed, in order to limit the losses to its national fund for insured deposits. This was standard FDIC procedure for a bank failure, but it illustrated how in a time of extreme stress, imposing haircuts on unprotected investors can accelerate the very panic you want to contain. The week after the run on IndyMac, depositors pulled more than $1 billion a day out of Washington Mutual, a much larger thrift with similar exposure to risky mortgages. They had seen the IndyMac precedent, and they didn't want to get stuck with haircuts if WaMu failed.

The FDIC's approach to haircuts would inspire fierce debate when WaMu stumbled in the fall. For the time being, though, IndyMac's indelible images of fear were just more evidence that things were going from bad to worse.

THE FINANCIAL system could easily absorb the $30 billion collapse of IndyMac. There was no way it could absorb the collapse of Fannie Mae and Freddie Mac. The two government-sponsored enterprises held or guaranteed more than $5 trillion in mortgage debt. They were funding about three of every four new U.S. mortgages, propping up what was left of the housing market. But they were heading for the abyss. Fannie's stock price plunged to $10.25 the day IndyMac failed, down 90 percent from its peak. Just about everyone except their captured regulator agreed they were woefully undercapitalized. One Wall Street analyst calculated that they had a capital shortfall of $75 billion. Despite Hank's pleas, Fannie had raised only $7.4 billion in new capital in 2008, while Freddie had failed to raise a dime.

I had been wary of Fannie and Freddie ever since I had watched the Clinton Treasury and Greenspan try without success to rein in their leverage. At the Fed, I had expressed similarly ineffective concern about their paper-thin capital buffers. Closely entwined with the government since birth, they were the most dangerous example of moral hazard in the financial system. Fannie and Freddie borrowed at artificially low rates, because markets assumed the government would never let them default, and poured the cash into mortgages, mortgage guarantees, and other highly leveraged bets on the U.S. housing market. They enjoyed access to cheap money, like banks, without the tougher constraints applied to banks.

Now those highly leveraged bets, so profitable for their shareholders and executives during the boom, were threatening to drown Fannie and Freddie in losses. The underwriting for the mortgages they

bought and guaranteed was more conservative than the private industry average, but in recent years, under pressure to increase returns to
shareholders, their standards had eroded. They had also built up a
huge portfolio of mortgage securities, including some backed by much
riskier subprime loans. With remarkably thin capital buffers, Fannie
and Freddie were acutely vulnerable to a nationwide housing swoon,
as well as a recession that was leaving more mortgage holders without
jobs and without the ability to make their payments.

But with private lenders and investors now in full retreat, the
housing market was as dependent on the GSEs as the GSEs were
dependent on the housing market. As Hank pointed out, when it
came to housing finance, Fannie and Freddie, along with the Federal
Housing Administration, were essentially the only games in town. If
they pulled back in order to reduce their leverage and husband their
capital, the death spiral of falling home prices, mounting foreclosures,
poisoned mortgage securities, and financial turmoil would intensify.
Somehow, Washington needed to restore confidence in Fannie and
Freddie. That would require government money.

That July weekend, after months of failed efforts to push Fannie and Freddie to raise more capital on their own, Hank decided
he needed to act before doubts about their viability became self-
fulfilling. On Tuesday, he asked Congress for legislation that would
give the Treasury almost unlimited authority to invest in Fannie and
Freddie, give their regulator the power to take them over, and give
the Fed a consulting role so we could dig into their books. I thought
the bill's substance was excellent, but the politics were brutal. Senator
Bunning scoffed that it made the Bear Stearns deal look like "ama-
teur socialism." Hank was also ridiculed for urging Congress to give
him immense and unprecedented powers so that he wouldn't have to
use them.

"If you've got a squirt gun in your pocket, you may have to take
it out," Hank explained to Congress. "If you've got a bazooka, and
people know you've got it, you may not have to take it out." That's

true, but when you talk about your need for a bazooka, people naturally assume you must face a serious threat to your security.

Nevertheless, by the end of July, the Democratic-controlled Congress overwhelmingly passed the bill, providing an almost blank check for a Republican Treasury secretary. The legislation also quietly raised the debt ceiling, a routine housekeeping measure that would become anything but routine in the years to come. But while Congress gave Treasury vast financial authority to inject capital into Fannie and Freddie, it denied Treasury any power over the management of the firms. That power went to their regulator, rechristened the Federal Housing Finance Agency. This awkward limitation, designed by Democrats to protect the new agency from political interference by a Republican president, would prove consequential later in the crisis when a Democratic president wanted to limit the damage to homeowners.

The legislation came close to formalizing the implicit federal guarantee behind Fannie and Freddie, but it couldn't improve their performance or their balance sheets. They soon announced more than $3 billion in second-quarter losses. Tim Clark, who led the Fed's dive into their books, concluded that their loan loss projections were half what they should have been. He thought much of their capital was an accounting fiction. His unvarnished assessment was that Fannie and Freddie were functionally insolvent.

Hank was going to have to use his bazooka after all.

ONE AFTERNOON that summer, I tried to lighten up the mood at the New York Fed with an impromptu contest for the best metaphor for what was happening to the financial system. "I've heard 'the wheels coming off the bus,'" I said. "We've talked about the engines falling off the plane." The usual suspects were wildfires and earthquakes, hundred-year storms and hundred-year floods. We also discussed cancer and contagion, sweaters unraveling and boulders rolling down a hill. I relayed one I had first heard from Goldman Sachs CEO Lloyd Blankfein: "The rivets are coming off the submarine."

Whatever the metaphor, things looked bad. Wachovia, the fourth largest U.S. bank, announced an $8.9 billion second-quarter loss. Thanks to some ill-fated financial ventures, the insurer AIG was up to $18.5 billion in losses over nine months. Both of those firms had ousted their CEOs, but neither had regained the confidence of the markets. Overall, financial institutions had already written down $300 billion in losses, and our research division estimated $650 billion in losses still to come, with the possibility of as much as $1.5 trillion.

Risk aversion was on the rise. The private equity investor Tim Collins told me he was moving all his liquid assets out of financial institutions and into TreasuryDirect, a program that lets individuals hold Treasuries directly in a government account. He didn't want even the slightest risk that his securities could get stuck in a failed bank, another textbook example of flight-to-safety panic.

THERE WAS nothing fun about that summer. I got a nasty case of poison ivy, so I worked for weeks with my legs slathered in Calamine lotion and wrapped in gauze. I once walked from my office to a conference room with a long train of Calamine-covered gauze trailing from my pant leg. Carole and I also had a horrible scare when Elise came down with dengue fever in a remote village in northern Thailand. Fortunately, we had family friends from my high school days who lived in Chiang Mai and helped her navigate the local hospital scene. But it was a painful, helpless feeling to know that she was so sick and so far away.

My main financial-world anxiety—and the market's, too—was still Lehman Brothers. Fuld kept asking me what I was hearing, but institutions were not lining up for the privilege of investing in his firm. Hank and I tried to encourage some interest from Bank of America, but CEO Ken Lewis, who had bought Countrywide despite its glut of toxic mortgages, told us he wasn't interested in Lehman. Fuld thought he could raise capital from the Korea Development Bank, but we had a hard time imagining the Koreans pulling the trigger. Meanwhile, banks, pension funds, and other institutions kept reducing exposure to Lehman.

That summer, Lehman and other weak firms frequently complained to me that stronger creditors were preying on them, demanding more collateral when they could least afford it. Fuld was particularly incensed about JPMorgan's margin calls. AIG's new CEO, Robert Willumstad, accused Goldman Sachs of being too aggressive in marking down the value of bonds it held that AIG had insured. I called Dimon and Blankfein to tell them not to overdo it, but I had no evidence that they were overdoing it. They seemed to be responding sensibly to the declining value of securities that Lehman and AIG held or guaranteed, and to the market's loss of confidence in those firms. I couldn't blame them for acting to protect their own firms.

Another common request I got that summer—from Fuld and others running or representing the weaker firms—was to reassure the public that there was no cause for alarm, that the financial system was safe and well-capitalized. But neither of those statements was true. I thought pretending otherwise to try to jawbone the markets would damage the Fed's credibility as well as mine. At that point, happy talk would have seemed so defensive and outlandish that I feared it would just convince the few remaining optimists that all hope must be lost.

I felt like I was watching a disaster unfold in slow motion, with no ability to prevent it and weak tools to limit the damage. Neither the Fed nor the Treasury had authority to inject capital into troubled institutions, except Hank's new power to invest in Fannie and Freddie. We had only limited tools to defend against a run on firms outside the commercial banking system, at a time when running seemed increasingly rational. The flood had already breached the levees, and all we could do was pile up more sandbags.

Throughout the crisis I often thought about the Serenity Prayer: *God, grant me the serenity to accept the things I cannot change, the courage to change the things I can, and the wisdom to know the difference.* It helped me to focus on what we could do, rather than obsess about what was beyond our powers. But I also thought about what I had said to Rubin during the Asian crises: Just because a problem has no apparent solution doesn't mean it isn't a problem. The summer of 2008 did not feel like a time for serenity about the things we could not change. And I was not serene.

I remember in August, when I was driving home after visiting my parents, I pulled off Interstate 95 at an exit in Warwick, Rhode Island, to finish a call to Rubin about the perilous state of the financial system. I don't remember the conversation itself—it's lost in the fog of war—but whenever I drive past that Warwick exit, I get a wave of the same crushing fear and nausea I felt that summer.

I was in the Adirondacks over Labor Day weekend, spending time with my family and trout fishing with Paul Volcker and Tim Collins. I took up fly-fishing late in life, and I don't do it much, but it's the most calming activity I know. It requires total focus. It blocks out the rest of the world, which was definitely a bonus that weekend.

I felt a bit guilty that I had gone fishing, because Hank had asked me to come to Washington to help him plan a resolution for Fannie and Freddie. They were dead men walking, struggling just to finance themselves. Foreign governments and other investors who had assumed their paper was as safe as Treasuries were screaming for U.S. government protection. But this was a Treasury operation, and I didn't think Hank needed me in the war room. He sounded worried that I was distancing myself for political reasons, but that wasn't it. I knew we were all in this together. I just wanted some downtime to hang out with my family and enjoy the rhythm of casting for trout before the crisis consumed everything.

Hank and his team did a fantastic job. By Monday morning, September 8, the Federal Housing Finance Agency had forced Fannie and Freddie into conservatorship and replaced the CEOs. Treasury also committed to backstop the firms with up to $200 billion in government capital, easing fears that Fannie and Freddie would default. That meant lower borrowing costs for the firms, lower mortgage rates for the public, and the removal of an existential threat to global finance. Hank took a lot of grief for firing the bazooka so soon after telling Congress he wouldn't have to, and his reversal did give the impression that we were lurching from emergency to emergency without a comprehensive plan. But he did the right and courageous thing, heedless of the political costs. And President Bush backed him all the way. I was deeply troubled by many of the Bush administration's economic policies, particularly its legacy of fiscal profligacy, which would complicate our later efforts to defuse the crisis and revive the economy. But I admired the President's willingness to support Hank's strategy when it wasn't popular.

The reaction to Fannie and Freddie quickly made the backlash over Bear look mild. Senator Bunning, who had said the Bear deal's assault on free enterprise made him feel like he lived in France, now said he felt like he lived in China. Senator Obama and the Republican presidential nominee, John McCain, both expressed outrage about public rescues of private firms, although they didn't directly criticize what Hank had done. McCain and his running mate, Sarah Palin, wrote a *Wall Street Journal* op-ed titled "We'll Protect Taxpayers from More Bailouts." Obama's campaign put out word that he didn't want a taxpayer-financed rescue of Lehman, which was also the emphatic consensus of both parties in Congress.

The economy was clearly deteriorating, with unemployment up to 6.1 percent, and no politician wanted to get on the wrong side of rising populist anger. I still had the luxury of laboring in relative obscurity, but as the public faces of the crisis response, Hank and Ben could not avoid the political arena. Hank's aides were pressing him to draw a line in the sand against bailouts. Some of Ben's advisers also wanted him to correct impressions that the Fed's money store was open.

That was a problem, because there was no chance a crisis this huge would be solved without putting more public money at risk. And Lehman was on the edge of the abyss. On Tuesday, September 9, after word leaked that the Koreans had lost interest in investing, Lehman's stock price dropped another 45 percent, while the cost of insuring its debt increased almost 50 percent. We had hoped the Fannie and Freddie rescues would buy Lehman time, but they clearly spooked some investors who hadn't realized the full gravity of the situation, accelerating the flight from Lehman. I interrupted Hank's lunch that day to tell him Lehman looked doomed. He asked if I thought it could last the week. I said probably, but the markets would need to see that we were working on a solution.

Hank said he'd reach out again to Bank of America, even though Ken Lewis had previously sounded dubious about Lehman. I mentioned that Merrill's John Thain and a few other market types had raised the possibility of a Long-Term Capital Management–style consortium of private firms helping out, even though I was doubtful that could work. Lehman was much larger than LTCM, and it would need much more money than LTCM had needed a decade earlier; the firms that would have to step up were also in much worse shape in a much worse economy. But dubious options were better than no options.

The stock market took its biggest hit since the start of the crisis that Tuesday, with financial firms such as Merrill, WaMu, and AIG getting pounded. In July, Bob Willumstad had visited the Fed and danced around the issue of whether we might be able to help if AIG's liquidity ever dried up; I had seen no reason to extend the privilege of Fed liquidity to an insurer. He came back that Tuesday to make his request for Fed help more explicit, this time with much more urgency in his voice. He emphasized that major Wall Street institutions hedged their risks through credit default swaps and other insurance contracts with AIG. At the time, I still thought it was almost inconceivable that the Fed would ever help out a troubled insurance company.

LEHMAN WAS beyond troubled. On Wednesday the 10th, Fuld tried to reassure the markets by preannouncing the firm's third-quarter earnings, but its $3.9 billion loss reassured no one. Markets especially hated Lehman's skeletal plan to spin off its real estate holdings, as if it could just stick its overvalued investments into a SpinCo box and proceed with business as usual. Fuld didn't seem to realize the endgame had begun. We still hoped to find a last-minute buyer, but my team began drawing up a Lehman liquidation game plan, drawing on our foam-on-the-runway work over the summer on how to cushion the damage from a failed investment bank.

Bank of America had agreed to give Lehman another look, but it hadn't even sent a due diligence team. Ken Lewis was in a dispute with the Fed related to his Countrywide purchase, and even after Ben promised to deal with it, Lewis told me he wouldn't even look at Lehman without assurances in writing. That seemed like an obnoxious demand at a time like this. "If you don't believe the word of the chairman of the Fed, we have a larger problem," I told him. Lewis agreed to send his team.

We wanted to have more than one bidder, so we were pleasantly surprised when the British bank Barclays also expressed interest in Lehman. Bob Diamond, an American who ran Barclays's investment banking arm, told me he'd only do the deal on the cheap; like a teenager playing hard to get, he also said he wouldn't make the first call. So I gave Fuld his number. A few minutes later, Fuld called back and told me Diamond had said he wasn't interested. I told him yes, Diamond was interested. Fuld called him again and Diamond again rebuffed him. Fuld angrily called me to complain again. This was starting to feel like an Abbott and Costello skit.

"I don't know what's going on here," Fuld said.

Finally, Diamond told Fuld he'd take a look, but the market was moving faster than he was. On Thursday, Lehman's stock price fell another 42 percent. Repo lenders were running from Lehman, just as they had run from Bear; they would reduce their lending by more than $50 billion that week. Hedge funds were scrambling to withdraw funds from the brokerage accounts they held at Lehman. JPMorgan demanded $5 billion in additional collateral from Lehman, and warned it might request $10 billion more over the weekend. Hayley Boesky, a PhD astrophysicist who was the New York Fed's head of market analysis, sent an email with the subject line: "Panic."

"On a scale of 1 to 10, where 10 is Bear-Stearns-week-panic, I would put sentiment today at a 12," she wrote.

Lehman's repo book was three times as large as Bear's. It had eight thousand subsidiaries around the world, more than one hundred thousand creditors, and more than nine hundred thousand outstanding derivatives contracts. It didn't seem likely to go quietly.

"There is full expectation that LEH goes, WaMu and then ML," Boesky wrote. That was shorthand for Lehman, Washington Mutual, and Merrill Lynch. "All begging, pleading for a large-scale solution which spans beyond just LEH."

ALL WEEK long, Hank had stuck to a consistent message in his private calls to the market: *The government will not subsidize the purchase of Lehman.* He warned Bank of America and Barclays that there was no political will for a Bear Stearns reprise. He did suggest in those calls that an LTCM-style consortium of private firms could help absorb some of Lehman's risk, but he insisted there would be no more taxpayer money for failed institutions. This wasn't really Hank's decision; he couldn't tell the Fed how to use its authority. But Ben had expressed similar aversions in our internal calls, though he did not rule out a role for the Federal Reserve.

As a private negotiating posture, I thought that made some sense. We didn't want Ken Lewis or Bob Diamond to expect taxpayer help to buy Lehman. And it was true that after Bear and Fannie and Freddie, Washington had become a cauldron of Old Testament populism and moral hazard fundamentalism. We didn't want to bolster the impression that government handouts were available upon request.

But whatever the merits of no-public-money as a bargaining position, I didn't think it made sense as actual public policy. The Bear intervention had been a well-designed solution to a serious problem.

I believed that if we could find a buyer to play the JPMorgan role and buy Lehman, and we had to take some risk to close the deal, it would be in the best interest of the country for us to do so, whether we liked it or not. In normal times, we wouldn't worry too much about the fate of an individual firm. But in a colossal crisis, you never want to allow a messy liquidation of a major institution unless you can draw a circle of protection around the rest of the system's core, a firebreak to contain the flames. And the Federal Reserve simply did not have the power to provide that critical protection. If Lehman failed, and the U.S. government publicly proclaimed that we were done with bailouts, rational investors would simply run from other financial institutions. I didn't mind no-bailouts as a negotiating stance, as long as we understood that, ultimately, private money wasn't going to defuse a global panic on its own.

By Thursday night, when Hank forcefully repeated his no-public-money stand during a conference call with Ben and SEC Chairman Chris Cox, I began to worry that he actually meant it. He declared that he didn't want to be known as "Mr. Bailout," that he couldn't support another Bear Stearns solution. I could hear the influence of his political advisers, who had been trying to steer Hank away from supporting any Fed role, urging him not to let me talk him into another Bear. I understood that Hank was under intense pressure; Congress was up in arms about his reversal on Fannie and Freddie, and many Republicans feared the bailout issue could put Senator Obama in the White House. Still, I thought we needed to "preserve optionality," as Bob Rubin used to put it. I didn't want us to commit to inaction and box ourselves in.

On Friday morning, it looked like Hank's team had done just that, converting a private negotiating stance into public policy. Major papers, newswires, and business TV channels had stories detailing the government's unwillingness to use taxpayer funds to rescue Lehman, all citing sources close to Hank. "Paulson Adamant No Money for Lehman," reported Bloomberg News. Hank's political aides had leaked his talking points: that markets had been preparing for a Lehman bankruptcy for months, that the Primary Dealer Credit Facility was now in place to smooth the process, that the Bush administration would not tolerate taxpayer-assisted deals. I told Hank this was a huge mistake, irresponsibly damaging to confidence. This was not the time to tell the markets they were on their own. By committing to do nothing now, we'd end up having to do more and put more taxpayer money at risk later.

This was one of the few times during the crisis when there was any distance between Hank and me. There was even some distance between Ben and me. I sensed their advisers pulling them toward political expedience, trying to distance them from the unpalatable moves we had made and the even less palatable moves I thought we'd have to make soon. The natural human instinct in a financial crisis, and especially the political instinct, is to avoid unpopular interventions, to let the market work its will, to show the world you're punishing the perpetrators. But letting the fire burn out of control is much more economically damaging, and ultimately more politically damaging, than taking the decisive actions necessary to prevent it from spreading beyond the weakest institutions into the core of the system. By pledging not to take on any more risk, I thought we risked fanning the raging flames.

These disagreements did not turn out to be consequential. Hank and Ben would have the courage to change course and do what needed to be done. We would talk constantly over the next few months, basically a never-ending conference call, making sure we stayed on the same page, preventing nervous colleagues from pulling us back toward inertia. But at that critical moment, I worried that all the anti-bailout rhetoric was jeopardizing our ability to find Lehman a buyer. Neither Bank of America nor Barclays seemed interested in an unassisted deal. And the markets were in full retreat from Lehman; by the final bell Friday, it was down to its last $2 billion in cash. If we couldn't find a solution over the weekend, we'd have a corpse on Monday.

We convened the leading financial CEOs at the New York Fed that evening for an emergency meeting. We met in a dark conference room behind wrought-iron gates on the first floor, where we could hear the rumble of the subway trains underground. Faces were drawn and tense. Careers and fortunes were in jeopardy. No one in the room could be sure their firm would survive. None of us had seen anything like this in our lifetimes.

Hank, who had just flown up from Washington, explained that Lehman was on the edge of failure, and that we had to explore ways to prevent that. One option, he said, was a merger with another firm, and there were two potential buyers. But neither of them was willing to take on all of Lehman's risk. Someone would have to finance the rest of the deal before the Asian markets opened Sunday night, and it wouldn't be the government. I echoed that no-public-money stance, though I carefully tried to frame it as a general Washington aversion.

"There is no political will in Washington for a bailout," I said.

Vikram Pandit of Citigroup soon raised a question on everyone's mind: What about AIG and Merrill? I told the group to focus on Lehman first, but Pandit was right to think beyond it. We had three existential crises that weekend, not just one.

Merrill's stock had lost more than a third of its value in a week. If Lehman went the way of Bear, Merrill was widely understood to be the next-weakest investment bank, the next obvious target for a run. Meanwhile, AIG's shares had lost nearly half their value in a week, and the spreads on its credit default swaps had spiked higher than Bear's before our intervention in March. A senior official in my markets group, Patricia Mosser, sent me an email shortly before I went into the Lehman meeting: "AIG is facing serious liquidity issues that threaten its survival."

While I was with the bankers, Hayley Boesky sent another email about panic among hedge funds.

"Now focus is on AIG," she wrote. "I am hearing worse than LEH. Every bank and dealer has exposure to them."

· · ·

THE SCENE at the New York Fed that weekend was a surreal frenzy of activity.

Hank and a few aides set up shop alongside my team in our temporary quarters on the thirteenth floor. It was a generic workspace—we called it our Holiday Inn Express—but it was functional and even advantageous for the crisis, bringing us together in a way our isolated offices on the executive floor couldn't. The rest of the building was swarming with bankers, lawyers, accountants, and analysts from a panoply of Wall Street firms with an array of interests, eyeing one another with suspicion but aware they shared a mutual interest in averting a systemic meltdown. We tried to keep some separation between the various swarms; a team from Lehman was holed up in our medical office. Hank and I stayed at each other's side, shuttling from conference room to conference room, from crisis to crisis, stepping out to take calls that rarely improved our mood. There was a lot going on.

We told the bankers from the night before to divide themselves into three groups: one to analyze Lehman's toxic assets to help facilitate a potential merger, one to investigate an LTCM-style consortium that could take over the firm and gradually wind down its positions, and one to explore ways to prepare for a bankruptcy and limit the attendant damage. Hank warned them all that we'd be watching carefully, that we'd remember who was and wasn't helpful. Bear Stearns had been the only major firm to refuse to join the LTCM consortium back in the 1990s, tarnishing its image on the Street. I reminded the bankers that reputational risk aside, Lehman's demise would threaten all of their firms, potentially crippling the financial system.

Saturday did not produce good news. Ken Lewis informed us there were about $70 billion worth of toxic assets in Lehman's portfolio that Bank of America wouldn't take, up from $40 billion the day before. Basically, BofA wasn't interested. Barclays told us it would have to leave behind $52 billion of Lehman's worst assets in any deal. And the Wall Street team scouring Lehman's books quickly concluded those

My family at home in Bethesda, Maryland, around 1966. My parents, Deborah and Peter; my sister, Sarah; and my identical twin brothers, Jonathan and David. I went to Wood Acres Elementary School, in the same neighborhood where Carole and I later lived after we moved back from Japan, and the same school our children attended. *(Courtesy of the Geithner family)*

Formative years in New Delhi, India, where we lived from 1968 to 1973. I attended the American International School from second through sixth grade. *(Courtesy of the Geithner family)*

With Carole Sonnenfeld at our Dartmouth graduation in June 1983.
(Courtesy of the Geithner family)

One of many summer vacations spent in Orleans, Massachusetts, on
Cape Cod, with Carole and our children, Benjamin and Elise, 1996.
(Courtesy of the Geithner family)

Treasury Secretary Bob Rubin takes a break from the annual World Bank Group–International Monetary Fund meetings, September 1997 in Hong Kong, to swear me in as assistant Treasury secretary for international affairs, as Undersecretary David Lipton looks on. *(Courtesy of the Geithner family)*

With international affairs colleagues Ted Truman (seated, foreground) and Mark Sobel (standing) in late 2000, in the Treasury Department's Andrew Johnson Suite—my office as undersecretary for international affairs and the temporary executive office used by Andrew Johnson in 1865 after he assumed the presidency following the assassination of Abraham Lincoln. *(Courtesy of the Geithner family)*

With Federal Reserve Chairman Ben Bernanke at the Fed's annual economic symposium, Jackson Hole, Wyoming, August 22, 2008. *(Andrew Harrer/Bloomberg via Getty Images)*

Meeting with Secretary Hank Paulson in his office at Treasury, after I had been named President-elect Obama's nominee for secretary, during the transition between the Bush and Obama administrations, November 25, 2008. *(Courtesy of the U.S. Department of the Treasury)*

The President's marathon meeting on the financial strategy on Sunday, March 15, 2009, in the Roosevelt Room of the White House. With advisers, from left: Gene Sperling, Larry Summers, me, Christy Romer, Lee Sachs, Jeremy Stein, Sam Hanson, Mary Goodman, Stephanie Cutter, and David Axelrod. *(White House/Pete Souza)*

Overleaf: Testifying before Congress amid the public outrage about the AIG bonuses, with Federal Reserve Chairman Ben Bernanke and Federal Reserve Bank of New York President and Chief Executive Officer Bill Dudley, March 24, 2009. *(Associated Press)*

Briefing the President aboard Air Force One en route to London for the first G-20 Leaders Summit of his administration, with National Security Advisor Tom Donilon, March 31, 2009. *(White House/Pete Souza)*

troubled assets were worth only about half what Lehman claimed. That would leave a substantial capital hole for a private consortium to fill in an industry-assisted deal, with about ten times the risk the Fed took in the Bear case with Maiden Lane.

Unfortunately, but not surprisingly, the team studying the LTCM option—putting some capital into Lehman before winding it down—decided it made no sense. Lehman's capital hole was just too big, and even if the consortium managed to finance the deal, it would have to guarantee Lehman's trading book in the heat of a run. Just as predictably, the team investigating what I dubbed "the lights-out scenario" concluded a Lehman bankruptcy would be devastating to the system.

That left an assisted deal for Barclays as the only option to avoid catastrophe. Grudging support was building for a consortium to finance Lehman's bad assets through a private vehicle reminiscent of Maiden Lane—the bankers called it "ShitCo"—so that Barclays could buy the rest of the firm and guarantee Lehman's trading book. Hank and I met with Dimon and then Blankfein, and they both said they thought the consortium would come through to help a competitor. But they also raised some uncomfortable questions: Did it really make sense to push major institutions to take on billions of dollars in additional risk, when capital and liquidity were scarce and no one thought resolving Lehman would be enough to calm the larger storm? What if we had to reassemble the consortium the following week to avert another failure? What if markets punished strong firms under the assumption that they were now responsible for rescuing their weaker competitors?

Dimon and Blankfein weren't being altruistic, but I thought they raised valid concerns. This would all become moot soon, but if the private consortium had balked at financing the entire deal with Barclays, I would have supported having the Fed assume some of the risk. I believe Ben and Hank felt the same way. Preventing a Lehman default had to be our top priority, because we didn't have the ability to limit the fallout from a messy failure.

"You need to know that if we can't work out a solution, we don't have the capacity to insulate you or the system from the consequences," I told the group.

Meanwhile, AIG was looking worse and worse. It had a trillion-dollar balance sheet, 115,000 employees, and a slew of solid insurance businesses. But a hedge fund–like subsidiary called AIG Financial Products had put its franchise at risk, selling insurance against the risk of a housing slump. It had exploited the strength of AIG's traditional businesses and AAA credit ratings to make gigantic commitments it couldn't keep. Now it was besieged by margin calls on its contracts insuring CDOs and other troubled mortgage securities, forcing it to scramble for cash just as it was being shut out of the credit markets. And the rating agencies, belatedly as usual, were threatening to dock AIG's credit rating, which would force it to post billions of dollars of additional collateral.

"They face the possibility of a multi-grade downgrade from Moody's on Monday, which would probably be the death knell," Don Kohn wrote.

AIG's main regulator, the Office of Thrift Supervision, had been oblivious to its troubles. Some of my New York Fed colleagues had met with OTS staff to discuss AIG that summer after one of Willumstad's hinting-at-danger visits to my office, and they had come away alarmed. But I went into that weekend with very little knowledge about the company, because, again, the Fed had no authority or responsibility to supervise insurance companies. Now Willumstad wanted the Fed to provide an open-ended loan, but he didn't seem to have a plan to strengthen AIG. As Don said, he wanted "a bridge to nowhere." It still seemed implausible to me that we would rescue the firm. But I assigned a New York Fed team to spend the weekend analyzing the financial world's exposure to AIG and the damage a default might cause to a fragile system.

"At the end we could blink if they are too connected to fail, but that will open up an unknown can of worms," Don wrote. "We should be sure that if we think about this it is a short-term bridge to a permanent solution."

On Saturday morning, Willumstad said AIG might need as much as $30 billion. But he clearly had no idea how bad things were. "We think they are days from failure. They think it is a temporary problem," Ben said in an email. "This disconnect is dangerous." By the end of the night, after scouring the firm's books, AIG's bankers concluded the firm actually needed something like $60 billion.

Nevertheless, I went home Saturday night feeling relatively optimistic about our two other existential crises. Hank and I had urged Merrill's John Thain to find a buyer as soon as possible, and he was now in talks with Bank of America about a deal. That helped explain BofA's lack of interest in Lehman—Ken Lewis apparently preferred Merrill's army of retail stockbrokers—but it also offered the tantalizing possibility of a rapid private-sector resolution of the Merrill dilemma. And Barclays looked like it was ready to move on Lehman. There were still some unanswered questions—and last-minute Fed assistance still seemed possible to me—but I thought we had a decent chance to avoid the trauma of a default.

THOSE HOPES were dashed quickly.

Early Sunday morning, I took a call from Callum McCarthy, a former Barclays banker who was the United Kingdom's top financial regulator. He told me his agency was unsure whether Barclays had enough capital to take on the risk of buying Lehman, or enough capacity to guarantee Lehman's book. He also told me Barclays wouldn't even be legally permitted to stand behind Lehman's trades before a shareholder vote that could take months to arrange.

I was absolutely stunned. We were on the brink of Armageddon. We had no alternative to a merger, no other plausible buyer apart from Barclays, and no idea Barclays's regulators had any problem with the deal. I couldn't believe that Barclays had gone this far without a green light from its supervisor, but here we were.

"Are you saying you won't approve this?" I asked.

McCarthy wouldn't say that, but he raised so many logistical and regulatory barriers that he might as well have said that. He suggested that the British banking sector had enough problems without taking on Lehman's. And he wouldn't answer my questions about how we could get his government to yes. I tried to emphasize that global stability depended on the deal, that delay was tantamount to a veto.

"Good luck," McCarthy replied.

I walked into Hank's temporary office. "We're fucked," I said.

We didn't believe we had the legal authority to guarantee Lehman's trading liabilities, even using our "unusual and exigent" powers under 13(3). And we didn't believe we could legally lend them the scale of the resources they would need to continue to operate, because we didn't believe they had anything close to the ability to repay us. Hank called Alistair Darling, the U.K. finance minister, to see if he could waive the requirement for a shareholder vote so that Barclays could guarantee Lehman's book immediately. Darling wouldn't do it.

"He said he didn't want to import our cancer," Hank told me.

He sounded shocked and deflated. When we went downstairs to tell the bankers that the consortium would not be necessary—and that they should prepare for a harrowing Monday—Hank announced in his inimitably blunt style that the British had screwed us. Chris Cox, a former congressman who still carried himself like a politician, then strangely thanked the bankers for their patriotic service to the nation. "Those were generous words—more generous than the people in this room deserve," I grumbled. I was in too dark a mood to congratulate bankers for trying to protect themselves from a life-threatening storm they had helped cause.

As frustrated as we were, the British regulators had legitimate concerns. Their banking system was five times larger than ours as a percentage of their economy; in some ways, it was also more vulnerable. They didn't think Barclays was strong enough to take on the vast bulk of Lehman's risk during a time when the world was deteriorating rapidly. It's possible that their concern was increased by their sense that the Fed wasn't willing to take part in the deal, since we hadn't committed to put skin in the game as we had with Bear. In the end, I'm confident the Fed would have helped finance a deal with a willing buyer, and I think Hank would have supported that, no matter what his people had told the press. But Fed assistance would not have eliminated the risk to Barclays, much less the British requirement for a shareholder vote, and I don't see how it would have changed the British position.

In any case, we were out of options. We had shown with Bear that we could facilitate the rescue of an investment bank by another financial institution, but without a willing buyer, we didn't think we could legally do the rescue ourselves. We had shown that we could push the boundaries of our authority to take on some modest risk, but the Fed's emergency authorities limited how much risk we could take; we were the central bank of the United States, and we weren't going to defy our own governing law to lend into a run. We could make loans to solvent institutions against solid collateral. We had some discretion about what we deemed solid, but we couldn't inject capital to repair Lehman's hole, and we couldn't guarantee Lehman's obligations.

Hank and I got on a speakerphone to brief Ben and Don that Barclays was out and Lehman was going to fail. "It's going to be a calamity," I said. They asked if I had an alternative plan, but I didn't. We were out of ideas for the moment.

At that point, all we could do was to try to limit the damage from Lehman's collapse. We decided to amplify the power of our liquidity programs, substantially expanding the scope of our lending facilities for investment banks and commercial banks to prepare for a further erosion of market funding. We agreed to accept any collateral that could be used in tri-party repo for loans through the PDCF. We would also exchange Treasuries for securities rated as low as BBB-minus through the Term Securities Lending Facility instead of insisting on AAA-rated paper. And we decided to continue to lend tens of billions of dollars to Lehman's broker-dealer arm, secured by its higher-quality assets, until it could wind down its trades. We hoped this could soften the blow to the system.

The only good news that Sunday evening—and it was very good news, though we weren't in a celebratory mood—was that Bank of America agreed to buy Merrill Lynch for $29 a share, a $50 billion transaction in the nick of time, removing at least for the moment another gigantic threat to stability.

AIG, by contrast, was still in dire straits. And my team studying the potential effects of its failure was deeply concerned about contagion. AIG insured the lives, health, property, vehicles, and retirement accounts of millions of American households, and it insured 180,000 businesses that employed two-thirds of the U.S. workforce. It also had $2.7 trillion of derivatives contracts, and its credit default swaps provided much of the financial system with protection against disaster. If it collapsed, the world's largest financial institutions would suddenly find themselves without the benefit of that catastrophic risk insurance just when they needed it most. A default could also create uncertainty around AIG's retail insurance businesses, and by extension, damage global confidence in the insurance industry.

Still, Willumstad's latest proposal—he wanted the Fed to lend AIG $40 billion to get the rating agencies off its back—seemed like another bridge to nowhere. Even though Lehman's imminent failure would make the system more fragile, and more vulnerable to the sudden collapse of another systemic firm, I still wasn't convinced we had a viable way to save AIG.

We had one additional problem that night: Lehman's board was refusing to admit it was lights out. During the crisis, we always tried to avoid panic by making big announcements on Sunday nights before Asian markets opened, so investors would have as much time as possible to digest the information. But Asia had already opened and Lehman had yet to announce its bankruptcy filing. The 158-year-old firm was still hoping for a last-minute reprieve.

Hank and I pressured Cox to stop hesitating and get Lehman to file. This would be the largest bankruptcy in U.S. history by far—Lehman was six times the size of WorldCom—and Cox was reluctant to tell its executives what to do. He didn't want their blood on his hands. But we needed to announce our expanded liquidity programs, without giving the impression they could be a lifeline for Lehman. Hank, who had lost patience with the SEC, yelled at Cox to pick up the phone and get Lehman to move.

"You guys are like the gang that couldn't shoot straight!" he said.

Cox eventually called Lehman's board, with my counsel Tom Baxter on the phone, and together they made it clear there was no other option. Lehman finally filed at 1:45 a.m.

I felt defeated. We had tried to do what we could with the powers we had, improvising strategies on the fly, but the fire was burning out of control. We had stretched the limits of the Fed's authority in all kinds of ways, but those limits were real. The Fed couldn't carry the burden of averting disaster on its own. We needed the full resources of the U.S. government to be deployed. The political system would have to help rescue the financial system. As Hank and I walked down a corridor back to my office, I said to him: "Now you've got to go to Congress."

Ben and I had been telling Hank for months that ultimately, there would have to be a comprehensive legislative solution to the crisis, authorizing the government to take a lot more risk. Hank had already used the authority Congress had given him that summer to commit $200 billion to shore up Fannie and Freddie, but it would take a lot more money and authority to shore up the rest of the system. Hank now agreed it was time to seek emergency legislation. The backlash would be brutal, but we couldn't keep doing late-night repairs with duct tape and comfort letters. We had to avoid another Lehman-style collapse. One would be awful enough.

I got a few hours of sleep that night in a bedroom in the New York Fed's Italianate "turret," a little alcove behind an elevator on the twelfth floor. Tom Baxter told me that during the 1990s, the convicted former CEO of the Bank of Credit and Commerce International had been held prisoner there during legal proceedings related to the BCCI scandal. I would sleep in that dark room for the next two weeks, when I slept at all.

• • •

MY MONDAY began with a call from the ECB's Jean-Claude Trichet, who had been so complimentary about our Bear intervention. Now he wanted to know, in a French-accented blend of astonishment and derision, whether we had lost our minds. How could we let Lehman go? Why would we want to create a global panic?

We hadn't done it on purpose. We had run up against the limits of our authority and the fears of the British regulators. But after all the no-bailouts rhetoric, the world naturally assumed we had consciously decided to teach Wall Street a lesson.

Much of the media reaction actually suggested Lehman's failure was a good thing, a fearless act of discipline on our part, a welcome corrective to a festival of moral hazard. On the left, the *New York Times* editorial page called it "oddly reassuring," while on the right, the *Wall Street Journal* declared "the government had to draw a line somewhere." I took no comfort from that nonsense. We hadn't chosen to draw a line. We had been powerless, not fearless. We had tried but failed to prevent a catastrophic default. That's still poorly understood, in part because Hank and Ben, who had the thankless job of explaining our actions, decided not to admit defeat in public. They thought at the time that confessing we didn't have the firepower to save Lehman would intensify the panic, which may have been right.

The panic was intense anyway. The financial markets, contrary to many confident predictions, did not behave as if they were prepared for Lehman's collapse. Stocks fell nearly 5 percent Monday, with financial stocks such as WaMu (down 27 percent) and Citi (down 15 percent) falling hardest. Hedge funds withdrew $10 billion from accounts at Morgan Stanley, and the cost of insuring against default by Goldman

Sachs nearly doubled, as markets began to lose confidence in the investment bank model no matter how strong the individual institution. The commercial paper market seized up; even General Electric, one of the highest rated firms in the world, struggled to borrow to roll over its massive financial subsidiary's short-term funding. And the yields on one-month Treasuries plunged from 1.37 percent to a mere 0.36 percent, a chilling flight to safety.

The most extreme flight was from AIG, whose shares dropped another 60 percent to less than $5 after drastic downgrades by the rating agencies, a harsh landing for a stock that traded above $150 at its peak. The state of New York gave the firm permission to use $20 billion from its regulated insurance subsidiaries to meet its margin calls at AIG Financial Products, but the temporary relief only highlighted its desperation. The company was bleeding to death.

The more our Fed team studied AIG and the insolvency regime for insurers, the less confidence they had in the potential for an orderly resolution. And the deeper they got into the firm, the more they feared its collapse would critically damage a system that was already on the brink. Virtually every major financial institution in the world had some exposure to AIG. Some of those positions were hedged, but it wasn't clear whether the hedges would be of much value in a collapsing financial system. And even if the direct exposures to an AIG default didn't seem crippling, the danger lurked in the market reaction to AIG's failure, which would increase the expected probability of other failures. No one would know who was safe, so everyone would tend to assume the worst about their counterparties, a recipe for escalating fire sales and liquidity shortages. A series of memos from my staff warned of multiple spillover effects. For example, European banks that had lowered their capital requirements by buying protection against credit risks from AIG would lose that protection, so they would suddenly face $18 billion in increased capital requirements at the worst imaginable time to raise capital.

There was little hope of finding a private-sector solution for AIG, but I thought we had to make a good-faith effort to explore one. After consulting with Willumstad, I asked JPMorgan and Goldman Sachs to send their top bankers to the New York Fed that morning, and see if they could arrange a credit line for AIG. "Do not assume you can use the Fed balance sheet," I said. The group soon concluded that AIG needed at least $75 billion just to stay alive. With capital markets freezing up after the Lehman default, it seemed implausible that banks would be able to find that kind of cash. They were hoarding liquidity. They didn't have billions of dollars lying around to risk on a massive insurer that was bleeding liquidity. They had to worry about protecting themselves.

That left the Fed as the only realistic option. Lending to an insurer still felt like a serious Rubicon to cross, but we had crossed plenty of Rubicons. As Ben pointed out, the troublesome parts of AIG behaved more like an investment bank than an insurer, and we were already lending to investment banks. Ben and Hank both recognized before I did that we had to do something about AIG.

It was hard to feel light while the world burned, but the acerbic Barney Frank, who shared my aversion to moral hazard fundamentalism, made me smile on a call that Monday. If nothing else, he mused, the terror of the free fall could dampen enthusiasm for government inaction, and shock the political world into taking the crisis seriously.

"Maybe this will shut up the crazies," he said.

You know things are dark when you have to convene a 3 a.m. conference call. I began the call with top Treasury and Fed officials by reviewing AIG's systemic risks. The U.S. financial system seemed even more exposed to AIG than it had been to Lehman. Europe and Asia were also more exposed to AIG. And not only was AIG larger than Lehman, with a more complex derivatives book, its decline had been much swifter, which would be even scarier to markets.

"If they default, you'll see default probabilities explode on all financial firms," I said. In other words, mass panic on a global scale.

A few days earlier, I thought there was no way we should help an insurance company. By early Tuesday, September 16, I had changed my mind. Letting AIG fail seemed like a formula for a second Great Depression. It was essential that we do everything in our power to try to avoid that.

That morning, JPMorgan and Goldman told me they definitely couldn't arrange a private loan to AIG. Now we had to decide whether we had the legal authority to act. By law, the Fed can only lend against reasonably solid collateral, but I thought AIG could clear that hurdle, even though Lehman had not.

Investment banks rely almost entirely on trust and confidence. They're nothing without their reputation for stability. That's why old bank buildings are usually made of stone, with massive pillars in front of them, and that's why Bear and Merrill—as well as Lehman— needed buyers once their own reputations for stability were shot. But AIG was different. It had more than a brand name. It had seventy-four million policyholders in 130 countries who paid it premiums. Unlike the investment banks, whose franchise value consisted mostly of the willingness of other firms to trade with them, AIG had a vast global empire of income-generating insurance businesses, which over time could offset the losses from its quasi hedge fund. I called Warren Buffett later that morning to see what he thought about the earnings power of AIG's traditional insurance subsidiaries. He was pretty positive about their underlying value, which made me more confident that we could meet the legal test of being secured to our satisfaction. Those insurance businesses would have a good chance of retaining their value if their parent company didn't go down.

I spoke to Ben Bernanke, Hank Paulson, Don Kohn, and Kevin Warsh early Tuesday morning before a regularly scheduled FOMC meeting, which my colleague Chris Cumming attended in my place so that I could deal with the crisis. I told them it now looked like AIG would need a loan of $85 billion, an almost incomprehensible amount at the time. "It has to be big if you want it to be decisive," I said.

I acknowledged that any rescue would create some moral hazard, not to mention a why-AIG-but-not-Lehman? public relations challenge. "I don't have the burden of explaining to the public the zig and the zag," I said. That unpleasant privilege, I pointed out, would fall again to Ben and Hank.

We would be exposing the Fed to the risk of an imploding insurance company, and there was a real possibility that our loan would simply buy the world time to prepare for a horrific default. Kevin was uncomfortable, understandably so. We all were. But I argued that rescuing AIG was our least-worst option. It would look like a lurch, but within the limits of our authority, it was our only hope of averting unimaginable carnage.

"We've got no viable alternatives," I said. "We're in the devastating position of having no power to fully protect the system from the consequences of default."

While we were considering whether to act, we learned that AIG was preparing to file for bankruptcy. I immediately called Willumstad. "Don't do that yet," I said. When he asked why, I told him the Fed was considering some help. That was the end of Washington's no-bailouts stance.

Ben decided we couldn't risk another sudden collapse of a systemic institution at a moment of such intense turbulence. And Hank agreed to write another comfort letter pledging Treasury's support for the Fed's efforts to save AIG.

We were in the grips of a financial hysteria much worse than I had seen in Mexico, Indonesia, or Korea. British regulators had frozen some of Lehman's client accounts, so overseas hedge funds were scrambling to retrieve their funds from Goldman Sachs and Morgan Stanley to avoid similar fates, even though both firms had reported decent earnings that day. Meanwhile, U.S. depositors were withdrawing about $2 billion a day from WaMu, twice as much as they had withdrawn after the run on IndyMac. The "TED spread," a measuring stick for fear in the banking system, was about to surpass the record set after the 1987 stock market crash.

Tuesday's most chilling development outside AIG was a money market fund "breaking the buck," which meant it could no longer promise investors 100 cents on the dollar. Money market funds were widely viewed as virtually indistinguishable from insured bank deposits, as similarly safe vehicles for storing cash with slightly better interest rates. But many money market funds had invested in commercial paper and other instruments that turned out to be riskier than they had thought. One fund, the Reserve Primary Fund, had even added to its stash of Lehman paper over the summer while everyone else was unloading it, which sparked a run on the fund after Lehman fell. The Lehman paper made up only about 1 percent of the $62 billion fund, but since the fund had no capital buffers to absorb losses, that was enough to create the stench of death; by that evening, the flood of requests for redemptions amounted to nearly two-thirds of the fund.

The Reserve Fund asked the New York Fed for help to avoid breaking the buck, but my team said no. We didn't think we could stop the run, and agreeing to their request would have amounted to an implied backstop for the entire $3.5 trillion money market industry. The Fed didn't have the legal authority to guarantee money market funds and protect their investors from losses.

"Ridiculous request," Don Kohn agreed in an email.

Still, the break-the-buck incident had cast suspicion on all prime money market funds. Institutional investors would withdraw more than $300 billion over the next week. The Reserve Fund debacle discouraged risk taking by other money funds, which meant even less buying of commercial paper and less lending through repo, which meant an even more intense liquidity crisis for banks and other institutions. Basically, short-term financing—whether secured by collateral or not—was vanishing. No collateral, no matter how safe historically, was viewed as truly liquid, because there was simply no liquidity in the system to buy it. This would have been the textbook definition of a panic, except no textbook had recorded anything like it.

It is a testament to the insanity of that time that the Reserve Fund news barely registered with me. Everything was falling apart around us, and I was consumed with designing a proposal for AIG. At 4 p.m., we sent its board the terms for its survival, very similar to the tough terms the private bankers had come up with when they were trying to raise private financing. The New York Fed, with the approval of the Fed board in Washington, would provide an $85 billion credit line to AIG at a penalty interest rate of more than 11 percent; in return, AIG would provide 79.9 percent of the firm, so taxpayers would get most of the benefits if it survived. Hank and I also informed Willumstad that he'd be out as CEO; Hank had persuaded former Allstate chief Ed Liddy to take the job. The government wouldn't have control of AIG, but we thought we had to install new leadership. Hank and I made it clear we needed an answer soon.

Willumstad quickly called back with AIG's lawyers, including the inevitable Rodge Cohen, to ask whether we would soften some of the terms.

"These are the only terms you're going to get," I said.

The board concluded—correctly, I thought—that AIG's share-holders would be even worse off in a bankruptcy, so they called back to accept an hour later.

AIG had told us earlier in the day that it would need $4 billion to make it to morning. Once again, they had dramatically underes-timated their problems. They now asked to draw down $14 billion. We had to keep the government's payment system open late to wire them the cash. And they had to rush collateral in the form of stock certificates and other securities over to the New York Fed in briefcases and grocery carts. They would need $23 billion more over the next three days.

Before that week, it would have been hard to fathom the Fed lend-ing into a run and being provided a four-fifths stake in a trillion-dollar insurance company. We had torn down yet another wall between the commercial banking sector and the rest of the financial system. We were appalled by what had happened at AIG, but we were determined to do whatever we could to stabilize the system, protect the broader economy, and avoid the kind of mass suffering Americans experienced during the Great Depression.

"Central banks exist to take out the extreme tail, the catastrophic risk," I said that night in a briefing for journalists. "In times of crisis, you will do things you thought you'd never do."

I knew we'd be accused of rewarding incompetence, of throwing public money down a rat hole. But I believed we had gotten taxpayers a reasonable deal, not just in the financial terms of the loan, but by avoiding even more severe damage to the economy. I'd soon get some early validation of that when Hank Greenberg, AIG's hard-driving former chief executive and a major shareholder in the firm, visited me to complain that the Fed had been given too much equity in AIG, too much of the upside. I was a bit shocked by the audacity; basically, he wanted us to give back a big chunk of the company. I told him we hadn't done the deal to make money, and we'd be happy to sell him back some of the equity if he'd be willing to take some of the risk. But what interested me was Greenberg's confidence that we'd get a positive return from AIG, rather than the tens of billions in losses that everyone else seemed to expect. He'd be right about that, but only because of the force of the government's actions to stabilize the company and the broader financial system over the next few years. He and other AIG shareholders would end up suing the federal government, claiming that we had been unjustly harsh to the firm we rescued.

The general reaction to the AIG loan was stunned outrage of a very different kind, and we made no progress in persuading Americans that the rescue had been a prudent and necessary act to protect Main Street from a failing financial system. I never watched TV news, unless you count *The Daily Show*, and I tried not to read press accounts of our actions. But I knew we were losing the battle for public support.

In a futile gesture against the overwhelming consensus, I did call a *New York Times* editor to complain about a damaging story portraying the AIG rescue as a backdoor bailout for Hank's former colleagues at Goldman Sachs. I had asked Lloyd Blankfein about Goldman's direct exposure to AIG; when he assured me Goldman's exposures were relatively small and fully hedged, I made him send me the documentation. Still, the *Times* wouldn't correct the record, and my call probably strengthened its suspicions. The same reporter later did a story portraying the entire crisis response team as servants of Goldman, accompanied by a vampire squid–like diagram with me in the middle. In the media, in the public, even in the financial community, we faced withering skepticism about our motives as well as our competence. After all, we had lent a mismanaged insurance company three years' worth of federal spending on basic scientific research.

Even Jamie Dimon told me he was surprised we had taken so much financial and political risk over AIG.

"I don't know if I would've done that if I were you," he said.

By Thursday morning, September 18, panic was engulfing the system.

Yields on short-term Treasury bills had dipped into negative territory, which meant investors were so afraid to invest they were paying the government to hold their savings. Banks such as Wachovia and Bank of New York were scrambling to prop up money market funds they had sponsored in order to prevent them from breaking the buck. The over-the-counter derivatives market was paralyzed. And the investment banks were under siege. Morgan Stanley's clients pulled an astonishing $32 billion out of the firm on Wednesday, more than the annual economic output of Panama or Jordan; its credit default swaps had tripled since Lehman fell. Even Goldman Sachs, the strongest of the investment banks, watched helplessly as half its $120 billion

in liquidity evaporated in a week. While the backdoor-bailout conspiracy theorists railed about Goldman making a killing, in the real
world, Goldman was getting killed.

Blankfein called me that morning before the markets opened.
I thought of him as one of the calmer, stronger, smarter forces on
Wall Street. He sounded shaken, though perhaps he was just trying
to make sure I was sufficiently scared. I don't remember what we discussed about Goldman's plight, but I do remember that a few seconds
after I hung up, I called him back.

"Lloyd, you cannot talk to anyone outside your firm, or anyone
inside your firm, until you get that fear out of your voice," I said.
"You can replace it with anger or you can cover it up. But you can't let
people hear you like that."

At that moment, fear was a sign you were awake and intelligent.
Anyone who wasn't scared had no idea how close we were to the abyss.

I was scared, too. It looked like the system was going to collapse,
taking down the strong firms along with the weak. We had just suffered a financial shock worse than the one that had led to the Great
Depression. Market volatility was more than a third higher than
it had been after the crash of 1929; bond spreads would rise more
than twice as high; the percentage of household wealth lost would
be more than five times worse than in 1929. When I spoke to Blankfein, I thought the investment banks were doomed, and I was worried
about several major commercial banks. As the unprecedented runs
on money market funds and commercial paper accelerated, a wave of
defaults by major nonfinancial corporations seemed likely as well. My
colleagues and I thought we were looking at another global depression
that would hurt billions of people.

The world was looking to us, and I knew the Fed alone didn't
have the authority to prevent disaster. It was a horrible feeling. I tried
not to be paralyzed by it or sit around whining about our limited
options. I tried to be disciplined about focusing on the problems in
front of us, thinking about ways we could help make things better,

trying to anticipate where the fire would spread next. Keeping busy helped. I spent countless hours on the phone, not only with Ben and Hank and my other colleagues in government, but with just about everyone who mattered in global finance, trying to get a feel for the texture of the markets, the new seams of panic. I talked with Carole, who listened patiently, asked good questions, and gave her thoughtful therapist take on the public reaction to our decisions. We often discussed medical analogies for the crisis—contagion, triage, intensive care, clogged arteries, and cardiac arrest.

I tried to work out every morning and used that time to think. During the weeks I slept in the turret, I would run along the Hudson, weaving through the early commuters as they trudged to work in the towers of Wall Street, trying not to dwell too much on our responsibility for their fate and the nation's fate. I ran without my security detail, although they later told me they tried to trail me in a car. I needed to keep moving, which was also my basic philosophy about the crisis. Inertia was the enemy. At my desk, I would scribble boxes and arrows and circles on sheets of Xerox paper, visual representations of our options, as if I were drawing up plays.

I didn't have a way to explain the terror of those days until later, when I saw *The Hurt Locker,* the Oscar-winning film about a bomb disposal unit in Iraq. What we went through on interminable conference calls in fancy office buildings obviously did not compare to the horrors of war, but ten minutes into the movie I knew I had finally found something that captured what the crisis felt like: the overwhelming burden of responsibility combined with the paralyzing risk of catastrophic failure; the frustration about the stuff out of your control; the uncertainty about what would help; the knowledge that even good decisions might turn out badly; the pain and guilt of neglecting your family; the loneliness and the numbness. I liked the protagonist's deadpan response when he was asked the best way to defuse a bomb: *The way you don't die.* In other words, the way that works.

Throughout the crisis, I felt better, or at least less terrible, whenever we were doing stuff, fighting back, trying new things. The Lehman aftermath was absolutely horrifying, transmitting panic through global markets like never before, but as Barney Frank's comment suggested, there was something liberating about it, too. It was an unwelcome vindication of the case for action. As much as the public hated bailouts, we were pretty sure people would hate the consequences of uncontrolled default even more. And I had learned during the nineties that the kind of actions that solve financial crises are never popular, that it wasn't worth trying too hard to make them popular.

The moral hazard fundamentalists did not stop pressing their case after Lehman. But now that the fire was burning out of control, they were less of a constraint. We could focus more on what to do, how to push the envelope of our existing authority, and how to get the additional authority we needed.

* * *

THE NIGHT Lehman fell, Hank had promised to seek legislation from Congress. But he didn't go to the Hill right away, and my staff feared the Bush administration was backsliding. During one meandering conference call, my trusted adviser Meg McConnell—a sharp and passionate economist whose criticisms could be withering, even on the occasions they weren't directed at me—suddenly pressed mute on my speakerphone. She seethed that Treasury needed broader rescue authority *yesterday*. The world was burning. What more was there to discuss?

"Just tell the secretary to tell the White House that if they don't get it quickly, there will be shantytowns and soup lines all across the country!" she yelled at me.

Hank kept his word, though. On Thursday afternoon, word leaked that Treasury planned to seek authority to buy some of the toxic assets weighing down the system, and the stock market promptly shot up 4 percent. That evening, Hank and Ben went to the Hill to urge congressional leaders to authorize hundreds of billions of dollars in emergency spending to save the economy. Ben warned that if they didn't act quickly, there wouldn't be an economy left to save. On Friday morning, Hank publicly announced that he would seek legislation empowering Treasury to buy toxic assets in order to unfreeze the credit markets—and that it wouldn't be cheap.

We didn't have time to wait for a bill to emerge and wind its way into law. The markets, to use Ben's medical analogy, were in anaphylactic shock. We had two death spirals we needed to stop immediately: the run on money market funds, which was killing the market for the commercial paper that provided America's top corporations with short-term operating loans, and the run on investment banks, which was threatening to ignite two more Lehman-style explosions.

The Fed had already put in place an alphabet soup of innovative credit and liquidity programs—the TAF, TSLF, and PDCF, largely designed by my staff in New York, working with a small group from Washington. In the days after Lehman, they created another one, the AMLF, an unwieldy acronym for the even more unwieldy Asset-Backed Commercial Paper Money Market Mutual Fund Liquidity Facility. The AMLF was an effort to revive the market for high-quality asset-backed commercial paper, which had shut down after Lehman fell, while easing pressures on money funds, which began dumping the paper after the Reserve Fund broke the buck. It used a slightly circuitous approach to arrest this cycle, lending to banks so they could buy asset-backed commercial paper from money market funds—with the Fed taking the risk. We announced it that Friday morning. Within two weeks, it was financing $152 billion worth of commercial paper, helping financial institutions and some of America's largest companies make payroll and make investments.

That same morning, Hank announced that Treasury would use the Exchange Stabilization Fund, the same fund we'd tapped to rescue Mexico in 1995, to guarantee shares in money market funds, a decisive and effective move. The announcement, combined with our moves to provide liquidity to the broader markets, helped prevent other funds from breaking the buck. It was an illustration of the power of government guarantees. When you can credibly commit to protect people from a catastrophic outcome, they don't have to act in anticipation of it. When you eliminate the incentive to run, you don't have to finance a run.

In fact, Hank's guarantees were so powerful that FDIC chair Sheila Bair called him to say they could trigger a run on the banking system and threaten her agency's insurance fund, by encouraging bank depositors with more than $100,000 in their accounts to shift their uninsured cash into money market funds. She was right—and to her credit, she had an alternative plan. She suggested Treasury should guarantee only investments that were in money funds before September 19, removing the incentive to shift cash out of FDIC-insured banks. Hank agreed.

In yet another announcement that busy Friday, the SEC temporarily banned the short selling of 799 financial stocks, a heavy-handed effort to stop the stampede of speculation and rumor mongering. We all had reservations about this. It seemed to signal a debilitating lack of confidence in those 799 firms. I thought there was some risk that preventing investors from hedging their exposures would actually accelerate the flight to safety through other mechanisms. It felt like trying to ban risk aversion, or the expression of negative opinions about firms that often deserved them. But Hank, who normally thought banning shorts was like burning books, believed short sellers were creating more stress than the system could handle. Cox wanted broad political cover before he would take action, so Hank asked Ben and me to encourage Cox to act. I figured it was worth a shot. I basically thought we should throw everything we had at the panic, and I really wanted us to stick together. So I told Cox I thought he should go ahead.

The ban's most immediate beneficiary appeared to be Morgan Stanley; CEO John Mack was publicly accusing the shorts of sabotaging his firm. Its liquidity pool had shrunk from $130 billion to $55 billion in a week; it was borrowing nearly $70 billion from the

Fed to make up the difference. Its stock price fell 60 percent before word of the short-selling ban leaked. One New York Fed bank examiner reported in an email that a Citi executive had told her: "Morgan is the deer in the headlights. . . . It's looking like Lehman did a few weeks ago." And everyone on Wall Street knew that if Morgan went the way of Lehman, Goldman would be next.

That would be more stress than the system could handle.

WE WERE under no illusions that the short-selling ban or even the prospect of broad congressional relief would magically stop the run on the investment banks. Morgan and Goldman needed immediate solutions. As Blankfein put it later, this would be their "existential weekend."

We had no good options, but we thought these last stand-alone investment banks might have a better chance at survival if we pushed them into the arms of commercial banks with stronger funding bases. Fed Governor Kevin Warsh, a Morgan Stanley alumnus, helped steer his former firm into merger talks with Wachovia. Wachovia, however, was as vulnerable as Morgan; during the bubble, it had acquired Golden West, a subprime mortgage lender that had even more toxic "pick-a-pay" option ARMs on its balance sheet than Countrywide or IndyMac. I was mindful of the old bank supervisor's cautionary tale about the drunk who tries to help another drunk out of a ditch, but ends up falling into the ditch himself.

At that point, however, we thought we had to explore any combination that could avert another Lehman scenario. I got Hank Paulson, Ben Bernanke, and Chris Cox on the phone together to put pressure on Lloyd Blankfein and John Mack to seek partners. I got Blankfein to call Vikram Pandit about merging Goldman with Citi, but they both hated the idea. I urged John Mack to call Jamie Dimon to push them to reunite Morgan Stanley with JPMorgan Chase, remnants of the original House of Morgan. Neither side liked that idea, either. With some encouragement from Rodge Cohen, who represented Goldman and Wachovia, we tried to broker a marriage of those two firms, but Goldman was daunted by what it found in Wachovia's books. We even considered Fed assistance, but the financials looked uncertain, and the optics were awful. Hank had just received a conflict-of-interest waiver to work on Goldman issues a few days earlier, while Wachovia CEO Bob Steel, another Goldman alum, had been one of Hank's deputies at Treasury until a few months earlier.

Nothing was working. John Mack talked to Pandit, but a Morgan Stanley merger with Citi would have raised similar drunks-in-a-ditch problems. China's sovereign wealth fund explored an investment in Morgan Stanley, but the talks fell apart quickly. Mack told us the Japanese bank Mitsubishi UFJ was interested in a major investment, but Hank and I were skeptical. We told Mack he needed a faster, more enduring solution, and we pressured him to try Jamie again. Mack basically told us to let him do his job. The perception that I was racing to arrange a bunch of shotgun weddings apparently led some Wall Street executives to dub me eHarmony.

On Sunday, Bill Dudley and Terry Checki, another top New York Fed official, walked into my office and said what I had been reluctant to admit to myself: There was no way we were going to be able to force Goldman and Morgan into the arms of Citi and JPMorgan, and even if we could we might just end up fatally weakening two banks at the center of the system. They had an alternative. We would convert both investment banks into bank holding companies like Citi and JPMorgan, if they would commit to raising a substantial amount of capital immediately. The change in status wouldn't do much to affect their access to financing from the Fed—they were already borrowing from the Fed through the PDCF and TSLF against a broad range of collateral—but it would create the impression that they were under the umbrella of Fed protection.

I didn't think that impression alone would save Goldman and Morgan Stanley, so the additional capital was non-negotiable; I said we wouldn't accept "naked" bank holding company designations. But they had less trouble raising capital than I had feared. As he had predicted, Mack secured a $9 billion commitment from Mitsubishi in exchange for 20 percent of his firm. Goldman Sachs attracted a $5 billion investment from Warren Buffett, a welcome show of confidence in America's financial system from America's top investor, and another $5 billion in capital through a public offering.

We had at least temporarily defused two more system-threatening crises. We had also extinguished the stand-alone investment bank model, ending an era of major Wall Street securities firms operating outside Fed supervision without meaningful constraints on leverage.

Some critics would later say we could have saved Bear and Lehman if we had offered them bank holding company status earlier, but Bear and Lehman were much weaker. The markets had lost confidence in their balance sheets, their ability to finance their assets, and their management. Simply changing their regulator wouldn't have erased the deep flaws in their businesses. Goldman and Morgan were perceived to be stronger, which is why Buffett and Mitsubishi invested in them in their darkest hour. They had stronger businesses and higher levels of capital and liquidity. The markets simply lost confidence in their ability to survive a general withdrawal of funding. Again, that's the definition of a financial crisis, a systemic loss of confidence that sweeps up the relatively strong along with the weak, the merely illiquid along with the insolvent.

Of course, in a financial crisis, insolvency can be in the eye of the beholder. If AIG had been forced to mark all its assets to their depressed market prices during a selling frenzy, then sure, it would've been insolvent. Just about every financial firm would've been insolvent. But we thought that once the crisis passed and asset prices once again reflected some notion of their true underlying value, there was a reasonable chance AIG's assets would be worth more than its liabilities. We were ultimately right, though we helped make that true by the cumulative force of the actions we took to rescue the financial system and broader economy.

By contrast, Lehman looked insolvent in almost any state of the world. There was a reason potential buyers were aghast when they saw its books. It had chased the boom for far too long; as late as May 2007, it led financing for a wildly overpriced $22 billion acquisition of the real estate firm Archstone. Bank of America, Barclays, and the Wall Street consortium all thought it had a capital hole in the tens of billions of dollars. One 2013 study estimated Lehman was at least $100 billion in the hole when it filed for bankruptcy, possibly as much as $200 billion. And unlike AIG, which had strong revenue-generating insurance businesses unrelated to its trading book, Lehman had nothing but its overvalued assets and its damaged reputation as a trading house. If we had done for Lehman what we did for AIG, we just would have financed a run on an unsalvageable institution. We didn't believe its core investment banking business was strong enough to generate the resources necessary to cover the losses in the rest of the firm.

Today, though, the world still believes we made a conscious choice to let Lehman go. That's the standard journalistic account, shared by many economists and financial players. It's understandable, considering what we did with AIG and others later, and considering the initial Washington comments; they were designed to avoid the damaging (though accurate) perception that we had been powerless to save a large and interconnected institution, but they helped feed the myth that we had chosen failure. Even some of my former colleagues at the Fed and Treasury still think we could have rescued Lehman; Alan Greenspan said so publicly. But I do not believe we could have done it without violating the legal constraints placed on the Fed, and without damaging our ability to deal credibly and effectively with the terrible challenges still ahead of us. To save Lehman, we would have needed a private company willing and able to buy most if not all of it, and we didn't have one.

Some critics have argued that in a truly existential crisis, central bankers have responsibilities that transcend the law. They say we should have done whatever had to be done to avoid a chaotic collapse of Lehman and worried about the consequences later. We had shown that we were willing to be creative, break precedent, and take substantial risk to try to preserve the stability of the financial system. But we were not going to grant ourselves extralegal power.

Even in a world where we somehow rescued Lehman, and then still went ahead and rescued AIG, we would not have eliminated the fundamental factors driving the crisis. The economy was collapsing, and the financial system would have kept lurching toward disaster—undercapitalized, overleveraged, still burdened by mortgage assets the markets wouldn't touch, still under threat of a broader run. It took the fall of Lehman and the impending collapse of AIG to persuade President Bush and Hank to seek legislative authority to try to repair the entire system. And even in the post-Lehman panic, Congress would not grant that authority until it had another opportunity to stare into the abyss.

IN THE heat of the existential weekend, Hank sent Congress his draft legislation for the Troubled Assets Relief Program, better known as TARP, or "the Wall Street bailout." His bill requested $700 billion to buy mortgage-related assets, with almost no limits on his authority. It described the Treasury secretary's decisions under TARP as "nonreviewable," stating that they "may not be reviewed by any court of law or any administrative agency." The entire draft was only three pages. It made no effort to establish conditions on recipients of the emergency relief or provide relief to foreclosed homeowners. It was really just a set of bullet points, even though it was presented as the basis for legislative text.

Congressional leaders, who had seemed shell-shocked but willing to act after Hank and Ben warned them about a second depression on Thursday evening, now just seemed angry. "This proposal is stunning and unprecedented in its scope—and lack of detail, I might add," said Senate Banking Committee Chairman Chris Dodd. "I can only conclude that it is not just our economy that is at risk, but our

Constitution as well." Many congressional Republicans, after eight years of almost unbroken support for the Bush administration, were even more hostile to Hank's draft. "It is aimed at rescuing the same financial institutions that created this crisis," declared Dodd's Republican counterpart, Richard Shelby. Editorial boards savaged the plan as an outrageous power grab and a taxpayer giveaway to Wall Street.

I liked it. While Hank's legislative tactics might have been a bit unsubtle, I thought his bill's sweeping grant of authority to the executive branch was essential. We don't expect Congress to micromanage battle plans during wars, and I felt the same way about financial wars. I had little faith in Capitol Hill's ability to design a smart bill with adequate firefighting tools at that fraught populist moment of fear and anger and ignorance. Congressional switchboards were lighting up with calls clamoring for Old Testament justice, but this was not the time to focus on punishing the arsonists. It was the time to focus on putting out the fire.

In fact, my initial concern with the language in Hank's proposal to Congress was that I wasn't sure it granted Treasury broad enough powers. Publicly, Hank was pledging to use the $700 billion to buy toxic assets, not explicitly to invest in financial institutions, but Ben and I wanted to make sure he also had the authority to inject capital directly into banks. We were pretty sure that would be necessary, as it had been for Fannie and Freddie; historically, that's how banking crises get solved. I thought toxic-asset purchases might be helpful, but I wasn't sure how they would work. But once I was sure the language in the bill was broad enough to allow capital injections as well, I was fine with it.

As long as TARP could be used to recapitalize the system, I just wanted Congress to pass it as fast as possible while screwing it up as little as possible. I know this sounds terribly antidemocratic, but it was ridiculous, at a time when we needed overwhelming force to do unpopular things, to expect elected officials to design the details of an exceedingly complicated rescue in the midst of a full run on the global financial system. I remember Rahm Emanuel, a House Democratic leader who needed his mouth washed out with soap even more than I did, called me to say he had a great fucking idea: What if we broke TARP into two $350 billion tranches, with separate congressional approval required for the second tranche?

"No, that's a terrible fucking idea!" I replied.

I argued that it would be hard enough to get politicians to take a tough vote to save their country once. Why try to force them to do it twice?

With his usual subtlety, Rahm let me know I was an idiot. He said Congress would never just hand Hank a $700 billion check. I realized he was not really asking my opinion about a plan he had in mind. He was informing me about a plan he had already put in motion.

I didn't press the point. I figured Rahm knew the politics of Washington better than anyone. And I had a couple more existential crises to worry about.

SIX

"We're Going to Fix This"

On Monday, September 22—one week after Lehman disappeared, one day after the independent investment bank model disappeared—France's president, Nicolas Sarkozy, summoned me to his suite at the Carlyle hotel. He was in town for the UN General Assembly. He wanted to talk about the crisis.

I had hosted a lunch for Sarkozy at the New York Fed back when he was a candidate, and I thought he was pretty compelling—direct, confident, admiring of the United States, open about France's challenges. This time, we had barely sat down before he started yelling at me about Lehman Brothers. He was upset about its ruinous collapse, but he was especially enraged about a story in that morning's *Wall Street Journal* about some assets Lehman had transferred out of Europe before going bust. President Sarkozy was convinced we had conspired to hurt French investors.

I was not in a diplomatic mood, and I cut off Sarkozy mid-rant.

"Mr. President, you've been badly briefed," I said. "Nothing you're saying is true."

President Sarkozy seemed surprised—he wasn't accustomed to

rude interruptions—and his aides seemed appalled. But he quickly calmed down, and we had a good conversation. He must have sensed my exhaustion. I had just been through a bad week for the ages. And the next week wasn't looking any better.

THE FALL of Lehman was a symptom of the unsustainable leverage and runnable short-term financing throughout the system that made the broader crisis inevitable. If Lehman had found a buyer or some other way to avoid a disorderly collapse, AIG or some other firm would have played the Lehman tipping-point role. Lehman was acutely vulnerable, but not uniquely vulnerable. It had built the farthest out in the floodplain, but it wasn't the cause of the flood. Ken Garbade, an excellent economist at the New York Fed, compared the financial system that September to an egg standing on its end. Any breeze could have blown it over.

That said, the fall of Lehman was a serious blow, shattering confidence around the world. It was the most destabilizing financial event since the bank runs of the Depression. Corporate bond spreads widened twice as much after Lehman as they widened after the crash of 1929. The Fed had to quadruple its foreign exchange swaps to meet the global scramble for dollars over the next two weeks. The $20-billion-a-month market for securities backed by credit cards, auto loans, student loans, and other consumer credit virtually vanished overnight. In the broader economy, businesses that saw demand and credit drying up—and saw their suppliers and customers facing the same problems—began downsizing their staffs and reining in their investments to prepare for the long winter ahead. There was political fallout, too; after Senator McCain observed on the day Lehman blew up that "the fundamentals of the economy are strong," Senator Obama took a lead in the polls that he never relinquished.

After Lehman, I lost whatever minimal tolerance I might have had for letting moral hazard or political considerations impede our efforts to attack the crisis. I supported anything that would discourage running or encourage investing; I opposed anything that would weaken confidence or stability. We had to do whatever we could to help people feel their money was safe in the system, even if it made us unpopular, even if it helped individuals and institutions that didn't deserve help.

But when the next financial domino fell, we didn't act to restore confidence. In one of the least appreciated episodes of the crisis, the U.S. government made things worse.

The domino was Washington Mutual, the nation's largest thrift, another big player on the frontier of the mortgage market. WaMu had been racking up losses throughout the crisis, and its stock price had dropped 90 percent. After Lehman fell, depositors pulled $17 billion out of WaMu in ten days, and even its forgiving regulators at the OTS could no longer vouch for its health. The FDIC usually waits until Fridays to close failing banks, so it has the weekend to prepare for a smooth reopening under new management, but WaMu faced such a frenetic run that the FDIC shut it down that Thursday.

WaMu was slightly smaller than Bear Stearns, with about $300 billion in assets, but it was by far the largest FDIC-insured bank ever to fail. It was ten times the size of IndyMac, and almost four times the inflation-adjusted size of Continental Illinois, the bank whose 1984 rescue by the FDIC spawned the term "too big to fail." A crisis so many had dismissed as a Wall Street problem, irrelevant to Main Street, had just claimed a major victim inside the traditional banking system.

Sheila Bair, a former Republican Senate staffer who was President Bush's FDIC chair, quickly agreed to sell WaMu for $1.9 billion to JPMorgan Chase, which would take over the failed bank's uninsured and insured deposits. But the FDIC did not require JPMorgan to stand behind WaMu's other obligations, as we had required it to do for Bear Stearns, leaving WaMu's senior debt holders exposed to severe losses. That sounded like a nice deal from JPMorgan's perspective—it had coveted WaMu's West Coast and Florida banking branches to complement Chase's traditional East Coast operations—but I thought it would be a disaster for the nation.

As the emerging-market crises and the entire history of financial crises made clear, imposing haircuts on bank creditors during a systemic panic is a sure way to accelerate the panic. Lehman had been a chilling reminder of how rapidly inchoate fear could escalate when lenders didn't get paid back. Bank creditors couldn't be sure which institutions might end up like Lehman or WaMu, so they ran from everyone rather than risk getting burned by a default. Even those who didn't think the situation necessarily called for running often felt like they had to run when they saw others running.

In most states of the world, haircuts are a perfectly sensible response to failure. In my time at the IMF, I had supported requiring haircuts for bondholders as a condition of assistance to Ecuador and Pakistan, because those crises were not systemic. There didn't seem to be much contagion risk. The message sent by those haircuts was that Ecuador and Pakistan had been unsafe investments, not that countries or even emerging markets were unsafe investments. Creditors lost money, but lending is a risky business.

The investors who bought WaMu's debt also should have known the risks; governments shouldn't get in the habit of guaranteeing bad bets. And the FDIC was required by law to resolve failed banks through a "least cost" approach that minimized the hit to its deposit insurance fund; standing behind WaMu's debts could have exposed the fund to serious losses. But Congress had provided the FDIC with a "systemic risk exception" that gave it the flexibility to protect bank creditors in moments of extreme instability. I couldn't imagine a more extreme situation. What was the point of systemic risk authority if it didn't apply to the worst systemic emergency since the Depression? Imposing losses when we had the power to prevent them would send a clear signal to other creditors of U.S. banks that they too were exposed to losses and should put their money somewhere safer if they didn't want haircuts.

It seemed obvious to me that in a moment of extreme vulnerability, haircuts would only intensify the crisis, but Sheila didn't see it that way. She was determined to guard against moral hazard and protect the FDIC insurance fund. She saw this as a teachable moment, a chance to show the world that the irresponsibility of WaMu and its bondholders would be punished. She made the same argument the Germans and other moral hazard critics had made against IMF assistance during the emerging-market crises: It will only encourage bad behavior in the future.

I thought that in the midst of the worst panic any of us had ever seen, any effort to minimize FDIC losses through haircuts in an individual case would lead to more bank failures and much bigger FDIC losses down the road. More failures would eventually require more aggressive government interventions, creating more moral hazard rather than reducing it. I couldn't understand why the risks in allowing WaMu to default on its debts weren't completely obvious, especially after Lehman's default had paralyzed credit markets and shocked the world. The FDIC was playing with fire. I called Ben, Don, and Hank to try to convince them to turn Sheila around.

"This is not the moment for more haircuts," I said.

They heard me out and acknowledged my concerns, but even though their support would have been needed for the FDIC to use its emergency powers, they couldn't compel Sheila to use those powers. And they were reluctant to pressure her. Sheila was a formidable advocate for her agency and its insurance fund, savvier about politics and the media than any of us. So despite my objections, the FDIC orchestrated a deal that let WaMu default on its creditors. Shareholders and subordinated debt holders were mostly wiped out, which was understandable. But senior debt holders were exposed to serious haircuts as well. The price of WaMu's senior debt traded at only 25 cents on the dollar the next day, Friday, September 26.

As soon as the deal was announced, the perceived risk of lending to U.S. banks increased dramatically. The markets ran first and fastest from Wachovia, a much bigger bank that was also in trouble, and now looked like it could be the next candidate for similar haircuts. The price of insuring Wachovia's senior debt against default doubled that Friday, while its ten-year bonds swooned from 73 cents on the dollar to 29 cents. Other banks were hammered, too. The cost of insuring Citigroup against default jumped almost 50 percent in a day. The U.S. government had sent a message that creditors of U.S. financial institutions were not safe, precisely the wrong message to send at a time of peril. Wachovia's creditors were so unnerved they demanded repayment of half the bank's *long-term* debt that day, trying to call in more than $50 billion in loans.

WaMu's demise did not get much media attention, partly because the world was still processing the shock of Lehman and AIG, partly because an amazing drama was unfolding that day at the White House. Senator McCain had suspended his campaign and swooped back into Washington, ostensibly to seek a solution to the crisis. But after President Bush convened a White House meeting with congressional leaders and both candidates, McCain and House Republicans seemed to scuttle the solution to the crisis, refusing to support TARP. Hank ended up getting on his knees to beg Speaker Pelosi not to abandon the bill because of Republican gamesmanship.

I understood why the campaign theater overshadowed the WaMu news. And we desperately needed TARP, so the political circus swirling around it was genuinely consequential. Still, WaMu was an overlooked mess that unnecessarily intensified the crisis. WaMu's demise was in some ways as damaging to confidence as the Lehman debacle, because WaMu's haircuts were totally avoidable. They sent a message to the world that the U.S. government was not seriously committed to defusing the financial crisis and containing the economic damage, even when it had the capacity to do so, even after the nightmare of Lehman. Perhaps the only good news was that the damage caused by the failure to protect WaMu's senior creditors led to some important changes in our approach to the intensifying crisis.

• • •

WACHOVIA WAS clearly the next domino.

It was a big domino, more than twice as big as WaMu, even bigger than Lehman, with a solid funding base of twenty-seven million deposit accounts. But the $800 billion Charlotte-based bank had been choking on Golden West's bad mortgages since the start of the crisis, and after WaMu's turbulent collapse, Wachovia was doomed. Depositors withdrew more than $5 billion from Wachovia on Friday. For the third straight weekend, we would have to try to find a solution for a failing giant before the markets opened Monday morning.

Wachovia had two suitors: Citigroup, which had been America's largest bank before Bank of America's recent acquisition spree, and San Francisco–based Wells Fargo, which was less massive but also less vulnerable. By Sunday, both banks had said they could not do a deal unless the FDIC took some of the risk on Wachovia's questionable assets. Sheila was resistant to anything that could expose the FDIC's insurance fund to losses, which would translate into higher premiums for all FDIC-insured banks. Sheila's WaMu plan had been designed to limit the immediate cost to the fund, regardless of the potential damage to the overall banking system. She wanted to replicate that strategy for Wachovia: sell off the bank, wipe out the shareholders and junior debt, and haircut the senior debt.

"I don't think the small banks should have to pay for the sins of the big banks," she explained on a Sunday conference call.

I lost my composure, and my words were pretty harsh. I felt guilty that I hadn't been more persuasive in preventing the panic-accelerating haircuts at WaMu. I was frustrated by what I considered the FDIC's narrow and parochial focus on protecting its fund during a global emergency, when our other tools seemed so limited. I had heard enough moral hazard fundamentalism. And I was sick of the insinuations, so prevalent in Washington, that any advocates of using emergency authorities to quell the panic must be acting at the behest of big banks. The stability of the entire banking system was at risk. The economy was already hurting badly. Trying to teach bondholders a lesson might have felt righteous, but it would ultimately entail more risk for the FDIC if it led to the failures of other banks. Repeating the WaMu haircuts for Wachovia's senior creditors could have triggered an uncontrollable run on the banking system, a proven formula for an economic depression. It made no sense to keep pouring fuel on a burning fire, accelerating the panic at a time when Hank was asking Congress for $700 billion to calm down the panic.

"The policy of the U.S. government should be that there will be no more WaMus," I said.

That evening, Ben and Don persuaded Sheila to invoke the FDIC's systemic risk exception for the first time in this crisis, setting aside the "least cost" mandate that would have required haircuts for bondholders. There would be no more WaMus. In a memo justifying the exception for Wachovia, the FDIC's staff made the late but accurate admission that "the closing of Washington Mutual" was a key source of stress in the system, right alongside Lehman and AIG. Another strict least-cost resolution, they said, "would almost surely have major systemic effects." No matter what was said publicly, they knew more WaMu-style haircuts could produce another Lehman-style catastrophe.

At 4 a.m. Monday, Sheila chose Citi's offer to buy most of Wachovia and stand behind its obligations for just $1 a share. Citi would place $312 billion of Wachovia's assets inside a "ring fence," partitioning them from the rest of its balance sheet, but would commit to absorb the first $42 billion in losses from those assets. The government would bear any losses above that, putting a ceiling on Citi's catastrophic tail risk, reassuring investors that Wachovia wouldn't drag Citi down if the assets turned out to be worse than expected. The FDIC staff concluded that the Citi proposal was unlikely to cost taxpayers anything, while the Wells offer would probably cost billions.

Even as she approved the deal, Sheila continued to emphasize her reluctance to put any public money at risk, implying she had bowed to pressure from Treasury and the Fed.

"I'm not completely comfortable with it, but we need to move forward with something," she said.

None of us were completely comfortable with it. Citi and Wachovia both had problems, and I knew their merger raised classic two-drunks-in-a-ditch issues. But all our options were terrible. And Wachovia needed a buyer with a big balance sheet to stand behind its debts, while Citi, which was too dependent on foreign deposits, would benefit from the more stable funding in Wachovia's domestic deposits. In any case, we couldn't afford another WaMu. This was another Band-Aid solution, but it beat bleeding to death.

Afterward, Ben wrote a note to Sheila that was full of praise—she wanted cover for a no-haircuts rescue—and correct about the deal's importance.

"You were able to turn what would have been the largest and most consequential bank failure in history into a medium-size, below-the-fold news story," Ben wrote. "I don't think markets appreciate the size of the bullet that was dodged, although everyone will understand it when the history is written."

We had elevated no-haircuts-in-a-panic to the level of doctrine. But we still didn't have the authority to make that commitment fully credible, to assure markets there would be no more WaMus or even no more Lehmans. We needed TARP.

After the Wachovia decision was in the FDIC's hands that Sunday night, I stopped by a dinner party at Henry Kissinger's apartment on the East River. I was late to the conversation, which inevitably turned to the financial crisis. With Kissinger's guests, I tried to draw a contrast with the chaos of the military conflict we were engaged in on the other side of the world.

"I know this looks like our Afghanistan," I said. "But we're going to fix this. We have the ability to impose a solution. We're the United States."

The House of Representatives would be voting on TARP the next day, and everyone wanted to know what would happen. I didn't know how the vote counting was going, but I felt confident, perhaps irrationally confident, that Washington would come around and do what seemed so evidently necessary to avoid a calamity.

"We'll get the authority we need," I said. "And then we'll put out the fire."

OVER WACHOVIA weekend, Hank worked out a deal with congressional leaders to expand his bare-bones TARP draft into bipartisan legislation. It included Rahm's plan to divide the $700 billion into two tranches, plus some executive compensation restrictions for TARP recipients. It also authorized a bunch of new oversight bodies, a nod to the backlash over Hank's "unreviewable" language.

Senate Finance Chairman Max Baucus had called me during the negotiations to complain about Hank's opposition to tougher comp restrictions. I had told him I was with Hank. I didn't think Congress should mess around with TARP as a way to reform executive compensation—not because I approved of the industry's lavish salaries and bonuses, but because reducing them seemed like a secondary objective in a crisis. And I wasn't going to undermine Hank's position. In general, I opposed conditions that would tie the administration's hands in using emergency authority. But the restrictions that ended up in the legislation, limited to golden parachutes and tax deductions, seemed pretty modest. I didn't like the idea of having to go back to Congress for the second tranche, either, but the bill still gave Treasury tremendous discretion over the money. For the most part, I thought the conditions were pretty harmless. And Hank was confident they would attract enough votes to get the bill into law, the most important consideration.

On Monday, though, the TARP legislation went down to a shocking defeat in the House, 228–205. Most Democrats supported it, but two-thirds of Republicans voted no. The stock market plunged almost 9 percent that day, the largest decline since the Black Monday crash of 1987, wiping out $1 trillion in wealth. Hank called me, as distraught as I had ever heard him. His voice broke as he told me how sorry he was.

"Tim, I couldn't get it across the line," he said.

In those days, I tended to be the most worried person in the room, but on this issue I was relatively confident. We were the United States of America. I couldn't imagine that Congress would stand by and let the economy sink into depression. I told Hank he would get what we needed soon. I also reassured him that he was doing a great job, and I meant it. I had tremendous admiration for him. He was decisive and fearless, always willing to take the heat. It was easy for me to clamor for unpopular actions behind the scenes, but Hank had to make the case in the public glare. He had been mocked as "Mr. Bailout," caricatured as a symbol of Wall Street corruption, portrayed as "King Henry" on the cover of *Newsweek*. Now he was being ridiculed as hapless and powerless. I knew the criticism hurt, especially the criticism of his motives; he was working around the clock to save the country from disaster. And while he felt awful that he hadn't been able to persuade members of his own party to put politics aside, that was their fault, not his.

The market crash seemed to focus their minds. Before Monday, the public reaction to TARP had been all anti-bailout anger, but now politicians started hearing from constituents whose life savings were disappearing. Senate leaders added some sweeteners to the bill, including extensions of dozens of tax breaks for businesses. The bill also temporarily raised the FDIC's deposit insurance limit from $100,000 to $250,000, to help protect the kind of account holders burned by IndyMac's haircuts, and to help prevent runs on traditional banks.

On Wednesday, October 1, the tweaked version of TARP passed the Senate with broad bipartisan support, 74–25. On Friday, it passed the House as well, as 57 representatives flipped from no to yes. The abrupt reversal evoked the Winston Churchill line about Americans always doing the right thing after trying everything else, but there was also something inspiring about it. A month before a high-stakes election, a Democratic-controlled Congress helped a Republican president with a 27 percent approval rating pass a wildly unpopular but desperately needed bill. We wouldn't see much of that kind of aisle-crossing during the next administration.

WHILE THE world watched the TARP debate, we were wrangling behind the scenes over an unexpected twist in the Wachovia deal. Citi's purchase had been announced Monday, and Wachovia had signed a weeklong exclusivity agreement for Citi to finalize it. But Wells Fargo made a new offer Thursday: $7 a share for the whole company, seven times Citi's offer, with no government help needed. Sheila decided that since Citi hadn't yet closed its deal, Wachovia was free to accept the better offer for its shareholders. She emphasized that the Wells deal was also better for taxpayers, since the FDIC wouldn't have to take any risk.

When I first heard the change was in the works, I was livid. On a series of conference calls, I once again argued that Sheila's position was untenable.

"The United States government made a commitment," I said. "We can't act like we're a banana republic!"

I was worried that scuttling the Citi deal could end up crippling an already vulnerable $2 trillion institution, weakening it at the worst possible time. Citi's stock price, after rising on the news of the Wachovia merger, would fall 18 percent on the news the merger was off, its steepest drop in two decades. Markets now assumed that Citi must have needed Wachovia's domestic deposits to survive. There was no bank more intertwined in global finance than Citi, which handled as much as $2 trillion of the world's payments every day, and CEO Vikram Pandit, understandably enraged, warned us there was now a good chance it could fail. "This is worrying," Ben emailed with classic understatement. Pandit argued that even putting fairness aside, the Citi merger would be better for systemic stability.

"I think he is probably right," Ben wrote.

While we were all concerned about damaging Citi, I was even more concerned that breaking a public promise would damage the government's credibility and destabilize the system. What firm would stick its neck out to backstop a failing company if it thought we'd keep shopping for a better offer after the deal was announced? I thought reneging on our word would make the U.S. government look unreliable.

There's no way to put a price on the government's credibility in a crisis. That was part of my reluctance to trumpet the strength of our weakened financial system when Dick Fuld and others wanted me to reassure the markets before the fall of Lehman. And that's why I had been so upset that the FDIC intentionally let WaMu default in the wake of all the damage caused by Lehman's failure. To resolve a crisis, a government has to show the capacity and the will to end it; it has to demonstrate through its deeds that its words can be trusted. *Credit* and *credibility* share the same Latin root. It was bad enough when Russian and Indonesian politicians broke promises. We were the United States.

"You can't run a government like this during a financial crisis," I protested.

Hank and Ben were sympathetic, but they let me fight that losing battle on my own. This was Sheila's call. There was no unified command structure in the U.S. government's financial wars. And in fairness, this time, Sheila probably didn't feel like she had much of a choice. Wells Fargo's privately financed $15 billion offer was certainly more attractive than Citi's taxpayer-assisted $2 billion offer.

Still, our constant zigzags looked ridiculous. We were lurching all over the place, and no one had any idea what to expect next. Hank said he wouldn't need to inject capital into Fannie and Freddie, then did what had to be done and injected $200 billion. Collectively, we helped prevent Bear's failure, then seemed to suggest we let Lehman fail on purpose, then turned around and saved AIG from collapse. Now we had announced and then unannounced a merger. Our inconsistency had multiple causes: the limits of our authority, which made us look like we were flailing; the balkanization of our authority, which put different tools in the hands of different officials with different strategies and different perceived responsibilities; and the inevitable messiness of fighting a crisis with limited time and incomplete information to make decisions. But whatever the cause, our unpredictability undermined the effectiveness of our response.

The broader authority in TARP offered the hope of a more comprehensive and consistent strategy. But first our strategy for TARP would have to evolve a bit, too.

• • •

HANK PITCHED the Troubled Assets Relief Program to Congress as a program to buy troubled assets. The plan was to restore confidence in financial institutions by purchasing $700 billion worth of the mortgage securities and other illiquid assets that were weighing down their balance sheets.

"The right way to do this is not going around and using guarantees or injecting capital," Hank told the Senate Banking Committee.

In Hank's view, even mentioning the possibility of direct capital investments would have been bad politics, raising the specter of nationalization. Government ownership stakes in private firms sounded un-American, and aid to the institutions that caused the crisis sounded corrupt. But within the Fed and the Treasury, there was a growing recognition that we couldn't defuse the crisis until we recapitalized the financial system. Current capital levels just weren't thick enough to absorb the magnitude of losses that could lie ahead.

Part of our increasing enthusiasm for capital was a result of increasing skepticism about asset purchases. My own skepticism had crystallized during the Fed's battles with JPMorgan over the Bear Stearns mortgage pool. Using TARP to buy assets would have been much more complicated and similarly slow; Treasury thought it would take at least forty-five days after passage before the program could begin. And it would have been incredibly challenging to figure out what the government should pay for assets the markets were no longer trading. If we set prices too low, we could have forced financial institutions to realize huge losses that could have threatened their solvency. If we set prices too high, the purchases not only would have looked like egregious giveaways to Wall Street, they would have been exorbitantly expensive for taxpayers. And Congress had given us only $700 billion to spend—a big number, but by no means an overwhelming number compared to the troubled assets in the banking system.

That was the main problem with using asset purchases to stabilize overleveraged financial institutions. Imagine a bank with $1 trillion in mortgage assets and $25 billion in capital, a 40:1 leverage ratio. To get it to a much safer 20:1 leverage ratio, the government could buy $500 billion of its assets, which would drain most of TARP on one institution. Or it could inject $25 billion in additional capital, achieving the same ratio with one-twentieth of the cash. Ken Garbade had first flagged this disparity back in March, suggesting in an email that direct capital investments "might be a more efficient way to contain the crisis." Asset purchases seemed like a way to burn through our cash without solving the problem, forcing us to go back to ask for more from a Congress focused on the next election.

At the end of September, I began a series of consequential meetings with Garbade, Meg McConnell, and other New York Fed economists to try to figure out how to advise Treasury to design TARP. We all agreed capital investments would be essential to stretch every dollar as far as it could go. In a September 26 memo titled "Escalation Options," Garbade and two colleagues noted that government capital had been part of the solution to most financial crises, including the

Depression. In this crisis, the Fed had provided plenty of liquidity—for commercial banks, investment banks, foreign banks, and money market funds—but we hadn't yet addressed the deeper solvency issues of undercapitalized institutions. They had already absorbed massive losses, and with even more massive losses potentially looming, most of them had no way to raise capital privately. Capital would be essential, even if it might not be enough by itself.

"The missing policy, to date, has been bank capital injections," the memo said.

I strongly agreed. So did Ben. And by the time TARP came up for a vote, Hank had come around to this view, too. He still expected to buy assets down the road, but he now believed injecting capital would be faster, more powerful, and more efficient.

I admired Hank's willingness to change course so quickly. But on a September 30 conference call, the day after the first disappointing House vote, I told Hank capital alone wouldn't save troubled firms.

"What you really need is the authority to guarantee their liabilities," I said.

Hank noted that the likelihood of Congress agreeing to guarantee trillions of dollars in bank debts—in addition to the $700 billion in spending the House had just rejected as overreach—was zero. He was right. But those meetings with Garbade and the New York Fed economists had persuaded me we'd need to deploy broad guarantees alongside capital injections to quell the panic and stabilize the system.

Capital was necessary to make banks stronger, but creditors were running away from banks regardless of their strength, and capital alone wouldn't stop a run already in progress. We needed to stop the run on liquidity first, and that would require guarantees. Just as FDIC deposit insurance prevented runs on insured deposits, and Treasury's money market guarantee was preventing runs on money market funds, the government needed to make it clear that until the crisis subsided, lenders would be able to provide credit to financial firms without fear of default. Across the Atlantic, we were seeing how the demonstrated willingness of the Europeans to inject capital had not prevented an escalating run on their banks—and the longer the runs continued, the more capital the banks would ultimately need. Ireland had moved first to guarantee its bank liabilities, and other countries were following suit, to avoid the spreading run on the European banking system.

Without guarantees, creditors would continue to run from banks, so banks would continue to hoard cash, market liquidity would continue to erode, and the run would intensify. Without more capital, banks would face increasing pressure to sell assets at distressed prices, which would create more losses and bigger capital holes; they would also have to pull back their lending, exacerbating what already threatened to be a severe downturn. So we needed both capital and guarantees. Capital was mostly about averting insolvency, while guarantees were mostly about preserving liquidity. But solvency problems could sap confidence and cause liquidity problems, while liquidity problems could force fire sales and cause solvency problems. Together, capital and guarantees could make the financial system stable enough to support growth again, instead of encouraging flight and working against growth.

Once TARP passed, I felt like we finally had some firepower to attack our capital problems. But I still had no idea how we'd get the authority to do guarantees. And while good news usually created lulls in the crisis where we could regroup and recalibrate our strategy, the passage of TARP did not quiet the markets at all.

THE WEEK of October 6 was the U.S. stock market's worst week since 1933. The S&P 500 dropped 18 percent. The "fear index," a measure of market volatility, hit an all-time high, while the spread reflecting stress in interbank lending also set a new record, four times its level before Lehman. Morgan Stanley returned to the brink, as rumors swirled that its deal with Mitsubishi might fall through; its stock price plunged while its credit default swaps soared. And AIG was burning through its $85 billion bridge loan so fast that we had to set up an additional $37.8 billion program. During the previous few weeks, we had committed more money to AIG than the federal government had spent on Social Security and Medicare.

Asian and European markets were in disarray, too. A *Financial Times* headline summed up the situation: "New Panic Is Proof of Big League Crisis." Ben and the ECB's Jean-Claude Trichet, with my encouragement, worked with Mervyn King at the Bank of England and several other central bankers to launch the first-ever coordinated global interest rate cut. That was a remarkable act of cooperation for central banks that had always prized their independence and sovereignty, but it didn't stop or even slow the collapse of the global markets.

In the United States, private credit was now virtually unavailable. The financial system was increasingly unable to play its most basic role in the economy: facilitating the flow of money from those who wanted to lend to those who wanted to invest or consume. The run on money market funds after Lehman, followed by the broader run on the banking system that consumed WaMu and Wachovia, had spilled into the unsecured commercial paper market where businesses with strong credit histories could raise money to finance their day-to-day operations. My team at the New York Fed, along with some staff from the board in Washington, developed another creative lending program to try to prevent the collapse of commercial paper, but we ran into resistance elsewhere in Fed headquarters.

Our proposed Commercial Paper Funding Facility required the most expansive interpretation of Fed authority yet. The Fed can only lend against collateral, and the CPFF was designed for unsecured commercial paper, which by definition is not backed by collateral. It's just corporate IOUs. My team proposed for the Fed to lend to a special-purpose vehicle that would buy the unsecured paper, in return for a fee that would provide some protection against losses. The Fed would take considerable risk, more risk than some members of Ben's team were comfortable with. But we didn't think the more conservative alternatives they preferred would be as effective in reviving the market.

The debate was slowing us down, and I feared we were on the verge of losing another critical part of the financial system. Companies such as Verizon, McDonald's, and Caterpillar as well as the financial firms at the heart of the crisis all needed to issue commercial paper to pay their bills. Late one night, I called Ben at home and appealed to our common desire to avoid what he liked to call "Depression 2.0."

"You can authorize this. You just have to decide whether you want to fix the problem or not," I told him. "There's no point in trying some kind of limp solution."

I was tougher than usual on Ben, but I wasn't telling him anything he didn't know. As always, he was calm and patient, analytical but comfortable making quick decisions. He had a quiet force to him.

"OK, I hear you," he said. "I got it."

Our teams quickly worked out a framework we could all live with, and we decided to roll it out the morning of October 7. At the last minute, it was Bill Dudley from my shop who actually suggested putting the brakes on the announcement, citing some operational concerns. And this time, it was Washington that insisted on full speed ahead. None of us were certain the CPFF would work, but we had to keep acting, keep moving, keep doing stuff.

"Look, we have no choice," Don Kohn wrote at 6:25 a.m. "We have to make this work, however complex. I think we should announce this morning."

We did. And we sorted out the technical issues quickly enough that the CPFF would start lending money in late October, providing companies with nearly $150 billion in liquidity in its first week. But the financial system needed help sooner than that.

• • •

WHAT IT really needed were comprehensive guarantees. I decided to call Sheila Bair to see if the FDIC could use its systemic risk authority to provide a solution.

I probably wasn't the best person to make the case to Sheila. We did not know each other well, and in our conflicts over WaMu and Wachovia I had been derisive of her arguments. While Hank and Ben had gently encouraged her to act in the interests of the system, selling her on the opportunity to be a firefighting hero, I had been more aggressive, dismissing her focus on limiting immediate risks to the FDIC insurance fund as parochial and shortsighted, warning that she was dragging us toward an epic disaster.

But I thought it was vital for some government agency to stand behind the debts of the banks, so depositors and lenders wouldn't have to assess which ones were good credit risks—because in the fog of a panic, nobody looks like a good credit risk. And the FDIC was the only plausible source of that authority. Congress had explicitly given it the ability to guarantee the debts of banks, even for banks that had already failed. I figured it was at least worth asking Sheila if she would guarantee the debts of banks before they failed—and not just one or two of them, but all of them.

Sheila politely listened to my pitch. I again made the case that the more risk the government could commit to take, the less risk it would ultimately have to take. If we had unlimited capital to inject into the banks, we wouldn't have needed guarantees, but we didn't have unlimited capital, and there was no way to know how much capital would be enough to reassure the markets. By standing behind the obligations of the banking system, the FDIC could help prevent an all-out run on the system. The world couldn't afford another Lehman—or another WaMu, though I didn't mention that sore subject—and we had to take extraordinary measures to prevent it.

To her immense credit, Sheila replied: "I think we might be able to do that."

Sheila and I would continue to have our differences, including on this very issue, but her willingness to use the FDIC's guarantee authority was one of the turning points of the crisis. She had already invoked the systemic risk exception after watching Wachovia disintegrate so abruptly in the wake of WaMu, and now she seemed open to considering a more sweeping use of that emergency authority. She had gotten her glimpse into the abyss, her taste of the burden of fear that Hank, Ben, and I had carried for more than a year.

As soon as I hung up the phone, I called Hank and Ben to report that Sheila might be willing and able to provide some form of broader guarantees. Hank invited Sheila to his office on Wednesday morning, October 8. Ben was there, too; I called in from New York. Hank began the meeting by telling Sheila it would be wonderful if she could apply the principles of the initial Wachovia plan in a broader way—in essence, if she could guarantee the liabilities of the banking system. She got defensive, reminding us there was only $35 billion left in her deposit insurance fund. Hank replied that if we couldn't guarantee the system, the run dynamic would feed on itself, more major banks would fail, and there would soon be nothing left in her fund. I made my usual case for overwhelming force being safer and cheaper than tentative half-measures.

It was clear Sheila had reservations, and she was too adept a bureaucratic warrior to let us box her in. But it was also clear she was willing to provide some kind of guarantees. And with TARP, we'd be able to provide capital as well.

Now we just needed to nail down the details. We had spent the past three frenetic weekends trying to save dying firms with systemic implications. We would spend the next weekend, Columbus Day weekend, trying to make sure we wouldn't have to do that anymore. We had been chasing an escalating crisis for more than a year, always behind the curve, patching together ad hoc fixes to try to hold the system together. Finally, we had a chance to design a more definitive solution.

• • •

I SHOWED up early Saturday at the south entrance of the Treasury building, the place where my government career began almost exactly twenty years earlier. The Secret Service didn't have me cleared in the system, so I had to wait outside for a half hour until they could verify that I had a meeting with Hank. My New York Fed colleagues and I sat down on the Treasury steps—in front of a statue of the first Treasury secretary, Alexander Hamilton, holding a three-cornered hat—and joked about all the reasons it might make sense to keep me out of the building.

It was a sunny, crisp, beautiful fall day in Washington, and even though the world was still disintegrating, I felt as light as I had in months. We finally had the outlines of a plan and the authority to execute it. We were going to deploy federal resources in ways Hamilton never imagined, but given his advocacy for executive power and a strong financial system, I had to believe he would have approved. It was Hamilton who had insisted on assuming the debts of the states and paying the new nation's creditors at face value to establish the U.S. government's reputation as a solid credit risk, even though haircutting foreigners and speculators who had bought Revolutionary War debt for pennies on the dollar would have been much better politics. He was America's original Mr. Bailout. As the inscription on his statue said: "He touched the dead corpse of the public credit and it sprang upon its feet."

One of our main tasks that weekend would be to persuade the FDIC to use the power of that public credit to provide guarantees that would help revive private credit. Ever since Sheila had acknowledged her authority to backstop the banking system, she had been backpedaling, proposing a variety of limitations and conditions that would have undermined the power of the guarantees. She wanted to absorb only 90 percent of the losses from bank debts, which potentially meant 10 percent haircuts. She also wanted to charge near-punitive fees for the guarantees. And she wanted to limit them to the new debts of banks with FDIC-insured deposits, excluding existing bank debts as well as all debts of bank holding companies and their broker-dealer subsidiaries.

Some Fed and Treasury officials shared the FDIC's unease about the scope and generosity of the guarantees. There was concern in some corners of the White House, too. But Sheila took the lead in trying to minimize the FDIC's risk, and we spent most of the weekend in tense negotiations. I pushed for the broadest possible guarantees, with fees modest enough that institutions would actually want to use them, and with no haircuts whatsoever. Once again, I was the bad cop, while Hank and Ben were conciliators. At one point, Sheila got so mad and dug in that Hank invited her into his office and essentially begged her to help us avoid Armageddon, promising to make sure she would get the credit she was due.

Ultimately, Sheila agreed to 100 percent guarantees—imposing haircuts would have been ludicrous—with fees that weren't prohibitive. But her efforts to limit the scope of the guarantees raised a thornier problem, a boundary problem. Once a government sets a dividing line between what's guaranteed and what isn't, it can spark a run from the debts and firms just beyond the line to the debts and firms on the safe side. We needed the guarantees to cover the obligations of bank holding companies, not just their FDIC-insured bank subsidiaries, or else the broader institutions and their nonbank affiliates would have come crashing down. The escalating guarantees in Europe were already creating the possibility that U.S. banks would be the only major banks operating without the full protection of their government behind them. Ireland's guarantees had prompted investors to shift cash from British banks to Irish banks, prompting the United Kingdom to offer its own guarantees; this arms race put additional pressure on us to follow suit.

In the congressional negotiations on TARP, Sheila had insisted on expanding FDIC insurance to cover checking accounts and other business transaction accounts at the seven thousand commercial banks in her jurisdiction. And she was now willing to provide guarantees for commercial banks insured by the FDIC. She just didn't want to extend them to the holding companies of banks and their nonbank affiliates, entities outside the formal boundaries of the bank safety net. That would have just added to the run on the most vulnerable parts of the system, which in turn would have put more pressure on the banking system.

After more haggling, we worked out a messy but acceptable compromise. The FDIC would backstop the *new* unsecured debt of bank holding companies as well as their commercial bank subsidiaries, but not of their broker-dealer subsidiaries, and not their existing debt. Ultimately, commercial banks would issue only about 20 percent of the debt guaranteed by the FDIC, so if we had agreed to limit coverage to those institutions, the guarantees would have packed much less power. Then again, they would have packed more power if the FDIC had agreed to guarantee existing as well as new debt; instead, we left existing creditors wondering whether more defaults and haircuts could be coming if the system ran into more problems. But the guarantees would help banks continue to finance themselves, which was critical.

Our other challenge that weekend was to figure out the structure of the capital investments—what kind of capital, who would get it, how to price it, and so forth. This would be the most sweeping government intervention in the private markets since the 1930s, and we had two days to design it. My bias was toward simple, workable, and powerful. Fed staff had floated several elegant pricing options for the capital injections, including a "co-investment" plan where private investors would do the valuations and put some of their own capital at risk alongside taxpayer dollars. It was a cool idea, and we would return to the concept later in the crisis, but it was way too complex a program to set up overnight. My staff often joked that whenever I referred to an idea as "elegant," I meant it was either too complicated or too difficult to implement, and therefore off the table.

"Important thing here is not to get hung up on the precise details but to get it done by Monday with the capital going in," Bill Dudley wrote me late Saturday night.

Ultimately, we decided the Treasury would buy up to $250 billion worth of preferred stock in participating firms from the first tranche of TARP. It would receive a 5 percent annual dividend, rising to 9 percent after five years to encourage firms to pay the government back. Treasury would also receive warrants to buy common stock, so taxpayers could get some upside if the firms recovered. Current purchases would be limited to nonvoting preferred stock, which would ease fears of nationalization. But preferred stock is less loss-absorbing than common equity, the most resilient form of capital, so the money we injected into the companies would look more like low-interest loans than true investments in their long-term health, reducing its power. We also decided that the terms of the injections would be the same for everyone—partly because differential pricing would have been too complex to design on the fly, mostly because we didn't want to slap weaker firms with the burden and the stigma of costlier capital.

Stigma was a real danger, which is why we also decided to make the capital all but mandatory for the largest firms. The United Kingdom had just announced a voluntary program, and only weak firms initially accepted the capital, prompting markets to punish them. The FDIC team argued it would be unfair to force capital into stronger U.S. firms. But the system as a whole was undercapitalized, and unless the broader shortfall was addressed, the crisis would keep migrating from the relatively weak to the relatively strong. The fire had not burned itself out when it consumed Bear or Lehman or AIG. It had gained strength, and no one was fireproof. Recapitalizing the entire system would benefit everyone, so allowing firms to opt out and still enjoy those benefits would have been truly unfair.

While we worked out the details of the capital and guarantees, the Fed's team was also finalizing our new commercial paper program, as well as an unprecedented expansion of our foreign exchange swaps that made unlimited dollars available to European, British, Swiss, and Japanese banks through their central banks. As important as the details were, we knew it could be even more important to convey a sense of overwhelming force, to reassure the markets and the public that the U.S. government stood behind the fragile system. We had to show we had the capacity and the will to end the repeated bouts of escalating panic.

In that email late Saturday night, after discussing where we stood on all of those programs, Dudley pointed out that a "coherent explanation of how it all fits together" could be as vital as any individual piece of the puzzle.

"This is about confidence mainly," he wrote.

BANKS WERE closed on Columbus Day, so Mitsubishi's executives personally delivered a $9 billion check to Morgan Stanley that Monday morning to close their deal and avoid a Lehman-style collapse. Hank and I had helped persuade the Japanese to close through some back-channel diplomacy, but we barely had time to breathe a sigh of relief that day. Hank had summoned the CEOs of nine of America's largest financial firms to the Treasury for a meeting that would help determine the fate of the global economy.

We wanted to inject $125 billion, half the initial program, into those nine institutions, which held more than half of the banking system's assets; our hope was that smaller institutions would then feel free to apply for TARP funding without stigma. We would invest up to 3 percent of each firm's risk-weighted assets: $25 billion for JPMorgan, Wells Fargo, and Citi; $15 billion for Bank of America; $10 billion for Morgan Stanley, Goldman Sachs, and Merrill Lynch, which was not yet part of BofA; $3 billion for Bank of New York; and $2 billion for State Street. We spent much of the morning stage-managing the meeting and refining the terms, focusing on how to make sure all nine banks accepted the new capital.

We agreed that Hank would begin with an overview of our plan, followed by Ben discussing its importance for stability. Sheila would then give the details of the guarantees, which we knew would be welcome news for the financiers. It would fall to me to explain the capital program, which would be less welcome for some of them, even though our investments in banks would be what most Americans saw as "bailouts." As we developed our scripts, I pushed hard to make the capital investments sound as close to mandatory as possible. We couldn't force participation, but we could make it sound inevitable. I expected some firms to resist taking new capital with government strings attached. But in a financial crisis, no firm is ever as well capitalized as it thinks. Lehman thought it had plenty of capital until it didn't.

Sheila and I also suggested that Hank should make the CEOs sign pledges to use their new capital to do more lending, which would help the economy; modify more mortgages, which would help struggling homeowners; and abide by the compensation provisions of TARP, which would appeal to some Old Testament impulses. Critics correctly identified these pledges as largely irrelevant shiny objects that we could point to when we were accused of ignoring Main Street. Politically, though, these fig leaves were better than nothing. Hank, Ben, and I believed the real way to help Main Street would be to prevent a financial meltdown that would launch a global depression, but that was harder to explain.

By 3 p.m., the nine bankers were seated at the long mahogany table in the Treasury secretary's historic conference room. The room was decorated with Renaissance Revival furniture and gas-lit chandeliers from the post–Civil War period, along with stately portraits of George Washington and Salmon Chase, the Civil War Treasury secretary whose face was on the first greenback. It had been the dignified setting for some of our brainstorming clusterfucks at Treasury during the emerging-market crises. This time, the crisis was in our own market, and we were about to engineer the most aggressive government intervention in our economy in nearly eighty years.

Hank was typically direct in his introduction, outlining the program and informing the bankers that they were all expected to accept the capital as well as the guarantees. "We're planning to announce that all nine of you will participate," he said. He suggested that there might be regulatory consequences for firms that didn't, and that any subsequent government interventions would be much less generous.

"This is the right thing to do for the country," Hank said.

When it was my turn, I announced how much each bank would receive, in alphabetical order from Bank of America to Wells Fargo. I emphasized that no one who rejected the capital would be eligible for the guarantees. It was a package deal, not an à la carte plan.

"You have to opt in to both for the program to work," I said. "We have designed this package to meet the needs of the system, and that should make it overwhelmingly compelling to each of your institutions individually."

I warned the bankers that if they all didn't accept the capital, TARP would become stigmatized, the system would remain under-capitalized, and they all would remain at risk. I also said it wasn't just "the system" that needed capital in this climate. Their individual firms did, too, even the ones that seemed strong. If the economy kept deteriorating, they would all need bigger capital buffers to finance themselves on reasonable terms and reassure the markets about their resilience.

"Some of you may say this is too much, but each of you may need to raise more, some of you a meaningful amount more, given the likely evolution of the economy," I said. "And if you wait, you will be raising it on substantially less favorable terms."

The two strongest firms in the room were JPMorgan and Wells Fargo. Jamie Dimon understood that in a crisis, banks can never have too much capital, and that JPMorgan would benefit from a healthier system. But Dick Kovacevich of Wells was openly hostile to our offer, even though he had just bought Wachovia and its mess of mortgages.

"Why would I need twenty-five billion dollars more capital?" he asked.

"Because you're not as well capitalized as you think," I replied.

That only seemed to make him angrier. Otherwise, though, the summit went much better than we had feared. The bankers seemed a bit shocked by the force of our actions, but they understood the existential imperative. "This is very cheap capital!" Citi's Vikram Pandit exclaimed. Merrill's John Thain, incredibly, asked for assurances about executive compensation, but his soon-to-be boss, Bank of America's Ken Lewis, scoffed that it was crazy at that moment to be discussing comp—or anything else, for that matter.

"We're all going to do this, so let's not waste time," he said. "Let's cut the BS."

Morgan Stanley's John Mack, hours after his firm was saved by a ten-figure check from a Japanese bank, was the first to sign his term sheet. He knew how hard it was to raise private capital in this market. By early evening, all the other CEOs had signed, too.

Even before we announced the terms, the market reaction was effusive. As news leaked out that we were taking action, the stock market soared more than 11 percent. The S&P 500 had its biggest one-day point increase ever.

We did a formal announcement the next day, then went to meet President Bush. The President was crisp, engaging, and gracious to all of us. He pulled me aside afterward to compliment me, presumably at Hank's request. "I hear you're the smart guy," he said. I didn't think much of Bush's tax cuts, his war in Iraq, or his conservative views on social issues, but I admired how he acted during the crisis. It couldn't have been easy for an ideological Republican to preside over such extraordinary government intervention in private enterprise. Bush was steady and calm, and he deserves great credit for being so supportive of Hank and the rest of us—in contrast to Senator McCain and many other Republicans on the Hill.

For the first time since the Bear rescue, I felt a sense of relief. I still felt numb, exhausted, and apprehensive about the dangers ahead. But we were finally trying to get ahead of the crisis. For weeks, I had been clamoring for us to do more, to take more risk, to provide more help to the financial system. And now we were acting more forcefully. I felt so grateful to Hank and Ben, who had to endure the slings and arrows of public outrage, while I got to stay behind the scenes, occasionally playing the heavy.

I guess I was starting to get a reputation. On Wednesday, Assistant Treasury Secretary David Nason forwarded me an email from a press aide: "CNBC just said that Tim Geithner was Paulson's Luca Brasi!" I wasn't entirely familiar with Don Corleone's savage hit man from *The Godfather,* but I had a feeling I wasn't being compared to a magnificent humanitarian.

"My cultural references are impaired," I joked. "Was he a really sweet guy?"

"Sure, as he killed people, he was quite kind," Nason told me.

THE MARKETS were happy about TARP, but they did not stay happy. The huge rally on Monday was wiped out Wednesday. The S&P 500 had an even worse day than it had after the House initially rejected TARP.

This time, the problem was not stress in the financial system. The measure of fear in interbank lending actually declined that week. Now the problem was stress in the broader economy. The new retail sales report was abysmal, consumer confidence had fallen off a cliff, and various measures of business confidence were hitting new lows. The September jobs report was the worst in over five years: 159,000 jobs lost, which would later be revised to 459,000 jobs lost, the worst in over three decades. Homes weren't being built, and cars weren't being sold. General Motors was so strapped for cash it was delaying payments to suppliers, and its stock price had dropped to the lowest levels since the Korean War. Chrysler's outlook was just as bad. The post-Lehman financial shocks had delivered such a massive blow to confidence that companies of all kinds were cutting jobs and costs and capacity as fast as they could, preparing for a prolonged economic contraction.

This is what we had been talking about when we had warned that Wall Street's problems could damage Main Street.

Meanwhile, the presidential campaign, once expected to be a referendum on a brutal quagmire in Iraq, had become a referendum on a brutal economy. And shortly after we announced the start of TARP, I got a call from my former Treasury colleague Mike Froman, a Citigroup executive who had gone to law school with Barack Obama and was now advising his presidential campaign.

The senator wanted to meet.

• • •

IN FEBRUARY, I had shown up at my polling station at a Larchmont elementary school to vote for Senator Obama. I had forgotten that as a registered independent, I wasn't eligible to vote in the New York Democratic primary. I had been a straight-ticket Democratic voter since the Clinton years, when the Republicans started veering far to my right. It was just my allergy to partisan politics that kept me from becoming a Democrat. And Senator Obama seemed like my kind of candidate—liberal on social issues, moderate on economic issues, pragmatic above all. I had read his memoir, *Dreams from My Father,* and found him appealing and impressive.

I was also impressed by Senator Obama's calm and responsible approach to the crisis, especially compared to Senator McCain's erratic pandering. Senator Obama kept in constant contact with Hank, who had nothing but praise for him. He never distanced himself from TARP, rounding up Democratic votes in Congress, passing up the opportunity to run against the Bush bailouts. Franklin Roosevelt had refused to lift a finger to help the outgoing administration relieve the suffering of the Depression, so he could draw a starker contrast with President Hoover after his own inauguration. Senator Obama did not follow that politically shrewd but costly example. He did whatever he could to help support our efforts to save the economy on President Bush's watch, even though it blurred his message of change.

I had heard about media reports floating my name as a possible Treasury secretary for Senator Obama, which seemed almost as implausible as the media reports floating my name as a possible Treasury secretary for Senator McCain. But I was flattered by his interest, and curious to meet him. On Friday, October 17, I went to see him in his room at the W Hotel in midtown Manhattan, and we talked for an hour. Just three weeks before the election, with the world watching his every move, he seemed totally relaxed.

He began by asking for an update on the crisis. Overall, I felt as upbeat as I had in fourteen months. I finally felt somewhat confident that we could avoid a reprise of the 1930s, but *upbeat* was a relative term.

"We've broken the back of the panic," I said. "But this thing isn't over. It's still terrible, and it's going to be for a long time."

Senator Obama then asked me a few questions about my background, so I described the arc of my childhood in India and Thailand. We discussed an odd family coincidence: When my father was running the Ford Foundation's Asia programs, the foundation had funded the work of Senator Obama's late mother, Ann Dunham, while she built a microfinance program in Indonesia.

Senator Obama asked all the questions, and he didn't reveal much, but we bonded a bit over our shared family tradition of international development work. He seemed genuinely curious, and I felt a lot more comfortable talking about myself than I normally would with someone I had just met. I explained that as cool and enriching as it had been to move around and live apart from my country as a kid, at some point I had decided I wanted to be an American. I had seen the outsized impact the United States had on the world, for better and for worse, and I wanted to be a part of making it better. He seemed to understand that. The senator then cut to the chase: "Tim, I might have to ask you to come to Washington."

"You shouldn't do that," I said. "Let me talk you out of that."

I wasn't being coy. I meant it. I liked my current job and my current life. I gave Senator Obama five reasons why he shouldn't try to make me Treasury secretary.

The first was the most important to me, though obviously less relevant to him. I had promised my family after I uprooted them from Washington that I wouldn't make them move again. They felt comfortable in Larchmont. Elise was a senior in high school, Ben was a freshman, and Carole had a rewarding job as a grief counselor. I didn't want to break my word.

The second reason was that there were better candidates out there.

"Like who?" the senator asked.

Bob Rubin and Larry Summers would be better, I replied. They both had already done the job extremely well. If Senator Obama went to the White House at this scary time—and the polls suggested he would—he'd want the best people around him.

My third reason was that in a period of turmoil and uncertainty, the public would want to see a familiar and reassuring face in charge of the country's finances. I had spent my career in obscurity, and I didn't think of myself as a reassuring presence. I looked young, I had never appeared on TV.

Number four was that at some point, we would solve the financial crisis, and the new president would be left with a slew of other challenges—health care, tax reform, the country's long-term fiscal mess—that had not been my life's work. I suggested that Senator Obama should look for someone with a broader range of experience, not just a crisis manager like me.

I thought the last reason was the one that made me a nonstarter: I had been deeply involved in the crisis response from day one. I was another Mr. Bailout, a political albatross, a vestige of the bad old days before Senator Obama arrived with his hope and change. Hiring me would look like an endorsement of all the unpopular stuff Hank and Ben and I had done.

"I've been up to my neck in this crisis," I said. "You're going to have a hard time separating from these choices if you ask me to work with you."

Senator Obama suggested he wasn't concerned about political appearances, but I said I wouldn't just be politically problematic. I believed in the merits of all that unpopular stuff that I had been part of.

"I'm proud of what we've done," I said. "I'm not going to renounce it or criticize it. And that would make it harder for you to chart a different course."

I liked him, and he seemed to enjoy the meeting, too. David Axelrod, his top political aide, would later joke that the senator and I had an instant "bromance." According to Axelrod, Senator Obama immediately informed his team that I would fit in perfectly; he supposedly told anyone who would listen that I had tried to talk him out of hiring me. The campaign was overwhelmed with jobseekers explaining why they would be perfect in Washington, so I guess my arguments against had a perverse effect.

It was not my intended effect. My reservations were real. And Carole didn't just have reservations; she was opposed. I felt guilty that I was even thinking about relocating again. I had also promised Carole that we would never again live apart, not for anything, and I knew we couldn't move the kids in the middle of the school year. I remember talking through my anxieties with my close friend and former Treasury colleague Josh Steiner, who was helping to run a team working on economic policy ideas for Obama. He listened patiently, then said: "Yeah, but if the president decides you're the best person for the job, are you prepared to say no?"

"Well, he's not going to decide that," I replied.

Over the next couple weeks, I thought about it more. Josh had a point. I did believe citizens have a certain obligation to serve their country if their president asks them to. And I definitely got caught up in the honor and excitement of it all. Obama seemed serious about policy and great at politics. I supported his general call for change, as well as his specific agenda of health care reform, public investments in research and infrastructure, and a more progressive tax code. With the passage of TARP, the main focus of the crisis response had shifted from the Fed to Treasury, and I did think my experience would be helpful to a new president inheriting a financial war. I worried about my weaknesses, but I persuaded myself that as long as I made sure Obama and his team understood them, really understood them, they weren't a good excuse to say no.

On Election Night, I watched the returns at home with my family. We were all ecstatic when Obama was announced the winner and gave his inspiring speech in Grant Park. I wish I could say Carole was so ecstatic that she urged me to follow the President-elect to Washington. She didn't. She hadn't wavered. She already thought I was too absent, too stressed out, sacrificing too much family life. She felt sick about the whole idea.

But I knew I wouldn't be able to say no if President-elect Obama asked.

FORTUNATELY, I had my job at the New York Fed to distract me from the speculation about my next job. Unfortunately, one of my main distractions was AIG, which was still hemorrhaging cash. It was about to announce a devastating $24 billion third-quarter loss. The financial crisis was a tough time to be any financial firm, but it was an impossible time to be a financial firm that provided insurance against the failure of other financial firms and financial instruments. As those firms and instruments lost value, AIG was getting crushed by incessant margin calls, prompting rating agencies to consider new downgrades, which would lead to additional margin calls. The company was once again on the brink of default itself, even after our twelve-figure assistance package.

Default was not an option, not unless we wanted a global stampede that could have made the aftermath of Lehman look relatively mild. But we didn't want to keep throwing money into a bottomless pit. AIG was starting to look like our Vietnam. We spent much of the week of the election trying to design a more lasting rescue plan that would stop the margin spirals and stabilize the company.

We decided Treasury would inject $40 billion in new capital through TARP, while the Fed would restructure our $112.8 billion in earlier support to AIG by creating two complex new Maiden Lane vehicles, similar to the structure used for Bear. We then transferred the mortgage-related paper that was prompting the margin calls into those vehicles. The idea was to help AIG continue to meet its obligations, while roping off the distressed assets that had propelled the company into a doom loop. We hoped this would be a tourniquet to stop the bleeding, rather than another mere transfusion of cash that would need to be followed up by still more transfusions.

The numbers were so large that we decided it was at least worth exploring whether AIG's counterparties would accept voluntary haircuts on their claims. A few cents on the dollar in concessions could have saved taxpayers perhaps $1 billion. But seven of the eight top counterparties flatly rejected anything less than 100 cents on the dollar. We could not force them to accept haircuts without forcing AIG into default. And we couldn't credibly threaten default to try to induce them to accept haircuts voluntarily. We were committing more than $150 billion to AIG to try to avoid a catastrophic default; the counterparties knew we wouldn't jeopardize the entire rescue, not to mention the stability of the global financial system, in a long-shot effort to shave a billion off the total. And even threatening default could have prompted the rating agencies to downgrade AIG, which would have required us to inject even more cash to keep it afloat. So the counterparties were all paid at par.

I thought our no-haircuts strategy was a no-brainer. The whole goal of our interventions was to calm the system. As we had seen with WaMu, which was less than one-third the size of AIG and much less vital to the broader financial system, haircuts send a destabilizing signal that more haircuts are coming, encouraging runs on financial firms. And if the federal government had invalidated AIG's contracts—or abused our regulatory power by muscling its counterparties into "voluntary" concessions—we would have sent a signal that no contracts were safe, even after the U.S. government and the Federal Reserve had gone to extraordinary lengths to save a systemic institution. We also would have dramatically weakened the power of the Columbus Day capital injections and guarantees. And we would have undermined the power of any future emergency assistance.

Nevertheless, our failure to impose haircuts on AIG's counterparties would become Exhibit A for the populist outrage and critique of our crisis response, grist for noisy congressional hearings and moralistic oversight reports. Our critics didn't explain how we could have imposed haircuts—many counterparties weren't even U.S. firms—or why haircuts (or even protracted negotiations over haircuts) wouldn't have produced downgrade and default. They simply found it obscene that our payouts to AIG flowed straight to financial giants such as Goldman Sachs. They didn't have better solutions; they just didn't like ours. We were often vulnerable to that kind of attack, because we rarely had good options. We just tried to choose the least-bad ones.

Goldman Sachs was a particular lightning rod, because Hank and the chairman of my board, Steve Friedman, had both run Goldman, while one of Hank's top aides on AIG issues, Dan Jester, and my markets chief, Bill Dudley, were former Goldman executives. It has become an article of faith in some circles on the left and right that the AIG rescue was *obviously* a backdoor bailout for Goldman. But it wasn't. The post-crisis investigations documented that Goldman's exposure to AIG through the trades in question was basically flat. AIG at one point owed Goldman about $14 billion, so the rescue looked like a windfall, but that was mainly part of Goldman's "matched book," where every dollar of insurance it bought from AIG was matched by a dollar it sold to another firm. So the $14 billion simply passed through Goldman to those other firms. And even if we hadn't stood behind AIG's side of the bargain, Goldman had protected itself against AIG's failure, too.

It's true that some of the firms from which Goldman had purchased that protection, such as Citi, had their own vulnerabilities, and might have struggled to honor their contracts if AIG had defaulted. In that sense, Goldman did benefit from our rescue, as did every bank and investment bank in the world. Default by AIG would have dramatically intensified the pressure on the entire system, bringing us back to the edge of financial Armageddon. And the acute pressures of the financial crisis were already damaging the Main Street economy. In that regard, everyone benefited from our decision to prevent AIG's failure, not just the millions of families and businesses around the world with AIG policies, but everyone with a job, a house, or some savings to lose. That's why we did what we did.

In early November, just before we announced the latest aid to AIG, I flew to Chicago to meet with President-elect Obama. The media were reporting that he was likely to choose either Larry Summers or me as his Treasury secretary. I usually made a point of not reading about myself in the news, but I did see some of the press I was getting during the cabinet speculation. I remember telling my family not to read any of it, because if they believed the good stuff, they might be more inclined to believe the bad stuff, and there would surely be bad stuff.

I had no idea.

In the airport lounge at O'Hare, I ran into Larry, who was, I'm pretty sure, in the process of checking the Intrade odds on Obama's choice for Treasury. It was kind of awkward for both of us. Larry helped launch my career at Treasury, catapulting me from noisy scribe to a series of increasingly senior positions. He had helped get me the New York Fed job, too. We were friends; we played tennis every spring with some former Treasury colleagues at the Bollettieri academy in

Florida. We had not always agreed on policy; we had fought about all sorts of things when he was my boss, and we had privately argued about much of my work during the current crisis. But now we were both candidates for a job that Larry had already done with distinction, at a time when he was eager to return to the public sphere. At the airport, I told Larry I had not sought the job and had urged Obama to choose him as secretary, which didn't really make the situation less awkward.

Obama met with Larry first, then me. The President-elect looked less relaxed than he had looked three weeks earlier in New York. He asked tougher questions, too. I remember thinking: Hey, I tried to talk you out of this. Why are you pushing me to talk you into this? At one point, he told me Rubin had said I wasn't very articulate, and asked me to respond.

"It's true," I said. "And it's worse than you think."

He also asked what I would do about housing. Three-quarters of a million homes had entered the foreclosure process in the third quarter, and with more homeowners starting to lose their jobs, delinquencies were rising fast. Fannie Mae had just announced a startling $29 billion third-quarter loss. There was intense political pressure for the government to match its largesse for banks with some largesse for ordinary homeowners. But that hadn't been my focus at the Fed.

"I don't know what I would do," I said. "But I'm sure we can do more than we're doing now."

The President-elect also asked me what I thought of Larry. I told him about Henry Kissinger's famous line that Larry should have a permanent White House office in charge of knocking down dumb ideas—a line that had first become public after I told it to a reporter years earlier. It's no secret that Larry is brilliant, but until you've been carved up by his intellectual scalpel, it's hard to grasp just how brilliant. There is no one better at exposing the flaws in an argument. I tried to convey to the President-elect that Larry was a uniquely compelling talent.

I returned to the airport after the interview. When I was in the security line, I got a call from Rahm Emanuel, the President-elect's new chief of staff. He wanted to know if I'd accept Treasury if offered, but also if I'd be willing to run the National Economic Council if I wasn't named Treasury secretary. I said I'd be willing to do Treasury, but not the NEC. The NEC director is usually the president's chief economic adviser, with an opportunity to influence an even broader array of issues than the Treasury secretary. But it is more about framing and coordinating policy than making or executing decisions. I didn't think it would make sense to abandon my New York Fed colleagues during the crisis to take a role like that. At Treasury, I would be more directly responsible for finishing what we had started, and then trying to fix the broken financial system.

A week later the President-elect called to ask if I'd be willing to work with Larry if he ran the NEC. I immediately said I would, even though I knew it would mean more awkwardness. Some of our former colleagues thought the idea of Larry at the NEC bordered on lunacy. It was hard to imagine a former Treasury secretary in an advisory role. And the NEC director is supposed to be an honest broker, making sure the president is exposed to diverse views, while Larry wasn't known for sublimating his own views. But he was the smartest economist I knew. And I thought Larry's imperious reputation was overstated; he's evidence-based, and he enjoys being challenged. In any case, I knew that if I became Treasury secretary, I'd be calling Larry no matter what he was doing. I valued his advice, and we would need all the talent we could get.

A few days later, while I was in the car heading home from work, the President-elect called to ask me to be his Treasury secretary. Hank had told me that when President Bush offered him the job, he had a list of carefully considered conditions, and had even given me his list as a model. I told the President-elect I didn't have any conditions. But I did have two things I cared about.

"One is that I want to make sure you know what you're getting with me," I said.

This was just reinforcement of our initial meeting in New York. I wanted to marinate him once more in my downsides: my lack of gray hair and gravitas, my lack of economic policy experience beyond financial and international issues, and most of all my unwillingness to distance myself from our financial rescue strategy. The President-elect said he understood all that.

"The second thing is I want to make sure you want a strong Treasury," I said.

I wasn't that worried about getting micromanaged, partly because I had a good feeling about my relationship with Obama, partly because I knew that after living the crisis I'd have a big knowledge advantage over my new colleagues. Still, I wanted to make sure that I wouldn't be expected to dance to the inclinations of the West Wing staff, although of course I didn't put it that way. The President-elect was very reassuring about my role, and he would more than keep his word.

We had guests at the house that night, so I couldn't tell Carole the news right away when I walked in the door. But she saw it in my eyes. I could tell she wasn't happy. I was ambivalent, too. My dread about the economy—as well as my guilt about what I was doing to my family—was stronger than my pride and excitement.

My impending nomination was leaked to the press at 3 p.m. on Friday, November 21, and the stock market promptly jumped 6.5 percent in the last hour of trading. It was tempting to see that as a flattering vote of confidence that the new president would succeed in preventing a second Great Depression, but I knew that praise from markets could be fleeting, and was not always evidence of good policy. Some simply viewed my appointment as a signal that we were likely to continue to provide government assistance to the financial system. As a matter of fact, when I got the call from Chicago, we were in the midst of engineering yet another rescue.

• • •

THIS TIME, the domino in danger was Citigroup, a behemoth three times the size of Lehman Brothers and far more integral to the functioning of global markets.

Citi was still a mess, choking on mortgages on and off its balance sheet, with a highly vulnerable funding base compared to other major U.S. banks. Its stock price briefly rebounded after its TARP capital injection, but the glow wore off quickly as its losses kept mounting. Its problems intensified on November 12, when Hank announced that the Bush Treasury would not be purchasing any illiquid assets after all. I agreed with Hank's decision, but the announcement seemed unnecessary, sucking hope out of the markets at a fragile time, pushing down asset prices and hurting confidence in financial firms at a moment when Citi looked like the weakest link. A week later, the off-balance-sheet SIVs that got Citi in trouble in the fall of 2007 faced such daunting losses that the company had to bring the rest of them back onto its balance sheet, spooking the markets yet again. Its stock price dropped below $4, down 93 percent from its 2006 peak.

Hank told me he felt responsible, but I told him this wasn't on him. There was plenty of blame to go around, some of it mine. Citi's many regulators, including the New York Fed, had failed to save Citi from itself during the boom. We had recognized its vulnerabilities too late. What mattered now was making sure it didn't implode and crater the financial system.

"We've got to make it clear we're standing behind Citi," I said on a November 20 conference call with Hank, Ben, Sheila, and the OCC's John Dugan.

The next day, two hours after the news of my nomination leaked, Ben forwarded me a document titled "Potential Actions to Support or Resolve Citigroup," which discussed possibilities such as receivership or bankruptcy. But we had no intention of letting that happen. The system couldn't have handled the sudden collapse of a $2 trillion institution that provided much of the world's financial plumbing. On a conference call Saturday morning, Hank nearly had a fit when Sheila suggested the FDIC could force Citi into receivership without melting down the system.

"If Citi isn't systemic, I don't know what is!" he replied.

Citi needed a solution that weekend, and because of my pending appointment, I decided to remove myself from the deliberations about what to do. The rescue package that the Treasury, the Fed, and the FDIC negotiated did what was needed to prevent disaster for the moment. It shored up Citi's thin capital buffer, injecting another $20 billion from TARP while ensuring more upside for taxpayers. It also reduced Citi's exposure to catastrophic tail risk by putting a government-backed ring fence around $306 billion of its assets. Citi would absorb the first $39.5 billion in losses on those assets, plus 10 percent of any losses above that, but Treasury would take the next $5 billion in the government's portion of losses through TARP, the FDIC the next $10 billion after that, and the Fed would absorb the rest in a worst-case scenario.

The markets responded well. On Monday, Citi's stock rose 58 percent, while its credit default swaps dropped by half. But I had no confidence that Citi was out of danger. I was in Chicago that morning for the official rollout of Obama's economic team, and Ned Kelly, a top Citi executive, called while I was on my way to the event. I asked him how the firm intended to turn itself around.

"I haven't the foggiest idea," Kelly said.

Larry and I met with the President-elect before the event at the Chicago Hilton, along with Christina Romer, who would lead his Council of Economic Advisers, and Melody Barnes, who would run his Domestic Policy Council. When Obama asked about the Citi rescue, I didn't want to go into the details of the whole complex mess. But Larry began explaining the capital injections, the ring fence, and other features he must have gleaned from our press release. He had nice things to say about our plan, but I knew more about it, and I knew it was nothing to get excited about.

"The details don't matter," I said. "It's duct tape and string."

As we prepared to face the cameras, I got the sense that Larry, Christy, and Melody were looking forward to making brief statements, and there was even talk of having us answer questions. I made it clear I thought that was nuts. The theme of the event was supposed to be reviving the economy, not bailing out the banks. That would change the moment I opened my mouth in front of the media.

"If you have me up there talking in the middle of this mess with Citi, the whole press conference will be about Citi and TARP," I told Rahm. "You don't want that."

He took my advice. The President-elect introduced me that day as "the chief economic spokesman for my administration," but I didn't speak. I stood silently in the background, a more familiar and comfortable role for me.

I knew I wouldn't have that luxury for long.

As I prepared to leave the New York Fed, it was hard to fathom how much we had done since the crisis began, and how much the financial world had changed.

The Fed had overseen an aggressive easing of monetary policy, reducing our target interest rate from 5.25 percent in September 2007 to as close as it can go to zero in December 2008. Ben had also launched a "quantitative easing" program, buying bonds to provide further monetary stimulus for the economy. We had expanded the Fed's balance sheet from $870 billion to $2.2 trillion with our new credit and liquidity programs, extending our lending far beyond the U.S. commercial banking system, financing a broad range of collateral for a broad array of nonbanks. We were lending hundreds of billions of dollars to the financial system every day, supporting the tri-party repo market and backstopping the commercial paper market, while the Treasury was guaranteeing money market funds. The Fed had become a true lender of last resort for the world, providing unlimited foreign exchange swaps to major central banks, even lending dollars to emerging markets in Brazil, Mexico, South Korea, and Singapore.

We had also used our authorities in all kinds of new ways to rescue failing financial firms, arrange shotgun financial marriages, and avoid cascading waves of financial failures. We had avoided an early disintegration of short-term funding by convincing Bank of New York Mellon to unwind Countrywide's repo book. We had helped guide a collapsing Bear Stearns into the arms of JPMorgan, taking on part of its risky mortgage portfolio. The Bush administration had placed Fannie Mae and Freddie Mac into conservatorship, injecting $200 billion in capital, ensuring they could help offset the disappearance of private mortgage credit. We had helped set up Bank of America's takeover of Merrill Lynch, JPMorgan's takeover of Washington Mutual, and Wells Fargo's takeover of Wachovia—all risky and messy deals, but all preferable to government takeovers or uncontrolled failures. We had rescued and re-rescued AIG. And we had ended the era of unregulated investment banks, letting Goldman Sachs and Morgan Stanley become bank holding companies while forcing them to raise capital.

With the passage of TARP, we hoped to move from ad hoc emergency interventions to a more coordinated approach. We persuaded the FDIC to provide powerful guarantees for the banking system, and we began providing huge infusions of new capital for vulnerable institutions. But we still had to intervene with more aid to prevent Citigroup's demise. And Hank, Ben, and Sheila soon had to do a similar deal for Bank of America, because Merrill Lynch was sinking again; its estimated fourth-quarter losses soared from $5 billion to $12 billion in a month, and Ken Lewis was threatening to abandon the merger. I did not participate in these negotiations, but Hank and Ben kept me in the loop, and I fully supported their efforts to make sure the merger went through and Merrill didn't become another Lehman.

It had been a brutal year. Of the twenty-five largest financial institutions at the start of 2008, thirteen either failed (Lehman, WaMu), received government help to avoid failure (Fannie, Freddie, AIG, Citi,

BofA), merged to avoid failure (Countrywide, Bear, Merrill, Wachovia), or transformed their business structure to avoid failure (Morgan Stanley, Goldman). The stock market dropped more than 40 percent from its 2007 peak. We did an extraordinary amount of unprecedented stuff, and we successfully slowed the run on the core of the banking system. But when I looked at the broader economic issues I would face at Treasury, everything else was still getting worse. The contagion had spread far beyond finance to the cars, homes, malls, and factories that made up the everyday American experience. No matter how much money the Fed pumped into the financial system, no matter how low it reduced interest rates, its efforts to strengthen growth were being undermined by the overhang of excessive borrowing that triggered the crisis and by a critically damaged financial system. Low rates didn't matter much when few Americans wanted to borrow and few banks wanted to lend.

We had slipped into an economic black hole. The loss of wealth from the declines in stock and home prices, much larger than the loss of wealth before the Depression, was depressing demand and confidence. The private sector was pulling back in preparation for a Depression-like scenario, which also depressed demand and confidence. Layoffs and foreclosures left families too broke and scared to spend, which again meant less demand and confidence, more layoffs and foreclosures.

Lehman, WaMu, and the trauma of the fall had been a financial earthquake, and now the economic tsunami was reaching the shore. The Labor Department reported a horrific 533,000 jobs lost in November, which would later be revised to 775,000, the worst month since World War II. Unemployment rose to 6.7 percent. Prices were falling at the fastest rate since the Depression, a reflection of vanishing demand. General Motors and Chrysler were hurtling toward bankruptcy. Again with my encouragement and support, Hank agreed to lend them $17.4 billion from TARP to tide them over until the new administration.

The President-elect would be inheriting an economy in absolute free fall, suffering not from a sudden loss of its ability to produce things, but from an acute shortfall of demand. And even though the panic in the markets had subsided a bit, the financial system was still broken. Our credit channels were frozen. Months of zigzags had left the world unsure whether the U.S. government was willing and able to prevent additional defaults by major institutions. And this was not a stable state. As the recession intensified, the price of securities would keep falling, increasing fears about the solvency of financial institutions.

"With the recent sharp deterioration in the already weak economic outlook, there is considerable potential for a severe adverse feedback loop between economic activity and the stability of the financial system," Larry and I wrote in an early policy memo to the President-elect. "Despite the dramatic actions already undertaken to strengthen our financial institutions and improve the functioning of our financial markets, nearly every segment of our financial system remains under extraordinary strain."

My brief optimism that we would avoid a reprise of the 1930s was gone. During this limbo period I went to see Ben and told him he needed to develop a plan for catastrophe. He needed someone else thinking about worst-case scenarios day and night, because I was already halfway out the door.

"I have a plan for catastrophe," Ben said with a smile. "My plan is to call you."

That was touching, but not comforting. In many ways, I felt like it was already all on me—the financial system, the economy, everything. And I didn't have a plan yet, either.

SEVEN

Into the Fire

On a conference call early in the transition, President-elect Obama wanted to discuss what he should try to accomplish in his first term. I responded first.

"Your accomplishment is going to be preventing a second Great Depression," I said.

After campaigning for two years on an expansive agenda of change, that was not what the President-elect wanted to hear.

"That's not enough for me," he shot back. "I'm not going to be defined by what I've prevented."

He wanted to reform health care, education, and the financial system that had dragged us into this mess. He wanted to reduce our dependence on foreign oil and other carbon-emitting fossil fuels. He wanted to give the poor and the middle class some tax relief while asking the wealthy to pay a bit more. I supported all those priorities, but during the worst economic meltdown in seventy-five years, I didn't think they could be our top priorities.

"If you don't prevent a depression, you won't be able to do anything else," I said.

"I know. But it's not enough," the President-elect repeated.

The conversation soon turned to the design of his fiscal stimulus package, an effort to pour hundreds of billions of public dollars into the economy to offset the collapse of private demand. The Recovery Act's temporary tax cuts and government spending would follow the Keynesian playbook for stimulating short-term economic activity and creating jobs during a downturn. At the same time, the President-elect wanted to use the stimulus to promote his long-term agenda, funding priorities such as clean energy, scientific research, and middle-class tax cuts. He kept asking us whether the Recovery Act ought to focus on a single transformative initiative, like a "smart electric grid" that could be a twenty-first-century analog of the interstate highways, or whether we should use it to usher in a variety of reforms and investments.

His ambition was compelling. Why not try to make the stimulus capture the imagination? Investing in renewable energy and scientific research would create jobs for solar installers and lab assistants in the near term, while laying a foundation for stronger growth in the future. Obama wasn't naïve about Washington; he just wanted to use his post-election political capital to do big things. He intended to expand the limits of what was possible, rather than shrink his policy ambitions to fit the existing political constraints. As Rahm said, a crisis would be a terrible thing to waste.

Still, the visionary brainstorming made me a bit uneasy. I wanted him to be able to do big things, too, but my immediate ambitions were narrower, dominated by the imperatives of the crisis. We needed to design a strategy to fix the broken financial system and a large fiscal stimulus package to arrest the economic free fall. We had to figure out a way to save the dying U.S. auto industry in order to prevent a regional depression in the industrial Midwest. We had to devise a plan to deal with the escalating housing crisis in order to protect millions of families at risk of foreclosure. At a time when the federal deficit was soaring past $1 trillion for the first time, we would also have to send Congress a budget laying out our tax and spending priorities, and demonstrating how we intended to limit the red ink once the economy recovered. Presidential transitions are usually a confused mess of jockeying for jobs and groping for ideas, but this one would be consumed by the economic emergency.

Larry and I would share responsibility for these challenges, though he would take the lead on the fiscal stimulus and I would carry most of the burden on the financial rescue. We asked the private equity investor Steve Rattner to lead a team dealing with the auto industry; he would work with Ron Bloom, an investment banker with roots in the labor movement. Peter Orszag, who would run the White House Office of Management and Budget, took the lead on budget matters. Christy Romer, the incoming head of the Council of Economic Advisers, would provide advice on all economic policy issues. And we had a team of experts helping us on housing.

The pace was frantic, the pressure overwhelming. I was worried the world was coming to an end and not sure we could stop it. I wasn't wrapped up in the spirit of limitless possibility and new beginnings that had driven the Obama campaign; I felt none of the spark and excitement that pervaded the halls of the transition headquarters. I remember one day, during the transition, the incoming cabinet and White House staff had to pose for portraits by the celebrity photographer Annie Leibovitz. All I could think was: What a weird and preening thing for us to do while the world is burning.

I missed Carole and the kids. I was flying up to New York to see them on the weekends, when I could, but even when I was with them, I wasn't really with them; I was lost in strategy about the crisis, or attached to a phone or two. In Washington, I stayed with my former Dartmouth classmate and Treasury colleague Dan Zelikow, who gave me refuge in a third-floor bedroom in his townhouse until the school year was over and my family could move down. I left for work so early and came home so late that I rarely saw Dan or his family, either. He later said I was like a ghost.

I spent my days in a spartan office on the eighth floor of the

Obama transition team's cramped, nondescript headquarters in downtown Washington, mostly attending marathon meetings with Larry and the economic team, some more productive than others. We endured so many PowerPoint presentations I began complaining about Death by Deck. There was a pretty good spirit of cooperation, but also some typical tensions over turf and power and who got to attend which meetings. Orszag, a former Clinton White House economist who had been running the Congressional Budget Office, was trying to establish early dominance over fiscal policy, signaling to Larry that there would be only one budget director. Romer, a newcomer to government and to a group that knew one another from the Clinton years, was trying to establish her credibility with the President-elect, and was understandably wary of being eclipsed by Larry.

I remember Larry asking me after one three-hour Recovery Act meeting in a windowless conference room how I thought it had gone.

"I guess it was pretty good," I told him. "I mean, you did ninety percent of the talking, but you were pretty interesting."

I was just teasing Larry, but we had some tensions, too, mostly over the financial rescue. Larry's mantra in those days was "discontinuity," the importance of distinguishing the Obama response from the pre-Obama response. Signaling a break with the past made sense politically, given how much America hated TARP, not to mention the yearning for change after the Bush years. It also made sense legislatively, since we had obligated almost all of the first $350 billion and needed Congress to authorize the second tranche. But I didn't like Larry's frequent derision of Hank and Ben; I was protective of them, and of course implicated in virtually everything they had done. One of Larry's memos to Obama was full of digs at "the mistakes of the past year and a half," the "erratic" and "ineffective" crisis response, and "the absence of any meaningful communication about objectives." Those critiques weren't entirely wrong, but Larry hadn't been there, and I didn't think he had earned the right to second-guess with that degree of confidence.

Larry was trying to respond to dual pressures: the imperative to fix what was broken and reduce the political risk for a new president coming fresh to the mess. I didn't share his confidence that we could fashion a crisis response that was both effective and politically popular. I saw former Mexican President Zedillo in Washington early in the transition, and he reminded me: "No matter what you do, no matter how you do it, the people are going to hate it." I understood the instinct to try to indulge the public's Old Testament cravings, but there was no way a few showy populist head fakes—guidelines pushing TARP banks to lend more or pay executives less—would make America happy about bailouts. And a genuinely populist approach to the crisis—punitive conditions that would demonstrate toughness at the expense of systemic stability—would violate the Hippocratic oath to do no harm, costing the taxpayers more in the end. The people would hate that, too. And they would really hate a depression. So I didn't care much about discontinuity. In fact, one of our first decisions was whether to replace Sheila Bair at FDIC and John Dugan at OCC, and we opted for continuity. Despite my reservations about Sheila and liberal complaints that Dugan was too close to the banks, I recommended that we ask both to stay on, and we did.

Our obligation was not to be different for the sake of being different, but to clean up the mess.

THE PRESIDENT-ELECT met with his senior advisers in Chicago on December 16, a four-hour meeting that would later attain mythic status as the opening scene of the Obama administration. Christy Romer, a noted scholar of the Great Depression, began with an overview of an economy careening toward another one.

"Mr. President-elect," she famously said, "this is your holy-shit moment."

If the main theme that day was the mess we were about to inherit, the main topic was the Recovery Act. We all felt the stimulus should be as big as possible and passed as soon as possible. Governments always face political pressure to tighten their belts during crises, be-cause families and businesses are tightening theirs. But for countries that can afford to borrow, austerity in a crisis is a dangerously mis-guided approach. Keynes recognized this "paradox of thrift," the idea that saving by individuals, considered virtuous in normal times, can cripple society's demand for goods and services during a downturn if everyone pulls back at once. One family's spending is another family's income; the less people spend, the less people earn, and the less people earn, the less they have to spend. That's when government needs to pump money into the economy to revive demand and restore confi-dence, even though politically, deficit spending can seem as profligate and counterintuitive in tough times as financial rescues.

I did not have strong convictions about the Recovery Act's exact contents. I was fine with well-targeted tax cuts, which can quickly get money into people's pockets and the broader economy. I was also fine with public works projects, which are slower but pack more eco-nomic punch. Direct aid to the unemployed and other victims of the recession would be fast and powerful, since they would be likely to spend the money right away. I was leery of the varied demands from congressional Democrats—as well as some members of the President-elect's staff—who wanted to plus up their favorite programs after eight years in the wilderness. But we didn't have time for protracted nego-tiations to optimize the package. I thought we should get as much as we could, as quickly as we could. The economic team seemed to agree on the big picture, so I didn't get too involved in the substantive details or the legislative strategy.

My focus was the financial system. In my part of the briefing for President-elect Obama, I warned that credit was still frozen and many major firms were still in danger. The system was broken, and if we couldn't fix it, the economy wouldn't recover no matter how much we spent on stimulus. I told the President-elect that we'd need to do more to recapitalize the banking sector, revive the flow of credit, and reassure the markets there would be no more Lehman-style fiascos.

I also discussed our early ideas for financial reform, pointing out that there was some tension between our long-term goals for the system, such as stricter limits on leverage, and our immediate crisis-fighting priorities, such as slowing down the deleveraging process. Eventually, we'd want financial firms to take fewer risks, but in this time of intense fear, we wanted them to take more risks in lending rather than pull back their credit. The financial system needed a version of Saint Augustine's plea: Lord, give me chastity, but not yet.

If the slow burn leading up to Bear Stearns had been phase one of the crisis, and the panic of Lehman followed by the emergency programs of the fall had been phase two, we were now entering a third phase, where the recession was accelerating, and the broader economy and the financial system were dragging each other down. I didn't lay out a new strategy during that Chicago briefing, because I was still working through a variety of ideas with Lee Sachs, Meg McConnell, and a talented young investor from the Blackstone private equity firm named Matt Kabaker. What I mostly tried to convey to the President-elect was that the situation remained terrible, and that we would have to do some terribly unpopular things, because a lot of firms that didn't deserve saving still needed to be saved.

Austan Goolsbee, a University of Chicago economist who had advised Obama ever since his original Senate campaign, then outlined our thinking on housing. It was a brutally complicated problem, affecting the profligate along with the merely unfortunate, and we felt intense pressure to do something big. There had been three million foreclosure filings in 2008, and, so far, federal efforts to ease the crisis had been limited in ambition and impact. One congressionally designed program known as Hope for Homeowners, an effort to reduce the mortgage debt of families in distress, had attracted only 312 applicants nationwide. And the futures markets suggested real estate prices still had a long way to sink, which meant a lot more suffering ahead—not just for speculators who had assumed the boom would never end and conspicuous consumers who had bought bigger houses than they could afford, but for hardworking homeowners who were underwater through absolutely no fault of their own.

I was no housing expert, but, again, my bias was to do the most aggressive interventions that were sensible and feasible. We had a team of talented and experienced progressives working on housing—including Michael Barr, a University of Michigan law professor who would become one of my assistant Treasury secretaries; Diana Farrell, a McKinsey director who would become one of Larry's deputies; and Shaun Donovan, who had run New York City's housing programs and would become secretary for Housing and Urban Development—but there were no easy solutions.

We looked carefully at all the grand plans floating around for universal mortgage refinancing or widespread principal reductions, but even if there had been some way to get them through Congress, we didn't think any of them would be a fair or economically effective use of taxpayer resources. Too much of the assistance would go to people who didn't need it, and the economic bang for the buck would be much less powerful than other stimulus alternatives, such as funds for infrastructure projects or preventing layoffs of teachers and first responders. The housing team had come up with a more targeted mortgage modification plan that would give lenders incentives to help at-risk borrowers (but not borrowers who could afford their mortgages or borrowers likely to default no matter what) by reducing monthly payments (but not overall principal amounts) in order to prevent some (but not all) foreclosures. We thought that could be done with $50 billion in TARP money, with the contributions of Fannie, Freddie, and the private sector multiplying that amount.

Orszag then laid out the harrowing budget situation. Tax revenues were drying up, automatic spending on safety-net programs such as food stamps and unemployment insurance was rising, and the 2009 deficit would exceed 9 percent of GDP. That wouldn't even include the cost of our stimulus plan. And our long-term budget deficits, driven in large part by rising health care costs, were completely unsustainable.

I stayed out of most of our arguments over specific programs, but I did push strongly for long-term discipline in our overall budget strategy—essentially, a fiscal version of Saint Augustine's chastity-but-not-yet prayer. I fully supported the Keynesian imperative of increasing short-term deficits to offset the cataclysmic fall in private demand, but I thought we had to reassure the markets that the stimulus would be temporary, that we would dial back deficits once the crisis passed, that we weren't drunken sailors. I argued for a credible medium-term plan to cut deficits to 3 percent of GDP, the level where our overall debt burden would stop rising as a share of the economy. Peter and Larry agreed. We got some pushback from Christy, Austan, and the most liberal member of our team, Jared Bernstein, Vice President Biden's chief economist. They worried about reining in President Obama's agenda before he even got to Washington. But the President-elect took our side. He had been critical of President Bush for putting expensive tax cuts and new spending on the national credit card, and he was serious about change.

I thought the President-elect seemed substantive, realistic, and comfortably in command. I liked his focus on getting the policy right first and worrying about the politics later; his pragmatic, whatever-works approach; his calm, no-drama attitude. But I didn't leave that meeting with much of the yes-we-can enthusiasm so prevalent in Obamaworld in those days. I felt weary and dark. It seemed like I was always sucking the hope out of the air in our meetings, explaining why the awesome new ideas weren't that awesome, and how the storm we were sailing into was even worse than we thought.

And I had my own brewing storm to deal with.

• • •

THE DAY after my nomination had leaked in late November, I got a call from Les Samuels, an assistant Treasury secretary for tax policy during the Rubin era. He was helping the Obama transition team with vetting, and he said he had a few questions about my tax returns.

He didn't sound too worried. I had made some careless mistakes, but they were innocent mistakes; I had disclosed them all to the campaign's vetting team in early November, and Samuels thought my accountants should have caught them. The Senate had not rejected a nominee for Treasury secretary since 1844, and during an epic financial crisis it seemed unthinkable. But Mark Patterson, a former Senate staffer who coordinated Obama's confirmations, told me afterward that the transition team had been instantly worried. The Senate Finance Committee, under Chairman Max Baucus and Republican ranking member Chuck Grassley, was known for putting tax records under the microscope; a nominee to run Treasury, which oversees the IRS, would be sure to get extra scrutiny. And in the partisan battlefield of modern Washington, there's no such thing as an innocent mistake. Patterson actually suggested to top transition officials that the President-elect ought to switch the jobs of Larry and me, so that I wouldn't have to face the Senate. He was told that unfortunately, that horse was already out of the barn.

My main problem involved unpaid payroll taxes from my time at the International Monetary Fund, a problem I thought I had already dealt with. American employees of the IMF had a complicated tax status—we were treated almost as if we were self-employed—and I screwed it up the whole time I was there. The IMF didn't withhold income taxes or payroll taxes, and its employees received bare-bones W-2 forms that didn't indicate that our wages were subject to payroll taxes. I paid my income taxes every quarter, but not my payroll taxes. After preparing my own returns for 2001 and 2002, I had accountants prepare my returns in 2003 and 2004, but they never corrected my error. In 2006, the IRS had audited me, and I had paid $17,230 in back taxes and interest, but I did not have to pay any penalties. My mistake was so common that the IRS announced a general settlement for IMF employees in my situation later that year.

The vetters also noticed that my back payments to the IRS had covered only my 2003 and 2004 returns. The IRS hadn't charged me for 2001 and 2002, because the statute of limitations had expired. I had simply paid what they asked. I hadn't stopped to think about whether I should pay for the prior years, another mistake. Samuels thought I should pay back taxes and interest for those earlier years, to go beyond mere letter-of-the-law compliance, and I agreed. I had my returns amended immediately, and wrote the IRS another check for $25,970 the day my nomination was announced.

On December 19, before my tax problems became public, I visited a Senate office building to answer questions from the finance committee's extremely thorough staff. I explained how I made my mistakes. I said they were dumb but honest mistakes. But the lead questioner, an IRS manager on detail to the committee, wasn't buying it. She suggested there was no way I could have missed the payroll tax problem, as if the only possible explanation was that I was venal, deliberately trying to evade taxes. I pointed out that my accountants had missed the problem, too.

"You should sue your accountants," said one of Senator Grassley's aides.

He sounded almost sympathetic. But the general tenor of the meeting was distrust bordering on contempt. One of "the Grassleys," as his staff was known, pointed out that there was no statute of limitations for fraud, prompting Patterson to ask if he was seriously accusing me of fraud. He just glared. Grassley's team grilled me relentlessly about the immigration status of a Brazilian woman who had cleaned our house once a week for a year. We had made sure when we hired her that she was a legal resident with a valid work permit, and we had paid our share of her payroll taxes. Her permit had expired a few months before she left us, and the Grassleys hammered me about that, but we would later prove that she had applied for the necessary paperwork and became a permanent U.S. resident a short time later.

It was my own screw-ups that made the inquisition possible, and I felt sick that I had put the President-elect in this position. Still, the IRS would soon send me a letter informing me that I wasn't liable for the 2001 and 2002 taxes I had just voluntarily paid, and explaining that I was entitled to apply for a refund. I decided not to avail myself of that particular privilege.

Grassley later admitted to another nominee that he wouldn't be able to pass his own committee's tax vetting. Another Republican senator privately commiserated with me about the hazing ritual.

"No one up here could withstand a tenth of this scrutiny," he said.

THE COMMITTEE released my tax information on January 13, 2009, and the reaction was as unpleasant as we expected. Jay Leno compared me to the actor Wesley Snipes, who was in jail on tax charges, and mocked me for copping to an honest mistake. "So the guy who's going to be in charge of the IRS is not a criminal," Leno quipped. "Phew, just incompetent." A relatively favorable *New York Times* story on my travails began: "If Timothy F. Geithner were a bank, he might well be considered 'too big to fail.'" A Pew poll had just found that only 1 percent of Americans knew who I was, so this would be my introduction to the public.

I met with the Senate Finance Committee to apologize and explain, but many of the Republicans were skeptical and derisive. One exception was Orrin Hatch of Utah, who promptly told the press he believed me and supported me. I don't know why he went out on that limb, but I was grateful. Another Republican privately told me not to take his opposition personally; it was just payback for Democratic opposition to President Bush's nominees. Yet another told me he would back me if I truly needed his vote, but otherwise he would oppose me to avoid looking Obama-friendly and potentially attracting a primary opponent.

Traditionally, Treasury secretaries had enjoyed a fair amount of bipartisan support. It worried me that my credibility was already under attack, when I was about to become the public face of our past and future rescues. I knew that any time I weighed in on tax policy I'd create a punch line for late-night comics. And it hurt to have my motives questioned. My daughter, Elise, was taking my new infamy especially hard; she's so protective of me, and took every slight personally. My mother ached over bad stories about me, too. For Carole, it was torture. The committee staff accused her of lying about our housekeeper, which was absurd, and she was furious and frustrated that she couldn't defend herself or me in public. She told me she wished she hadn't been so careful to hire legal workers over the years; otherwise, I could have been disqualified from my position. Ben said less, as teenage boys tend to do, but I knew this was tough on him, too.

As the frenzy swirled, I went to see Baucus and Grassley to ask if I would have their support. "If I don't have your confidence," I said, "I'm not sure I can do this job effectively." Baucus was critical but supportive. Grassley remained noncommittal. As Patterson said, even Republicans without real objections to me had political incentives to let me twist in the wind.

"They're going to wait and see how this plays out," Patterson said.

Around that time, I ran into David Axelrod in a narrow hallway in the transition office and suggested that it might make sense to withdraw my nomination to protect the President-elect.

"Axe, I don't want to be a burden," I said. "If you guys decide you want to go a different direction, I'll be OK with that."

"No, we're sticking with you," he replied.

I made a similar offer to Rahm. He was similarly unmoved, although I'm sure he and Axelrod thought about whether it might make sense to pull the plug.

"You're going to be fine," Rahm said. "They just want to cut you and make you bleed."

I tried not to wallow too much in the furor. I remember one day Larry, who had endured his share of public controversies, stuck his head into my office to say hey, you're handling this well. He said I "presented a good sense of equanimity," a nice and very Larry way to put it. But my confirmation was a real drain on my time and mental energy. I had constant meetings with lawyers and accountants, hearing-prep sessions with a "murder board" of role-playing colleagues, plus a series of obligatory courtesy calls with senators. I remember one awkward meeting with Senator Bunning, who had repeatedly denounced our crisis response as socialism. We talked about baseball—he was a Hall of Fame pitcher—and mused about moral hazard, but we both knew we weren't going to bridge our differences.

I was also devoting a lot of time to recruiting. I was going into the world's most powerful finance ministry at the most perilous time in generations, and Treasury was very thin. The office most critical to the financial rescue had only a handful of career civil servants, compared to about two hundred in the international division where I had first worked. And Treasury's top twenty leadership positions all required Senate confirmation.

Early on, those senior jobs were hard to fill. Jack Lew, President Clinton's former budget director, initially seemed interested in being my deputy, but changed his mind after Secretary of State Hillary Clinton asked him to be her deputy. Tom Nides, a Morgan Stanley executive, seemed willing to come help me run the department, but he decided to stay in New York until his firm was in better shape. There was plenty of interest in joining the administration, but it was hard to find candidates with financial experience who were confirmable, given the prevailing fever of loathing for the financial sector. And it seemed like half the candidates we considered for Senate-confirmed positions failed our internal vet because of their own tax issues, which would have been ironic if it hadn't been so debilitating.

I did find some great people right away for jobs that didn't require Senate confirmation. Mark Patterson, who guided me through my own confirmation, agreed to be my chief of staff. After spending most of his career as a staffer for Democratic senators, he had worked for a few years as a Washington hand for Goldman Sachs, which I knew would raise some eyebrows, but I didn't care, because he was so outstanding. Patterson would set the tone for my hiring motto at Treasury: *No jerks, no peacocks, no whiners.* Lee Sachs, an incredibly thoughtful and knowledgeable financial wizard, would be my counselor on all financial market issues, with Matt Kabaker as his deputy. Gene Sperling, the policy savant who had run the National Economic Council during Clinton's second term, also agreed to be my counselor. Gene would take the lead on tax and budget issues, while helping me navigate the intersection of policy and politics in Washington. Meg McConnell also helped out during those critical early days, but she hated Washington's political and bureaucratic games, so she would return to the New York Fed after a few months.

Because of my tax issues, my own confirmation hearing was delayed, which meant the new president would start his job without an appointed Treasury secretary in place to help him navigate the crisis. I felt like I had already let him down. But he called me one night—after I had fallen asleep—to tell me to hang in there, the controversy would pass. I don't know what I had done to earn his confidence, but he made a point of trying to bolster mine.

"I don't care about this stuff," he said. "You're my guy."

ON INAUGURATION DAY, the Obamas and the Bidens went to morning services at Saint John's Church, along with the cabinet and other administration officials. Carole and I got to watch the charismatic pastor T. D. Jakes give a sermon on Daniel 3:19, the story of three Hebrews cast into a fiery furnace after refusing to worship false idols. Jakes compared the biblical fire to the economic inferno that now confronted the new administration; the Hebrews, he preached, survived the flames because they stood firm for what they believed was right.

"You cannot change what you will not confront," Jakes said. "The problems are mighty and the solutions are not simple. Everywhere you turn there will be a critic waiting to attack every decision you make. . . . But you cannot enjoy the light without enduring the heat."

It was an inspiring message. And as we made our way to the viewing stand at the Capitol, it was remarkable to look out at the millions gathering on the Mall, voting again, this time with their feet, for hope.

It was a moving day. Carole and I sat with Chief Justice John Roberts at lunch, and we even stopped by an inaugural ball that night, because it felt like the thing to do.

But I was still full of foreboding and darkness. My relatives had descended on Washington for the event, hoping to attend my swearing-in as well—my sister had flown in from Thailand—but my tax mess had scuttled those plans. I was embarrassed by the public debate about whether I was both venal and incompetent or merely incompetent. Mostly, though, I was thinking about the financial system, worrying about how to prevent it from combusting again, and how to get it working again.

It was below freezing that day, but as Carole later said, it really did feel like we were walking into the fire.

MY SENATE confirmation hearing was the next day. I didn't want my family to stay for it, and I didn't let my kids skip school for it, although Carole and my father came to support me. I knew it would be ugly. Republicans were having a field day with the idea that I wanted to raise America's taxes without paying my own. And there wasn't a lot of enthusiasm in either party for the financial rescues I had helped engineer. The Senate had just narrowly agreed to release the second tranche of TARP, with only fifty-two senators voting to avert another panic. After thirty-four Republican senators had supported giving the original TARP authority to the Bush administration, only six voted to extend the authority in the Obama administration. Despite the historic crisis, the President wasn't going to get a honeymoon, and neither was I.

New York Senator Chuck Schumer introduced me at the hearing. And Paul Volcker, who had agreed to chair the President's new Economic Recovery Advisory Board, also testified on my behalf, lending his gravitas to my cause. But most of the three-and-a-half-hour grilling was pretty dismal. Republican Senator Jon Kyl of Arizona all but called me a liar, saying it was "incomprehensible" I could have been so clueless about my taxes, scoffing that my explanations "strain credulity," pointedly reminding me that I was under oath.

"Would you answer my question rather than dancing around it, please?" he demanded.

The senators then submitted 289 additional written questions that I was supposed to answer that night, so the committee could vote the next morning. We had a team of staff working all night. I left at 2 a.m., and Patterson asked me to come back at 5 a.m. to review the draft answers; when I returned, we couldn't buy coffee because nothing was open yet.

And we did mangle one answer. Several senators asked if I would label China a "currency manipulator," so I wrote an equivocating reply stating only that we would encourage China to let the yuan appreciate. I believed that using the manipulator label, especially before I was even confirmed, would be counterproductive, offending the Chinese and making them less likely to strengthen the yuan. But Obama had described China as a currency manipulator during the campaign, so in the early-morning confusion, my diplomatic dodge got replaced with his campaign rhetoric. The answer sent a provocative, unintended signal to a wary, ascendant power, complicating my early dealings with my Chinese counterparts. I would have to clarify in my early calls that no decision had been made, and that we would try to conduct our future diplomacy in private.

I ended up developing very good relationships with the Chinese. It probably helped that I spoke some Mandarin, and that many top government officials—including Wang Qishan, my primary counterpart—had met my father during his time in Beijing for the Ford Foundation. I would help bury a bill by Senator Schumer to punish China for currency manipulation; I asked him if he wanted to call his legislation "Schumer-Hawley," after the protectionist Smoot-Hawley bill that deepened the Great Depression. But behind the scenes, the President and I would put relentless pressure on the Chinese to let their currency rise. And over time, we helped persuade them that a stronger yuan served their own interests, improving the purchasing power of their growing middle class. The yuan would appreciate 16 percent in real terms during President Obama's first term, and China's trade surplus would be cut in half, to the considerable benefit of U.S. businesses and their workers.

By January 26, when the Senate finally voted on my nomination, I was the last nominee still working out of the transition office. The elaborate security apparatus was gone; the maintenance staff had already started knocking down walls and ripping out phone lines. Carole and my father watched the roll call on C-SPAN, as the Senate confirmed me 60–34, the narrowest margin for any modern Treasury secretary. I didn't bother to watch. I was scared about the future and scarred by the process; I was bleeding more than Rahm had predicted. It was clear that I'd be starting my new job deeply damaged, surrounded by questions about my competence and integrity, at a time when the country needed confidence in both.

We then drove to Treasury for my swearing-in ceremony in the historic Cash Room, where bankers and ordinary citizens used to come to exchange gold and bonds for U.S. currency. President Obama, Vice President Biden, Larry, and Ben were all there, along with many of Treasury's career civil servants who had worked with me in the 1990s. I appreciated the support, but I couldn't really enjoy the moment. It had never been my goal in life to get a big Washington job and the trappings that come with it, although I did think it was cool when I found out my Secret Service code name would be "Fencing Master." I hoped I could be useful, but it was hard to get too excited when everything seemed to be going to hell.

Our challenge, I said in my remarks, would be "to restore confidence in America's economic leadership around the world." The President also spoke of the "devastating loss of trust and confidence" in U.S. financial markets.

"You've got your work cut out for you," he said.

The next morning, I briefed the President in the Oval Office about the five big bombs we had to defuse—Fannie, Freddie, AIG, Citi, and Bank of America—as well as the deeper problems in the financial system. That was the meeting where I told him how bad things really were, and he told Larry and me that he wanted to rip off the Band-Aid, that he wanted a strategy to put a quick and definitive end to the crisis.

Our skeletal team was working on it.

OUR INTERVENTIONS in 2007 and 2008 hadn't ended the crisis, so I spent much of the transition trying to figure out what would.

The Fed, the Treasury and the FDIC had done a lot to stabilize the financial system. Our innovative credit and liquidity programs for banks and nonbanks, our backstops for commercial paper and money market funds, and our swap lines for central banks in developed and developing countries had all helped prevent complete financial collapse. We had avoided a number of devastating explosions by rescuing some huge firms, including the five bombs that were once again on the brink of failure. We had helped guide many of the system's weakest links—Countrywide, Bear Stearns, Merrill Lynch, WaMu, Wachovia—into the arms of more stable partners. The Columbus Day capital injections and FDIC guarantees had eased the panic. The world's most powerful government was now providing support, in various forms, for financial institutions and markets with more than $30 trillion in liabilities.

So why was the financial system still falling apart?

The most obvious catalyst was the collapse of the broader economy, reflected in the devastating decline of consumer and business confidence in the United States and around the world. American households lost 16 percent of their wealth in 2008, driven by falling home prices and stock prices, a decline five times larger than the 3 percent loss of wealth during the financial shock that precipitated the Depression in 1929. The disappearance of wealth, disposable income, and jobs was dragging down private demand, which further depressed asset prices, putting more pressure on banks to hoard liquidity and restrict credit, which in turn sucked more financial oxygen out of the economy. Economic distress meant more delinquent mortgages, which meant more troubled mortgage securities weighing down banks, which meant less lending and more economic distress. This vicious cycle of financial and economic contraction was gaining momentum, and no one was sure how it would end. Fear of a depression was making a depression more likely.

Unemployment had climbed to 7.3 percent in December, as businesses slashed staff and canceled investments to prepare for tough times ahead. Circuit City filed for bankruptcy, following the Sharper Image, Linens 'n Things, and other familiar retailers. Manufacturers such as Boeing, Caterpillar, and Pfizer announced mass layoffs. The CEO of Corning, Inc.—which makes the Gorilla Glass found on smartphones and laptops, and which announced 3,500 layoffs that January—later told me he thought the corporate world had overreacted, cutting too far too fast out of fear of an uncertain future. But it was a terrifying time, and it was worse than anyone could yet comprehend. We thought we were losing about 500,000 jobs a month; the initial government estimates were later revised to more than 750,000. The initial GDP release estimated the economy had contracted at an annual rate of 3.8 percent in the fourth quarter of 2008; that was later revised to an 8.3 percent decline. Those numbers were depression numbers.

The question was how we could turn things around. In a normal recession, loosening monetary policy to lower the cost of borrowing is a relatively quick and effective way to boost the economy. But the financial system is the conduit between the Fed and the economy, and the financial system was broken. In an epic financial crisis that followed a major credit boom, easy money had much less power. Interest rates were already effectively zero; most banks had little ability and even less desire to lend; businesses had little desire to borrow; and consumers already had too much debt. As central bankers say, it felt like the Fed was pushing on a string. It had begun the first round of quantitative easing, or QE1, buying GSE mortgage bonds to help reduce the cost and increase the availability of mortgages. This was an innovative way to do monetary stimulus at a time when short-term rates were as low as they could go; the Fed would later expand the program to Treasuries to try to drive down long-term rates more generally. It was helpful at a time when the economy was still struggling, but it would not be enough on its own.

We needed an expansionary fiscal policy alongside expansionary monetary policy. A year earlier, Hank had helped forge a deal between liberal Democratic Speaker Nancy Pelosi of San Francisco and conservative Republican Minority Leader John Boehner of southwest Ohio for a $150 billion fiscal stimulus package, about 1 percent of GDP. But those tax rebate checks had been too small and too long ago. We were going to have to do much more to offset a year of recession and the huge loss of wealth that followed the financial panic of the fall. The Obama fiscal stimulus plan had already grown from $175 billion late in the campaign to more than $500 billion in early December, when Christy Romer pulled Larry and me into a conference room in the transition office and said we were still thinking too small.

"This thing needs to be much bigger—at least eight hundred billion dollars," she said.

Larry and I agreed. We all wanted as much as the political system could deliver. Our constraint was Congress. At the time, $800 billion over two years was considered extraordinarily aggressive, twice as much as a group of 387 mostly left-leaning economists had just recommended in a public letter, more than the entire New Deal in inflation-adjusted dollars. And most of the Recovery Act—safety-net spending, tax cuts for workers, highway and subway repairs, aid to help states avoid layoffs and service cuts, and much more—seemed like solid stimulus. I wasn't worried that some of its infrastructure projects might not be "shovel-ready"—or that some spending on Obama agenda items such as clean energy and medical research would take time to get into the economic bloodstream—because I thought the economy clearly would need support for a while. I just wanted the legislation passed quickly so that the money could start to flow.

That would be harder than it should have been. Every major Republican and Democratic presidential candidate had proposed a stimulus package in 2008, but after the election, Republicans who happily voted for the Bush stimulus at a much less dire moment turned the Obama stimulus into partisan poison. The President tried to reach out to them, inviting them to the White House, visiting them on the Hill, accommodating their demands for $300 billion in tax cuts in the package. But when the House passed the Recovery Act in late January, every Republican still voted no. It was kind of rich to hear them thunder about runaway deficits after they spent eight years squandering the Clinton surpluses, leaving the country short on fiscal firepower to try to prevent a depression. And it was maddening to watch them try to obstruct a new Democratic president's jobs bill in an economic emergency, after Democrats helped an outgoing Republican president pass TARP in a financial emergency. None of us expected a Washington lovefest, but we had hoped that some Republican support might be available for a new president who had inherited a crisis for the ages. The GOP's reflexive opposition to the Recovery Act was a signal that we shouldn't count on Republican cooperation going forward.

In any case, fiscal stimulus and monetary stimulus were not my main responsibilities. Larry oversaw the Recovery Act. And now that I had left the Fed, I had no responsibility for monetary policy. At my going-away dinner at the Fed board, Richmond Fed President Jeff Lacker, the inflation hawk who was one of my most ardent critics, gave a funny and gracious speech reminding me I'd no longer be able to print money at Treasury. "That's our job," Lacker said. "Remember that."

But the credit markets were a central part of my responsibility, and they were frozen. I thought we could provide direct help to the broader economy if we could get credit flowing again to creditworthy borrowers.

One reason Americans can usually get a credit card or borrow at reasonable rates to buy a car or grow a business is that lenders can package the loans into "asset-backed securities" and sell them to investors. But after the Lehman panic, when no one knew what anything was worth, these securitization markets shut down. Investors stopped buying the loans, so many lenders stopped making them. The spreads on auto loans and student loans quickly tripled.

In November 2008, the Fed had announced a new program designed to bypass the banks to kick-start the securitization markets: the Term Asset-Backed Securities Loan Facility. We designed TALF to create investor demand for high-quality asset-backed securities by accepting them as collateral for Fed loans. There was also a twist: Treasury would provide $20 billion from TARP to absorb losses on the securities, and the Fed would leverage that capital to provide $200 billion in financing to help investors buy them. Leverage had created a lot of problems, but now we could harness its power to stretch TARP dollars much further.

When I started at Treasury two months later, the Fed was still trying to figure out how to design TALF. My team proposed expanding it to $1 trillion before it even started, while broadening it to accept securities backed by all kinds of consumer and business credit: equipment loans, small business loans, commercial mortgages, and perhaps even residential mortgages in addition to car loans, student loans, and credit card loans. Ben agreed.

TALF wouldn't get much media attention, but it would be remarkably effective, reviving stalled credit markets that were vital to the American Dream. The securitization markets for auto loans, student loans, and other consumer loans that had disappeared after Lehman quickly rebounded after the launch of TALF. It would be one of the least controversial planks of our strategy, because it wasn't about the banks.

But we still had to figure out what to do about the banks.

• • •

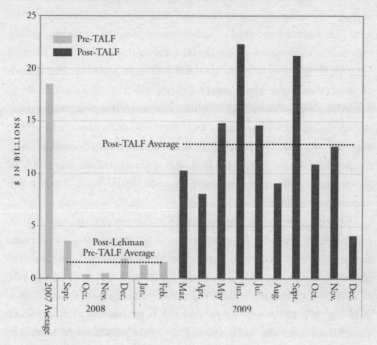

TALF Revived Consumer Lending Markets
Consumer Asset-Backed Securities Issuance

The markets for auto loans, credit cards, and other consumer credit (excluding mortgages) that could be packaged into securities averaged nearly $20 billion per month in 2007 before grinding to a halt after Lehman fell. The Fed-Treasury TALF program brought these securitization markets back to life. They averaged about $13 billion per month after TALF launched in March 2009.
Source: U.S. Treasury Department.

THE IMPLOSION of the economy was not the only source of instability in the financial system.

The ad hoc, inconsistent crisis response of 2008—which was mostly but not entirely a result of the limits on the Fed's and Treasury's authority before TARP—had added to the pervasive uncertainty about what remained at risk and what we might do next. Even where we had authority to act, we had not established clear rules of the game. Investors were not only unsure how to evaluate the health of institutions during a financial crisis and an economic collapse; they were also unsure how the U.S. government might handle institutions that started falling into the abyss. Bank shareholders had no idea whether they would face substantial dilution, or a government nationalization that could wipe them out. Creditors were still worried about Lehman-style defaults and WaMu-style haircuts. We hadn't fully committed to removing catastrophic risk from the system, and we had adjusted our approach so often that our commitments wouldn't necessarily be trusted, anyway. There was a general sense that the U.S. government might not have the will or even the ability to do what was necessary to end the crisis.

Our Columbus Day interventions had been helpful, but not all-powerful. By limiting its guarantees to the new (but not existing) senior debts of commercial banks and bank holding companies (but not nonbanks), the FDIC had left creditors with exposure to debt that was outside that circle of protection at risk of serious losses. And because the initial TARP capital injections were in preferred rather than common stock, the market saw them more as additional medium-term debt for the banks than as permanent loss-absorbing capital. The system's capital—its defense against insolvency in case of serious losses—still seemed inadequate. That was a problem, because major banks still had huge piles of distressed assets on their books, and were still anticipating huge losses. Citi announced an $8 billion fourth-quarter loss. Bank of America wrote down even more losses to account for Merrill's deteriorating mortgage portfolio.

These illiquid assets were another major source of uncertainty. Reasonable people could disagree about their true value, and it mattered whether they would be worth 90 cents or 75 cents on the dollar in a calmer market. But their value in the current market was deeply distressed, often less than 50 cents on the dollar, because almost nobody was buying them. Bank balance sheets are opaque, and in such fragile and turbulent times, investors and lenders tended to assume the worst about assets and institutions. Imagine you had to sell your house tomorrow in a market where no one could get a mortgage. You'd have to sell it at a tiny fraction of its potential value. At my farewell dinner at the Fed, Jeff Lacker had quipped that my colleagues had considered giving me one of our Maiden Lane vehicles as a going-away present, since they probably wouldn't exceed the Fed's $25 gift limit. At the time, those assets were distressed enough to make the joke funny.

The markets had welcomed TARP, but they no longer believed that TARP was big enough to fill the system's capital hole. The President had pledged to use at least $50 billion to address the housing crisis, so we now had about $300 billion left to repair the financial system. Fortunately, we wouldn't need TARP money to recapitalize Fannie and Freddie, because the separate authority Hank had gotten to put capital into them was essentially unlimited; otherwise, they were hemorrhaging so badly they could have drained most of the cash we had left. But the rest of the financial system was bleeding, too. My former colleagues at the New York Fed privately estimated that the banking sector alone could still face $836 billion in additional losses in a "stress scenario" and as much as $1.246 trillion in an "extreme stress scenario." That didn't include losses at nonbanks such as AIG, GMAC, and GE Capital. It certainly didn't include General Motors or Chrysler, which would also need TARP to survive.

Overall, the Fed calculated that banks could need as much as $290 billion in additional capital in the stress case and up to $684 billion in the extreme case, about 80 percent of it for the fifteen largest banks. That was more than TARP could handle. And now that financial rescues had become political kryptonite, Congress had become yet another source of uncertainty, unlikely to provide more funding if TARP ran dry. Somehow, we needed to get more power out of our remaining cash.

• • •

OUR OPERATING assumption was that we needed a "capital plus" strategy: capital plus some form of asset purchase or loss-sharing arrangement to take some additional risk off the banks. The idea with the most support in financial circles, and some populist circles, was to revive the original TARP plan by creating a government "bad bank" to buy illiquid assets from the actual banks. There was a widespread belief, often tinged with moral fervor, that we needed to cleanse their balance sheets of toxic junk, to "scrub their books" so they could lend again.

Sheila Bair was the most aggressive government advocate of a bad bank. My former colleagues at the New York Fed were pushing related proposals for a "ring fence" that would reduce the risks faced by banks by providing government guarantees for some of their scarier assets, a variant on the second round of the Citi and Bank of America rescues.

I was eager for a consensus solution, but I wasn't sure the bad-bank or ring-fence proposals could work in practice, and Larry was typically relentless in exposing their shortcomings. With more than $1 trillion in toxic assets still locked in the banking system, the cost of buying them or guaranteeing them could far exceed what we had left in TARP. My painful experience negotiating the relatively modest Bear Stearns asset pool—as well as my exposure to the Paulson Treasury's internal debates about asset purchases—had also left me skeptical of government efforts to buy or ring-fence distressed assets from banks that had the chance to live. Nobody had good answers to the problems of how we would decide which assets to buy or guarantee, how much to pay for them, and how to avoid getting taken to the cleaners by banks that knew the details of their assets much better than we did. Hank had brought in some top experts on securities auctions to try to solve these problems in the fall, only to abandon the effort as unworkable—and if anyone had good incentives to make asset purchases work, it was the secretary who had pledged to use the Troubled Assets Relief Program to buy troubled assets.

Ultimately, the problem of having the government set prices for assets that the market wouldn't touch seemed insurmountable. If we set the prices too high, we'd burn though TARP, providing a huge and politically inflammatory subsidy for the banks without eliminating all the bad assets on their books or all the uncertainty about their future. And we'd probably get stuck with the worst assets, exposing taxpayers to potentially brutal losses. But if we set prices too low in order to husband our TARP dollars, banks would refuse to sell unless we somehow forced them to sell, in which case they'd take the brutal losses themselves. That would expand their capital shortfalls, eventually requiring many more TARP dollars. And no matter how we decided to price the assets, the process would be long and contentious, creating more uncertainty and run risk while it played out.

While I was thinking about this pricing problem, I remembered a suggestion that Warren Buffett had made in the fall of 2008, when we were deciding what to do with the first tranche of TARP. Buffett had written Hank a letter suggesting that Treasury could partner with private asset managers to create an investment fund, then let the private managers decide what to buy, solving the pricing problem. Banks would get a new source of demand for assets they wanted to sell, but they would not be forced to sell at fire-sale prices that would require them to take damaging losses. And the private managers would not be tempted to pay too much for the assets, since their own money would be at risk alongside TARP money.

I reread Buffett's letter, and I thought the idea made sense. I also thought it might appease the demand in the financial and political arenas for some kind of government effort to buy illiquid assets. But a program limited to voluntary asset purchases, while avoiding the bad bank's price-setting problems, would necessarily be a modest program, an effort to chip away at bad assets rather than scrub anyone's books. It would also be complex and difficult to design, which was why Hank hadn't embraced it during the panic of the fall.

During the transition, my team began working to convert Buffett's concept into the "Public-Private Investment Program." They ultimately devised a smart and workable structure for PPIP, as well as another dismal crisis acronym. But we knew we still needed a more comprehensive plan to stabilize the financial system.

OVER CHRISTMAS, I escaped to Mexico to spend another family vacation glued to my phone. One evening at sunset, I called Larry from the beach to suggest a new idea for deploying TARP. I thought this new approach could recapitalize the banks, restore confidence over time, and make the financial system investable again. I first described the plan as a "valuation exercise."

We would come to call it the stress test.

The plan aimed to impose transparency on opaque financial institutions and their opaque assets in order to reduce the uncertainty that was driving the panic. It would help markets distinguish between viable banks that were temporarily illiquid and weak banks that were essentially insolvent. Then it would help stabilize the strong as well as the weak by mobilizing a combination of private and public capital. The stress test would end up having many other virtues I didn't foresee at the time. Kabaker later dubbed it "the gift that keeps on giving."

There were two parts to the plan. First, the Fed would design and execute a uniform test for the largest firms, analyzing the size of the losses each institution would face in a downturn comparable to the Great Depression. For years, the banks had conducted ad hoc stress tests built around rosy scenarios they chose themselves; at the Fed, I had pushed for more rigor and less optimism, but I had never gotten much traction. Now the banks would have to prove they had enough capital to survive a true worst-case scenario, with the loss estimates determined by the independent Fed.

It was unsettling to think about what the stress test might expose, but no news can be even more destabilizing than bad news. During a crisis, investors and lenders without information tend to assume the worst and run. Of course, bad news could trigger a run, too, if it was worse than people expected. There was a real possibility that the stress test would expose unmanageable losses. But we were already living with that fear. It seemed better to dispel the uncertainty.

I did think there was some chance that the news would be better than expected, that the fears of widespread insolvency would prove excessive. Unlike the bad bank, the stress test would be forward looking. It would analyze future income as well as future losses. And each firm's potential losses would be calculated according to an estimate, however imperfect, of the underlying long-term value of its assets, not the current fire-sale value in a market without buyers. So banks would be forced to hold capital against losses they'd incur on assets they planned to hold to maturity—potentially serious losses, because a depression would create rampant defaults in mortgages and other loans. But the banks would not be forced to hold capital against losses they'd incur by unloading assets at depressed prices during a panic—potentially catastrophic losses, because few investors had cash available to buy the assets and no one knew what they were worth.

The stress test would provide information, and hopefully a measure of confidence. The second part of the plan would provide capital.

The Fed would determine how much more of a capital buffer each bank would need to weather a catastrophic downturn, and would give each firm a chance to raise the funds privately. But if a bank failed to raise enough capital on its own, the Treasury would inject extra capital to fill the gap. In either case, shareholders would be diluted—they'd own a smaller share of the company—and the firms with the biggest problems would face the most dilution. Depending on the size of the government stake, management might be replaced. Some banks might end up effectively nationalized, with the government holding a majority of shares. But that would be a last-resort solution, not a preemptive solution. The scale of Treasury's investment and the extent of nationalization would be determined by the scale of the firm's capital hole and the willingness of private investors to plug it. Ultimately, I thought that by making it clear we would recapitalize the banks to levels that would allow them to withstand depression-style losses, we could make a depression less likely.

On that December call, Larry was understandably skeptical, and typically full of questions. How would the stress test work? Why would the Fed's loss estimates be credible? What if we didn't have enough TARP money left to fill the gaps? I certainly didn't have all the answers yet. As we discussed the issue in the following weeks, Larry worried that the markets would see the stress test as a bogus sideshow, an effort to delay the day of reckoning for insolvent banks, a tentative solution that would dodge the bold choices needed to end the crisis.

Sometimes it was hard to tell if Larry was punching holes in an idea because he had a genuine problem with it, or just because he was a world-class hole-puncher. But in this case his initial discomfort reflected some real differences that we would continue to debate in the subsequent months, disagreements over how deep the banking system's problems really were. As pessimistic as I was about the state of the banks, Larry made me sound cheery. He thought the rot went much deeper.

Larry believed the only credible way to assess the capital shortfalls of various institutions was to evaluate their assets at something close to current market prices. By that measure, during the worst period of illiquidity and fear since the Great Depression, just about every major institution was insolvent. So Larry worried that the stress test would be viewed as a whitewash, a mechanism to prop up zombie banks. I thought Larry's focus on the current prices of mortgage-backed securities and other illiquid assets in the banking system was misguided, since they had been artificially depressed by the crisis. It seemed plausible that the assets might turn out to be worth significantly more than they could fetch during a panic, and that many of the major banks would turn out to be solvent. Most of my former colleagues at the Fed and my new team at Treasury agreed that the banks clearly needed more capital, but were not necessarily beyond the point of no return. We thought the stress test could demonstrate that, while also revealing how much capital each bank needed.

Larry had worked part-time at the hedge fund D. E. Shaw, and I started describing his take, a bit unkindly, as "the hedge fund view." Hedge fund executives tended to see the banks as dumb, lumbering giants, which wasn't necessarily wrong. But since hedge funds "marked to market" every day, updating their books to reflect current asset prices, they also thought banks should have to do the same thing. This didn't make much sense. Banks had more stable sources of funding and different accounting rules. They were permitted to value some assets on a hold-to-maturity basis because they held some assets to maturity; the value of those assets would be determined by a borrower's ability to pay, not day-to-day price shifts in the market. Historically, traditional bank accounting had often been abused to cover up losses, but suddenly changing the rules to make the banks take massive losses during a crisis would have forced them into fire sales and killed them.

Some investors, including many hedge funds, had an interest in forcing the banks to unload distressed assets, so they could scoop up the assets on the cheap. That wasn't Larry's interest. He just found the hedge fund view of the market more compelling than mine. He didn't propose an alternative solution, which was not atypical for Larry, but he was consistently skeptical of the stress test as a solution to the system's capital deficiencies. He just thought it would delay the inevitable pain.

I couldn't say for sure that Larry was wrong. My view was: Let's see. If Larry was right and the system was irretrievably broken, the stress test would expose huge shortfalls, banks would fail to raise private capital, and the government would have to carry the burden of recapitalizing the financial system on its own. But if Larry's view was right, we were doomed to end up in that situation no matter what we did. On the other hand, if Larry was wrong and most of the big banks were fixable, the stress test's results could rally private capital off the sidelines to help fix them; we would also avoid having the tax-payers take on huge amounts of unnecessary risk, and we would be on a much quicker path to stabilize the system. In an uncertain situation, it seemed sensible to push for more information. There would be risks in whatever we did, but I thought the stress test could reduce the risks.

Larry can't help but argue every side of every issue, and at one point he found a simple way to make my case for me. If you go to the hospital with a leg injury, he said, you don't want amputation to be the first option. Maybe when all is said and done, you'll end up losing the leg, but you want your doctor to try some other options first.

I didn't think we were ready to amputate.

On my third full day as secretary, January 29, I was supposed to have my first one-on-one meeting with President Obama. As I was about to walk into the Oval Office, Stephanie Cutter, a veteran Democratic operative who was handling our communications strategy, told me we would have a "pool spray," a photo opportunity for the White House press. The President and I would make brief remarks about executive compensation, responding to a report that Wall Street firms had paid their executives big bonuses while piling up record losses in 2008.

"Here's what you're going to say," Cutter said.

She handed me the text, and I skimmed the outrage I was expected to express. I'm not very convincing as an angry populist, and I thought the artifice would look ridiculous.

"I'm not doing this," I said.

Instead, I sat uncomfortably next to the President while he expressed outrage.

Americans were furious about bailouts for overpaid bankers, and the White House political team wanted us to show we were on the side of the backlash. Axelrod and Press Secretary Robert Gibbs were clamoring for some public displays of Old Testament justice. I got that. Symbols did matter. On my first day as secretary, we had pressured

Citi to cancel a tone-deaf plan to buy a new corporate jet; the headline in the *New York Post* had been "Just Plane Despicable." A week later, the President and I would announce a set of compensation reforms for senior executives at TARP firms, designed by a Treasury team led by Gene Sperling. The reforms were stringent enough to infuriate Wall Street, but not nearly stringent enough to satisfy the public outrage.

That's what made me uncomfortable. The public outrage was appropriate, and I understood why the President wanted to embrace it, but I didn't see how we could ever satisfy it. We had no legal authority to confiscate the bonuses that had been paid during the boom. We had no power to set compensation for most private firms. We had more authority over firms receiving TARP funds, but we couldn't reduce bonuses to levels that the public might find acceptable without unleashing an exodus of talent from those banks, reducing their prospects of navigating their way to safety. In any case, I thought the public's rage on these issues was insatiable. I feared that the tougher we talked about the bonuses, the more we would own them, fueling unrealistic expectations about our ability to eradicate extravagance in the financial industry.

My view was that our best response to all the anger would be to do all we could to end the crisis, repair the damage it had inflicted, and revive the economy so that more people could get back to work. That was our most important obligation, as well as the best path to a measure of justice for victims of the crisis. I also hoped that we could channel the country's populist outrage into support for comprehensive long-term reforms of the financial system, as well as the President's many other initiatives designed to create equal opportunity for more Americans. But at this point, the most important thing was to repair the banking system, not to get caught up in vilifying it.

By early February, our small team at Treasury, working closely with the Fed, had devised the broad outlines of a three-part financial strategy: the stress test followed by capital injections to stabilize the largest banks, the public-private investment funds to buy distressed assets, and the TALF expansion to resuscitate credit markets. At the same time, we needed to make a more credible commitment that we would allow no more messy failures of systemic firms, and no more haircuts of senior bondholders—in other words, no more Lehmans or WaMus. And we needed to launch our new housing plan, which we hoped would ease pressures on some of the victims of the crisis, even though we knew we wouldn't be able to prevent millions of foreclosures.

We spent hours in meetings trying to build consensus for this approach, with Larry as well as the FDIC, the Fed, and other regulators. I wanted everyone on the same page to give the plan credibility, to reduce the risk of more confusing lurching. I kept saying we could not afford to come across as Afghanistan, crippled by tribal warfare among regulators. I told everyone that I wanted us to agree on a plan and sign our names in blood, to show the world we would use the combined force of our agencies to fight the crisis.

But we had a hard time generating enthusiasm for our strategy inside the government. It seemed awfully generous to the banks, yet our decision not to buy toxic assets seemed like a problem for the banks. Most of the dissenters had smart concerns but no alternatives, a phenomenon I was familiar with from our internal debates over the previous year and a half. I often reminded them: *Plan beats no plan.*

Sheila did propose a plan of sorts, a bad bank that she called an "aggregator bank," in which the government would buy toxic loans from financial institutions. This idea had the same pricing problems as the other asset purchase plans. If the pricing was too generous, it would look like an expensive gift to the banks and leave taxpayers with too much risk. If the pricing was too harsh, it wouldn't strengthen the banks. Either way, it would take too long to put in place. Larry and I didn't think it made sense, and neither, ultimately, did the Fed. But Sheila continued to talk it up in interviews in the more generous form, and her aides leaked that it was likely to happen in articles with headlines such as "Obama Team Considers New 'Bad Bank'" and "'Bad Bank' Plan Gets Momentum to Revive Lending."

The markets loved those articles, because the government-run bad bank sounded like a way for Wall Street to dump its garbage on Uncle Sam at generous prices; financial stocks had two days where they jumped double-digit percentage points in late January when press accounts were fueling bad-bank rumors. My team wanted to start preparing the markets for our actual plan, but I told them I didn't want us fighting leaks with leaks. My staff got so annoyed by the drumbeat of FDIC-planted stories that at one point they gave Sheila's aides a harmless snippet of wrong information, just to see if it would end up in the media. It quickly did.

Everyone seemed to have anxiety about our strategy, and I warned the President in a February 5 memo that our approach did have real risks. There would be a long period of uncertainty before the stress test was done, a time when fears of potential dilution or even nationalization "could reignite the run on financial institutions." We thought we'd need a lot more money soon, and "a long political fight about additional resources and authorities will raise anxiety globally." We were in uncharted territory, with "little consensus among knowledgeable academics and experts," so we could expect withering attacks no matter what we did. And the five financial bombs, along with other wobbly institutions, would need help in a hurry, "possibly before this plan will start to show results, which will add to fragility."

That memo wasn't a decision memo. There weren't agree-disagree boxes for the President to check. It was an informational memo, letting him know exactly what we were doing, marinating him in our unpleasant choices, giving him a chance to object if he wanted a different approach. He didn't object. He asked smart questions, and subjected my recommendations to no-holds-barred debate with my colleagues. But he hadn't run for president to be a financial engineer. He relied on us to figure out what needed to be done, and he gave me a lot of deference on the substance.

After all, he had a lot on his plate. He was suddenly commander in chief, waging wars in Iraq and Afghanistan. He had a government to run, which posed enormous staffing challenges; his nominee to run health care reform, Tom Daschle, had just withdrawn because of tax issues. (I knew my own tax issues had magnified the focus on Daschle's, yet another source of guilt during my early days on the job.) The White House was also finishing negotiations on the Recovery Act, and not a second too soon. The economy had shed another 600,000 jobs in January—later revised to more than 800,000—and unemployment was up to 7.8 percent.

President Obama had walked into a nightmare. These had been America's worst three months for jobs since World War II ended and the defense industry shut down its wartime factories. We were all relieved that three moderate Republican senators agreed to back the stimulus, ensuring a filibuster-proof majority to try to stop the economic free fall. But the compromises necessary to lure those Republican votes and keep Democrats on board would be a harbinger for the Obama presidency. The three Republicans, along with quite a few Democrats, limited the size of the package to $800 billion. That included a $70 billion fix to the alternative minimum tax that nobody in the administration wanted to include, because it provided almost no stimulus. But the President needed the legislation, so he had to take whatever he could get. We didn't have time for endless negotiations; we wanted the stimulus to start flowing immediately.

In any case, now that the stimulus was done, we had to get moving on the financial mess. After a couple of delays to try to build consensus, we settled on February 10 for my fateful speech to unveil our plan.

"But we don't have a plan," Meg protested.

She had a point. We didn't have many details in place, but I decided that we needed to lay out the framework of our strategy for the markets as soon as possible. The vacuum of information and constant speculation was too damaging. I didn't want expectations to continue to be distorted by inaccurate leaks. And I thought a deadline might force resolution of our remaining internal disagreements.

The run-up to my speech was horribly tense. White House staff wanted the speech to reassure the public by emphasizing our determination to get tough on Wall Street and save taxpayer dollars. My Treasury team wanted to reassure the markets by emphasizing our determination to do whatever it took to prevent more bank failures. The results were predictably schizophrenic. I remember Larry came over to my grand new office, with twenty-foot ceilings and an Alexander Hamilton portrait over the fireplace, to read an early draft. He proceeded to eviscerate it as unworthy of the office I occupied—the same office, he did not need to mention, that he used to occupy.

"I can't tell you what to do, but I wouldn't give a speech like this," he said. I felt the same way about the early drafts, and the later drafts weren't poetry, either.

The night before my speech, my team was still negotiating with the FDIC, the Fed, the OCC, and the OTS over a joint statement of support, and with the White House over a fact sheet for the press. We wouldn't finalize the terms of the joint statement until after I began speaking, so instead of going out to the press in advance of my remarks, the statement wouldn't be ready until after markets had already reacted and reporters had filed their stories.

My team spent most of the night before the speech in a second-floor corner office at Treasury, arguing and rewriting and then arguing some more. At one point, Lee exploded at Gene when he tried to rebrand our capital plan as a "Financial Stability Trust," which might sound good to the public but might also be confusing to the markets. Meg was hunched over a computer, stripping out the remaining populist rhetoric, while Gene and Lee hovered behind her, debating with each other about what needed to be put back in.

"You guys seem to be on the same page," she said sarcastically. "Why don't you type?"

At one point, Meg noticed that a strawberry Pop-Tart she had bought from one of Treasury's vending machines had vanished. She looked over at Gene, who shrugged and admitted he had eaten it. He said he would buy Meg another in a tone suggesting he comprehended neither the enormity of his crime nor the inadvisability of messing with Meg when she was tired and hungry.

"When, Gene?" she demanded. "When are you going to get me another?"

I had a bad feeling that the speech the President had foreshadowed as my "moment in the sun" would be a mess. (The billionaire Pete Peterson, my former board chairman at the New York Fed, later asked me if the President had intentionally made me a fall guy, which, of course, he hadn't.) I was supposed to do a few rehearsals to learn how to use the teleprompter, but I kept putting them off; I finally did a couple of half-hearted run-throughs that evening, repeatedly stopping to edit my text as I went along. I also had no time for prep sessions for my national TV appearances after the speech. Rubin used to do roughly sixty minutes of prep for every minute on *Meet the Press*; I did zero minutes of prep for the first TV interviews of my career.

I knew I could now move markets any time I opened my mouth; I stashed a *New York Times* headline about minimalism in Japanese design in my office drawer when I was a young civil servant to remind myself never to say too much. I also knew that my first words to the world could do a lot to build or destroy confidence. "Talk is cheap— or really expensive," I kept telling my team. I meant that credible rhetorical commitments to the safety of the system could reassure lenders and investors even more than money in the window, while loose language stoking fears about haircuts or nationalization could be instantly destabilizing.

Back when I was in my first senior position at Treasury, I used to explain to new recruits that deciding on the right policy was only 10 percent of their challenge. And it was important to decide early, so they would have time for the other 90 percent—negotiating the substance, framing the narrative, figuring out how to execute. But I had spent so much time devising our financial stability strategy and fighting over its substance that I had spent virtually no time on getting the explanation right. I had neglected the theater, even though I had no real personal experience with the theater. I was probably in some denial about my transition from anonymous mandarin to public figure. The weekend before my speech, I mentioned to Mark Patterson that I was pleased I could still walk around in public without being recognized.

"That's not going to last much longer," Patterson said.

MY SPEECH, as I mentioned in the introduction to this book, sucked.

Barclays Capital's chief U.S. economist called my speech "shock and ugh." Martin Wolf's *Financial Times* column about the already-doomed Obama presidency called our plan "yet another child of the failed interventions of the past one and a half years: optimistic and indecisive." The consensus view was that my inept delivery and lack of detail had dramatically increased uncertainty in the financial system. The conservative columnist Jim Pethokoukis summarized my message as: "We have a plan to have a plan." He added a one-word editorial comment: "Ouch."

Ouch was right. I had announced a series of novel, complicated programs with no precedent in crisis response, while providing few clues about what would be in them or how they would work. Not even Paul Krugman, the Nobel laureate economist and progressive *New York Times* columnist, could figure out what we intended to do. "I really don't know, at least based on what we've seen today," he wrote. And Krugman had one of the least hostile reviews of my speech, at least acknowledging the possibility that it could conceivably be "a Trojan horse that smuggles the right policy into place." Most commentators simply took it for granted that my public debut had been an unmitigated fiasco, before moving on to speculation about how long I would last as secretary.

"Mr. Geithner . . . doesn't know what he's doing, and pretty soon, everybody's going to find out," the hedge fund investor Jim Rogers scoffed on Bloomberg TV.

The speech had a bunch of big commitments, without much

explanation of what they meant. I said we would mobilize up to $1 trillion each for both the investment fund and the credit program, to make it clear they would be substantial relative to the size of their markets. And I tried to draw a definitive "no more Lehmans" line in the sand: "We believe that the U.S. has to send a clear and consistent signal that we will act to prevent the catastrophic failure of financial institutions that would damage the broader economy." But those new commitments just reinforced the public's view that we would continue to throw money at Wall Street, while the parts of the speech designed to ease some of the public's outrage about bailouts—pledging a new era of transparency and tough conditions for TARP recipients—just seemed to unnerve investors. Lacking detailed information about our plans, everyone assumed the worst, as if I were a toxic asset myself.

It's not a good sign when stocks plummet during a Treasury secretary's first speech. But as bad as my speech and my delivery were, the reaction of the markets had a lot to do with their expectations, fueled by pre-speech leaks, that we would announce a bad bank to buy troubled assets at inflated prices. The public was outraged that we still seemed to be bailing out banks, but investors were disappointed that our plan didn't sound like enough of a bailout.

With a Democrat in the White House, the markets were also afraid that the stress test would be a prelude to nationalizing banks, even though we repeatedly insisted that wasn't our goal. In fact, I envisioned the stress test as an effort to prevent unnecessary nationalization. But we wouldn't know for sure whether we would have to take over any insolvent institutions until the stress test was complete and we could see how bad things really were. That would be a terrible source of uncertainty in the coming months.

That evening, as the condolence notes rolled in, I told my team I was sorry I had put us in such a tough position, by going public with so few details and botching the theater. I warned that the next few months would be tough, because critics would be ripping our plan to shreds, and we wouldn't have much of a story to tell beyond: Hang on, trust us, it's better than you think. But we just needed to keep putting flesh on the bones of our plan.

"The only way we're going to get out of this is to get the details right and execute," I said. "This is the plan. We know it's a good plan. We just have to demonstrate that."

I wanted our work to have a cadence. I said we should roll out new details every week or so, as fast as we could finalize them, gradually building credibility and reducing uncertainty.

"The world needs to see that we're going to keep at it until we fix it," I said.

It wasn't fixed yet, though. The markets kept falling. The media kept pounding. I left two days after the speech for a G-7 meeting in Rome, where my fellow finance ministers, some of whom I had known since my days as Larry's noisy scribe, seemed pleased to see me but genuinely worried about my plan. They didn't understand it, either.

It's hard to describe the stress of knowing that the world was depending on our plan to prevent a catastrophe, and that nobody seemed to think it was any good. I remember in the Oval Office the morning after my speech, when the President had asked what the hell had happened, my colleagues kind of turned toward me with body language that implied: Don't ask us, ask Tim. And it really was all on me. All I could do was keep my head down and try to focus on my work. I had started carrying a Buddhist amulet that my aunt Lydia had given me in my wallet, along with a Unitarian prayer to the Spirit of Truth that I found soothing in turbulent times:

> *Grant us to feel thy shadow near*
> *So may we find the strength to stand face forward,*
> *Courage to walk toward the dawning day.*

They were comforting words, but honestly, my problem wasn't really strength or courage. My problem was that there was no way to know for sure if our plan would work.

On February 18, on the way back to Washington after President Obama announced our housing program in Mesa, Arizona, we met in his office on Air Force One. Financial stocks had plunged 20 percent since my speech. The President was clearly nervous that we were heading for a cliff. He wanted to know how bad the losses in the financial system were going to be, how much government help the banks were going to need, and when we were going to find out.

My response, unwelcome again, was that we would have to wait for the Fed to finish the stress test. We would move forward with our housing initiatives. We would go ahead and launch our other programs to revive the credit markets and invest in distressed assets. But none of that would dispel the uncertainty.

"We'll pressure the Fed to speed this up, but we won't know how this ends until they're done," I told him. "It's scary. It's risky. And there's no way we can know if it's going to work. But we're stuck letting this play out."

HOUSING WAS at the heart of the crisis, and the housing initiatives we unveiled in Arizona would be especially controversial. The President's announcement, and the perception that we were bailing out deadbeat homeowners, inspired the CNBC commentator Rick Santelli's infamous rant that day calling for a new Tea Party, galvanizing an antigovernment movement on the right that would scramble the politics of the Obama years. At the same time, the left would view our efforts to address the foreclosure crisis as woefully inadequate, and as the most damning evidence that we cared more about Wall Street than Main Street.

We couldn't legally force private owners of mortgages to give borrowers a break during tough times. The situation got especially complex when loans were sliced and diced into multiple mortgage securities owned by a range of investors, including pension funds, mutual funds, hedge funds, and banks. The complexity of this system and the convoluted web of property rights would make it much harder to implement programs to help homeowners. And while we did commit $50 billion in TARP funds for that purpose, we estimated that about eight million homeowners were at risk of foreclosure, and millions more were in distress. Trying to figure out which ones to help was a thorny policy problem.

Our goal was not to subsidize borrowers who splurged on overpriced McMansions and vacation homes and investment properties, or took out home equity loans to buy swimming pools and fancy cars. We knew that a few outrageous stories of aid to reckless speculators and scam artists could cripple support for our entire housing program. We also wanted to avoid spending billions of taxpayer dollars to restructure mortgages for families who would lose their homes even with government help; inevitably, some innocent victims of the crisis would have to move into cheaper homes or rental properties. And while we didn't worry excessively about the moral hazard implications of our programs, we had to be careful not to create perverse incentives for less vulnerable homeowners to stop making payments in order to qualify for help.

Our biggest debate was whether to try to reduce overall mortgage loans or just monthly payments. The main problems with loan reduction were its huge up-front expense and minimal bang for the buck; the benefit to homeowners would be spread out over the life of their mortgages, when we wanted to maximize the benefits we could provide immediately. Some proposals for broad-based principal reduction for underwater homeowners seemed particularly wasteful, since roughly three-fourths of those families were still current on their mortgages. Homeowners who couldn't afford their payments were the imminent foreclosure risks. And theoretically, payment reductions could benefit creditors as well as borrowers if they helped get mortgage payments flowing and avoid defaults. Most creditors weren't eager to get stuck with millions of foreclosed homes after a historic real estate bust, when a glut of inventory was further depressing resale values.

So we decided to focus our program on reducing monthly payments, rather than the overall principal, for at-risk homeowners. It felt like the least-bad option. We thought there were as many as three to four million borrowers who would be likely to face foreclosure without government help but might be able to stay in their homes with more affordable payments. The banks and investors who held their mortgages could cut their losses, too; recovery from foreclosure is typically only half the loan size, and was less than that during the crisis. Larry did point out that debt crises rarely end before governments help reduce excess debt burdens, but nobody had a feasible proposal for a cost-effective, well-targeted, large-scale debt reduction program for homeowners that could get through Congress.

The big news out of Arizona was our Home Affordable Modification Program, which provided incentives for mortgage servicers to reduce payments on owner-occupied homes down to 31 percent of the borrower's income. HAMP was modeled in part on work the FDIC had done with IndyMac's mortgages, but with more of a focus on rewarding successful modifications. We thought it was narrowly targeted for maximum effectiveness at minimum cost. But Santelli and the conservatives who responded to his Tea Party rant thought we were transferring their hard-earned tax money to profligate freeloaders. Meanwhile, liberals would spend the next several years citing our overly optimistic estimate that HAMP would help as many as three to four million homeowners as evidence of the failure of our housing initiatives.

In addition to HAMP, the President announced the Home Affordable Refinancing Program, or HARP, an effort to help millions of borrowers refinance their mortgages. He also called on Congress to pass "cram-down," a borrower-friendly bill that would have allowed mortgages to be restructured in bankruptcy court, but Rahm would soon inform him we didn't have the votes even for the very narrow version being kicked around in Congress, despite Democratic control of the Hill. I didn't think cram-down was a particularly wise or effective strategy, anyway. The bankruptcy courts were already overwhelmed, and the bill had the potential to push up mortgage costs for all borrowers—though perhaps only slightly given its limited scope—which would have further weakened the recovery.

The largest and most important housing initiative we unveiled in Arizona, although it wasn't widely viewed as housing policy at the time, was a new $200 billion capital commitment for Fannie and Freddie, which were burning through the $200 billion they got during Hank's tenure and were again under fire in the markets. Along with the Federal Housing Administration, they were virtually the only remaining sources of housing finance, essentially keeping the mortgage market afloat. Stabilizing them would be vital to stabilizing the broader housing market—and to keeping mortgage costs low, so that homeowners could enjoy the tax-cut-like benefits of refinancing.

Our lifeline to Fannie and Freddie would be pilloried as another wildly expensive financial bailout, but it wouldn't require additional congressional action or TARP money, so it would be relatively easy to execute. At a time when home prices had already fallen more than 30 percent, and futures markets were expecting another 20 percent decline, our $200 billion commitment would help steady a $20 trillion real estate market, while helping millions of homeowners to refinance. Saving Fannie and Freddie not only avoided catastrophe, defusing two of our financial bombs; it laid some groundwork for recovery.

THAT LEFT three bombs still ticking. The most worrisome, yet again, was AIG.

The Fed and the Treasury had sunk $150 billion into the company, but it was starting to look like a bottomless pit. AIG was about to report a mind-boggling loss of $61.7 billion in the fourth quarter of 2008, about a billion dollars per business day. It was once again on the brink of a ratings downgrade, which would trigger tens of billions of dollars in margin calls, bringing the firm back to the edge of a catastrophic default.

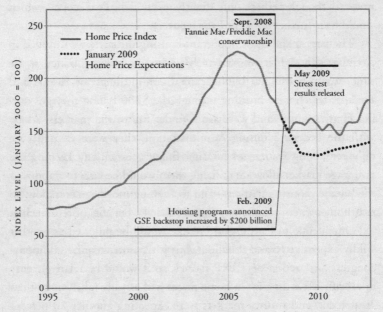

Government Programs Helped Stabilize Home Prices
S&P/Case-Shiller 10-City Composite Home Price Index

In January 2009, home prices had already fallen 30 percent and were pro-jected to plunge 20 percent further. But actions by the government and the Fed to support the economy—and specifically to support Fannie and Freddie, hold down mortgage rates, and help prevent foreclosures—helped stabilize prices in 2009 and facilitated a recovery of prices that began in 2012.

Sources: Bloomberg and U.S. Department of Housing and Urban Development.

On the one hand, we needed to salvage AIG to prevent a return of the panic. On the other hand, AIG increasingly looked unsalvage-able. We had a "blue team" analyzing the best way to pump more money into the firm to stop the bleeding for good. But we had just tried to fashion a permanent solution for the company three months ago. So we also set up a "red team" to study if it would be possible for AIG to go into bankruptcy without mass contagion. When I polled both teams at a February meeting in my small conference room, there was growing support for letting AIG go bankrupt, especially if AIG could separate its rogue Financial Products unit from its healthier insurance subsidiaries—or, as somebody suggested, "take FP out back and shoot it."

One of the investment bankers whom Hank had hired at the end of 2008 to run TARP suggested the world might not end if AIG collapsed.

"I remember when Lehman filed, and the next week, life went on," he said. "Joe Schmo went to the ATM and didn't even notice it."

I was a bit stunned to hear that version of history. Lehman's filing had sent the worst shock through global markets in generations. It had taken trillions of dollars in guarantees by the U.S. government to break the panic, to make sure average Americans could still withdraw cash from ATMs when they wanted. And I thought AIG, the insurer of choice for troubled financial institutions and financial instruments, still posed even greater systemic risks. Perhaps I had some post-traumatic stress disorder from Lehman, but only because Lehman had been truly traumatic.

"You may not have felt anything," I replied. "But for those of us who saw it up close, believe me, we're not doing that again."

I had just pledged in my speech that the failure of systemic firms was no longer an option. Now we had to prove we intended to keep our commitments. Some red-team members suggested we could argue that AIG was an exceptional case, so letting it go would not reflect on our commitments to other firms. I asked if they were absolutely certain the world would believe us, because otherwise an AIG collapse could tear down the system. If we pulled the plug on AIG after investing such extraordinary resources in its survival, we would send a powerful message that our words didn't mean much, that we couldn't or wouldn't act to save systemic firms, most likely sparking a run on the remaining weak links.

"If we renege on AIG, Citi and Bank of America are next," I said.

"Until someone can show me there's a firewall high enough to protect the rest of the system from AIG's failure, we're not going there."

This is a classic problem in crisis response. The overwhelming temptation is to let the most egregious firms fail, to put them through a bankruptcy-type process like the FDIC had for community banks and then haircut their bondholders. But unless you have the ability to backstop every other systemic firm that's in a similar position, you'll just intensify fears of additional failures and haircuts. We didn't have that ability. Lee used to say it would be nice if we were the Adam Sandler character in the movie *Click* who could freeze time with a remote control. Then perhaps we could wind down AIG in an orderly fashion, and persuade the markets there was no need to panic. But in the real world, people react in real time, in dynamic and uncontrollable ways that reflect their perceptions and fears. We could hope our decisions about AIG would have minimal impact on other firms, but we couldn't be sure its failure wouldn't topple the entire financial system.

Citi was already under siege, as was Bank of America. On Friday, February 20, Citi's stock price dropped below $2. The cost of insuring BofA's bonds rose 15 percent. The markets had lost confidence in the quality of their capital, a slightly technical but extremely serious problem. Citi had enough "regulatory capital" to meet the requirements we had imposed at the Fed, but less than 20 percent of that capital was common equity from shareholders, the highest-quality capital, the permanent investments that can absorb losses and protect a troubled firm from insolvency. If you counted only common equity, Citi and BofA were now two of the most highly leveraged banks. Citi had more than $60 in assets for every $1 in top-flight capital, while BofA's ratio was nearly 40:1. And markets had stopped trusting lower-quality capital, even the preferred investments we made through TARP.

This was mostly foreseeable, and I should have paid much more attention to Citi's lack of common equity while I was at the Fed. Even the capital we pushed Citi to raise in late 2007 and 2008 came in the

Markets Were Very Concerned About
Large Financial Institutions Failing
Average Credit Default Swap Spreads of Six Large Institutions

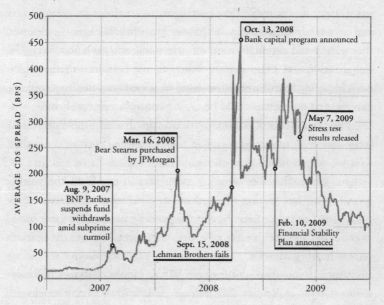

This market measure of the default risk of large financial institutions' senior debt increased sharply after Lehman's failure. While it receded temporarily following the initial TARP capital injections in the fall of 2008, confidence in the biggest banks only began to recover after the stress test results and the cumulative effects of our other policy initiatives in 2009.

Source: Bloomberg (represents the unweighted average of five-year CDS spreads of Bank of America, Citigroup, Goldman Sachs, JPMorgan, Morgan Stanley, and Wells Fargo).

lower-quality forms that investors now found meaningless. But now we had a more immediate problem. Rumors were swirling that we were going to nationalize Citi and BofA, so investors, fearful of getting wiped out, were running from them.

We were, in fact, preparing to take a larger stake in Citi to address its capital problems, but we were hoping to keep government ownership below a majority stake if at all possible. It was also true that inside the administration, we were discussing the possibility that bad stress test results could force us to take substantial equity stakes in some banks, perhaps amounting to effective nationalization. In our internal strategy discussions, some participants—at times including Larry and his adviser Jeremy Stein, his former Harvard colleague—suggested that widespread nationalization was inevitable and even necessary. Nationalization was a threatening word for investors in a market economy, implying that shareholders could be wiped out, creditors could be haircut, and politicians could be taking control of private firms.

The proponents of nationalization inside the administration were indeed pushing to impose losses on bank creditors, arguing that otherwise we would never have enough TARP dollars to recapitalize the system. External voices were no more reassuring. Even the world's most famous free market advocate, Alan Greenspan, declared in February that "it may be necessary to temporarily nationalize some banks in order to facilitate a swift and orderly restructuring." As the markets started hearing rumblings that we too were talking about nationalization and haircuts—sometimes from White House officials who brainstormed with academics and market participants—bank stocks fell and default risks increased.

This was deeply damaging at an exceptionally fragile moment. After outlining our programs before we could spell out the details, we were extremely vulnerable to speculation about our true intentions. The fear that we might re-create the conditions that unleashed the panic of the fall was undermining everything we were trying to do to put out the remaining fires. Lee kept saying he could feel the markets tremble with every exploratory call to New York from a White House staffer. There was an element of self-fulfilling prophecy at play. If the markets thought the administration thought the banks were doomed, the markets could doom the banks.

Of course, there were still a lot of good reasons to be worried about the world, no matter what was leaking out of our meetings. That Sunday, Larry and I sent the President an unbelievably dark memo. We noted that of the nation's four largest banking institutions—Citi, BofA, Wells Fargo, and JPMorgan—JPMorgan was the only one that wasn't "in distress." We said there was "a significant chance" that Citi and BofA would end up in the hands of the government. We warned that AIG was not only a devastating problem in its own right, it reflected deeper problems in its industry that imperiled similarly massive life insurers such as MetLife and Prudential. And we calculated that after financing the TALF credit facility, the PPIP investment funds, our foreclosure relief programs, the auto industry rescue, and whatever emergency interventions we'd need while the stress test was under way, we would likely have less than $100 billion left in TARP to recapitalize the banks.

"That is surely not enough," we wrote.

We would end up including a $750 billion placeholder for additional financial rescues in our first budget, more than we would request for the Pentagon.

But our first task, we told the President, was "immediate reassurance." The world had listened to my speech, and it hadn't believed my no-more-Lehmans promise. Our pledges to try to keep the banking system private hadn't seemed credible, either. We decided that before the markets opened Monday morning, the regulators would need to sign in blood on another joint statement, basically repeating the never-again message I had failed to get across in my speech two weeks earlier. "We reiterate our determination to preserve the viability of systemically important financial institutions," it said. In other words: No, seriously, we mean it. "The strong presumption . . . is that banks should remain in private hands," the statement concluded. In other words: please stop running away from Citi and BofA.

It's never good when the markets won't take the word of a Treasury secretary, but I didn't think there was much I could do to change that except back up my words with actions and give investors a chance to judge what we actually did. The wait for the stress test results would be excruciating. We would have to rely on the patience of the markets at a time when patience seemed almost irrational. And there was a very real possibility that the results would be terribly disappointing. We could talk about leaving banks in private hands, but we wouldn't be able to do that if it turned out they were truly insolvent. The President wanted us to rip off the Band-Aid, but we knew we might not like what we found underneath.

"There is the risk that our overall approach to large financial institutions will be overwhelmed by events in the most negative economic scenarios," we wrote in our memo. "We may, by being proactive, be blamed for causing the problems we are seeking to preempt. Further, there is the risk that . . . we will pull the 'Band-Aid' off a wound that we lack the capacity to sterilize and thus exacerbate problems."

In other words, even if we executed our plan properly, a depression remained a serious risk.

"On balance, though, our judgment is that the risks of alternative paths are even greater."

At least that was my judgment. I believed our plan was the least-bad option. We just had to roll it out, piece by piece, and hope it could win the confidence of the markets. The good news, although it certainly didn't seem that way at the time, was that my early struggles had set expectations about as low as they could go.

EIGHT

Plan Beats No Plan

On February 25, the Fed rolled out more details of the stress test that it would administer to the nineteen largest banks. Expectations were low, and we did not exceed them. The general reaction was that it looked like a whitewash, a bogus exam designed to give a clean bill of health to a gravely ill banking system.

The stress test was supposed to evaluate whether the banks had enough capital to survive a brutal downturn, and the critics didn't think the Fed's assumptions about the trajectory of the economy looked brutal enough. They complained that the Fed's "stressed" scenario for growth and jobs—the economy shrinking 3.3 percent in 2009, unemployment rising to 10.3 percent in 2010—sounded less like a doom-and-gloom scenario than a likely scenario. They turned out to be right about unemployment. But the Fed's assumptions for housing prices—down 14 percent in 2009 in a likely scenario, 22 percent in the stressed scenario—turned out to be much darker than reality.

The Fed's most important assumptions were the loss rates that bank assets would face in the stressed scenario, because those would determine how much capital the banks would need to raise. And those assumptions would be appropriately dark, even worse than the losses during the Great Depression. But the Fed did not release those assumptions at the time. As a result, many analysts—including all three quoted in the *New York Times* the next day—suspected the stress test would be too weak, an elaborate ruse to produce reassuring news.

"It sure sounds to me like they are designing this to make it sound like the banking system is in great shape," one banking expert told the *Times*.

That wasn't true. The Fed would play it straight. We knew that if the stress test results didn't seem credible, the markets would ignore them and assume the worst. But few outsiders seemed to have faith in the process. Behind closed doors, even Larry suggested the fix was in, complaining that the Fed was too cozy with banks, and that I was too protective of the Fed.

In fact, we didn't know how well the financial system was prepared for a severe downturn, so we designed our program to recapitalize it no matter what the stress test found. After the Fed identified how much capital each bank would need to survive the stressed scenario, the banks would have six months to raise enough capital from private investors to plug their shortfalls. If they couldn't, the Treasury would invest enough TARP capital to make up the difference. Our investments would again be in preferred shares, but they'd be "convertible" into common equity, so recipients would be better prepared to absorb losses.

There was one serious problem with this approach. The overarching goal of the stress test was to reduce uncertainty, but there would be tremendous uncertainty until the stress test was complete. For months, markets wouldn't know which banks would need to raise capital and how much they would need to raise. Shareholders wouldn't know how much dilution they were going to face, and if the government ended up taking equity stakes at extremely low prices, the dilution could be massive. We were already seeing accelerated flight from bank stocks, which was further depressing their prices and the potential dilution investors would face, which in turn was further accelerating flight from bank stocks.

Our solution to this death spiral was what Lee dubbed "the Geithner Put." He later teased me that it would be immortalized as the biggest put in financial history, which is why I prefer to think of it as the Kabaker Put; I'm sure Matt would enjoy having a put named after him. In any case, it effectively created a floor under bank stock prices, stopping the death spiral and encouraging private investments in financial firms that otherwise would have looked much too risky.

What the put did was fix the conversion price that Treasury would pay for stock in a bank just below the stock's price in the run-up to my February 10 speech, even if the market price dipped much lower. It did not eliminate the risk for bank investors, but it eliminated a lot of the uncertainty that was frightening them, and it reduced the risk that they would get totally clobbered. They might fall a few feet, but unless their bank was in terrible shape, they wouldn't fall a few stories. The media paid almost no attention to the put, which was just as well; it probably would have been trashed as a giveaway to bank investors. But our goal was to recapitalize the system, and every dollar of capital that private investors could inject would be a dollar that wouldn't have to come from taxpayers.

The hedge fund manager David Tepper later told the press that in February 2009, while the world was mocking my speech, his Appaloosa Management fund began buying bank stocks, because he read our public statements and thought our strategy sounded sensible. He continued to increase his investments in Bank of America and other troubled firms after we announced the put, and in 2009 his fund reportedly enjoyed some of the best returns ever recorded on Wall Street.

"You seemed to be keeping your word," Tepper told me after I'd left Treasury. "And I figured if you didn't keep your word, I could sue you."

Of course, our goal wasn't to help Tepper make billions of dollars for himself and his investors. Our goal was to get the economy growing again, and that required stabilizing the banks so they could start lending again. Tepper simply listened to what we said, watched what we did, and bet that we would succeed.

OUR BASIC strategy was to follow through on what we said we would do, and hope the system would hold together until the stress test was complete and our other rescue programs had time to get traction. But Citigroup and AIG were still on the brink of failure, and the collapse of either one could have made the fall of Lehman look mild.

With Citi, we faced a dual challenge. The bank clearly needed more capital to survive—and not just any capital, but common equity. Treasury was the most likely source of new capital. But rumors that we intended to nationalize the bank were shaking confidence in the entire banking system, because nationalization would mean steep losses for investors. We didn't want to let Citi fail, but we also didn't want to nationalize banks unless absolutely necessary; we had to dispel rumors of a government takeover if we didn't want a broader run on the system.

Instead, we settled on a solution where Citi's private preferred stockholders would convert their shares into common equity, and we would convert an equal amount of the government's TARP preferred shares. This conversion would enhance Citi's ability to absorb losses without additional TARP funds. It would also demonstrate that our initial TARP injections of preferred stock into other firms could be a source of greater firepower in the future. And while it would increase the government's stake in Citi to as much as 36 percent, we would not take a majority position, reassuring the markets that we wanted to avoid nationalization.

On February 26, the day after we rolled out the stress test, my exhausted team pulled an all-nighter to finalize the terms of the conversion, while Citi worked with investors such as Singapore's government fund and a Saudi prince to ensure their participation. By 5 a.m.

on the 27th, all that was missing was a signature from Treasury—and since I was still the President's only Senate-confirmed official at the Treasury, the signature had to be mine. But nobody knew where I was. A young staffer who had been assigned to catch me on my way into the office had gone to sleep on Kabaker's couch after setting his alarm to go off early. But I had arrived even earlier to work out in the Treasury gym.

Lee finally found me on a treadmill in the department's basement. I paused the machine and signed, adding $50 billion in common equity to Citi's buffer against losses.

As vital as it was to show we weren't looking to nationalize systemic firms, it was even more vital to show we wouldn't let them fail. We had to demonstrate that we were serious about no-more-Lehmans. Otherwise, private investors wouldn't put cash at risk to help recapitalize the financial system, and we weren't sure we had enough resources to do it through TARP. When it came to AIG, even after our extraordinary commitments, the markets weren't convinced we were willing to stand behind the company, and the rating agencies, with their exquisite timing, were threatening new downgrades. On March 2, we announced another $30 billion commitment to help AIG meet its obligations, and the rating agencies agreed to hold off. We were all in.

The political reaction was predictably fierce. AIG had explored the frontier of recklessness, and taxpayers were outraged that they were repeatedly paying to keep it afloat. That outrage was about to explode.

ON TUESDAY afternoon, March 10, I got some ugly news. Our TARP team had learned that AIG was about to pay $165 million in bonuses to employees in the Financial Products unit that had helped blow up the firm. The bonuses amounted to less than 0.1 percent of the U.S. commitment to AIG, but it was hard to imagine worse optics.

We went back and forth in my office trying to figure out whether we could legally block the bonuses, and whether it even made sense to try. Our lawyers thought AIG was contractually committed to paying the bonuses, and they did not believe we had the legal means to block them. I was instinctively skittish about the U.S. government breaking contracts, especially at a time when all sorts of commitments had been called into question. We weren't Venezuela. And I worried that if the U.S. government tried to impose a solution in one case, even this egregious case, we would send a message that no contract was safe, a destabilizing message during a crisis. As Lee Sachs liked to say: "In a storm, the world needs anchors." The rule of law was arguably our most important anchor, especially during this limbo period when fears of nationalization and federal interference were pervasive.

We had dealt with this bonus issue in a more general and theoretical form in early February, before we knew about AIG's situation. Senate Banking Committee Chairman Chris Dodd, facing a tough reelection battle in Connecticut, had inserted a populist executive compensation amendment into the Recovery Act, capping bonus payments for TARP recipients and empowering Treasury to "claw back" existing bonus arrangements. In discussions with Dodd's staff, my team had proposed a variety of changes, including a suggestion to remove the retroactive claw-back provision. We thought it would infringe the sanctity of contracts and change the terms of the TARP rescue. Senator Dodd agreed and stripped the provision out of the bill, while rejecting most of our other recommended fixes.

When the AIG news arrived a month later, I still worried that unless we had a clear legal basis, we could not force a financial firm to violate a contractual obligation without unleashing a new wave of panic and uncertainty. It would send a message that the protections of the law might not apply when politically inconvenient. It could make customers and counterparties wonder whether their contracts might be violated next, sparking runs on other financial institutions, and it could encourage talented employees of TARP-funded firms to flee. It could also make firms less willing to participate in TARP out of fear that we would retroactively change the conditions, weakening the power of our crisis-fighting tools.

But these concerns had no public constituency. The mess at AIG took the bonus issue out of the realm of theory. It was going to be impossible to explain.

The public was understandably incredulous that major TARP recipients had expressed their appreciation for their taxpayer-financed rescues by paying out boom-level bonuses in January 2009. And of course, I had helped design the original AIG rescue when I was still at the Fed. At the time, my staff and I had been too consumed with trying to contain the post-Lehman panic to even consider whether we could do anything about executive compensation. We had structured the rescue to distance government officials from managerial and commercial decisions inside the firm; AIG had promised those bonuses well before it began receiving government assistance. But now AIG's independent decisions were ending up on our doorstep anyway.

The AIG bonus scandal would take the media frenzy and the public anger to new levels, and I knew it would be another devastating blow to confidence in our crisis response. The next day, I called Ed Liddy, the new CEO of AIG, to say, essentially: What the fuck?

"This is going to kill us—and you!" I said.

Liddy said he had tried to renegotiate the bonuses, but his employees refused to accept anything less than they were promised. His attorneys believed that if the bonuses weren't paid in full, the employees would sue for breach of contract and the firm would be on the hook for as much as triple the amount, including damages. He said he could only try to renegotiate future payouts. I knew that wouldn't mollify anyone, but I did not believe I had any legal basis to stop contractually promised payments, and I thought the public relations value of trying to intervene would pale in comparison to the damaging specter of the U.S. government trying to break a private contract.

On the way to a meeting in the West Wing, I stopped by Rahm's office to tell him about the AIG mess. Rahm was the center of energy and activity in the West Wing, and we had a great relationship. He was constantly checking in with me to hear how the markets were doing, to plot strategy, to get a jump on what might go wrong next. He did not try to micromanage me on policy, and he was very creative about protecting me from other potential sources of interference in the White House. He wanted to keep close track of what we were doing, weigh in on our communications strategy, and make sure there were no unexpected surprises. I wanted that, too. I wanted to expose the White House to our unpalatable choices, and make sure it had a measure of ownership of our decisions, but without dragging the President too far into the muck of the details.

But there was no way I could protect the White House from this. It was hard to imagine a more politically damaging news story than taxpayer-funded bonuses for the arsonists who set the system on fire. And I told Rahm we didn't think we had any legal basis to intervene.

"We don't really have a choice," I said. "It's going to be a nightmare."

It was already hard to fathom the mess that had been dropped in President Obama's lap. Rahm called it "the gift bag." February was the worst jobs month yet, with unemployment rising to 8.1 percent. The S&P 500 had fallen to new lows the day before I learned about the bonuses, down 57 percent from its peak. The President publicly said it looked like a good time to buy stocks, which struck me as an unwise thing for him to say, although investors who took the financial-adviser-in-chief's advice would have more than doubled their money in four years. Meanwhile, car sales at Chrysler and GM had fallen in half, a disaster for their workers and suppliers, and an ominous sign for the entire manufacturing sector.

I was far away that Saturday when the AIG bonus news became public, attending a meeting of G-20 finance ministers in Horsham, an out-of-the-way town in the English countryside. It fell to Larry to go on the Sunday television shows to defend our position, repeating the word "outrageous" again and again, while trying to point out that we're a nation of laws. It didn't matter. The words "AIG" and "bonuses" in the same sentence were enough to convince most Americans that we were on the side of the bad guys.

• • •

HORSHAM WAS as cold as one would expect of England in March, and the chill invaded the stone-walled lodge where the ministers met. I was already run down after months without much sleep, and I caught some kind of flu. On the military plane that took us home Saturday night, I was coughing, aching, and unhappy. The summit had not been a great success; the headlines were mostly about international tensions. And I had to review materials for a meeting the next day with the President and his economic and political advisers, many of whom were deeply skeptical about our financial repair plans. We would have to make the case for staying the course.

I'm not a screamer, but I got a bit loud that night on the phone with Lee and Kabaker, and not just because the reception over the Atlantic was spotty. I was irked by a PowerPoint presentation that they had negotiated with Larry while I was away. The offending slides confronted the hypothetical of a bank that couldn't raise enough private capital to fill the hole identified by its stress test: What would we do if we had to inject so much TARP capital that the bank was effectively nationalized? Lee and Larry had agreed to present two options to the President. One was the Treasury plan for a "conservatorship approach," which would allow us to handle a bank in a way similar to the government's handling of Fannie and Freddie, so we'd have the discretion to wind down our investments gradually to minimize shocks to the system and losses for the taxpayers. The other was Larry's "rapid resolution exit," which would require an immediate restructuring of the bank, including immediate liquidation of bad assets.

Both options had their theoretical merits, but I didn't think Larry's approach was feasible or desirable. Somehow, though, Larry had talked Lee and Kabaker into making his strategy sound like a cool hawkish approach that would make the President a populist hero, while ours sounded like an equivocating dovish approach that would make the President seem cowed by the banks.

"There's no way you can present it like that! You're making the dominant option look pathetic!" I said over the crackling on the line. "You can't say we're dove and he's hawk. There's no dove. You've got to make it Hawk One and Hawk Two!"

I was concerned that everyone on board could hear me, including Robert Zoellick, the Republican diplomat whom President Bush had chosen to run the World Bank. I didn't want to advertise our internal divisions and add to the sense of disarray. But Hawk One/Hawk Two was important. It wasn't just about framing an arcane debate over resolving failed banks; it was about framing the larger debate about our plan. Larry and others were suggesting we were shying away from tough choices just as Japan had done after its banking crisis, setting up the United States for a Japan-style lost decade. We thought our strategy was plenty tough.

After all, we intended to force big banks to raise the capital they needed whether they wanted it or not. A credible stress test would ensure that the shareholders of the banks that needed the most capital would face the most dilution. The banks least capable of filling their gaps on their own would end up with the largest proportion of government ownership, but even the banks that did manage to raise capital from private investors would dilute the ownership stakes of existing shareholders. I remember once while Larry and I were sitting outside the Oval Office, I tried to convince him that this meritocratic form of triage would be brutal to the shareholders of the institutions that most deserved brutality, while avoiding the panic-inducing consequences of nationalization or liquidation.

"I don't see why you want to portray this as so generous to the banks," I said. "They're going to be diluted in proportion to their sins."

But Larry wasn't impressed by that argument, and he was a formidable debating opponent. He knew the President liked the idea of firm, decisive action that would end the bailout era and put the mess behind us. He often implied that while the President stood for bold problem solving, I stood for tentative half-measures. At one meeting in the Oval Office, Larry explained that the President was over *here,* as he extended his arm to his side, while Tim was over *here,* as he extended his opposite arm.

"I'm much closer to you, Mr. President," Larry said.

• • •

ON SUNDAY, March 15, from 3 p.m. until well past 10 p.m., President Obama and more than a dozen of his economic and political advisers discussed our financial crisis response in the Roosevelt Room. Lee and Kabaker had edited their deck to make it clearer that both options were hawkish, but Larry was in classic form, disparaging our strategy as "watchful waiting" for a patient that needed "radical surgery." Echoing the President's own words on my first day as secretary, he said the time had come to rip off the Band-Aid and let the system begin to heal. His recurrent theme was that our plan was too reminiscent of Japan, which had kept its zombie banks alive and suffered the consequences of its timidity, and not enough like Sweden, which had nationalized banks and enjoyed a buoyant recovery.

The President was sympathetic to Larry's views, which some accounts of the Obama administration have used to suggest that he wanted to abandon our plan.

"We don't want to do Japan," he said at one point.

The Roosevelt Room meeting was a spirited debate at a time when I was not exactly at the commanding heights of influence. My team and I spent most of the meeting on defense. The relentless criticism of "Tim's plan" was a reminder that this all was on me, that even my colleagues inside the administration—led by Larry, who had supported my career since I was his noisy scribe—were unimpressed. The President clearly wanted to hear what disturbed them about our plan, and he let them vent for hours.

But we had already announced the outline of our plan. We had launched several specific components of the plan. We couldn't scrap or dramatically revamp it before we knew the results of the stress test without risking even more turmoil in the markets. The Roosevelt Room meeting was an opportunity for our colleagues who felt uneasy about the plan to express their criticisms and angst. It was also a chance for the President to get immersed in the debate in case he wanted to adjust our plan down the road. It wasn't a referendum on whether to proceed.

The main policy issue we debated was the Hawk One/Hawk Two hypothetical of what to do if the government needed to take a majority stake in a bank, either before or after its stress test and capital-raising period were complete. Larry and others wanted us to commit to forceful restructuring policies in advance—breaking up or carving up the hobbled banks, replacing management, unloading assets, perhaps even haircutting certain creditors to help cover the losses.

My basic response was: Sure, that might make sense in some cases. We'll see. We couldn't know what would be optimal months in advance; it would depend on the bank and the state of the world at the time. We couldn't decide now, and it made no sense to tie our hands. We were also constrained by the limits of our authority, which didn't really allow preemptive nationalization. We still had no way to wind down large complicated financial firms, and the FDIC could step in to take over smaller banks only when they were on the verge of failure or technically insolvent under existing regulatory requirements, which none of them were at that point. We were also constrained by the limits of our remaining financial resources. Whatever the possible virtues of a "rapid resolution" strategy, it would be expensive. Hours into the meeting, we got to the last slide in our deck, which noted almost in passing that Hawk Two could require $200 billion to $400 billion in additional capital, more than we had left in TARP.

Rahm practically leapt out of his seat.

"What are you talking about?" he said. "There's no more fucking money!" The last thing he wanted was to force the President to ask Congress for another TARP.

The skeptics had a lot of legitimate concerns, but few feasible solutions. Larry and Christy made economic arguments that the banks were in worse shape than we thought. Political advisers made political arguments for more Old Testament justice. Again, my response was: You might be right, and you might get what you want. We'll see. The results of the stress test would reveal the health of the banks. Their success or failure in raising private capital would determine how tough we would be. We couldn't responsibly short-circuit the process before we knew how it would play out. For now, the debate was purely theoretical.

It was certainly a theoretical debate worth having. I wanted the President and our internal critics to understand exactly what we were doing. And the President was right: We didn't want to do Japan. Although it wasn't entirely fair to Japan, that was shorthand for turning a blind eye to the remaining capital hole in our banking system, for hoping that if we waited around long enough the economy would improve enough for the assets to recover their value and lift the banks out of trouble. That's what Larry meant by "watchful waiting."

But that wasn't our strategy. The stress test was the opposite of turning a blind eye; it would subject the banks and their assets to unprecedented scrutiny and transparency. And unlike the early Japanese strategy of "regulatory forbearance," their see-no-evil approach of letting undercapitalized banks slide, we would make sure banks ended up with enough capital to survive a severe downturn, whether the capital was injected voluntarily by investors or forcibly by us. Finally, if a bank did turn out to be insolvent, we didn't intend to follow the Japan model of letting it limp along for years, too weak to lend, dragging down the economy. Our approach to banks that needed another significant dose of government capital, whether it mirrored Hawk One or Hawk Two, would look more like Sweden than Japan.

Among the opponents of "doing Japan," there was a lot of enthusiasm for "doing Sweden," shorthand for biting the bullet and nationalizing up front. This affection, however, was based on a bit of myth about what actually happened in Sweden. Lee and Kabaker explained that Sweden had exhausted every other option during the first two years of its crisis before turning to nationalization. Then it nationalized only two of its six major banks—and only after it fully guaranteed the liabilities of its entire banking system to prevent the fire from spreading. Sweden's banks were also much smaller and less global than ours, at a time when the rest of the world economy was much healthier and the global financial system was much less fragile.

What we tried to push back against was the idea that preemptive nationalization was an appealing option, a cool way to look muscular and advertise our determination to tackle problems. We thought it would be a financial, political, legal, and logistical nightmare. We knew it might eventually be necessary for the weakest institutions. The government had already placed Fannie and Freddie into conservatorship and their CEOs had been replaced. AIG had to replace its CEO, and it was in the process of dramatically downsizing its sprawling businesses. But the notion that we should even consider nationalizing a large swath of the banking system as anything but a last resort, just because it felt resolute and cleansing, seemed irresponsible and unwise.

If we nationalized a major bank, we would not only own all its legacy losses and risks, which could be hugely expensive for taxpayers; we would own its management issues and compensation messes and who knew what other surprises. Congress would feel like it owned them, too, and would be tempted to interfere in the bank's business decisions for political purposes. Bill Isaac, a former FDIC chairman, had put it well in a *Wall Street Journal* op-ed that had resonated with me, recounting how the 1984 nationalization of Continental Illinois, a tiny bank by modern standards, had been a terrible mess that lost taxpayer money and dragged on for seven years. Lee compared nationalizing a big bank to invading Iraq.

"If you want to go in, you better be sure there are WMDs," he said. He echoed Colin Powell's famous Pottery Barn rule: If you break it, you own it.

In other words, before we decided to take responsibility for a troubled bank, we'd better be sure it was truly insolvent. And we thought the best way to judge that was through the stress test. Our critics said we should just take over Citigroup, to signal discontinuity and intolerance for Wall Street excess. That struck me as a rash effort to claim a scalp; we had just orchestrated the share conversion to strengthen the company, going out of our way to avoid taking a majority stake, and Citi was actually starting to show signs of stability.

More important, we had already announced a process through the stress test that would give the world a better sense of how much more capital Citi and the other banks would need, and would give them a chance to raise that capital on their own. Why would we go out of our way to abandon that process, another wrenching lurch in strategy, in order to take over a multi-trillion-dollar international banking operation? How would that help the rest of the still-fragile financial system? What impact would it have on the markets, particularly the shareholders and bondholders of other banks awaiting stress test results? My team thought the most likely result of a preemptive nationalization of Citi would be a run on Bank of America, potentially followed by Wells Fargo, Morgan Stanley, and Goldman Sachs. We could quickly end up owning half the banking system. In a crisis, you can't nationalize one firm and haircut its creditors unless you are prepared to guarantee the obligations of every other similarly situated firm. Sweden had done that, but it's not the kind of thing you do if you have other options.

In any case, our plan was already in motion. We knew it had risks. We couldn't be sure it would work. But our critics didn't have feasible plans of their own. As they kept pushing the President to be proactive and tough, I kept asking them to flesh out the alternatives and walk us through them. How would that work? Where would you get the authority? How about the money? Then what happens? What's the exit strategy? I tried to remind everyone that concern is not a strategy, and that plan beats no plan. I wanted the President to see there weren't plausible alternatives to proceeding with the stress test, and we were still preserving all our options for the next stage.

After a few hours of asking hard questions and listening to the debate, President Obama said he was going to get a haircut and dinner. He told us to get on the same page before he got back. As the meeting broke up, I thought I heard him ask if five guys could follow him to the Oval Office. What he in fact asked was whether anyone wanted Five Guys, a hamburger chain I had never heard of, although I would later discover my son Ben liked it, too.

Once the President left, Rahm, Axelrod, and Robert Gibbs ordered cheeseburgers from the White House mess, but the economic team just sat around arguing, fueled only by occasional dips into a bowl of Hershey's Kisses. Rahm returned to the subject of Hawk One/Hawk Two. He made it clear that if we needed hundreds of billions of extra dollars to resolve banks Larry's way, then we weren't going to do it Larry's way. Period. Someone then asked Larry what we should do if we couldn't get more money.

"We'll have to do Tim's plan," Larry said.

I was later asked about an author's claim that the President decided in the Roosevelt Room that we should nationalize Citi, and that I had slow-walked his instructions. That was not true. The plan for Citi was no different from the plan for the other firms, which was to see how it did in the stress test, see if it could raise capital privately, then figure out if we needed to do more. The President understood the risks of lurching into a preemptive nationalization strategy, and he never told me to pursue that path.

I remember an amusing moment during the break, when Larry suddenly looked perplexed, as if he had just discovered something unexpected in a familiar place.

"You know, this stuff is really hard," he said.

"Welcome to my world," I replied.

We thought we showed the President we had a good plan, not just *a* plan. It wasn't just the least-bad option. But the President certainly got a crash course in its risks. Many of his senior advisers, the people he trusted to promote his interests and philosophy, thought it was bad policy and bad politics. And our newest controversy was going to do more damage to confidence in the wisdom of our overall strategy.

"Mr. President," I said near the end of the meeting, "this AIG thing is going to get ugly." We discussed the problem with the bonuses, and why we didn't believe we could stop them.

"Let me get this straight," the President said. "We're going to pay bonuses to the very people who caused all this damage to the financial system? And, by the way, a lot of them live in London so we won't even collect taxes on their bonuses?"

Yeah, basically. The President winced. He had been remarkably supportive of our approach. He had been amazingly supportive of me. He had already shown his willingness to stand behind deeply unpopular decisions that made his political advisers cringe. But it would be hard to top the unpopularity of this one.

THE NEXT day, the President and I announced a new small business lending initiative in the East Room. After I laid out the details in my usual colorless fashion, the President said he wanted to take a moment to discuss his outrage about the AIG bonuses.

"I've asked Secretary Geithner to use [our] leverage and pursue every single legal avenue to block these bonuses and make the American taxpayers whole," he said. "I want everybody to be clear that Secretary Geithner has been on the case."

I read a draft of those remarks the morning of the event, and I wasn't pleased. We didn't think we could claw back the bonuses that had already been obligated, and even if we could modestly reduce future payouts, raising public expectations seemed unwise. I thought the President should stay as far away from the issue as possible. I didn't see the need to remind everyone that I was "on the case," either.

But the country wanted blood. That week, the House of Representatives rode the wave of populist anger by passing a confiscatory

90 percent tax on Wall Street bonuses, though the bill would die quietly in the Senate. While grilling CEO Ed Liddy at a hearing, Barney Frank, usually a paragon of reason, demanded the names of AIG's bonus recipients; Liddy, who had joined the firm after its downfall out of civic duty and had agreed to a one-dollar salary, had to read aloud an anonymous letter threatening to track down AIG executives and strangle them with piano wire before Frank backed off.

The AIG bonuses quickly became shorthand for government coddling of Wall Street, and I was perceived as the coddler-in-chief. Once when Paul Volcker saw me talking on my cell phone as he walked down the aisle of the New York–Washington shuttle, he mock-whispered: *Just say no!* Volcker was joking, mostly, but the general perception— dating back to a *Washington Post* column during my confirmation calling me a "Goldman Sachs alum"—had hardened that I was just another banker at the helm of Treasury, doing the bidding of the banks. New York Mayor Michael Bloomberg once introduced me at a public event as a Goldman guy; CBS newsman Harry Smith referred several times to my Goldman past during an interview; even Rahm's wife once told me I must be looking forward to returning to Goldman.

Around that time, Senate majority leader Harry Reid—the only politician I knew who could match my clipped brevity on the phone— invited me to attend the regular lunch of the Senate Democratic caucus, our supposed allies on the Hill. But liberal populists dominated the room, and they didn't display much affection toward me. I remember Senator Bernie Sanders, the lefty firebrand from Vermont, yelling about how the President had only Wall Street people around him. I listed some of the progressive economists on the President's team, including Christy Romer, Jared Bernstein, Gene Sperling, and Alan Krueger, my chief economist at Treasury. I explained that I had never worked on Wall Street. But the prevailing mood was dismissive. Afterward, I told Pete Rouse, a legendary behind-the-scenes Senate power broker who was now the President's counselor, how badly the meeting had gone. I said I thought I should tell the President.

"Don't worry about them," Rouse told me. "They've probably already forgotten every word they said."

I had to testify about the bonuses, too, a hearing I remember mainly because my daughter, Elise, running on a treadmill at the gym, saw me on TV sitting in front of a "Fire Geithner" banner held aloft by some Code Pink activists. Michele Bachmann, a conservative from what would soon be known as the Tea Party wing of the Republican Party, kept demanding that I point out the section of the Constitution that approved what we had done, as if the congressional approval of TARP was null and void because the Constitution didn't specifically mention bank rescues. Liberal Democrat Maxine Waters suggested we were doing the bidding of Goldman Sachs. Another conservative Republican, Jeb Hensarling, went after me with echoes of Watergate.

"Mr. Secretary, the public needs a straight answer," he said. "What did the Obama administration know, and when did they know it?"

The challenge during these long and stormy congressional grillings was to endure them, to be civil in the face of the grandstanding. Alan Greenspan once told me his coping mechanism for enduring hearings was to think about lunch. But while the Hill theater didn't usually matter much, the overall bonus furor was compounding the reputational damage for AIG, driving the company back toward the financial abyss. Customer renewals in AIG's key insurance business declined sharply in March, and the company's credit ratings were at risk yet again. Even though we had already committed an unfathomable $182 billion to AIG, some members of my team still thought we might have to break up the firm through a bankruptcy-type process. We had only $110 billion left in TARP to fix the banks as well as the auto industry, so the idea of tapping those funds to resolve AIG immediately was not appealing. But there were still a lot of enthusiasts for that idea, despite my warnings that it could revive the panic.

The politics of crisis response were unspeakably awful, and I thought the White House's efforts to align itself with the populist fury were growing increasingly futile. On March 27, the President invited the CEOs of the major banks to the White House, where he famously said our administration was the only thing standing between them and the pitchforks. I guess the idea of the meeting was to show the President pressuring bankers to show restraint on compensation, but the overall effect was to reinforce the sense that we weren't willing to do much about it—and that the financial elite was welcome at the White House. The President once told me he felt uncomfortable playing a populist, like he was wearing clothes that didn't fit. He wasn't going to be a convincing Teddy Roosevelt, lambasting the "malefactors of great wealth." And the bankers weren't going to impose public-sector salaries on themselves and their senior executives. They were surprised and resentful about the public antipathy, and they thought we were feeding it.

There was just a vast chasm of misunderstanding separating the bankers, the public, and us. At one point in the meeting, JPMorgan Chase's Jamie Dimon told the President he could lend me his team to help draft our proposed financial reforms. This was not a tempting offer. Dimon would later express genuine irritation to the President that we hadn't taken him up on it, as if it would have been a feather in our caps to let Wall Street's most powerful firm help write our new Wall Street regulations. After the White House meeting, one banker told the press the session showed "we're all in this together," which was not quite the message the White House wanted.

We never really figured out how to navigate the populist waters. One of my advisers, Jake Siewert, suggested I see President Clinton on a later trip to New York. Jake had been Clinton's press secretary, and he thought it would be helpful for me to discuss the politics of populism with the master practitioner; we had a nice conversation over takeout soul food in the former President's Harlem office. I remember he was on a diet, so he ordered something healthy and picked fried chicken off everyone else's plates. He had lots of excellent political advice; for example, he urged us to continue to push hard to raise taxes on the top income bracket, but cautioned me to make sure I didn't look like I was happy about it. Unfortunately, when it came to the anger about bailouts and Wall Street, he said the American people were just too angry to be appeased.

"You could take Lloyd Blankfein into a dark alley and slit his throat, and it would satisfy them for about two days," he said. "Then the bloodlust would rise again."

Of course, it wasn't much fun to be on the receiving end of so much of that anger. My colleagues kept asking with deep concern if I was OK, as if I had contracted some pitiable disease. I tried to keep presenting a good sense of equanimity, but I knew I was a political liability.

One morning before we walked into the Oval Office, Larry mused that the President probably thought he was getting a Rubin-Greenspan dream team when he hired us, another above-the-fray "Committee to Save the World." It wasn't turning out that way, and there was something poignant about that.

"It must be hard for him," Larry said.

"REGARDLESS OF whether he stays, resigns, or is fired, there is universal agreement that Treasury Secretary Tim Geithner is 'embattled,'" began a *Slate* article in late March. After listing several examples of the media calling me "embattled," the author compared my status to other embattled figures—such as former Illinois Governor Rod Blagojevich, a Democrat indicted for corruption, and former Idaho Senator Larry Craig, a Republican arrested for lewd conduct in an airport bathroom—to gauge my chances of survival. He concluded they weren't zero, because "if Geithner stepped down under a cloud, that could send investor confidence, and thus the markets, into the ground."

That particular spring, that counted as optimism. The President kept expressing confidence in me publicly, in press briefings, on *60 Minutes,* even on *The Tonight Show,* but that just fueled more speculation that I was on my way out. I sometimes joked about my inevitable firing with Axelrod. "The sooner, the better," I said. More seriously, I told Rahm several times that I'd resign if he thought it would help the President. He told me, in colorful terms, that my resignation was not desired. Still, I recognized that if our overall strategy failed miserably, I would be the fall guy, and rightfully so.

I was pretty disciplined about ignoring my press clippings and limiting my cable TV diet to *SportsCenter*. But I worried that the cumulative damage of all these controversies, and especially the white-hot rage over AIG, would make it impossible for me to be effective. That spring, I asked my friend Michelle Smith, a savvy Washington hand who had worked with me during my first stint at Treasury and was now Ben's communications director at the Fed, whether I would ever recover enough for me to do my job properly. She said she thought I would, but that it could take another year. I was beginning to think it would be hard to wait that long.

In some ways, those days were easier than the worst of 2008, because I believed we had a reasonably good plan, even though I may have been the only one who thought so. I didn't feel helpless. But it was still a searing time. I was living apart from my family, feeling lonely. I was racked with guilt about what I was exposing them to. Carole felt as acutely as I did the huge burden of responsibility my job entailed, the pain of my failure to give more confidence to a wounded country. She didn't take my advice to avoid reading the news, and she took the constant attacks on me personally. At one point, David Axelrod called her to thank her for her sacrifice, because it really was a sacrifice.

I was lucky to have friends in Washington from graduate school and my earlier stint at Treasury, who knew me before I became a public figure, who didn't care about my standing in the Beltway constellation. And it was somewhat freeing to be a reluctant warrior. I hadn't sought the job, and I had no aspirations for another job in public life, so I could try to do it as well as I could without worrying too much about the personal fallout. I remember Bob Rubin reminding me over dinner to just make sure I was true to myself, to do what I believed was best and right, not to bend too much to the political imperative.

This was partly his way of gently chiding us for doing too many public events designed to align ourselves with Old Testament concerns, but it was good advice. Generally, I tried to focus on what I could control.

Unfortunately, there was a lot I couldn't control. I was still the President's only Senate-confirmed appointee at Treasury, running a department with 120,000 employees during a crisis. When Jim Lehrer of PBS came to Treasury to interview me, he was stunned by how empty it was on the third floor, where the senior staff was supposed to sit. We could hear our footsteps echoing through the halls. It was hard to find confirmable candidates at a time when most forms of financial expertise and experience were considered disqualifying. One candidate to be my deputy didn't work out because she had been a top SEC official during the boom, another because she had served on the boards of AIG and Goldman Sachs. I even tried to bring in Rodge Cohen, who had represented just about every troubled Wall Street firm during the crisis, but he withdrew as well, probably a wise political decision.

I finally had the inspiration to call Rahm and ask him to send over Neal Wolin. After Oxford and Yale Law School, Neal had worked for Bob Gates at the CIA; he had been Treasury's general counsel during the Clinton administration; he had run a major insurance business; and now he was a deputy White House counsel. Rahm immediately told him to get the fuck over to Treasury to help me, without even specifying a job. Neal says the call where I actually asked him to be my deputy a few weeks later lasted less than thirty seconds.

One of Neal's first excellent insights was that we simply couldn't function as long as the AIG bonus mess was smoldering in our laps. "It's sucking the life out of everything," he said. His idea was to bring in Ken Feinberg, who had overseen the September 11 victim fund, as an independent "special master" to oversee compensation at TARP firms. Feinberg would do a great job reining in some of the industry's excesses; he was not the slightest bit intimidated by the titans of finance. And it would be good for me not to have to get too deep into the messy and time-consuming process of pushing down the levels of compensation in individual firms, even though we'd still get blamed for whatever excesses remained.

Otherwise, I tried to keep us moving, laying out the details of our new programs, showing the markets we would do what we said we would do. And, gradually, even in the depths of AIG hell and bailout rage, we started to see the early signs of light.

• • •

IN LATE March, the President was as worried about our plan as anyone. The uncertainty of waiting for the stress test was agonizing. The derision of my colleagues, the press, and the public was troubling. So was the market reaction. We had already rolled out new financial programs to support the housing market through mortgage modifications and new aid for Fannie and Freddie, to revive consumer and business lending through TALF, and to repair the banking system through the stress test and capital assistance. Investors remained unimpressed.

During one Oval Office meeting not long after the Roosevelt Room showdown, the President asked me: "Tim, are you sure your plan is going to work?"

I said no. I was not sure. I explained that it had taken economists decades to reach a rough consensus on what policymakers screwed up in the Great Depression. Nothing in life was certain. "But I'm confident that our plan is better than the alternatives, Mr. President," I said. He presumably would have liked a more definitive show of confidence.

On March 23, we finally got some positive feedback from the markets, after we unveiled some details of our Public-Private Investment Program for buying toxic assets. Prominent economists and journalists portrayed it as yet another giveaway to Wall Street, "a vulture fund relief scheme," as Martin Wolf of the *Financial Times* put it. Paul Krugman dubbed it "financial hocus-pocus" and "cash for trash," while the economist Jeffrey Sachs, who had already accused us of ripping off taxpayers to enrich bankers, called it "even more potentially disastrous." But the markets loved it. Stocks rose 7 percent, the first day of mostly good news in my two months at Treasury. Investors, who had been disappointed after Hank twice abandoned plans to buy toxic assets, and then again when my initial speech hadn't lived up to the leaked expectations about asset purchases, were excited again.

I thought the giddy investors and our angry detractors were all overreacting. The PPIP fund was not a decisive element of our strategy, and while it did offer some incentives for private asset managers to invest in distressed assets, it was not nearly as generous to Wall Street as everyone thought. Overall, the government would take more downside risk than our private partners, while any profits would be split evenly. In a market dominated by sellers, we thought it was important to put the massive firepower of the government on the buy side. But the private funds would still have to put money at risk if they wanted to buy. And financial firms with troubled assets would be under no obligation to sell.

That was why we liked the PPIP. Market forces would determine the prices of distressed assets, reducing the risk that taxpayers would overpay and provide a massive backdoor bank bailout, as well as the risk that banks would be forced into fire sales and massive losses. But that was also why we had modest expectations for what it might accomplish.

Ultimately, the PPIP would help catalyze more activity in illiquid markets, but it would directly finance only about $22 billion in asset purchases, a far cry from the $1 trillion potential amount we had initially announced. If it had been the money-for-free boondoggle that our critics described, there would have been a lot more interest. At the time, though, we were happy the markets were happy. I hadn't anticipated such a spark in confidence. As for our critics, well, the market rally just reinforced their view that everything we did was too generous to Wall Street.

I remember one revealing exchange when I testified before the Congressional Oversight Panel, a TARP monitoring body led by the Harvard law professor and noted consumer protection advocate

Elizabeth Warren. This time, the Code Pink signs behind my head said "Give Us Our \$\$\$\$\$ Back!"—which we ultimately did with interest. Damon Silvers, an AFL-CIO attorney and a member of the panel, was grilling me about PPIP, trying to get me to admit it was a heads-Wall-Street-wins-tails-taxpayers-lose scam, when the cross-examination took a personal turn.

"Let me stop you right there," Silvers said. "What I don't get—and I practice law, and you've been in banking—is a deal—"

"I've never actually been in banking," I interrupted.

"Well, a long time ago," he said.

"Actually, never," I replied.

"Investment banking," Silvers retorted.

"Never investment banking," I said. "I've spent my entire life in public service at the Treasury and the Federal Reserve."

"All right," Silvers conceded. "Very well then." And then he continued his attack on PPIP as a shocking handout to financial interests.

THE ECONOMY shed another 800,000 jobs in March, pushing the unemployment rate to 8.7 percent. The human costs of joblessness were devastating, but the jobless number was also a political disaster that would undermine our efforts to ease those human costs. In January 2009, Christy Romer and Jared Bernstein had issued a forecast suggesting the Recovery Act would keep the jobless rate below 8 percent, giving Republicans an enduring anti-stimulus talking point. Clearly, the problem was that the pre-stimulus situation had been worse than we realized, not that the brand-new stimulus had already failed, but Republicans would cite that forecast incessantly. Economically, their argument that stimulus was actually making things worse was ridiculous, but politically, it packed a punch. It was short and simple, in contrast to our long and complicated explanations about counterfactuals. It was another reminder of the perils of prediction, making us look like an economic gang that couldn't shoot straight.

Partisan spin aside, it was true that two months into President

Obama's term, things felt worse—especially in the industrial Midwest, where some factory towns had 20 percent unemployment. And GM and Chrysler had burned through their Bush administration bridge loans, so we had to decide whether and how to try to save them. I had no background in manufacturing, but I thought it would be crazy to let GM or Chrysler collapse in the midst of a deep recession if we could somehow help them become viable again.

In our strategy debates at the White House, Christy Romer, Austan Goolsbee, and others argued that letting Chrysler die would give GM a better chance to live, but I never got the sense the President considered that option too seriously. Our team analyzing the auto industry believed that Chrysler had a decent chance to survive if it restructured and completed a merger with the Italian automaker Fiat. With hundreds of thousands of jobs at stake, we weren't going to consign a potentially salvageable company to the scrap heap. That would have caused substantial new damage to an economy that was still contracting, offsetting the benefits of the stimulus.

I had a lot of confidence in "Team Auto," an experienced group of investors, lawyers, and financial advisers led by Steve Rattner and Ron Bloom. The team reported to Larry and me, but I generally left the details to them. Rattner didn't even consult me before he fired General Motors CEO Rick Wagoner; if anything, that move increased my confidence in Team Auto. They balanced a solid understanding of the industry's importance with an appropriate disdain for its leadership's unwillingness to change. In our meetings, President Obama kept telling them to be tough, to ignore the politics, to focus on how the companies could become competitive again. GM's management assumed that we would keep sending them checks, that we wouldn't dare force America's most iconic company to restructure through bankruptcy, but that was a serious miscalculation.

On March 30, the President announced that we would provide additional TARP loans to keep GM and Chrysler afloat, but with aggressive deadlines for them to propose viable restructuring plans or else face government-facilitated bankruptcies. "Year after year, decade after decade, we've seen problems papered over and tough choices kicked down the road, even as foreign competitors outpaced us," he said. "Well, we've reached the end of that road." By the end of the spring, both firms would be in bankruptcy, and Team Auto would be restructuring them.

Once again, we hit the political sweet spot where the right, the left, and much of the middle disapproved of our actions. Most of the country saw the GM and Chrysler rescues as new big-government bailouts for mismanaged firms. But the industry and its Democratic defenders saw the stringent conditions as a betrayal, especially compared to our approach to the financial industry. Bankruptcy would mean haircuts for creditors—as well as hardships for autoworkers, retired autoworkers, and auto dealers—that we hadn't imposed during our bank rescues.

"The banks have received ten times more money than the auto industry. And yet they seem to be receiving very different treatment," Elizabeth Warren observed when I testified before her oversight panel. She challenged me directly: "Do you think the banks are better managed than the auto companies were?"

Not necessarily, but GM and Chrysler weren't viable in their current forms. The stress test would help determine the extent to which that was true for the banks. More important, the financial industry is very different from the auto industry and every other industry. A bank's most important asset is its reputation for creditworthiness; its entire business depends on customers and creditors trusting it with their money. Banks are also much more reliant on short-term financing, and they are much more vulnerable to failure if that financing dries up.

As we had seen with the Lehman collapse and WaMu haircuts in the fall of 2008, banks are also inherently more vulnerable to contagion. The automakers did not rely heavily on runnable short-term financing, and lenders could more easily tell which of them were in trouble. Using the bankruptcy process to reduce their debt obligations would send a message about the dangers only of lending to failing car companies, not car companies in general. By contrast, confidence is the lifeblood of the entire financial industry, and in a crisis, investors have a much harder time distinguishing the strong from the weak among banks than they do in other industries. That's why haircuts for bank creditors or disorderly failures of systemic banks during a panic can trigger runs on the entire financial system, especially when the system is relying on short-term funding that can flee in an instant. Financial failures are different from auto failures or any other failures, which is why Congress equipped the FDIC with special bankruptcy-like powers to deal with failing banks.

We thought that was pretty solid logic. But we were under no illusions that the public would embrace it. We just had to focus on what approach was most likely to work, and hope the public would judge us on the results rather than the optics.

AT THE start of April, President Obama and I went to London for his first G-20 conference, a high-profile test of the international community's ability to work together to attack the crisis. During the Depression, nations had turned inward, erecting new trade barriers in a damaging race to the bottom, embracing austerity while global demand withered. We were determined not to repeat those mistakes. Our fortunes were closely tied up with the rest of the world, and it would be tough to turn the U.S. economy around if the global economy continued to contract.

Some G-20 nations, particularly Germany and France, wanted the meetings to focus primarily on long-term international regulatory reforms that could help mitigate the next crisis. But this crisis was still burning. Larry and I thought our main imperative should be building consensus for a coordinated short-term program of economic stimulus and financial support that could alleviate the crisis and boost global demand. The President decided we would push for both.

A powerful stimulus effort would require a serious mobilization of resources for emerging economies. At an early stage in our internal discussions, Mark Sobel, a veteran Treasury civil servant who held my old international job, and the Fed crisis maven Ted Truman, whom I had recruited to Treasury to help oversee our international efforts, proposed that we should push to expand the IMF emergency fund that we helped create after the Mexican peso crisis. Sobel suggested we try to increase its financing from $50 billion to $300 billion, to make sure it had enough firepower to support countries in trouble.

"Let's do five hundred billion," I said. The magnitude of the collapse had been huge, and there was no point in undershooting. Just like that, we decided to propose $500 billion.

At the meeting of finance officials in Horsham, I had pushed to get the major G-20 countries to commit to a substantial fiscal stimulus program; my staff suggested a target of 2 percent of GDP. But I hadn't made much headway. The post-summit *New York Times* headline was "No Clear Accord on Stimulus by Top Industrial Nations." In Europe, support for stimulus was already fading. The Germans talked up the moral virtues of fiscal discipline for the world. There was talk that the French, who were also promoting a premature shift to austerity, might actually walk out of the London summit. Many foreign governments blamed U.S. profligacy for the crisis, and didn't think we were in a position to tell them how to restore growth.

The world desperately needed more stimulus, and Larry wanted us to push much harder to get the rest of the G-20 on board with a specific quantitative commitment. I was worried that the summit would end in division, giving the President an early failure on the international stage. So I told Larry's deputy, David Lipton, to tone down the confrontational rhetoric in the press and to stop raising expectations we might not be able to meet. "We need a 'Kumbaya' moment," I said. I had known many of the other finance ministers for years, better than I knew many of my new colleagues in the administration, and I knew they didn't like lectures from the White House. Given the damage our crisis had caused and the extent of the failures in our financial system, we had to approach the negotiations with a measure of humility, and try to rebuild some credibility internationally.

So we toned down the rhetoric and worked to build consensus. The results far exceeded expectations, and the agreements we announced in London helped begin to restore stability in the global economy. There was no specific target for fiscal stimulus—that was never going to happen—but we got a general commitment "to deliver the scale of sustained fiscal effort necessary to restore growth." More concretely, the G-20 agreed to deploy $1.1 trillion in new international financing to fight the crisis, including the full $500 billion for the IMF emergency fund. We committed not to introduce new measures of trade protection. And we agreed on the broad outlines of future financial reforms, including higher capital standards. This time, the media takeaway from the summit was about coordination and cooperation.

"World Leaders Agree on Global Response," the *Wall Street Journal* headline said.

London was an important success for the President, and it felt particularly satisfying to me. Despite our own economic weakness, and lingering resentments over U.S. foreign policy in the Bush years, we had set the agenda. After the summit ended, a beaming President Sarkozy walked up to President Obama and me, pumping his fists and chanting "Geithner! Geithner!"—as if I were his favorite soccer star.

It was a goofy gesture, and the President looked at me with raised eyebrows as if to say: What's up with this? But it was nice to feel less embattled for a moment.

I RETURNED home to our crisis, bruising congressional hearings, and meetings, lots of meetings, endless meetings. Meetings are life in Washington. Often they're just for show, a way to suggest motion or commitment to an issue. Sometimes their main purpose is to make people feel included. But occasionally they're the real thing, a forum for actual policymaking. I got into the habit of walking into crowded meetings in Larry's office and joking: "Is this a real meeting or a fake meeting?" In other words, are we talking about a policy that requires a decision, or just talking? When it was a real meeting, I'd usually suggest that we skip the throat-clearing and fast-forward to the end of the PowerPoint deck so we could get to the debate about options. I wore my impatience too openly.

Still, talking could serve a cathartic purpose. That April, as we waited for the stress test results, I held a series of follow-ups to the President's Roosevelt Room meeting at Treasury, to give our internal critics an in-house outlet to continue to vent about the risks in our plan and propose ways to make it better. Larry and his colleague Jeremy Stein did push several sensible ideas that we would incorporate into the stress test, including tougher loss assumptions, a higher capital target, and more transparency, and the war-gaming of our overall strategy did help flesh out its strengths and weaknesses. But when they proposed more radical departures in strategy, I mostly just tried to wear them out, explaining the problems with their alternatives. Sometimes, after Larry would propose some new approach, I would look at him and say: "Larry, I heard what you like about that. Why don't you make the case against?" And he was really good at that, often better than I was at explaining why his shiny new idea had its own crippling faults. Gene Sperling said later that no alternative plan presented in those meetings could withstand thirty minutes of debate.

I wasn't always on my best behavior. I got irritated when the critics offered anxieties without alternatives. When they did propose solutions, I could be pretty dismissive as I sucked the hope out of them. I remember before one late-afternoon meeting with this group of internal critics and advisers, I scheduled a one-on-one dinner with Larry at 8 p.m., so he would have an incentive to end the meeting; he always thought he had a better chance of getting me to see things his way if he could get me alone. I told the Treasury team before the meeting not to bring any food, in hopes that everyone would get hungry and lose interest. But 8 p.m. came and went. Around 9:30 p.m., my senior adviser, Sara Aviel, brought in some orange matzo boxes that had been left over from someone's Passover seder.

"Sara, no!" I shouted, only half in jest. "Don't feed them! It will only encourage them!"

One frequent theme in these sessions was the idea that my former Fed colleagues and I were so scarred by Lehman Brothers that we were afraid to do anything that might unsettle the financial system. Larry and Jeremy Stein would say I suffered from "Lehman Syndrome," a kind of financial post-traumatic stress disorder. Sperling sometimes quipped that whenever anyone mentioned the words "systemic risk," everyone's IQ instantly dropped fifty points.

I pleaded guilty to Lehman Syndrome. I thought that if you weren't traumatized by the fall of Lehman and terrified by the thought of another Lehman, you weren't paying attention. I was sometimes uncharitable about the "chicken hawks" of the crisis, the financial equivalent of ardent Iraq War supporters who had never fought in war and had the luxury of distance from the battlefield. Letting systemic firms fail, nationalizing them, haircutting their creditors—it all sounded alluring when you hadn't lived through the consequences. I preferred to err on the side of avoiding another calamity. One meeting about AIG devolved into psychoanalysis, with various colleagues offering theories of how the crisis had warped me.

"OK," I said after twenty minutes of speculation. "We're done with that."

Subjecting our plan to criticism—you could call it stress testing the stress test—helped make the President somewhat more confident in our approach. On April 27, for instance, he hosted a White House dinner for some of America's leading economists, including critics such as Paul Krugman, Jeff Sachs, and Joseph Stiglitz. The President began with a pointed reminder that our strategy was my baby. "I'd like to hear your views," he told the group. "You already know what Tim thinks." The President invited each of them to speak, and most of what he heard was the familiar complaints that our plan was limp and unambitious, a recipe for zombie banks, too generous to the financial system. When the President asked each of them what they would suggest we do instead, he was exposed to an outside version of what he had heard inside the White House: more concerns and critiques, a few ideas, but nothing that sounded achievable, nothing that didn't bring problems of its own.

Krugman was typically thoughtful, and in some ways I found his critique the most gratifying. He said that while he wasn't certain, he'd be inclined to do more nationalization, especially Citi and Bank of America. But he acknowledged that if we did that we would have to guarantee the rest of the system to guard against runs, just as I had been saying internally. "That could be expensive," he conceded. I knew the President read Krugman's columns—including some that first floated Sweden as a model—and I was happy to hear him validate my warnings. Early in the meeting, the President had mentioned how Larry and I often invoked the Hippocratic oath: First, do no harm. Now the economist widely regarded as the intellectual leader of the nationalization brigade was acknowledging that preemptive nationalization could do significant harm without a dramatic expansion of government guarantees.

Krugman later downplayed how expensive it would have been to seize Citi and BofA, since their market capitalizations had dwindled. But we didn't have the authority to do preemptive nationalization and comprehensive guarantees. And even if we had been able to take over two megabanks that held a quarter of U.S. banking assets, we would have faced the unappealing Hawk One/Hawk Two choice of either liquidating quickly, which would have created huge fire-sale losses for taxpayers, or trying to run the sprawling institutions for the long haul, which would have created all kinds of different problems.

During this uncomfortable limbo period before the stress test was done, we came under pressure to do all sorts of things to demonstrate initiative. Several of the President's advisers in the West Wing suggested that I fire Bank of America CEO Ken Lewis, who had engineered the troubled acquisitions of Countrywide and Merrill Lynch, and was pretty clearly on his way out anyway.

"Tim, I'm trying to look out for you," Gene Sperling told me. "If he's going anyway, why don't you push him out?"

I understood the impulse to chop off a banker's head and mount it on a stake, but while Bank of America had taken lots of risk and had received extraordinary assistance, we didn't control the firm. If the firm failed to raise private capital after the stress test and we ended up having to take a majority interest, then its management would be replaced, as had occurred at Fannie, Freddie, AIG, and GM. But if we arbitrarily decided that Lewis had to go before the stress test revealed his firm's plight, we'd undermine our own plan.

"I know you're looking out for me," I told Gene. "I'm just not going to do things for message reasons."

We just had to wait.

WAITING WASN'T easy. The markets were bouncing all over the place. From Inauguration Day through April, the S&P 500 index of financial stocks *averaged* a 5 percent daily shift; in normal times, a 1 percent swing is a big day. In White House staff meetings, Larry used to talk about how we never knew if the stock market was going to crash the next day and send us straight to the 1930s. The stress test would reveal whether the banks faced manageable difficulties, which could end the harrowing volatility, or giant capital holes, which would require drastic new measures.

My former colleagues at the New York Fed were doing most of the analytical work on the stress test, but they kept a close hold on it that spring. They were trying to estimate future revenues as well as losses, an entirely new exercise for bank supervisors, made even more complex by this unusual moment of uncertainty. So their numbers were in flux. They didn't want us to design policies based on preliminary data that could shift dramatically, which was sensible but frustrating.

"I'm the fucking Treasury secretary and I can't see these numbers?" I groused during one conference call.

As we tried to pry results out of the Fed, we continued to debate various questions about the design of the stress test. One involved transparency. Fed supervisors were compiling loss estimates for all nineteen firms, broken down by asset classes such as residential mortgages, commercial real estate, business loans, credit cards, and so on. They were also compiling revenue estimates, which they would combine with the loss estimates to calculate each bank's capital gap. I thought the Fed ought to make these results as transparent to the public as possible, not just for the system overall but for each individual firm. I thought the best way to reduce uncertainty would be to allow investors to look under the hoods of the banks, so they could decide how stressful the stress test really was.

But from the outset, Fed officials were reluctant to publicize bank-specific numbers. They feared that publicizing their guesses about future losses and capital positions could undermine confidence, prompting investors to run from banks that looked weak. They were also concerned that releasing detailed results compiled with proprietary bank data would hamper their access to that data in the future. "It violates confidentiality of supervisory information and will irreparably damage the credibility of the supervisory process," they wrote in an early memo.

Larry and I believed that we needed the fullest plausible disclosure, that even bad news would be better than no news. Investors were already assuming the worst about many banks. And I worried that voluntary disclosures by stronger banks alone could be even more stigmatizing to weaker banks than mandatory disclosures for all. I made the case to Ben and he ultimately agreed, overruling the traditional conservatism of the Fed staff. The stress test would end up revealing each bank's capital gaps, projected losses, and even losses by asset class. There was a bit less transparency for revenue forecasts, but in general the Fed adopted the anti-Japan approach, coming as close as U.S. bank supervisors ever had to flinging open the system's books.

Our other big debate involved the "bogey," the capital level we would force banks to meet in a worst-case scenario. We all agreed we needed a new measuring stick that emphasized common equity, despite the legal and logistical hurdles of establishing new capital rules in just two months. The last set of international rules, known as Basel II, had taken nearly a decade to finalize. But as Citi and Bank of America had learned, markets no longer trusted capital that wasn't common equity, so the Fed quickly devised a new measure known as "Tier 1 common." The key question was how much common equity each bank would have to hold.

Initially, some Fed staffers advocated ratios as low as 2 percent of the bank's risk-weighted assets, but we raised the choice to 3 percent or 4 percent. Higher requirements would force banks to raise more new capital, and Lee was nervous that a tougher bogey could scare away private investors, especially if the stress test projected disastrous losses. But Larry and Jeremy Stein consistently argued for the higher number. And I encouraged Ben to adopt the stricter 4 percent standard. Again, to his credit, Ben agreed, overruling some of his staff. This exercise wouldn't work if the markets didn't think it was tough and credible. A disastrously high number for the system's capital needs could kill us, but a laughably low number could hurt us, too.

By the second half of April, we were finally seeing the Fed's preliminary data—and to our relief, it did not seem disastrous. I told the President it looked like we would probably be able to recapitalize the system with our existing TARP resources, just two months after we had budgeted that $750 billion placeholder for a second TARP. In an April 24 briefing for the President, we said nine of the nineteen stress-tested institutions—we called them "winners"—did not appear to need any new capital. We believed five more institutions would be able to raise the capital they needed soon, so they could help finance an expanding economy.

But we also identified five "negative outliers" that looked like they would have significant capital holes. Bank of America faced the biggest shortfall, and we were concerned that if it was unable to raise enough private capital, the government could end up with a majority stake. And the General Motors financing arm, GMAC, while not as gigantic, was a complete mess, facing huge losses and plummeting revenues.

Lew Alexander, a former Fed and Citigroup economist who had joined our team at Treasury, drafted an "opposition research" memo with potential critiques we might face after the results were released, starting with the stress test's insufficiently dark macroeconomic assumptions. In April, unemployment rose to 8.9 percent, already approaching the stress test's pessimistic scenario of 10.3 percent. "Even if we convince them the methodology for estimating the losses, revenues and all the other components is sound, the results will be suspect on that basis," Alexander wrote. He also warned that after several gloomy estimates by private analysts, the relatively manageable numbers we expected might be perceived as "simply too small."

The Fed's numbers kept fluctuating as the May 7 release approached, and my team remained skittish. We were drafting an op-ed to accompany the release, and Matt Kabaker thought some revisions by a speechwriter, declaring the system had "a substantial cushion of resources to withstand the challenges ahead," sounded overconfident.

"My own view is that the future economic outlook is sufficiently uncertain and bleak, and the impact this test will actually have is sufficiently in flux, that the declaration of victory this draft represents is inadvisable," Kabaker wrote. Steve Shafran, who had worked for Hank and stayed on as an adviser to me, agreed that it was too early to dance in the end zone. "Besides, the Treasury secretary is supposed to be dour and conservative—anything else is off-key," he wrote. Lee chimed in as well: "Some hedging language is appropriate. Highly likely a pullback coming."

I added plenty of qualifications to the draft. But the results we ultimately released were quite reassuring. In the stressed scenario, the

Fed projected about $600 billion in additional losses across the nine-teen firms, in addition to the $400 billion they had already lost dur-ing the crisis—huge by historical standards but not insurmountable.

The news about capital was even better. After taking account of some modest future earnings, as well as existing reserves and capital, the stress test found that as of January 1, the nineteen firms needed an additional $185 billion in capital. But those firms—mostly Citi—had already increased their common equity by $110 billion since Janu-ary 1. That meant the ten firms that still needed capital would have to raise only another $75 billion. We thought they could do most of that without new TARP dollars.

Bank of America had the largest need at $33.9 billion, a significant but manageable problem for such a giant institution, especially after the Citi share conversion of TARP preferred shares into common equity provided a model. Wells Fargo—whose CEO, Dick Kovacevich, had scoffed that he didn't need more capital when we unveiled the TARP injections, and had called the stress test "asinine"—was next with $13.7 billion. Citi needed only another $5.5 billion, because it had already increased its common equity by $87 billion. The only institu-tion that seemed to be in deep trouble was GMAC, which was diag-nosed with an $11.5 billion capital shortfall, almost twice the amount of its common equity.

The next morning, I walked into the Oval Office for the Presi-dent's daily economics briefing with a report from Bridgewater Asso-ciates, the world's largest hedge fund firm. Many experts, including Larry, regarded Bridgewater's *Daily Observations* as among the smart-est and most credible sources of private-sector economic analysis—and among the darkest about the banks. In front of the economic team and the President's political advisers, I handed that day's *Obser-vations* to the President.

The headline was "We Agree!"

"The Stress Test numbers and ours are nearly the same!!!" the re-port began. "The regulators did an excellent job of explaining exactly

Bridgewater®
Daily Observations
May 7, 2009   © 2009 Bridgewater Associates, Inc.

Ray Dalio
Jason Rotenberg

United States

We Agree!

The Stress Test numbers and ours are nearly the same!!! The regulators did an excellent job of explaining exactly what they did for this stress test, and showing the numbers that produced the results. They did virtually exactly what we did since we started putting out our loss estimates nearly two years ago, and their numbers are essentially the same as ours. The differences between our numbers and theirs are more a matter of terminology than of substance. For example, the biggest difference between their estimates and ours is due to the number of years they and we are counting – i.e., their loss estimate is for the losses that will occur over the next two years and ours is for the total amount of losses that will be taken on these assets over the lives of these assets. As there will be losses in years 3, 4, etc., in addition to those in the first two years, naturally the total losses (i.e., ours) will be greater than the losses incurred over the next two years (i.e., theirs). We won't conjecture why they did it that way, though we do know from our projections that the maximum capital needs (i.e., when earnings fall short relative to losses) is probably at the end of two years. Anyway, that accounts for most of the difference in our total loss estimates, and in addition we may also have a slightly worse economic scenario than they do. Once these adjustments are made, we see essentially the same picture.

The table and chart shown below convey the reconciliation.

Two Year Loss Estimate and Capital Needs ($Bln)		
	Fed Stress Test	Bridgewater Estimates
Losses Over Next Two Years	-600	-552
Gross Capital Raises Needed	-185	-177
Plus Adj. for Asset Sales and Conventions	110	110
Net Capital Needs	-75	-67
% of Banks Needing Capital	47%	68%

1
Bridgewater® Daily Observations 05/07/2009

The financial markets ultimately judged the stress test to be credible, and investors were willing to provide the bulk of the new common equity required to stabilize the financial system. I shared this Bridgewater analysis with the President the day after the stress test results were released. Bridgewater's positive assessment soon became the consensus view in the markets.

Source: Bridgewater.

what they did for this stress test, and showing the numbers that produced the results."

I wasn't dancing in the end zone, but that was a good day for the home team.

NINE

Getting Better, Feeling Worse

Most Americans never heard about the stress test, and for many of those who did, it sounded like another Washington joke. *Saturday Night Live* had a field day with it, having an actor playing me open the show by earnestly announcing that we had given every bank a passing grade, since we didn't want to "unfairly stigmatize banks who scored low on the test because they followed reckless lending practices or were otherwise not good at banking." The fake me then griped that Citigroup hadn't taken the written portion of the stress test seriously enough, revealing an answer sheet with "Geithner sucks!" scribbled next to every question. He also chastised GMAC for answering "taxpayer bailout" to every question, although he acknowledged that had been the correct answer to most of them.

I'm sure a lot of the public saw me as that hapless, cowed-by-the-banks caricature. And I had no expectations that the stress test would transform my reputation inside the Beltway, either. It was at the White House Correspondents' Association dinner that same Saturday night that President Obama quipped that one of his goals for his second hundred days in office would be to housetrain his new dog, Bo, so that he wouldn't treat me like a fire hydrant.

Nearly two years into the financial crisis, I was an official punch line. But another funny thing happened after the stress test: The crisis started to subside.

By the time I briefed the President on the system's progress a month later, the ten major firms with capital needs had raised their common equity by $66 billion without additional government help, leaving a mere $9 billion shortfall. And we thought all the firms except GMAC had credible plans to fill their capital holes through the private markets. After all our Hawk One/Hawk Two arguments about whether and how to nationalize major banks, after all our anguish about our dwindling TARP funds and the dim prospects of Congress approving more, those debates looked moot. We no longer thought the financial system would need lots more government assistance. We certainly didn't think we'd need another TARP.

As Lew Alexander had predicted, critics accused us of papering over the deeper problems in the banks, telling a happy story that the markets wouldn't believe. "A rigorous audit it wasn't," Krugman wrote the day of the release. But it was a rigorous audit, and the transparency allowed everyone to see that. Despite its comparatively benign assumptions about unemployment, the stress test assumed a two-year loan loss rate of 9.1 percent, higher than the peak rates during the Great Depression and dramatically higher than anything since. The ultimate test of the stress test was whether private investors would take the risk of investing new capital in banks, and they would do that on an impressive scale, driving BofA's stock price up 63 percent that week, and Citi's up 35 percent. The broader markets were reassured, too. The equity market's "fear index" dropped to its lowest level since the fall of Lehman. So did interbank lending spreads, as banks became less reluctant to lend to one another.

There had been lulls in the panic in the fall of 2007, the following winter before Bear, and the spring after Bear. But there had never

The Stress Test Was Truly Stressful
Commercial Bank Two-Year Loan Loss Rates

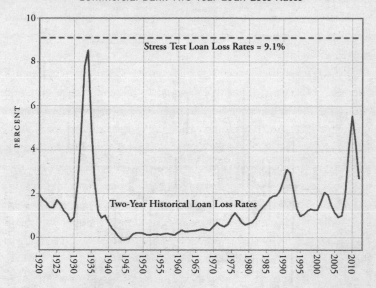

The line running across the top of this chart—included in the Fed document announcing the stress test results—showed that the stress test assumed bank loan losses even worse than during the Great Depression. Perhaps more than anything else, this brutally tough assumption helped convince investors that the test was credible.

Sources: Federal Deposit Insurance Corporation, Federal Reserve Board, and International Monetary Fund.

been a real sense of stability. Now nearly every financial indicator was heading the right way. During the week of the stress test, the price of credit default swaps for the six largest banks dropped by a third. And by the time the results were in, the index of financial stocks had more than doubled since hitting bottom in early March. As our strategy became clearer, and fears of widespread nationalization faded, confidence returned to the financial system, and confidence bred stability. The system had become investable again.

Some suggested this was mostly just good luck. My team had

The Panic and the Rescue

Stock Market Performance—S&P 500

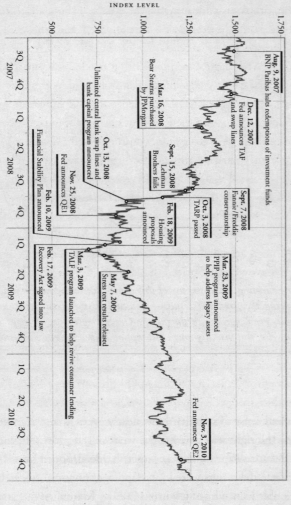

INDEX LEVEL

Aug. 9, 2007
BNP Paribas halts redemptions of investment funds

Dec. 12, 2007
Fed announces TAF
and swap lines

Mar. 16, 2008
Bear Stearns purchased
by JPMorgan

Sept. 7, 2008
Fannie/Freddie
conservatorship

Sept. 15, 2008
Lehman
Brothers fail

Oct. 3, 2008
TARP passed

Oct. 13, 2008
Unlimited central bank swap lines and
bank capital program announced

Nov. 25, 2008
Fed announces QE1

Feb. 10, 2009
Financial Stability Plan announced

Feb. 18, 2009
Housing
proposals
announced

Feb. 17, 2009
Recovery Act signed into law

Mar. 23, 2009
PPIP program announced
to help address legacy assets

Mar. 3, 2009
TALF program launched to help revive consumer lending

May 7, 2009
Stress test results released

Nov. 3, 2010
Fed announces QE2

The S&P 500 stock index is an imperfect but useful proxy for the arc of the crisis. The markets continued to deteriorate even after our extraordinary actions in the fall of 2008, only turning after the Recovery Act, the stress test, and the other financial initiatives of 2009.　Source: Bloomberg.

always suspected the banking system was more solvent than it looked, but we had no way to be sure; if the stress test had revealed catastrophic problems and unmanageable capital shortfalls, it might have backfired. But the test was tough, transparent, and well-designed, which helped reduce uncertainty in the markets. And our promise to inject TARP capital into banks that needed it, combined with the FDIC's guarantees of financial liabilities and our public no-more-Lehmans pledges, bolstered confidence that we were standing behind the system. Along with the President's fiscal stimulus, the Fed's monetary stimulus, TALF to restore consumer credit, and the PPIP funds to revive the market for toxic mortgage assets, we sent a concerted message that we would do whatever was necessary to put the crisis behind us. By requiring banks to hold enough capital to survive a depression, we made a depression less likely.

Now the markets were stabilizing. In a financial crisis, when people think things are bad, things can get really bad, but once people decide things are getting better, that can be self-reinforcing, too. In early June, with banks raising so much capital on their own, we announced that we were putting on hold our initial plan to have the PPIP fund buy their troubled loans, although it did buy a modest amount of their troubled securities. Meanwhile, the Fed's emergency liquidity programs, which had been pumping $1.5 trillion into the financial system at their peak in late 2008, would drop below $400 billion by the end of the summer. These programs, widely viewed as giveaways, had been designed to be expensive for borrowers when the panic eased, so banks, investment banks, and issuers of commercial paper had an incentive to repay the Fed and exit as soon as the opportunity presented itself.

We also gave nine of the largest banks permission to repay $67 billion of TARP capital and exit the program, an even more powerful signal of relative normalcy. Jamie Dimon had brought a fake $25 billion check to the White House meeting of bankers in March, his brash way of suggesting that JPMorgan didn't need our help, but we had refused to let firms return our capital before the stress test could determine how much they needed and whether they could raise it privately. At the time, we had worried that even after the stress test, allowing some banks to repay might prompt markets to run from banks that didn't. By June, those fears had subsided.

The repayments were clearly good news for firms such as JPMorgan, Goldman Sachs, and Morgan Stanley, which got to escape the stigma of TARP and its attendant restrictions on compensation, dividends, and extravagant corporate retreats. But they were also good news for taxpayers, who cleared nearly $6 billion in profits from those nine firms. And they were good news for the financial system, expanding TARP's firepower in case we needed to deal with new problems such as commercial real estate or municipal bond markets. During an Oval Office meeting with Larry and the President, I joked that TARP would now have plenty of cash to restructure GM and Chrysler.

"Don't worry, Mr. President," I said. "The banks will pay for Larry's auto losses."

That actually turned out to be right. TARP's bank capital programs would end up earning nearly twice as much for taxpayers as it would cost to restructure GM and Chrysler.

The success of the stress test was encouraging, but at the time, we had seen too many false dawns to let our guard down. The crisis was still percolating through the economy, posing all kinds of dangers. One day I got an email from Gene Sperling warning me that California, the world's eighth-largest economy if it were its own country, could not issue $17 billion in bonds it needed to meet its obligations. "The California crisis might be real," Gene wrote. He suggested that we could use TARP to create a Fannie-type enterprise for state and local governments. But we weren't confident we had the legal authority, and the practical complexities were daunting; Congress was also hostile to the idea of rescuing states. Ultimately, we decided not to try, and California ended up having to pay its employees in IOUs for a time.

Global confidence in U.S. economic power was badly shaken. When I spoke that spring at Beijing University, where I had studied abroad during college, one student asked if Chinese investments in U.S. government bonds were safe. I said those assets were absolutely safe. During the crisis, investors around the world had sought refuge in Treasuries, because they were perceived as the safest investment on earth. But my assurance was met by snickers of laughter from the young audience, a pretty remarkable show of how far the United States had fallen.

On June 9, Meg McConnell sent me a long email fretting about a litany of dangers that still threatened the financial system: rising personal and corporate bankruptcies, soaring commercial real estate vacancy rates, lingering weakness in European banks, and much more. "Kind of scary when you think about it," she wrote. Meg has a feel for the dark side of any situation, and while I wasn't quite as concerned as she was about the exposure of Swedish banks to the Latvian exchange rate, I agreed with her main point: Our interventions to prevent bad outcomes had broken the panic, but the global economy was still terribly weak, and if we began allowing the kind of bad outcomes we had pledged to prevent, the panic could return.

"Things are likely still very fragile," she wrote.

We had a test case in July with CIT Group, a midsize commercial lender that had received $2.3 billion from TARP in late 2008 and now had major liquidity problems. It had appealed to the FDIC and the Fed for some relief, but Sheila had refused, arguing that CIT wasn't viable and wasn't systemic. My colleagues at Treasury were less confident than Sheila that its failure wouldn't destabilize the system, and on the Friday when its survival was in doubt, our crisis response team settled in for a weekend of work on a possible rescue. The company's CEO, apparently less concerned, abruptly ended a call with Lee that afternoon because he had to catch a flight to Nantucket. We were mindful of Larry's dictum that "you can't want it more than they do," that it's futile to try to save people who won't try to save themselves.

CIT was less than one-fifth the size of Bear Stearns, and much less active in the repo and derivative markets. Still, Lee was deeply worried about the economic fallout as well as the message we would send if we let one of the nation's largest small business lenders fail after receiving funding through TARP. But Sheila thought the system could handle it, and an effective plan required her approval. The FDIC officially rejected CIT's request for relief, forcing the firm to find a high-cost private loan that was basically a bridge to bankruptcy.

This time, the markets seemed to agree with Sheila. CIT caused little damage to confidence, although its bankruptcy did cost taxpayers their $2.3 billion TARP investment. Lee says that was the moment he finally felt like the crisis was winding down.

I still wanted us to stay vigilant—to keep thinking about what Kabaker called the "bad room" would look like. I had my team put together a deck of "Policy Alternatives if Conditions Deteriorate" that included all kinds of frightening scenarios. We weren't out of the woods yet, which would affect an important and delicate personnel matter facing the President.

BEN'S FOUR-YEAR term as Fed chairman was expiring in January 2010, but we would need to get a successor nominated and confirmed well before that. Early in the summer of 2009, I went to the President to begin the planning. He said his preference was to appoint Larry. He felt comfortable with Larry. I knew Larry wanted and expected the job. The President and I agreed he would be outstanding.

But as we discussed the choice of Ben's successor, we also discussed whether this was the right time for a change—at the Fed and at the White House. We were still at a vulnerable moment. The President still had an ambitious economic agenda. As we talked through it, the President said continuity might not be a bad idea.

I knew some in the President's progressive base would object if he kept a Republican in such a crucial economic job, but Ben had done an outstanding job fighting the crisis, keeping his promise to the public to do whatever he could to help avoid Depression 2.0. He was now presiding over a creative experiment through QE1, buying $1.75 trillion in Treasuries, high-quality mortgage securities, and Fannie and Freddie debt to provide extra support for the economy. I still talked to him just about every day, and I doubt there's ever been a closer relationship between a Treasury secretary and a Fed chairman.

And despite our financial strategy disputes, I thought Larry was an invaluable adviser to the President, the same awesome devil's advocate who Kissinger said should have a permanent White House office. Larry never made heroic efforts to conceal his own views, but he was open to alternative views, even if he wasn't always polite about the ones he found wanting. There was certainly some tension on our economic team, some resentment that Larry and I had too much sway, some grumbling that Larry's meetings devolved into unfocused seminars. But I've attended plenty of decorous policy meetings with written agendas distributed in advance and formal speaking orders that amounted to nothing. I thought Larry's messy, sprawling clusterfucks mostly led to deeper thinking and better decisions.

I told the President I thought the current arrangement was working well, and I said this didn't seem like a great time for change at the Fed. He liked the idea of keeping Larry by his side and Ben at the Fed. I spoke with Ben, and the President invited him over to the Oval Office, where Ben said he was willing to stay, although he wasn't sure he wanted to serve a full additional term. He was tired, and the worst of the crisis seemed to be over. When it became clear the President wanted continuity, Larry was disappointed, but I think he also recognized it wasn't an ideal time for a change. He was tired, too, and he considered leaving the administration. But the President, Rahm, and I all leaned on him to stay, and he relented.

We still needed all hands on deck. We were relieved that the financial fires were receding, that the financial markets were recovering, that Americans whose savings had been vaporized during the crisis were recouping some of their losses. But the primary goal of our financial engineering had always been to revive the broader economy, and times were still very tough on Main Street. We could see early signs of economic growth in the data, but people weren't feeling it on the ground.

• • •

THE ECONOMY shed about three hundred thousand jobs a month from May through August 2009, which was horrible. But it was less than half the rate of job losses in the previous six months. Economists would later peg the end of the Great Recession to June 2009. The financial system was still damaged, but it no longer seemed to be tearing down the broader economy. And the Recovery Act was working, pouring cash into the economy. GDP still contracted by 0.4 percent in the second quarter, but again that was significantly better than the 5.4 percent decline in the first quarter. While Republicans mocked the stimulus as "Porkulus," a big-government grab bag, its tax cuts and government investments were clearly helping to prevent things from getting much worse.

Unfortunately, "Things are getting worse at a much slower rate" is not a convincing message of hope. Neither is "Things would be even worse if we hadn't acted." It's hard to inspire the public with counterfactuals. And the one economic statistic everyone understands is the unemployment rate, which happens to be a lagging indicator after severe recessions, trailing the recovery in economic growth as businesses wait to see whether the improvement is real. By summer's end, even though job losses were slowing, the jobless rate had soared to a gruesome 9.6 percent.

Even mild financial crises leave terrible economic damage in their wake, and this had obviously not been a mild crisis. We knew our policies were limiting the carnage, and all the data bore that out, but what Americans could feel and see was the carnage. The President's approval ratings, after hovering in the sixties during his early months in office, dipped to the low fifties that summer, and would never really recover.

Even amid the signs of hope, we had a rich flow of new messes. For example, AIG turned a profit in the second quarter, another promising sign of stability. But after CEO Ed Liddy stepped down from his dollar-a-year job, the press soon reported that his replacement, former MetLife CEO Robert Benmosche, was spending much of his first month on vacation at his vineyard in Croatia. Benmosche then invited a reporter to his eight-thousand-square-foot villa on the Adriatic Coast, where he described his new $7 million compensation package as "bottom end," complained of "lynch mobs" protesting the AIG bonuses, and mocked our economic policies as totally incompetent. We heard a lot of right-wing criticism about big-government intervention that summer, but we hadn't expected it from our fresh recruit to run the largest beneficiary of our interventions. Benmosche would turn out to be a strong CEO of AIG, but at the time he seemed like a stranger-than-fiction plot to make us look inept.

We still were living with the pervasive perception that President Obama had rescued the arsonists. Even Axelrod and Gibbs once suggested during a White House meeting that Americans were understandably angry at the administration because we had given the banks hundreds of billions of dollars. I reminded them that the Obama administration hadn't given the major banks any new money. We had forced them to raise private money. But if the President's top political aides thought we had pumped more cash into Wall Street, what were the chances that average Americans would understand the distinctions? We were still getting hammered over bonuses and bailouts, by the left and the right and a litany of government overseers, with virtually no acknowledgment that the financial system and the economy had stabilized.

THERE WAS a new spasm of outrage in July when the special inspector general for TARP, a former prosecutor named Neil Barofsky, released a report proclaiming that the government's crisis interventions had exposed taxpayers to $23.7 *trillion* in potential losses. As

Politico noted, that was more than our GDP, more than the inflation-adjusted cost of every war the United States had ever fought, about a hundred times the cost of NASA's moon mission.

As a measure of the size of the markets we backstopped, the figure was in the ballpark, a kind of unintended compliment regarding our success at deploying overwhelming force. But as a measure of potential losses, $23.7 trillion was absurd. For losses to climb that high would require every mortgage backed by Fannie or Freddie to default, every house behind those mortgages to be worth nothing, and every U.S. bank that had received TARP funds to fail. Nevertheless, this $23.7 trillion sound bite was soon rocketing across the airwaves, a gift-wrapped talking point for our critics. It would have been laughable if it weren't so damaging.

Oversight is vital, especially when vast sums of taxpayer dollars are at stake, and skepticism is in order when the government floats cash to well-connected private firms. But Barofsky's desire to prevent perfidy was untainted by financial knowledge or experience. He assumed our motives were self-evidently sinister, as if we had helped banks for fun and profit rather than to cure a metastasizing financial crisis. He was outraged by every program, uninterested in context, unmoved by evidence of success, never burdened by having to examine alternatives. He would hire a staff to scrutinize TARP that was almost as large as the staff we had to manage TARP, and he would requisition firearms and bulletproof vests for his antifraud troops. Neither he nor his well-armed team ever produced a follow-up report to explain how the actual cost of TARP's bank investments to taxpayers turned out to be zero—less than zero, really, because they turned a substantial profit for the taxpayer. Hank Paulson apologized to me twice during our work together—once for initially failing to persuade the House to pass TARP, and once for bequeathing me Barofsky.

Watchdogs weren't the only voices adding to the deep public despair about the crisis and the rescue. That was the Tea Party summer, when grassroots conservatives rallied against the President's supposedly

The Scope of the Financial Rescue
Market Size and Crisis Response

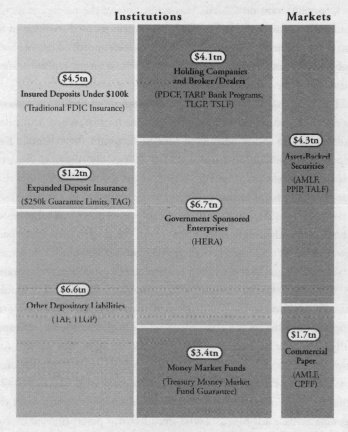

Institutions | **Markets**

($4.1tn)
Holding Companies
and Broker/Dealers
(PDCF, TARP Bank Programs,
TLGP, TSLF)

($4.5tn)
Insured Deposits Under $100k
(Traditional FDIC Insurance)

($4.3tn)
Asset-Backed
Securities
(AMLF,
PPIP, TALF)

($1.2tn)
Expanded Deposit Insurance
($250k Guarantee Limits, TAG)

($6.7tn)
Government Sponsored
Enterprises
(HERA)

($6.6tn)
Other Depository Liabilities
(TAF, TLGP)

($3.4tn)
Money Market Funds
(Treasury Money Market
Fund Guarantee)

($1.7tn)
Commercial
Paper
(AMLF,
CPFF)

Our alphabet soup of crisis response programs provided support directly and indirectly to firms and markets with about $30 trillion in financial liabilities. The diversity of programs was necessary to extend a safety net against panic broad enough to cover the institutions and markets most critical to economic growth. This is an imperfect representation of the scope and diversity of programs, as there is some double-counting across sectors due to the overlapping nature of our support.

Sources: Federal Deposit Insurance Corporation, Federal Reserve Board, U.S. Treasury Department, and company filings. (Data as of June 30, 2008; Government Sponsored Enterprises include only Fannie Mae, Freddie Mac, and the Federal Home Loan Banks, and do not include other GSEs or Ginnie Mae.)

far-left, debt-exploding, freedom-killing agenda. I used to joke that I was personally responsible for the birth of the Tea Party, because Rick Santelli's rant on CNBC was a response to the mortgage modification program, and the Tea Party movement focused so much of its initial fire on the financial rescue. But it quickly morphed into a clearinghouse for anti-Obama and anti-government anger, raging against the stimulus, health reform, taxes, spending, and debt.

I sometimes wondered where this newfound right-wing enthusiasm for fiscal discipline had been during the Bush years, when unfunded wars, tax cuts, and a new Medicare prescription drug benefit had helped turn the Clinton surpluses into deficits. By contrast, Obamacare included reforms aimed at reining in the rising medical costs that threatened our fiscal future, and the Congressional Budget Office estimated that it would reduce future deficits overall despite its subsidies to extend care to the uninsured. Then again, the original Tea Party protested an unelected king who raised taxes, while Obama was an elected president who had lowered taxes, so consistency wasn't really the point.

The rise of the Tea Party reflected and also intensified the Republican Party's decades-long drift to the far right. I don't think we ever expected many Republicans to cooperate with the President, especially after their lockstep opposition to the stimulus, but we still underestimated the relentlessness and effectiveness of their opposition. I considered the President a moderate, market-oriented Democrat—he wouldn't have chosen Larry and Rahm and me if he weren't—but the Republican base saw him as a wild-eyed leftist, a perception fed by Republican politicians in Washington. I don't know how many of them truly believed the President was turning the country into a socialist dystopia, and how many were just afraid of Tea Party primary challenges, but it didn't really matter. After their wounding electoral defeats in 2006 and 2008, opposition to Obama brought them together.

I remember on my first trip to Beijing as secretary, an embassy official called to tell me that Mark Kirk of Illinois, one of the few nominally moderate Republicans left in Congress, had just held an unusual meeting with Chinese officials. Kirk had advised them not to buy Treasuries or other U.S. government debt, warning them that our spending was driving us toward default, and that the Fed was creating hyperinflation. I couldn't believe it. Not only were those fears delusional, but he was undermining American interests on foreign soil. I called him on his way out of China to explain that there was this noble tradition in politics that you don't criticize the United States while you're abroad—and you definitely shouldn't say we're going to default on our debts. But partisan politics no longer seemed to stop at the water's edge.

The impossibility of achieving true bipartisanship in Congress meant the President had to keep the Democrats with him if he wanted to pass anything. This was especially true in the Senate, where Republicans were using the filibuster with unprecedented regularity, blocking just about anything that didn't have the sixty votes needed to overcome it. For the second half of 2009, the Democrats had exactly sixty senators, which led to side deals like the "Cornhusker Kickback" that clinched Nebraska Senator Ben Nelson's vote on Obamacare. But as the President's policies became less popular, many Democratic senators began keeping their distance. Moderates from Republican states didn't want to look like big spenders. Liberals thought we were too restrained in our spending and too close to Wall Street. With lockstep opposition from Republicans, it became increasingly difficult to get anything through Congress.

The President was often blamed for gridlock in Washington, but I thought he got a remarkable amount done despite a polarized Congress. I found that much of the criticism of his effectiveness as an executive—especially from CEOs who didn't have to overcome filibusters—reflected a misunderstanding of the constitutionally imposed balance of power in Washington, the limits of executive authority in economic policy, and the constraints imposed by a determined opposition that had the votes to block action. I thought he was smart, thoughtful, hardworking, demanding (but not harshly so), confident (but not overly so), relentlessly practical, and relatively indifferent to short-term political costs. He did his homework. He listened. He delegated. Some found him distant, but I saw him show plenty of warmth and emotion and dry humor. He was especially sweet to my mother, who gave him a lucky stone from the Cape. He wasn't paralyzed by the ugliness of choices or the prospect of criticism. He handled adversity remarkably well, which was fortunate, because he faced a lot of it.

He was human, of course. Sometimes I thought he wore his frustration too openly. He harbored the overly optimistic belief that since his motives and values were good, since his team was thoughtful and well-intentioned, we deserved to be perceived that way. But I didn't find most criticisms of the President compelling. I could relate to the distance he kept from the Washington establishment. I liked the audacity of his aspirations, his instinct to expand the frontier of the possible, his effort to achieve fundamental Democratic Party objectives but also his willingness to defy his Democratic base. He focused on doing the big things he always said he would do. When a president has political difficulties, the Beltway inevitably debates whether the problem is his bad policies or bad message or bad personality or bad leadership, but I didn't think that explained the Tea Party summer and the paralysis that followed.

Our main problem was the economic fallout from a vicious crisis. Unemployment was 9.6 percent and still rising, so we looked ineffective. As Jon Stewart said while introducing a *Daily Show* segment about a homeowner who had moved from Westchester to Washington but couldn't sell his home: "We all know the economy, uh, sucks." The homeowner in question was me.

"Hold on. Timothy Geithner, the man responsible for getting us out of this economic shitstorm, cannot sell his house?" the correspondent, John Oliver, asked with mock horror. That's right, replied a local real estate agent. "Oh, God," Oliver gasped. He spent a lot of the segment making fun of pictures of the blue tiles in my son's bathroom, as if to suggest they should disqualify me from public service.

Carole and Elise had been inside baking brownies for her high school graduation party when Oliver and his crew showed up to film outside. They were trapped inside the house until he left, and they were pretty upset. Even though *The Daily Show* was my favorite TV show, and I was certainly a fair target, I was angry at the invasion of our privacy. I hated the idea that my family was by extension subjected to ridicule. I also hated the idea that Elise was graduating from high school, and that my work had kept me away during so much of her last year at home.

As the financial crisis began to ebb, my fear and anxiety morphed into numbness and exhaustion and anger. I felt singed. I remember talking over dinner with my close friend Josh Steiner, who had lived through the political attacks on the Clinton administration during his Treasury days, about what was harder to deal with emotionally, fear or anger. He said that anger made it much tougher to keep focus and perspective, and I agreed. I was always pretty good about tuning out fear and focusing on my work, trying to preserve that impression of equanimity, but I had to make a conscious effort not to let the anger eat away at me.

THE TRAJECTORY of the economy continued to improve for the rest of 2009, which is to say it shed jobs less rapidly—down to about two hundred thousand a month for September and October, averaging less than one hundred thousand a month in November and December. The economy actually began growing again in the summer, and expanded at an impressive 3.9 percent clip in the fourth quarter. Home prices stabilized. In December, Bank of America and Wells Fargo fully repaid their TARP funds, and even Citigroup paid us back most of what they owed; by year's end, we had recouped about two-thirds of the federal outlays for bank rescues. I was finally confident that the U.S. portion of the financial crisis was over.

The media seemed to recognize that, although it was curious how often that fact was reported in the passive voice, as if the crisis had simply ended of its own accord. It was amazing to see how quickly the overlapping government watchdogs scrutinizing TARP pivoted from dire warnings that our investments were exposing taxpayers to vast losses to equally fervent complaints that we hadn't ensured taxpayers enough of the profits. At a meeting that fall with the four major TARP oversight bodies, their redundancy on stark display as they crowded into Treasury's large conference room, I told them we planned to put them out of business early by getting the government's money back as soon as possible. They didn't seem to find that as worthy of celebration as I did.

We were fortunate that things stabilized as rapidly as they did, but it wasn't an accident. We had put the lurches and zigzags of 2008 behind us, finally deploying overwhelming force to stand fully behind the financial system, finally removing the catastrophic risk of another Lehman or another WaMu. We had defused the bombs of Citi, Bank of America, Fannie, Freddie, and even AIG. We had made a credible commitment through the stress test to recapitalize the system to survive Depression-like losses, through government force if necessary, which made a depression less likely. We had created a new backstop for the credit markets and a public-private fund to buy troubled assets. And by making the system investable again, we had reduced the burden of the rescue for the taxpayer. We had resisted pressure to liquidate firms or nationalize them prematurely, even though some smart people thought we were temporizing.

Jeremy Stein, who had joined Larry in pushing for more proactive federal intervention, told Lee and Matt Kabaker that summer that the banking system had been in better shape than he had thought, and that we had been right to let the stress test play out.

"We were wrong," Stein said. That was gracious of him, but the market's response to the stress test took us by surprise, too.

Our financial repairs would not have turned things around by themselves. They worked in conjunction with the Fed's aggressive

Extraordinary Commitments, but Not for Long
Government Commitments During the Financial Crisis

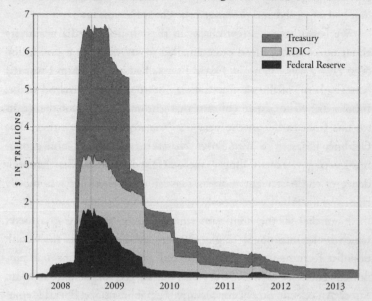

*Our direct commitments to the financial system—a combination of guaran-
tees, capital injections, loans, and other support—totaled nearly $7 trillion
at their peak. The aggressiveness and design of our response helped us end the
panic and exit those programs remarkably quickly, with a positive return to the
taxpayer as well as a tremendous boost to the economy.*

Sources: Federal Deposit Insurance Corporation, Federal Reserve Board, and U.S. Treasury Department.

monetary stimulus through QE1 and our aggressive fiscal stimulus
through the Recovery Act; they were all necessary, and they were mu-
tually reinforcing. They put a floor under home prices, equity markets,
and the economy, breaking the vicious cycle of housing losses, financial losses, and economic losses chasing one another down the drain.
They helped restore confidence so families and businesses could begin
to spend again, so it no longer seemed necessary and rational to hunker
down in preparation for the apocalypse. Our international work also

had a powerful effect on the global economy, restoring trade finance, preventing the competitive currency devaluations and protectionism that had worsened and prolonged the Great Depression.

We began to see a few cracks in the relentless media negativity about our work. Axelrod once emailed to say that the right-leaning *New York Times* columnist David Brooks had just told him I was the "unsung hero" of the administration. "Start singing!" Axelrod wrote. Brooks did write a nice column that chronicled some of the greatest hits from earlier in the year—a *New Republic* essay titled "The Geithner Disaster," a *Wall Street Journal* survey of forty-nine economists who gave me a failing grade—before concluding that "the evidence of the past eight months suggests that Geithner was mostly right and his critics were mostly wrong."

Nevertheless, the dominant story at home was unemployment, which broke into double digits in October. The air was thick with populist recriminations, many directed at me, contrasting our purported generosity to Wall Street with our alleged indifference to Main Street. An eclectic mix of conservative Republicans and liberal Democrats in Congress and in the media began calling for my resignation. Barofsky fueled the fire in November with another tendentious report suggesting we should have haircut AIG's counterparties, a report that never explained how we could have used the threat of default to extract concessions without crashing the global financial system and triggering a second depression. Barofsky acknowledged in his report that our fears that violating AIG's contracts would have accelerated the panic were "certainly valid concerns," but that didn't interfere with his condemnation.

I would appear at sixty-seven congressional hearings during my tenure as secretary, and one of my more memorable exchanges occurred with Kevin Brady, a Texas Republican on the Joint Economic Committee, after Barofsky's report came out. Brady began with a barrage of talking points about how America was bleeding jobs since the passage of the stimulus, when in fact the stimulus had slowed the bleeding;

how our out-of-control spending had blown up the deficit, when in fact we had inherited a record deficit; how the world was preparing to abandon the dollar as its reserve currency, which was simply false; and how business investment was down because of fear about health care reform and tax increases, rather than the epic financial crisis we had just endured.

"The buck, in effect, stops with you," said Brady, a former U.S. Chamber of Commerce executive. "Conservatives agree that as point person you failed. Liberals are growing in that consensus as well. . . . Will you step down from your post?"

I was usually disciplined about letting congressional bluster wash over me, and I started my reply with my usual attempt at calming civility. "Congressman, it is a great privilege to serve this President, and I am very pleased to have a chance to address the range of concerns you gave." But I decided not to let his rant go unanswered.

"I agree with almost nothing in what you said," I continued. "I welcome the advice you're providing, after you left this President an economy falling off the cliff, the value of American savings cut almost in half, millions of Americans out of work, the worst financial crisis we have seen in generations."

Brady mocked my observation that before the stimulus, the economy was disintegrating, while after the stimulus, the economy had started growing.

"That created several quadrillion new jobs, is that right?" he scoffed.

"Congressman, it is just a basic fact: A year ago, this economy was falling at the rate of six percent," I replied. In fact, it had been more than 8 percent, but we didn't know that yet. "We were losing between half a million and three-quarters of a million jobs a month, and that process was accelerating, not slowing, until the President of the United States took office."

Brady seemed frustrated that I was responding with facts. He did not respond in kind.

"Mr. Secretary, the public has lost all confidence in your ability to do the job," he declared. "It is reflecting on your president."

Your president. That said it all. I tried to explain how our tough choices had helped avert disaster, how eight years of Republican irresponsibility had made our job harder, how President Bush had inherited a $5.6 trillion ten-year surplus before leaving President Obama an $8 trillion ten-year deficit. But to the Tea Party wing of the Republican Party, anything "our" president did was anathema.

"You have to take responsibility for your decisions," Brady continued.

"I take responsibility for anything I am part of doing," I replied. "What I can't take responsibility for is the legacy of the crisis you bequeathed the country."

"This is your budget! This is your bailout! This is your stimulus!" he shot back.

"I take full responsibility for those with great honor and pleasure," I said.

It was around that time that Sandy Weill, the former Citigroup CEO, was quoted saying that I needed to lighten up. He said I looked like I needed a massage and a vacation.

THE RECOVERY Act had provided vital fiscal stimulus, and it would continue to pour money into the economy in 2010, but it wasn't big enough to fill the gaping hole the crisis had torn in U.S. output, or the brutal contraction in government spending at the state and local levels. We needed even more stimulus.

Every member of the President's economic team agreed about that, although Christy Romer and Jared Bernstein—and sometimes Larry, too—were the most vocal. We devoted most of our meetings that fall to strategizing about how to design our next round of stimulus. We all knew that after the early Keynesian successes of the New Deal, FDR had abandoned fiscal expansion too quickly, helping to kill a fledgling recovery in 1937 by trying to balance his budget while there was still mass unemployment. None of us wanted to repeat that mistake and cause a double-dip recession. We all wanted to keep trying to offset the historic drop in private demand. I wasn't enthusiastic about every line item of the Recovery Act, but its major components—tax cuts for workers, a temporary expansion of the safety net, aid to cash-strapped states, and investments that would put people to work on roads, sewer plants, and medical research—were pulling us back from the abyss.

Unfortunately, "stimulus" had become a dirty word in American politics. With unemployment in double digits, this yawning gap between the perception and the reality of the Recovery Act was probably inevitable. The stimulus was a jobs bill passed at a time when jobs were vanishing; our insistence that it was preventing much worse pain, while true, was not compelling to people in acute pain. Republicans were calling for massive and immediate spending cuts, trying to reinvent themselves as deficit hawks, feeding on public unease with trillion-dollar deficits and impatience with the pace of recovery. Many Democrats were also reluctant to support anything that could conceivably be described as "stimulus" in a thirty-second attack ad. And the public was dubious of the idea that when families and businesses were tightening their belts, those of us in government should borrow more money from China so we could loosen ours.

In our internal debates that fall, we did not spend much time arguing over a massive "second stimulus." Rahm and the President's legislative staff made it clear there was no appetite for that on the Hill. So we focused on a more modest but still significant mix of extensions to Recovery Act programs and proposals for new tax cuts and infrastructure spending. I thought the most plausible and responsible legislative strategy was to pair proposals for short-term stimulus with proposals for medium-term deficit reduction—the Saint Augustine approach of fiscal chastity, just not now. I thought requesting "naked stimulus," more money without offsetting cuts or a credible plan to reduce deficits down the road, would be a waste of time and political capital. But Larry warned that even appearing to embrace deficit reduction during such a severe downturn would be seen as a 1937-style embrace of austerity, conceding the battle over Keynesian economics without a fight. He made the somewhat prescient argument that we would end up getting cuts we didn't want, but not the stimulus we needed.

In those internal debates, I was usually the fiscal hawk, arguing that we had to show the world we would address our unsustainable long-term fiscal path even as we pushed for more near-term stimulus. I told Larry that winter that we needed to get ahead of the fever that was building for austerity. I thought we should try to frame the debate by proposing a long-term fiscal plan, including entitlement reforms to put Medicare and Social Security on more sustainable paths. He said that would be a dumb validation of austerity arguments, needlessly alienating our Democratic allies, and a waste of time, since Republicans would never go along. And I had some sympathy, probably unwisely, for a plan floating around in Congress to create a bipartisan deficit reduction commission. It seemed like it was worth a shot.

But I was not an austerian. I was an Augustinian. I did not want to hit the economic brakes. I just thought, perhaps naïvely, that showing our willingness to hit the brakes in the future would give us a better chance to persuade Congress to let us keep our foot on the gas pedal now. I remember early in the administration, Larry was appalled by a White House event where the President ordered $100 million in budget cuts, which Larry saw as economic malpractice at a time of vanishing aggregate demand. But while the theater of the event was pretty transparent—$100 million was a rounding error in the federal budget—I thought it made sense to express solidarity with Americans concerned about government waste, even though I thought we needed to do more short-term stimulus.

I believed that progress toward a long-term plan for deficit reduction was important, but I never thought it was a higher priority than economic growth; in fact, I didn't think we could reduce future deficits without reviving the economy first. The Great Recession's shriveling of tax revenues and increases in temporary safety net spending were primary drivers of our current fiscal imbalance. When the unemployed had jobs again and businesses had profits again, they would pay more taxes and require less help from the safety net, and near-term deficits would shrink again.

The turnaround of the financial system and the remarkably quick return to economic growth did make me more confident than I should have been about the economic outlook. I believed the worst was behind us, and I told the President that. I took too much comfort from Fed forecasts consistently projecting growth rates between 3 and 4 percent. But the President did not stop pushing for us to do more for the economy. And we continued to push for more stimulus in every budget and every fiscal negotiation. We didn't get as much as we wanted, but that wasn't because we embraced austerity, or because the President pursued health care reform instead of "focusing on jobs." I never saw his other priorities get in the way of his focus on the economy.

The problem was in Congress. By late 2009, Republicans were holding up the extension of unemployment benefits during the worst recession in seventy-five years. They opposed small business tax cuts that had, until that point, been central to their agenda. After complaining that the Recovery Act didn't include enough infrastructure, they began opposing infrastructure. And the idea that conservative Democratic senators in states such as Arkansas, Indiana, and Nebraska would have embraced big spending proposals if only the President had used his bully pulpit to crusade for them is fantasy. We would squeeze several modest stimulus bills through Congress in 2010—including tax cuts for small businesses and state aid to protect teaching jobs— by offsetting them with equivalent budgetary savings over ten years. But we never got more than a few Republican votes for any of them. Naked stimulus would have been a nonstarter. And legislation that can't actually pass Congress can't stimulate the economy.

The President stopped using the s-word in 2009, and he would talk more about deficit reduction in 2010, a rhetorical pivot that angered some liberals. He was a Keynesian, but he didn't see the point of belaboring Keynesian arguments that the public wasn't buying. He would also create a bipartisan fiscal commission, after Senate Republicans blocked an effort to create one through legislation. He would appoint former Republican Senator Alan Simpson and former Clinton White House Chief of Staff Erskine Bowles to co-chair the commission, which was assigned to recommend policies to cut the deficit to below 3 percent of GDP by 2015.

Somehow, we convinced the left that we were committed to austerity and the right that we were runaway spenders. As usual, our policies were in a political no-man's-land. Nobody seemed to think we were striking the right balance.

• • •

BY THE fall of 2009, our housing policies were probably even less popular than our fiscal policies.

One of every eight mortgages was in foreclosure or default, a disaster for suffering families as well as communities blighted by abandoned homes. And some of the initiatives the President had launched in Arizona in February to try to reverse the slide were off to an embarrassingly slow start. The HARP program, designed to help 4 to 5 million borrowers refinance their mortgages, had helped refinance less than 100,000 homes in its first six months. The HAMP program, our effort to reduce the mortgage payments of another 3 to 4 million homeowners at risk of foreclosure, had facilitated less than 2,000 permanent loan modifications. It had produced temporary relief for another 360,000 homeowners, but a thicket of problems related to mortgage servicers was blocking their path to permanent relief.

This mess quickly became Exhibit A for progressives who believed we cared more about Wall Street than Main Street. I held a bunch of meetings with angry Democrats—in Speaker Pelosi's office, Senate Majority Whip Dick Durbin's office, and all over the Hill—who derisively questioned the depth of our commitment to help homeowners. Elizabeth Warren, one of our most ardent and eloquent liberal critics, devoted a series of hearings to the start-up difficulties of HARP and HAMP, as well as her larger problems with TARP.

"The people who funded the bailout, the American taxpayers, are bombarded with news that the Wall Street firms that benefited from TARP assistance are reporting windfall quarterly profits . . . while unemployment remains close to 10 percent, loan defaults continue to rise, and the foreclosure crisis has no apparent end in sight," she said at a hearing in October. I thought she put the dilemma quite well.

The next day, Warren stopped by my office. I told her we were as frustrated as she was at the glacial early pace of our housing efforts.

"At some point, you should tell me what you propose we do," I said.

Warren seemed taken aback. To her credit, and to my surprise, she admitted that she hadn't really thought about what specifically we should be doing differently. But she promised to think about it and get back to me.

A few days later, she called back with three ideas. One was reasonable but modest. Another we were already working on. The third was large-scale principal reductions, which we didn't think would be a cost-effective use of our limited resources. Housing was an impossibly complex issue that didn't lend itself to simple solutions, and the limitations of our housing programs were a lot easier to identify than they were to fix. We were under intense pressure to improve these programs—not only from our many critics, but from the President, who was deeply dissatisfied with our early results, and constantly pushed us to do better. He often sent us the heartrending letters he had received from families facing foreclosure; they clearly haunted him. We were dissatisfied and frustrated, too. Some of our programs were stumbling out of the gate. Others weren't ambitious enough. We would keep looking for ways to expand their power, reach, and effectiveness throughout the President's first term.

If there had been a game-changing housing plan that could have provided much more relief, we would have embraced it. We had some

of the nation's best progressive talent working on housing. We also
had powerful incentives to throw everything we had at the problem;
the press was killing us and so were our political allies. The head of
the National Council of La Raza once warned me that if we didn't
start doing more to prevent foreclosures, Hispanic groups wouldn't
work for the President's reelection.

We tried to do what we could within the constraints we faced. It
wasn't enough. But it was more than most people realized.

WE HAD three basic housing objectives. We achieved the first two without much drama or media attention. The third would be a struggle.

Our first goal was to arrest the dizzying drop in home prices. The
most important thing we did to stop the slide, other than our efforts
to arrest the broader economic and financial free fall, was to stabilize
Fannie and Freddie so that mortgage credit could keep flowing at a
time when private capital was fleeing the sector. Even with unemployment rising and defaults increasing, home prices stabilized in mid-
2009, and gradually began to rise in the following years. The end of
the real estate slump helped avoid further damage to the typical family's largest source of wealth and savings, and was critical to restoring
the economy to growth. It wouldn't have happened without our $400
billion lifeline for Fannie and Freddie.

Our second objective, related to the first, was to keep mortgage
rates as low as possible. Our rescue of Fannie and Freddie was vital
here as well, since they were now the dominant drivers of mortgage
credit. The government backstop maintained their access to cheap
money, which held down rates for ordinary families. The Fed's purchases of mortgage-backed securities through QE1, along with more
modest purchases by the Treasury, also helped keep rates historically
low, putting extra money in the pockets of millions of Americans. And
our HARP program, along with a streamlined refinancing program
for Fannie and Freddie, helped borrowers refinance their mortgages at
those low rates even if the decline in home values left them underwater.

Despite its slow start, HARP would help three million homeowners refinance. That was short of the program's initial target, but by 2014, another twenty-three million U.S. homeowners would refinance their mortgages outside of HARP, a huge though unheralded stimulus.

Our final goal, helping vulnerable families stay in their homes, was more complicated.

By the fall of 2009, two million U.S. mortgages were in foreclosure and another seven million were at serious risk of foreclosure. About eleven million homeowners were underwater—one in every five mortgages—with a total of about $700 billion in negative equity. Our resources could make an important difference in the lives of some vulnerable families, but they were far too limited to fix America's housing problems, much less its larger economic problems.

It was also going to be extremely difficult to decide whom to help and how to help them. Even after the horrific recession, roughly nine out of ten homeowners were still paying their mortgages on time, often at significant hardship and sacrifice. We didn't want to spend tax dollars helping borrowers who could afford to stay current without our help, but there were also real fairness issues, as well as political issues, around using tax dollars to help their neighbors who got in over their heads. And politics aside, as we studied potential housing programs, we were troubled by their limited bang for the buck. The logistics were daunting. The incentive problems were complex. If our ultimate goal was to improve the lives of families in need, rather than claim we had "fixed housing," there were much more efficient ways to help.

We did not believe, though we looked at this question over and over, that a much larger program focused directly on housing could have a material impact on the broader economy. Jan Eberly, the assistant secretary of economic policy, took a fresh look at these alternatives later, and her analysis concluded that even if the federal government had borrowed and spent $700 billion to wipe out every dollar of negative equity in the U.S. housing market—a "principal reduction" program of utopian proportions—it would have increased annual personal consumption by just 0.1 to 0.2 percent. The projected impact on employment was relatively modest, too, amounting to a cost of about $1.5 million of federal spending per job created. By contrast, our auto rescue cost about $14,000 for each of the one million jobs it saved. In other words, even if Congress had authorized the mother of all principal reduction programs, as expensive as TARP and almost as expensive as the Recovery Act, it wouldn't have changed the trajectory of the recovery.

Our main foreclosure prevention program, HAMP, was much more narrowly targeted. It was designed to help homeowners who seemed likely to default in their current situation but likely to stay current if their mortgage payments could be reduced for several years. Borrowers with expensive homes or second homes or rental properties weren't eligible. We didn't want to spend our limited resources helping speculators hang on to investment properties they had hoped to flip in the boom. We knew HAMP would help borrowers, who would avoid the trauma of foreclosure, as well as mortgage servicers, who would receive generous incentives to track down eligible homeowners and modify their mortgages. Many creditors howled in protest, but they would ultimately benefit, too, receiving more income from HAMP borrowers paying reduced mortgage payments than they would have gotten from foreclosure sales during a foreclosure epidemic when banks were already awash in inventory.

We knew it would be tough to identify the universe of eligible homeowners and get them into the program quickly. HAMP borrowers could get relief for up to three months through a "trial modification" with minimal documentation, but then they would have to provide proof of eligibility to receive a permanent modification. We ended up requiring a mountain of paperwork for permanent relief, in part to appease critics such as Barofsky, who warned that the limited safeguards in our initial proposal were an invitation to fraud; we decided that in this case he had a point. But Larry warned that we were so worried about "false positives," providing aid to the undeserving, that we would allow too many "false negatives," denying aid to the deserving. He had a point as well.

By the fall, it was clear that HAMP's reliance on the broken infrastructure of the mortgage servicing industry was a serious problem. This was probably unavoidable; we didn't have the authority to start up a new government agency or hire thousands of loan specialists ourselves, and even if we'd been able to get the authority from Congress, it would have been a long and messy process. But the servicers, many of them owned by banks, had little experience modifying loans, and nowhere near the capacity or the resources they would need to modify millions of loans. They had been completely unprepared for the housing crisis, and had laid off staff in droves after the bubble popped. Now we were asking them to conduct a challenging and time-consuming form of triage, and they were terrible at it—slow to hire, slow to figure out how to provide relief, just slow. In fairness, many of the borrowers they were supposed to track down were hard to find and harder to engage; homeowners also struggled to find every required document. But many incompetent servicers found ways to lose those documents multiple times.

As the disappointing numbers rolled in that fall, and it became clear that many homeowners in the trial period wouldn't or couldn't produce the documents they needed for permanent relief, we discussed whether we should just grant a permanent loan modification to everyone with a trial modification, to help as many homeowners as possible. But we decided that could produce too much opportunity for scandal and abuse that would threaten support for the entire program; we had seen the dangers of "no-doc loans" and "liar loans" during the boom. We were spending the public's money, and we had an obligation to protect the integrity of the program.

The President kept urging us to think big, to think bold, to consider anything that would help homeowners in distress. We even revisited our debates about broad-based principal reduction. But as I testified before Warren's panel in December, the biggest driver of the foreclosure crisis wasn't underwater mortgages. It was the weak economy. Too many unemployed and underemployed workers were having trouble making their mortgage payments. We could spend hundreds of billions of dollars paying down negative equity without changing that reality. It wouldn't matter how many mortgages we modified if the borrowers didn't have income. We couldn't fix the economy by fixing housing, but we could do the reverse.

"Our judgment is the best thing we can do is to help get the economy growing again, bringing unemployment down as quickly as we can, and to continue to make sure we're providing overall stability to the housing market," I told Warren.

The most important thing we could do to fix our housing problems—other than stabilize the real estate market, keep mortgage rates low, and provide targeted foreclosure relief, which we were already doing—was to help promote an economic recovery that could create more jobs and income for average Americans. I had once told the President—and he often quoted this back to me—that if he had another $100 billion to spend on the economy, we wouldn't recommend he spend it on housing. It would make much more economic, moral, and practical sense to provide relief to families through tax cuts, unemployment insurance, or safety net spending, or to save the jobs of teachers and first responders via aid to states, or to finance infrastructure projects that would put people to work building schools and fixing roads and creating a smart electric grid. Housing programs are pretty weak job creation and income support programs, while the opposite is not the case; job creation and income support programs are excellent ways to help families afford their mortgages or rent.

STILL, OVER the rest of my time at Treasury, we would make an extensive set of changes and additions to our initial housing initiatives to try to expand their reach.

We added programs to provide relief to the unemployed and to help overstretched homeowners move into affordable rentals. We made

HAMP's financial incentives much more generous in order to accelerate the modifications. We set up a program to evaluate mortgage servicers and withheld incentive payments from the worst performers. We provided new incentives to reduce burdensome home equity lines of credit and other second mortgages, which had been obstacles to modifications of first mortgages. We provided billions of dollars to the states hardest hit by the housing bust to help fund their own programs, and billions more to state housing finance agencies across the country. We even added a narrowly targeted principal reduction program for some HAMP recipients.

We also tried to push the Federal Housing Finance Agency to pursue a similarly targeted program for loans backed by Fannie and Freddie. But acting FHFA director Edward DeMarco, a competent but cautious civil servant who did not want to inflame our Republican critics, refused to allow any principal reductions, even though FHFA's own analysis showed they would save the government money in about half a million cases. It was amazing how little actual authority we had over Fannie and Freddie, considering they were entirely dependent on Treasury's cash to stay alive. Some liberals later blamed the President for their failure to provide relief, since he could have fired DeMarco at any time. But we couldn't just appoint a new director on our own. The President did nominate well-respected North Carolina Banking Commissioner Joe Smith to replace DeMarco, but Senator Shelby blocked him, claiming he would be an administration "lapdog," even after North Carolina Senator Richard Burr, a Republican who actually knew Smith, endorsed him as "the best nominee" and "a perfect choice." After that experience, we had a hard time finding any willing candidates.

This was frustrating, but I don't think a more compliant FHFA would have produced a dramatically different result. And while our numerous expansions of housing programs helped many Americans, they were still modest relative to the size of the problem. They certainly didn't change the widespread perception that after embracing a strategy of dramatic force and creativity to save greedy financiers, we left innocent victims of the crisis adrift, vulnerable to the predations of the very banks and investors who had benefited most from our largesse. I once played a prank on Gene Sperling, pretending I had told a reporter he was the secret architect of HAMP—not just the substance, but the communications and messaging strategy. My press secretary got so worried that Gene would have a heart attack that she called to spill the beans; that's how universally reviled HAMP was.

HAMP would end up permanently modifying about 1.3 million mortgages through 2013, saving the median homeowner more than $500 a month. That's a lot less than the 3 to 4 million we unwisely suggested HAMP would aim to help at the rollout in February 2009, a number that would be thrown back in our faces from that day forward. But the industry permanently modified another 3.9 million mortgages without government assistance, so the number of homeowners with more sustainable loans was about what we had hoped. Another quarter million homeowners have avoided foreclosure through alternative programs we implemented, and the Federal Housing Administration has mitigated the losses of 2 million more. If we had somehow managed to triple the HAMP modifications, we wouldn't have substantially increased the overall number of modifications, just the share supported by the government, and we wouldn't have made a serious difference in the post-crisis economy. The foreclosure crisis was caused by big macro forces—a frenetic credit boom, a brutal recession, a dizzying drop in home prices—and big macro forces would be required to end it.

That said, our housing efforts got off to a rough start, and I set too high a bar for expanding them later on. I was also an ineffective advocate for what we were trying to do. I often met with social service agencies from the low-income housing world, and I frequently made the kind of empathy mistakes that frustrated Carole, pushing them for solutions and inundating them with the constraints we faced instead of listening patiently to their stories and feeling their pain. I wanted to hear about what was working and what wasn't and how we could realistically help. I once interrupted an advocate early in her passionate description of the human costs of the crisis, saying I knew things were terrible out there. "Let's stipulate that," I said. "Let's talk about what we can do." Afterward, Sara Aviel walked me back to my office and told me: Don't ever ask them to stipulate the pain and suffering.

"Let them have their moment to explain," she said.

I made similar mistakes when we arranged a series of dinners to reach out to disgruntled progressive leaders. Instead of listening sympathetically to their complaints and promising to do better, I would defend our strategy, provide lists of all the constraints we faced, and explain why their alternatives wouldn't work any better. All I managed to do was persuade them that I wasn't on their side. John Podesta, the former White House chief of staff who ran the Center for American Progress, told Patterson after one dinner that I needed to stop trying to explain all the barriers that made it harder to do more on housing.

"He said you're only making it worse," Patterson told me.

In many ways, 2009 was an extraordinary year for the new administration. We helped end the financial crisis and the Great Recession faster than we had ever thought possible. The U.S. economy was growing again, and by March 2010, it would be adding jobs again. In April 2009, the IMF predicted we would spend up to $2 trillion bailing out the U.S. banking system; by the end of the year, it already looked like taxpayers might turn a profit on our financial rescues. A paper by the economists Alan Blinder and Mark Zandi estimated that without our fiscal, monetary, and financial interventions, GDP would have been about 11.5 percent lower, and we would have lost an additional 8.5 million jobs. Meanwhile, GM and Chrysler were out of bankruptcy and poised to return to profitability. The Recovery Act was pouring transformative resources into the President's long-term priorities, including clean energy, education reform, electronic medical records, and scientific research. And both houses of Congress had passed a version of health reform, bringing a long-standing progressive dream to the brink of reality.

Politically, though, it was a brutal year. The right hated us, and the left wasn't interested in defending us. Republicans won gubernatorial races in New Jersey and Virginia, states the President had won a year earlier. And in January, Republican Scott Brown stunned the world by claiming the late Ted Kennedy's seat in deep-blue Massachusetts, ending the filibuster-proof Democratic majority in the Senate.

That same day, I went to see the usually dour Senate Minority Leader Mitch McConnell, and he was in a pretty good mood. At that point it looked like Obamacare might be dead, although congressional Democrats would later find a way to push it across the finish line. The President's disapproval ratings were getting much closer to his approval ratings. McConnell bluntly told me Republicans intended to stick with their strategy of obstructionism, blocking whatever the President wanted, because it was working for them electorally.

"The one exception," he said, "might be financial reform."

That was why I had come to talk to him. The financial regulatory system was broken, and we needed legislation from Congress to fix it. I didn't want a future Fed chairman or New York Fed president to feel as helpless to confront a gathering storm as Ben and I had felt. I didn't want a future Treasury secretary to face the constraints Hank and I had faced after the storm hit. But if the forty-one Senate Republicans stuck together, they could prevent us from reforming the system, and I wanted to know if McConnell planned to do that.

McConnell is a calculating politician, and I find many of his beliefs and his methods offensive, but he can be appealingly candid. He didn't seem to have much personal enthusiasm for financial reform, and certainly not for our vision of reform. Still, he suggested he was not burning with desire to unite his caucus in a battle against a cause that enjoyed broad public support, and risk reinforcing the Republican image as the defenders of Wall Street and the rich.

"It's possible that you might be able to get some of our guys, maybe five to ten, on financial reform," he said. "Everything else, we'll fight you. And it's going to work for us."

We could worry about everything else later. We needed to pass financial reform now. The worst of the financial crisis was over, and the President wanted to sign a bill before Americans forgot just how horrifying and devastating it had been.

TEN

The Fight for Reform

Financial crises cannot be reliably predicted, so they cannot be reliably prevented. They're kind of like earthquakes that way, or they would be if earthquakes were triggered by manias and fears and human interactions. We know some of the warning signs, most notably credit booms, substantial and sustained increases in private borrowing relative to income. But we can't outlaw stupidity or irrational exuberance or herd behavior, and we can't anticipate with any confidence exactly when manias will turn into panics. We can't count on fallible central bankers or regulators to stop financial booms before they become dangerous, because by the time the danger is clear, it's often too late to defuse the problem.

Still, governments can do a lot to reduce the damage of financial disasters, just as they can with natural disasters. In the same way building codes can require sturdier construction in fault zones or elevated structures in floodplains, strong financial regulations can limit the severity of future crises. Even though governments can't eradicate crises, they can reduce the system's vulnerability to crises, as well as the risk that crises will spiral out of control. This crisis wouldn't have been so bad if the United States hadn't been so woefully unprepared.

The President did not want that to happen again, and neither did I. We wanted to reform the system to make it more resilient, less vulnerable, and better at providing the credit and capital economies need to grow. We wanted to address the root causes of the crisis and our inability to contain it, so that history wouldn't repeat itself. To return to my favorite analogy, we wanted better fire prevention, fireproofing, and fire inspections, along with better-equipped firefighters for the inevitable times when our precautions wouldn't be enough.

The fundamental causes of this crisis were familiar and straightforward. It began with a mania—the widespread belief that devastating financial crises were a thing of the past, that future recessions would be mild, that gravity-defying home prices would never crash to earth. This was the optimism of the Great Moderation, the delusion of indefinite stability. This mania of overconfidence fueled an explosion of credit in the economy and leverage in the financial system. And much of that leverage was financed by uninsured short-term liabilities that could run at any time.

This combination of a long rise in borrowing fueled by leverage in runnable form is the foundation of all financial crises, and it would have been dangerous in any financial system. But it was much more dangerous for us, because many of the overleveraged major firms that were borrowing short and lending long were outside our traditional banking system. These institutions were not constrained by the regulatory safeguards that applied to banks, which was why so much risk migrated in their direction, and they did not have access to the government safety net designed to contain runs on banks. The safeguards for traditional banks weren't tough enough, either, but what made our storm into a perfect storm was nonbanks behaving like banks without bank supervision or bank protections, leaving by some measures more than half the nation's financial activity vulnerable to a run. When the panic hit, and the run gained momentum, we did not have the ability to protect the economy until conditions were scary enough to provoke action by Congress.

Those were the main causes of the crisis. You could say that on the front end, the long period of low interest rates in the United States and worldwide helped fuel the crisis, because it helped fuel the mania that inflated the bubble, encouraging more borrowing, more home-building, more risk-taking. This was a necessary condition, though not a sufficient condition. And on the back end, the inadequacy of our firefighting tools—our inability to manage the failure of large complex institutions in an orderly fashion, our limited authority to stop a panic outside the banking system—helped prevent us from containing the crisis. This was an accelerant.

But the root causes, as usual, were mania, leverage, and runnable short-term financing. That's how our financial system became that scene from *It's a Wonderful Life*.

THERE WERE all sorts of other problems in the system, and they gave rise to a variety of theories purporting to explain the crisis. The problems were so many and so varied that the crisis became a kind of Rorschach test; you could find at least some evidence to support almost any theory that confirmed your prior ideological biases, no matter where you stood on the political or economic spectrum. Some of these problems did contribute to the crisis and did magnify the damage caused by the crisis, but they were not principal causes of the crisis. They would not have been so material without the more fundamental forces of the mania—the excessive belief that past would be prologue and the good times would continue to roll—that fed the excess borrowing.

Some critics, for example, saw the core problem as the gradual rollback and Clinton-era repeal of the Depression-era Glass-Steagall limits on bank activities, which allowed commercial banks with insured deposits to get mixed up in investment banking. But most of the firms in the center of the crisis—Bear, Lehman, AIG, Merrill, Fannie,

With President Obama in London at the meeting of the G-20, where the major economies of the world committed to avoid one of the central mistakes of the Great Depression by working together to address the crisis, April 2, 2009. *(White House/Pete Souza)*

Larry Summers and I face the President in the Roosevelt Room of the White House, January 14, 2010. *(White House/Pete Souza)*

President Obama congratulates Senator Chris Dodd (D-Conn.) and Representative Barney Frank (D-Mass.) after signing the Dodd-Frank financial reform bill in Washington, July 21, 2010. *(Associated Press)*

Presenting Chinese Vice Premier Wang Qishan with an authentic New York City Fire Department hat—a reference to the "firefighter" nickname that the vice premier earned in China for being the "go-to guy" for handling tough issues like SARS, the Olympics, and Guangdong's financial crisis in the 1990s, Washington, January 18, 2011. *(Courtesy of the U.S. Department of the Treasury)*

Before the House Budget Committee on Capitol Hill—one of sixty-seven congressional hearings in which I testified as Treasury secretary, February 16, 2011. *(Jim Watson/AFP/Getty Images)*

Meeting with the President in the Oval Office of the White House, April 9, 2012. *(White House/Pete Souza)*

With the national security team at the arrival ceremony for South Korean President Lee Myung-bak on the South Lawn of the White House, October 13, 2011. *(Kevin Dietsch—Pool/Getty Images)*

Meeting with German Finance Minister Wolfgang Schäuble during his vacation in Westerland, on the North Sea island of Sylt, July 30, 2012. *(Associated Press)*

Gathered with the Treasury senior staff and a few special guests in the secretary's small conference room for the final morning meeting of my tenure, January 25, 2013. Standing, left to right: Marisa Lago, Cyrus Amir-Mokri, Dick Berner, Wally Adeyemo, Charles Collyns, David Cohen, and Sara Aviel. Seated, left to right: Neal Wolin, Tim Massad, Leslie Ireland, Jenni LeCompte, Mark Patterson, Matt Rutherford, Gene Sperling, Mark Mazur, Jan Eberly, Carole Geithner, Chris Meade, me. *(Courtesy of the U.S. Department of the Treasury)*

At my Treasury desk, August 21, 2009. *(Courtesy of the U.S. Department of the Treasury)*

Freddie—were basically unaffected by the repeal of Glass-Steagall, be-cause they were not commercial banks. And traditional banking—making loans, especially real estate loans—ended up being pretty risky, too. WaMu, Wachovia, IndyMac, and hundreds of smaller insti-tutions that blew up in the crisis were basically overextended banks and thrifts, not the far-flung financial conglomerates made possible by the disappearance of the Glass-Steagall partition. It is true that Citi and Bank of America might have been less risky and had fewer problems if they had not been allowed to build and buy vulnerable investment banks. But the most damaging failures happened to firms operating on just one side of the divide.

Some on the right have tried to blame the crisis on Democratic-led efforts to combat discrimination against low-income and minor-ity borrowers, such as the Community Reinvestment Act of 1977 or Fannie and Freddie's affordable housing programs. But the erosion in underwriting standards, the rush to provide credit to Americans who couldn't have gotten it in the past, was led by consumer finance com-panies and other nonbank lenders that did not have to comply with the Community Reinvestment Act—which, after all, discouraged red-lining for nearly three decades before the crisis. These firms took credit risks because they wanted to, not because they had to; they believed rising home prices would protect them from losses, and their investors were eager to finance their risk-taking. Fannie and Freddie lost a lot of market share to these exuberant private lenders, and while they did be-latedly join the party, the overall quality of the mortgages they bought and guaranteed was significantly stronger than the industry average.

Another popular villain was size, the notion that crises happen when big financial institutions get too big. In an ideal world, the government would be indifferent to the failures of banks, and that is harder when banks are bigger. But the Great Depression began with a cascade of failures of small banks. Bear Stearns wasn't even one of America's fifteen largest financial firms in March 2008; it was still so interconnected with the financial system that its failure at that fragile moment would have caused panic in the derivatives markets, the repo markets, and the financial markets in general, just as we saw later with Lehman. In a system vulnerable to panic following a long credit boom, even relatively small institutions can cause systemic damage when they fail in messy ways. Big banks, of course, can cause even more damage—which is why they should be subject to tougher regulations—but they are also better equipped to absorb losses that would kill a small bank. And if big firms such as JPMorgan, Bank of America, and Wells Fargo hadn't been big enough to absorb failing firms such as Bear, WaMu, Countrywide, Merrill, and Wachovia, our crisis would have been much worse.

Related to the theory that size caused the crisis was the theory that moral hazard caused the crisis, that "too-big-to-fail" banks took on so much risk because they knew the government would bail them out if they got in trouble. There was certainly moral hazard in our system. Traditional banks did enjoy a mix of explicit and implicit government protection, advantages that were not sufficiently offset by constraints on their risk-taking. But that wasn't our main problem. Again, the worst of the crisis took place outside the traditional banking system, where private financial markets had willingly financed huge amounts of leverage in more loosely supervised firms such as Bear, Lehman, and AIG. Those firms had no reason to expect emergency assistance, and neither did their shareholders or creditors, because the U.S. government had no history of intervening to rescue nonbanks. There was no precedent for guarantees of money market funds or government support for the commercial paper market, either. In fact, even after we helped JPMorgan acquire Bear, the financial markets continued to pull back from the surviving investment banks. The prospect of a similar "rescue" was not much comfort to other systemic firms or potential investors; Bear ceased to exist and its shareholders lost a fortune. The moral hazard theorists simply underestimated the mania, the power of Hyman Minsky's theory, which I first read in 2007, that stability can breed instability.

That said, moral hazard was a legitimate problem. Fannie and Freddie exploited their access to cheap capital—a result of the widespread (and ultimately correct) assumption that the government would stand behind their obligations—to take on way too much leverage and risk, a classic example of moral hazard. The large banks also enjoyed lower-cost financing because of their access to a government safety net, which was one reason they got so large. And there was a real danger that moral hazard created by our actions to resolve this crisis could plant the seeds of a future crisis. I still didn't think firehouses caused fires—as Stan Fischer put it during the emerging-market crises, condoms don't cause sex—but resolutions of financial crises always create some moral hazard, and I wanted our reforms to limit moral hazard going forward.

It was also tempting, and intuitively satisfying, to blame the crisis on the deceit and fraud and other misbehavior that flourished during the boom—duplicitous brokers luring borrowers into mortgages they couldn't afford, Bernie Madoff types running wild, securities firms dumping toxic products on unsuspecting clients. These abuses were terrible and unfair, but they were more a feature of the mania than a significant cause of the crisis, fueled by the dominant belief that risk-taking was no longer particularly risky. Promises of easy money seemed plausible in those days, because a lot of easy money was being made. Wei Xiong, a Princeton economist, told me later about a study he coauthored analyzing the personal housing transactions of those involved in the mortgage securitization business during the boom. They got caught up in the frenzy like everyone else, buying bigger homes for themselves and speculating in the real estate market even as prices defied gravity. Throughout the financial system, "insiders" were putting their own money where their mouths were; many of them ultimately lost a lot of money doing so.

But even if predatory behavior wasn't the main cause of the crisis, even if some toxic products were sold without a full understanding of their toxicity, ordinary Americans deserved more protection from predatory behavior and toxic products. The financial crisis exposed our system of consumer protection as a dysfunctional mess, leaving ordinary Americans way too vulnerable to fraud and other malfeasance, while leaving the financial system vulnerable to sudden crises of confidence. Many borrowers, especially in subprime markets, bit off more than they could chew because they didn't understand the absurdly complex and opaque terms of their financial arrangements, or were actively channeled into the riskiest deals. Underwriting standards deteriorated dramatically, producing flimsy loans that were quickly packaged into complex securities; the eagerness of investors to buy them does not excuse the shoddiness of the products.

This was another area where our weak and disjointed regulatory system, riddled with gaps and evasion opportunities, cried out for reform. Government oversight just hadn't kept up with the fast-growing and fast-changing frontiers of finance, from the exotic innovations in mortgage markets to the explosion of complex derivatives. The financial cops weren't authorized to patrol the system's worst neighborhoods, and they weren't aggressive enough about using the authority they had. While we clearly needed better safeguards against systemic risk in these new frontiers outside the traditional banking system, we also needed to make sure individual Americans weren't left vulnerable to predation and abuse there.

But again, the most powerful theory of the crisis was simple. It started with a long mania of overconfidence, the widespread belief that house prices would not fall, that recessions would be mild, that markets would remain liquid. The mania fueled too much borrowing, too much leverage, and too much runnable short-term financing, with too much of it happening outside the traditional banking system. Borrowers took too many risks; creditors and investors were way too willing to finance those risks; the government failed to rein in those risks, and then was unable to act quickly or forcefully enough when the panic hit. Meanwhile, the actions the government finally took to end the crisis created new dangers of moral hazard. And our Wild West system of consumer protection was a national disgrace.

The question was what to do about this mess.

I DIDN'T think there was much we could do about manias and beliefs. We couldn't ban fads or mandate judicious thinking. But there was a lot we could do about our other vulnerabilities, starting with stronger shock absorbers across the entire financial system.

I always thought our top reform priority should be more conservative rules requiring financial institutions to hold more capital, take on less leverage—the flip side of capital—and maintain more liquidity. The rules would have to be applied broadly and globally, to prevent risk from migrating from banks to nonbanks and from U.S. firms to foreign firms. By forcing financial institutions to maintain a larger cushion of capital to protect themselves from potential losses, restricting their ability to borrow to finance risky investments, and making sure they could meet their short-term obligations if their funding ever dried up, we would limit their vulnerability to runs, while also limiting the system's vulnerability to contagion if a major firm did fail. We couldn't squelch the natural cat-and-mouse game between innovation and regulation, but more conservative capital and liquidity requirements could provide a baseline of safety, especially if we built in the capacity to expand their scope over time, and if we required financial firms to take periodic stress tests based on genuinely dark scenarios. The crisis was a reminder that they wouldn't prepare for a storm while the sun was shining unless regulators forced them.

In addition to the shock absorbers for individual firms, I thought we also needed stronger shock absorbers in the markets where firms were connected, such as tri-party repo and especially derivatives. By requiring more collateral (or "margin") behind trades, we could limit leverage in the system, while also limiting the systemic damage from the failure of individual firms.

Derivatives didn't cause the crisis, and they even played a useful role helping businesses, farmers, banks, and investors to hedge risk before and during the crisis. But in the midst of the panic, derivatives did help make it worse. The derivatives dealers who demanded more collateral to protect themselves against the rising risks of default helped increase those risks. The complicated spaghetti of the derivatives market magnified the fear and uncertainty caused by the implosion of major derivatives traders such as Bear, Lehman, and AIG. We needed to make derivatives trading more transparent, while requiring firms to collect and post more collateral in advance to avoid the vicious dynamics of margin spirals. And we needed to require "central clearing" for most derivatives trades, establishing an intermediary with a strong financial foundation that would stand between counterparties so that a default by one firm was less likely to set off a cascade of additional defaults. Lee Sachs had pushed this idea inside the Clinton administration, and I had taken up the cause at the New York Fed, where our plumbing work with the Fourteen Families laid the foundation for central clearing.

Those ideas were all financial equivalents of requiring fire-resistant building materials or smoke-activated sprinklers. But they wouldn't mean much without more effective fire inspectors and stronger enforcement of the fire code. Our current oversight regime, with its competing fiefdoms and overlapping jurisdictions and perverse incentives encouraging firms to shop around for friendly regulators, was an anarchic mess. Vast swaths of the financial system had no one in charge. Others were swarming with regulators engaged in tribal warfare. I often compared the situation to the wild frontiers of the Afghanistan-Pakistan border region or the Balkans a century ago. We needed a simpler structure that would make sure the more conservative rules we envisioned were applied more evenly and more broadly across the financial system, with clearer accountability for monitoring risk within every major firm and especially across the entire system.

At the same time, we needed a dramatic overhaul of our inadequate and fragmented consumer protection regime. The rules governing consumer finance were too weak. The authority for enforcing them was spread across seven federal agencies and fifty states. Thousands of companies were extending credit with no meaningful oversight, from payday lenders to auto dealers, leaving Americans unprotected from abuse. President Obama believed he had been elected to fix problems like that.

Finally, we needed to bolster the government's ability to fight fires. One top priority was "resolution authority," what Jamie Dimon called "bankruptcy for big dumb banks," the power for government to manage the failure of systemic institutions through an orderly process, like the FDIC had for normal banks. With more authority to unwind major firms more deliberately, we'd reduce the danger of catastrophic Lehman-type failures and the need for AIG-type rescues. But we also wanted to preserve the firefighting authorities that helped us stem the panic—most important, the Fed's general authority to provide liquidity and the FDIC's authority to guarantee bank debt during times of systemic distress. We couldn't end bailouts by proclaiming an end to bailouts, or, worse, by stripping away the government's bailout power; we couldn't eliminate panics by promising not to act in the face of the next panic. On the contrary, giving crisis responders the power to use overwhelming force to quell a panic makes panics less likely. We needed to try to reduce the risk, in Charles Kindleberger's framing, that future manias would turn into panics and then crashes.

We began debating all these financial reform issues in the early days of President Obama's transition. But the first question we had to answer was a less technical question of sequencing: When should we pursue legislative reforms? Financial reform would consume a lot of political oxygen. Our overriding priorities in those days were ending the crisis and reviving the economy. There were some near-term tensions between financial reform, which would ultimately require banks to take less risk, and economic recovery, which would depend on banks getting out of their defensive crouches and taking risks again. There was a case to be made for Saint Augustine–style caution—tougher capital and liquidity requirements, just not yet. Paul Volcker, the venerable leader of the President's new economic recovery board, reminded us that getting reform right was more important than passing reform quickly. This was complex stuff, and transformative opportunities like this didn't come along often.

Rahm, as usual, wanted immediate action. Politically, he believed that offense, a strategy of relentless initiative, was the best defense. He saw "Wall Street reform" as a great issue to build momentum, set the agenda, and force Republicans to choose between siding with Wall Street and giving the President a bipartisan victory. And regardless of Rahm's political considerations, I thought it made sense to strike while the pain of the crisis was raw and the financial establishment was weak, rather than wait for memories to fade and the empire to strike back. I wanted to seize the first-mover advantage in setting the terms of the debate, both in the United States and globally. I also believed an early push for reform could provide a productive outlet for the public's Old Testament anger, a positive expression of what I called "the atonement agenda." I didn't want populist fury to muck up our crisis response with damaging short-term conditions, but I thought it could help us pass tough new long-term rules of the road.

The President decided to push sooner rather than later. I proposed that we should draft the first version of the legislation ourselves, and he readily agreed. We had left the drafting of the stimulus to congressional Democrats, and we would give the Hill even more control over health care reform. But I feared that Congress didn't have the necessary technical expertise to craft effective financial reforms, and that if we didn't take the initiative, financial lobbyists as well as ideological extremists on the left and the right would have too much influence over the shape of the bill. So even while the crisis was still burning, our reform team was meeting daily, scrambling to prepare legislation to ease the next crisis.

We weren't scrambling fast enough to suit Rahm. He initially hoped to get our legislation through the House before that G-20 sum-mit in London in April 2009, an insanely ambitious timeline. He then said he'd settle for a full legislative draft before the summit. At a meet-ing in Rahm's office in March, my deputy Neal Wolin said that wasn't possible, either. This would be a complex bill, likely to run hundreds of pages. Rahm pointed to a desk with a computer.

"Sit the fuck down and start typing," he snapped. "And don't get up until you're finished."

THE GOAL of financial reform, as Larry liked to say, was to make the system safe for failure. It wasn't to prevent the failure of individual firms that take on too much risk, but to make the aftershocks of fail-ure less threatening to the system as a whole. I believed the key to achieving that goal would be improving our shock absorbers. In an uncertain world, with fallible human beings running and supervising financial institutions, we needed cushions to protect the system from their inevitable mistakes. In other words, we needed more capital, less leverage, more liquidity.

But we didn't want Congress designing the new capital ratios or leverage restrictions or liquidity requirements. Whatever their flaws, regulators were much better equipped than politicians to determine, say, the precise amount of common equity a bank should have rela-tive to its risk-weighted assets, or the amount of cash it should hold to meet potential withdrawals. History suggested that Capitol Hill would be too easily swayed by the clout of the financial industry and the politics of the moment; we didn't think that was the place for the intricate work of calibrating the financial system's shock absorbers. The Fed was not a very popular institution at the moment, but it had a lot of technical expertise as well as political independence, and we thought it was much better suited for the job.

We also thought these problems demanded global solutions. This was a global crisis, and we had been hurt by weak regulatory stan-dards overseas, not just by our failures at home. If we had unilaterally imposed strict new limits on risk, without encouraging higher standards globally, we simply would have reduced the market share of U.S. firms around the world, without making the global system more resilient. So starting at that G-20 summit in London, we began leading the push for tougher international financial reforms, including the new capital, leverage, and liquidity requirements that became known as Basel III; broader oversight of derivatives markets; and better ways to deal with the failures of global banks. This would require a messy, protracted process of behind-the-scenes diplomatic negotiation, but it would be absolutely crucial to strengthening the system.

We would pursue the rest of our reforms in Washington, and the process there would be messy and protracted as well. There were vast sums of money at stake, and a vast array of powerful lobbies with interests in the outcome. Passing comprehensive legislation in Washington is always a challenge, and it would be even harder at a time when the President faced such determined Republican opposition. The fact that this particular comprehensive legislation involved regulatory reform would only add to the degree of difficulty, because the affected agencies all had congressional defenders looking out for their turf, as well as influential supporters in the financial industry.

In fact, as we started to debate reform inside the administration and on Capitol Hill, many of our thorniest questions involved which regulators would do what in the future. Just about everyone agreed that the current oversight regime was a ludicrously balkanized mess, but the same tribal warfare that hobbled the regulatory system would hobble our efforts to rationalize it.

For example, we thought one obvious fix would be to merge the Securities and Exchange Commission and the Commodity Futures Trading Commission, two market regulators whose overlapping mandates routinely produced duplication and confusion. But the CFTC, through a quirk of history, was under the jurisdiction of the congressional agriculture committees, which did not want to surrender their power over a slice of the financial system—or their access to campaign donations from financial interests. I asked House Financial Services Chairman Barney Frank whether he thought we could round up the votes.

"Sure, you can merge the SEC and the CFTC," he said. "You just can't do it in the United States."

We faced a similar quandary with bank supervision. The Fed oversaw the holding companies that owned banks, while an individual bank might be regulated by the Fed, the Office of the Comptroller of the Currency, the Federal Deposit Insurance Corporation, the Office of Thrift Supervision, a state banking supervisor, or some awkward combination of those choices. This led to venue shopping and other forms of regulatory arbitrage, as well as blind-men-and-the-elephant problems where no regulator had a truly comprehensive view of an institution or the responsibility for monitoring it. Ideally, we would have liked to consolidate the OCC, FDIC, and OTS into a single national regulator for depository institutions, with a dominant ongoing role for the Fed. But we decided that politically, that was another nonstarter.

I was uneasy about the distractions of trying to reorganize the military while we were fighting a war. With Congress so starkly divided along partisan lines, we couldn't afford to lose any votes over turf, or waste half our time fighting rear-guard actions against regulators protecting their prerogatives. Ultimately, the only agency we'd propose to eliminate was the hapless OTS, which had invited banks to come under its umbrella to take advantage of its softer supervision, and had brushed off concerns about sinking thrifts such as Countrywide and WaMu.

In a Roosevelt Room meeting with the President that spring, Diana Farrell, the McKinsey veteran who was Larry's deputy, made an impassioned plea for a more ambitious regulatory overhaul. The irrationality of the organization chart offended her management-consultant sensibilities, and rightfully so. But I pointed out to the room that in domestic policy as in foreign policy, there are wars of necessity and wars of choice. Reform was a necessity. Reorganization felt like a choice that could mire the bill in the quicksand of interagency warfare; we wanted regulators focused on helping us fix the broken financial system, not fighting for their bureaucratic survival. Farrell was right that we were putting politics ahead of our policy analysis, but the ideal policy wasn't achievable. That point was neatly illustrated later when Senate Banking Committee Chairman Chris Dodd released a plan to merge the supervision functions of the OCC, OTS, FDIC, and the Fed into one mega-agency. It was dead on arrival.

Some of the most controversial turf issues involved the Fed, which was facing an intense political backlash over the crisis, the bailouts, and the bad economy. I thought the Fed should be made the nation's "systemic risk regulator," with the authority and the responsibility for identifying dangers across the entire financial system, setting broad constraints on leverage and other risks, and even expanding the scope of those shock absorbers and other safeguards over time. As risk migrated in the future, we wanted the Fed to be able to designate the future equivalent of nonbanks such as AIG or GE Capital as systemically important, so they would be subjected to tougher supervision, and could be resolved safely if they got into trouble.

I had a long history with the Fed, so I was never going to be perceived as an unbiased arbiter of the relative merits of the various supervisors and regulators. For all the Fed's weaknesses, I still thought it had the smartest staff in the regulatory community, the best vantage point on the system, and the most independence from politics. But Chairman Frank told me anti-Fed sentiment was just too strong to expand its powers. Chairman Dodd, the other key player in the reform bill that would come to be known as "Dodd-Frank," complained that it would be "like a parent giving his son a bigger, faster car right after he crashed the family station wagon."

Sheila Bair was especially aggressive in trying to clip the Fed's wings and expand the FDIC's authority, arguing that if the FDIC was going to be stuck taking on the risks of resolving big banks after they failed, it needed a bigger role overseeing them before they failed. She was relentless and effective lobbying Dodd, Frank, and other members of Congress. She also tried to go around me to Rahm without much success. One of her crusades—embraced by most of the other independent regulators and the lobbyists for much of the financial industry—was for an interagency council to get many of the powers to oversee systemic risk that we hoped to bestow on the Fed. This view got a lot of traction on the Hill, but I saw the council as a way to avoid any centralized accountability. I remember testifying before the Senate that you can't convene a committee to put out a fire. We already had a committee called the President's Working Group on Financial Markets, and I had seen its limits up close. "There isn't going to be any fucking council," I scoffed in one meeting with industry executives. I spoke too soon.

The one area where we did propose a massive reorganization was consumer protection. The President was especially passionate about defending ordinary families from financial abuse. At one early Oval Office meeting to discuss credit card reform, he told us about the outrageous rates he had paid as a young community organizer. He soon signed a bill forcing transparency into the credit card business, while cracking down on arbitrary fees and rate resets, an important prelude to his more comprehensive consumer reforms.

On the broader issues, our team of reform architects drew inspiration from a 2007 article by Elizabeth Warren advocating that mortgages and other financial products should be regulated like toasters and other consumer products, perhaps by an agency like the Consumer Product Safety Commission. The case for a new institution to force change and signal a commitment to change was compelling to all of us. It felt like a just cause and a war of necessity.

Despite our trepidation about turf battles, we decided to try to strip the consumer functions out of the Fed and other regulators, housing everything in a new consumer financial protection agency. Banks certainly liked dealing with bank supervisors on consumer issues, but many consumer experts believed it was unrealistic to expect safety-and-soundness regulators that had to make sure banks were financially stable to be equally vigilant about making sure they weren't taking advantage of customers. As Larry told the President, the airline safety board shouldn't be in charge of protecting the financial viability of the airlines.

The President liked the idea of a new independent agency to protect Americans from financial predations. And his political advisers were happy to take a stand that would please liberal activists, who had been remarkably unenthused about his unprecedented stimulus, his audacious commitment to comprehensive health care reform, and much of the rest of his early presidency. Rahm thought a new consumer agency would resonate with the rest of the public, too, building support for the larger bill and putting our opponents on the defensive. It was a lot easier to understand than inscrutable reforms such as "resolution authority" or "derivatives clearinghouses."

The big banks and much of the traditional business lobby decided to wage war on the new consumer protection agency. This was helpful for us, and quite dumb of them. A stronger regime of consumer oversight posed no serious risk to competent, ethical banks, and could even help them avoid losing business to less regulated competitors. But some of Washington's most powerful trade groups chose to direct their opposition to our only reforms that enjoyed broad public support, invoking ridiculous fears that we were planning to regulate butchers and florists. Later in the process, Neal Wolin would show me a draft of a blistering speech he planned to give at the U.S. Chamber of Commerce, exposing holes in the chamber's mendacious campaign against the agency. He asked if I was comfortable with it, and I said absolutely.

"I could not give that speech, but you definitely should," I told him.

Many business and financial executives did not wait long after the President helped rescue the economy and their bottom lines to conclude that he was relentlessly hostile to their interests. Carole would sometimes read me quotes in the press from CEOs saying their banks would have been fine without government help, and remind me about their distress calls to our home during the crisis. I hosted regular dinners at Treasury with a changing mix of CEOs from across the country, many of whom genuinely seemed to believe I was an outlier in an implacably anti-business administration. I tried to remind them that the President had paid a huge political price for financial and economic interventions that had provided a huge boost for their businesses and their stock prices. After listening to one long complaint about government meddling with the private sector, I told the story of Lyndon Johnson's response to Charles de Gaulle's demand that the United States remove our soldiers from France: Would you like us to remove the graves, too?

"That was a good story, but they had no idea what you were talking about," Neal told me after dinner.

We knew financiers and other businessmen would fight Dodd-Frank, but at times I was more concerned about the damage caused by opposition from regulators. It wasn't that I expected them to embrace all the President's reforms. I had seen plenty of parochialism during the crisis. But I was surprised by the intensity of their self-serving lobbying, not just over consumer issues, but over almost everything. That summer, just as we released an eighty-eight-page white paper detailing our reform proposals and rolled out the bulk of our legislation, the various regulators were swarming the Hill. In late July 2009, I invited them to a meeting at the Treasury, and told them in unusually intemperate language that by going around us to Congress to advance their own interests at one another's expense, they were undermining the prospects of passing a strong, coherent bill.

"You're having a lot of fun right now, fucking with us, trying to protect your own turf," I said. "You're going to screw up the chances for meaningful reform. And you should know that at some point at the end of this process, we're going to be in the room and you're not." I wanted them to know that if they kept undermining the cause, we would be in a position to undermine them, although I guess "undermine" might not have been the exact word I used to convey that sentiment. Some of the objects of my affection in the room leaked the highlights of my remarks to the *Wall Street Journal,* which ran a story about my "expletive-laced critique," headlined "Geithner Vents at Regulators as Overhaul Stumbles."

I wish I could say I was being strategic, but it was just a frustrated rant, and, of course, it had no positive effect. Three days later, Neal forwarded me an email from Elizabeth Warren, reporting that President Obama's SEC Chair, Mary Schapiro—usually one of the most cooperative regulators, and a supporter of our overall reforms—had lobbied Republican Senator Susan Collins against our proposed consumer agency.

"If true (who knows), egregious," Neal wrote.

ONCE WE released our legislative draft, the House of Representatives, as they say in Washington, had to work its will.

The House is a majoritarian institution, and Democrats had a solid majority, so we knew we could pass something. We also had a great ally in Chairman Frank, one of the sharpest members of Congress. I had first met Barney while working on Third World debt relief in the Clinton administration; I remember he once pulled me out of a meeting in the majority leader's office late at night to shout at me about something the IMF had done. He was not going to be overly deferential to us on financial reform, either, but fortunately, we agreed on most of the substance. He had to be attuned to the political needs of Democrats on his committee—liberal populists who wanted to burnish their anti–Wall Street credibility as well as moderates with major financial interests in their districts—but when we had differences, we tried to work them out.

In September 2009, for example, Barney was about to release draft language for the consumer agency, and Assistant Treasury Secretary

Michael Barr, a law professor and former Rhodes scholar who ran point for us on reform, thought it was riddled with problems. "Important areas of consumer protection would literally disappear," he wrote to Barney's staff director. Barr emailed me as well: "I don't want to slow things down, but this thing is a real mess." But Barr went over to the Hill the next day and smoothed out the more damaging wrinkles with Barney's staff.

Barney was ideally suited to carry such a politically fraught bill. After nearly three decades in Congress fighting for liberal causes, he had enough credibility with the left to resist extreme populist measures that could undermine the financial system, but he was not swayed by overwrought industry warnings that any stricter regulations would kill jobs and strangle businesses in red tape. He had no illusions about cooperation from House Republicans, who had marched in lockstep against the stimulus and would do the same against health reform, but he also made it clear to his fellow Democrats that they couldn't all get everything they wanted and still pass a bill. Barney was a realist who understood the politics of the Hill and wouldn't let the perfect be the enemy of the good.

These politics were unusually complex. It usually takes several hours for a congressional committee to "mark up" legislation so it can be considered by the full House. Barney's financial reform markup in the fall of 2009 took seven weeks. The special interests were out in full force, and the big Wall Street banks, despite their deep pockets and fearsome reputation, were not even the most influential. The smaller community banks, with members in every congressional district, got themselves largely carved out of the new consumer agency's direct supervision, despite our resistance. They also helped engineer a shift in the FDIC's insurance fund to make the bigger banks pay a bigger share of the premiums, which we supported. The big banks had become so politically toxic that they had to recruit other special interests to advance their objectives, such as the U.S. Chamber of

Commerce, as well as specific industrial companies and agricultural businesses that used derivatives.

The combination of lobbyist warfare, regulatory infighting, Republican intransigence, and Democratic divisions would make Barney's legislative sausage-making a real challenge. One painful example was a giveaway to the influential auto dealers lobby, which also had a presence in every congressional district. Even though House Republicans had no interest in supporting the overall Dodd-Frank bill, they united behind an amendment by Congressman John Campbell, a former auto dealer from California, to exempt his old profession from the consumer agency's oversight. That was terrible policy; for most families, vehicles are the most important purchases other than homes, and the amendment left them vulnerable to scams. But enough Democrats bent to pressure from car salesmen back home to get it through the committee.

The lockstep Republican opposition to the legislation also meant that subsets of the Democratic majority could make ransom demands in exchange for their votes. The Congressional Black Caucus threatened to oppose reform until Barney agreed to add $3 billion for mortgage relief for the unemployed and $1 billion to help cities buy foreclosed properties; those were worthy causes, but they illustrated our political tightrope. The centrist New Democrat Coalition, which had some members with close ties to the financial industry, then threatened to block the bill unless we barred states from passing consumer regulations tougher than federal rules. They backed down after Neal Wolin deftly brokered some compromise language, but again, the impossibility of Republican cooperation gave lawmakers on the Democratic side enormous power to extract concessions.

Nevertheless, House Democrats passed a bill in December—again, with zero Republican votes—that generally aligned with most of our proposals. It required supervisors to impose tougher regulatory requirements on the large, systemic banks than on regional and community banks. It created new powers for monitoring systemic risks, although it bestowed those powers on an interagency council instead of the Fed. It required a broad swath of derivatives to be centrally cleared, traded with more transparency, and subjected to tough margin requirements, although it allowed too many exceptions for specific interests. And it approved a strong stand-alone consumer agency, despite the carve-outs for auto dealers and community banks.

The House bill also created new resolution authority for big failing firms, but the result was a confused combination of anti-bailout fever and some misguided FDIC ideas. The bill envisioned 10 percent haircuts for secured creditors of firms that had to be unwound, which was a surefire panic accelerant. It also curtailed the FDIC guarantee authority that had been so crucial to the success of our crisis response, compromising a vital tool in the government toolbox. And instead of financing the bankruptcy-like process with an open-ended government credit line and recouping the costs from the industry afterward, the bill created a $150 billion fund that would be financed in advance and fully controlled by the FDIC. This was awful policy; the fund wasn't even close to big enough to unwind multiple trillion-dollar banks during a crisis. It was awful politics as well, enabling Republicans to mock the entire bill as a "bailout fund."

Still, we were pleased the House had passed the most ambitious financial rules reform since the New Deal. We hoped the Senate could fix its shortcomings.

WE WERE also making progress internationally.

In London in April 2009, we had proposed the creation of a stronger global coordinating body for financial reform, called the Financial Stability Board. I envisioned it as a new "fourth pillar" of international economic coordination, joining the International Monetary Fund, the World Bank, and the World Trade Organization. We gave the major emerging-market economies, such as China and India, a seat at the table so that they would be part of designing the new rules, and therefore more willing to impose them on their own growing financial markets. At a G-20 summit in Pittsburgh in September, we helped forge a consensus for significantly tougher worldwide capital standards—with even higher levels required for systemically important firms—along with stronger liquidity buffers and new leverage requirements. We were the main source of initiative, though we had a lot of support among other countries damaged by the crisis. By the start of 2010, the international community had agreed on reforms that would dramatically strengthen the system's shock absorbers.

This was pretty amazing. The last new international capital rules had taken six years to negotiate. We had reached consensus on much stronger, more complex, and more comprehensive reforms in less than a year. Much of the detailed negotiations of specific numbers and formal regulations still lay ahead, along with the challenge of implementation, but this was lightning speed for an international endeavor.

Amid all this global progress and cooperation, our occasional disputes got much more attention, especially my minor spat with British prime minister Gordon Brown, a Scottish Labour Party politician whom I had first met when he was the United Kingdom's finance minister and I was a midlevel Treasury official. In November 2009, mired in a tough campaign for reelection, Brown had his political advisers reach out to David Axelrod to try to get the administration to support a global tax on financial transactions. The so-called Tobin tax was a perennial populist favorite, conceived as a way to reap revenues from financial interests and discourage financial speculation. It had been tried in many countries, and the United States even had a very small tax on equity transactions to help fund the SEC. But Brown's proposal would have been easily evaded by sophisticated investors, would hurt mostly retail investors, wouldn't raise much revenue, and would have no effect on speculation. I told Axelrod we couldn't support it. He wasn't eager for the President to endorse a global tax increase, anyway.

Later that month, Brown and I met privately before a G-20 summit in St. Andrews, Scotland, and he again pitched the Tobin tax. I told him we couldn't back it, but we were open to other ways of recovering the costs of financial rescues. I said we were already considering a tax on bank leverage, which we thought would be much more effective in discouraging risky behavior as well as raising revenues to make taxpayers whole. I tried to make it clear I wanted to help him avoid a public conflict with the United States, but he wanted a Tobin tax.

Later that day, I sat for an interview with Sky News, the British version of Fox News—also owned by Rupert Murdoch, consistently hostile to Brown and Labour. They asked if I would support Brown's financial transaction tax, and although I expressed support for his broader objective of getting the financial industry to pay for its rescues, I said we wouldn't back a Tobin tax. This set off a press frenzy; Brown's top adviser told Axelrod that I had delivered "quite a hard slapdown." Brown called me to complain that I had embarrassed him on right-wing TV, but I had warned him where I stood. He said he really needed me to support him. I again said I couldn't do that. Brown's people pressured the White House to walk back my public statement, and my team in Washington asked me if I wanted to clarify it.

"Clarify what?" I asked.

There was no realistic prospect of a global Tobin tax. It certainly had no chance without our support, so we became a convenient villain. President Sarkozy later told a group of world finance officials in my presence: "We could do it if it wasn't for Tim!" But even the continental Europeans couldn't agree on one for Europe.

Many G-20 countries would end up embracing the better-designed bank leverage tax that we proposed in the United States to cover the expected losses in TARP. But we got no traction in Congress, even among Democrats, even though we called it a "fee" to try to avoid anti-tax hysteria. Ultimately, it didn't really matter, since the estimated cost of TARP, more than $100 billion at the time, would gradually dwindle to zero.

• • •

POLITICALLY, WE were still facing a tough road ahead on financial reform. In late December, Axelrod sent me some polling data: 61 percent of Americans thought banks had too much influence over our administration. The banks certainly didn't think so, but that didn't matter. We were still in political no-man's-land, doing enough for the right to hate but not enough for the left to like. Conservatives thought we were profligate socialists, and liberals thought we were in bed with the banks.

In fact, we were at war with the banks and other special interests that were trying to water down our reforms. Payday lenders didn't want to be regulated by the new consumer agency; insurance companies didn't want to be designated as systemic firms; corporations (often fronting for Wall Street) argued that they shouldn't have to trade their derivatives on exchanges. My team, led by Neal Wolin and Michael Barr, fought back, and the President and I backed them at every turn. I remember Boeing's CEO came to tell me that the status quo was better for Boeing because they could get better terms through private arrangements with their derivatives dealers. "Look, if everyone is coming in and telling me they're getting special deals from their dealers, maybe nobody is getting a good deal," I told him. After Neal's confrontational speech about the consumer agency, lobbyists for the chamber and several major financial trade groups came to see me to complain that Treasury officials were fighting them on everything.

"My team is beating back your proposals because they're bad for the country," I told them. "And we're going to keep doing it."

From my perspective, the flak we were taking from every side reflected the impressive extent to which policy trumped politics in the Obama administration. The President repeatedly made it clear that he wanted us to do the right thing even if it wasn't the popular thing, to be guided by evidence rather than polls. He showed a remarkable degree of deference to our substantive policy judgments. We discussed the political ramifications of our decisions, but on the central questions of economic and financial policy, politics didn't drive our decisions.

I admired the President's conviction that we should do whatever we thought was necessary to end the crisis, fix the economy, and reform the financial system, then let the public judge the results.

Of course, where we had to legislate to achieve results, where it was not just a question of how best to use authority Congress had already given the President, we had to be more sensitive to the politics. This was especially true on financial reform. The widespread perceptions that we were too close to financial interests were harming our efforts to craft a legislative coalition. As the MSNBC host Rachel Maddow once told me, it was hard for many Democrats to trust me as the architect of tough reforms, since to them I was the face of the unjust Wall Street bailouts.

The President, annoyed and baffled by the suspicion of our motives, was eager to push back against the dominant narrative. We were fighting for sweeping reforms, including a new consumer agency that advocates had considered a pipe dream, but the public and the press seemed to take it for granted that we were doing the bidding of banks. "They really think we're bent," the President once marveled after telling me about a critical column he had just read.

I advised him to stop reading that stuff, but he was a voracious consumer of news, and he knew that looking bent wouldn't help us keep Senate Democrats on our side. President Obama never pushed me to support bad policy for political reasons, but he did ask us to try to avoid gratuitous attacks on Democrats when we fought bad proposals with popular appeal. And he did keep asking me whether we were being tough enough on the major banks. He was particularly interested in a proposal by Paul Volcker to prohibit traditional banks from engaging in "proprietary trading," from speculating on their own account while enjoying access to cheaper capital as a result of their access to the government safety net.

Volcker made the case in multiple meetings that banks shouldn't be able to behave like hedge funds, taking trading risks that could force the Fed or the FDIC to ride to their rescue if the bets went bad. He believed that the high-flying investment bank culture, fueled by surreal compensation packages that in some ways rewarded short-term risk-taking, had infected traditional banks that now competed for their business. He sketched out a proprietary trading ban on a single page, and pitched it as a simple way to rein in the speculation that he thought had turned Wall Street into a casino. It would be a partial substitute for the old Glass-Steagall restrictions on banks engaging in nonbanking financial activities, an effort to restore the conservative ethos that Volcker recalled from his days as a commercial banker.

Larry and I were skeptical. Proprietary trading by banks played no meaningful role in the crisis. For traditional banks that failed, the main problem was traditional loans, mostly mortgage loans. And the firms that caused the most damage—the investment banks, the GSEs, an out-of-control insurance company—were not traditional banks with insured deposits. It was true that some banks—Citi and Bank of America after its purchase of Merrill—put a lot of risk in their investment bank affiliates, risk that increased their vulnerabilities. But we thought a proprietary trading ban would be hard to define, and might end up impairing a valuable source of liquidity to markets. We didn't want to stop banks from hedging risks or matching up buyers and sellers of securities, and it would be hard to distinguish these hedging and "market making" activities from mere speculation.

But in January 2010, even before Scott Brown scuttled the filibuster-proof Democratic majority, the prospects for reform passing the Senate seemed bleak. Just when we could finally use some populist energy to build support for our bill, it had morphed into disillusionment about our efforts to reduce unemployment and foreclosures, along with cynicism about our desire for real reform. Volcker had a lot of credibility with the left, and he was regarded as less than enthusiastic about the reform legislation, even though he supported most of what we were doing. His concerns—and the perception that those concerns were not getting traction in the Treasury or the White House—were seen as evidence that we were soft on reform.

I was usually an internal voice against conceding to political imperatives, but I thought the benefits of getting Volcker more fully committed to the Dodd-Frank cause were compelling enough to try to make the substance of his idea work. I didn't know if it would do much to make the system more stable, but I thought we could design it in a way that would minimize the potential damage to useful financial activity. After a lunch with Volcker on Christmas Eve, I went to the President and told him I thought we could put together a proposal that might get Volcker on board. For me, this was purely legislative calculation. I neglected to tell Larry that I had evolved on the issue, and he was not happy; he thought I was making a stupid and craven concession to populism. But the President was pleased. We drafted some legislative language, and Axelrod came up with the idea of calling it the Volcker Rule.

On January 21, 2010, President Obama announced our new proposal in the Diplomatic Reception Room in front of Dodd, Frank, our economic team, and Volcker himself. We had informed Dodd and Frank, but we had not consulted them. Dodd was irritated because he thought we were going to screw up his negotiations in the Senate. Frank was irritated because it made our approach look "tougher" than his, when he had left similarly populist provisions out of the House bill out of deference to our opposition. Larry was irritated because he thought I was surrendering on substance to appease the Old Testament crowd. But there was a decent policy argument on moral hazard grounds against allowing banks backed by the government to run hedge funds and private equity funds. And the President used the ceremony to try to jump-start momentum for our broader reforms.

"What we've seen so far, in recent weeks, is an army of industry lobbyists from Wall Street descending on Capitol Hill to try and block basic commonsense rules of the road that would protect our economy and the American people," the President said. "If these folks want a fight, it's a fight I'm ready to have."

At the time, the announcement was mocked as a cynical reaction to Scott Brown's victory the day before; we had planned it before we knew about Brown, but no one believed that. My newfound support for the Volcker Rule was certainly political, but it was driven by my desire to pass the broader reforms, and the timing really was a coincidence. Because my lack of enthusiasm for earlier versions of Volcker's proposal was not a secret—and a photo of the announcement caught me staring at the floor—the President's embrace of the Volcker Rule was also seen as a rebuke to me. That was comical but convenient, because if I had been viewed as its champion, it would have had less power with the Democratic left.

I remember Bob Rubin, who was always suspicious of populism, told me he didn't think the Volcker Rule was a good idea.

"I assure you that if you were sitting in my seat, you'd think it's an excellent idea," I told him.

THE SENATE tends to be somewhat less majoritarian and partisan than the House, partly because of the sixty-vote hurdle to overcome filibusters, partly because six-year terms give senators at least some relief from the permanent campaign, partly because they represent entire states rather than gerrymandered and often homogeneous House districts. Long before Scott Brown's election meant we'd need at least one Republican senator to pass financial reform, Chairman Dodd, who had spent thirty years in the Senate, was trying to build bipartisan consensus on the banking committee. He announced early on that he would try to negotiate terms with his ranking member, Richard Shelby, a conservative Republican from Alabama. We were worried about the potential price of accommodation, but Dodd knew the Senate better than we did, and he said he had never passed major legislation without a Republican partner.

I didn't know Dodd well, and we had gotten off to a rocky start during the AIG flap; our staffs had blamed each other for his Recovery Act language that barred us from going after bonus contracts retroactively. He was a savvy and seasoned Washington insider, but he faced an uphill reelection battle. We worried that would make it hard for him to hold the line against populist pressure, and might make him cautious about moving the bill. After he decided not to run for reelection in January 2010, we sometimes worried he would be *too* anxious to pass a bill that would burnish his legacy, cutting deals at the expense of the President's priorities. And in the White House, there was some skepticism about Dodd's efforts to find common ground with Republicans. We hadn't seen a lot of hope yet for bipartisan consensus in Washington, and among other roadblocks, Republicans were making it pretty clear they could never support legislation that included an independent consumer agency, which we considered non-negotiable.

At times, Senator Shelby could seem genuinely interested in bipartisan reform. At one early dinner at Treasury, he expressed enthusiasm for higher capital requirements, central clearing of derivatives, and other administration priorities. But after the Tea Party summer put Republicans on notice that their base would rebel against any compromise with a tyrannical socialist President, Shelby became much more antagonistic. Even behind closed doors, we could sense his staff pulling him back from engagement. At one meeting in Dodd's hideaway in the Capitol, Shelby was edging toward a compromise on some contentious issue when he suddenly stopped in midsentence. He had caught the eye of one of his top aides, who was glaring and shaking his head.

"But, of course," Shelby hastened to add, "the outcome would depend on what my caucus is willing to do."

We doubted the Republican caucus would do much. We had seen Senator Baucus spend precious months wooing Republicans to support Obamacare; in the end, not one Republican voted yes. The Senate was still marginally less partisan than the House, but during the Obama years, the margin was shrinking rapidly. Senator McConnell, who was heralding Republican opposition to reform on fund-raising trips to Wall Street, would later declare that his number one goal was to limit President Obama to one term, an admission surprising only for its candor.

Sure enough, in early February 2010, Dodd announced that he and Shelby had reached an impasse. Dodd then announced he would begin new negotiations with Republican Senator Bob Corker of Tennessee; by early March, that courtship had fallen apart, too. We got a sense of how seriously the committee's Republicans wanted to engage when they filed hundreds of amendments before Dodd's markup—including dozens to move the bill's effective date back ten days, eleven days, twelve days, and so on—and then decided not to offer any of them, essentially declaring that they didn't want anything to do with financial reform.

Still, Dodd's patient, persistent bipartisan outreach was critical to persuading the Senate's moderate Republicans—Brown along with Susan Collins and Olympia Snowe of Maine—to consider supporting the bill. Dodd's good-faith efforts to find common ground also helped persuade moderate Democrats to support a bill with little bipartisan support; like Baucus on health reform, Dodd showed his caucus that broad bipartisan consensus was impossible. Ultimately, Dodd was a dealmaker, and a very skillful legislator. At times, we disagreed with his accommodations, like when he agreed to scrap new fiduciary requirements for brokers and investment advisers at the request of South Dakota Democratic Senator Tim Johnson. "Bad and pointless loss for investor protection," Barr wrote to me. "Still waiting for more shoes to drop."

But the new fiduciary duties got restored at the end. Senator Dodd worked very closely with us, and when we told him we had a real problem with changes he was considering to build support, he tried to respond to our concerns. At one point, Michael Barr and Laurie Schaffer, Treasury's banking lawyer, stopped by my office to tell me Dodd wanted to eliminate much of the Fed's supervisory responsibility. My instant reaction was no way—or, as I sometimes abbreviated it, NFW. The United Kingdom had separated its lender-of-last-resort function from its supervision function, with disastrous results; its central bank, lacking the situational awareness that comes with supervisory boots on the ground, badly underestimated the crisis and allowed a run to cripple Northern Rock. But after the President invited Dodd to the Oval Office and expressed similar NFW sentiments in more polite terms, Dodd changed his mind. He pushed us to be more practical, and to bend where we needed to, but he knew he needed the President to get the bill done.

We had a similar uh-oh moment, with less satisfactory results, over derivatives regulation. In early April 2010, Senate Agriculture Committee Chair Blanche Lincoln of Arkansas, a moderate Democrat from a deep-red state, sent Barr some weak compromise language on derivatives that did not include mandatory clearing of derivatives and did not require derivatives to be more openly traded. We knew this was politically sensitive—Lincoln was up for reelection, and she was in trouble—but after a weekend of talks with the White House, we let her know the President would oppose her language if she introduced it in its current form. We were stunned when she then replaced her bank-friendly language with a dramatically different proposal, a blast of populism that essentially would have barred commercial banks from the derivatives business.

After her tack to the right fizzled, Senator Lincoln was now tacking left. She wanted to outflank a liberal Democratic primary challenger who had been bashing her as a tool of the banks. Her staff was also trying to get back at us for rejecting her initial language; they called the new provision their "fuck-you-with-a-cherry-on-top." But we didn't see how the new Lincoln amendment, so broadly and sloppily written, would reduce systemic risk. Banning FDIC-insured banks from using derivatives would just drive more derivatives into uninsured nonbanks. Banks needed to use derivatives to hedge their risks, and I didn't see why they shouldn't be allowed to help their customers hedge risks as well. I explained all of this to the President, and he agreed with the substance of our concerns, but this was one of the times he told me to be careful about how we fought back. The Lincoln amendment quickly became a new rallying cry for the left, and evidence of my opposition would only strengthen their conviction it was necessary and just.

There was yet another populist spasm that April, after the SEC filed fraud charges against Goldman Sachs and a young trader named Fabrice Tourre, who had written emails calling himself "the fabulous Fab" and mocking the mortgage securities that Goldman was selling its customers. Tourre was charged with failing to disclose critical information to the buyers of a complex security that Goldman had created with input from another customer who wanted to bet against the housing market. I was surprised to see this case become such a symbol of Wall Street's perfidy; these actions deserved sanction, but the victims were not particularly sympathetic, just large financial interests who were taking opposing bets on the housing market. But Democratic Senator Carl Levin of Michigan created compelling theater by torturing several Goldman executives at a hearing, repeatedly asking them about deals their underlings had described as "shitty." This was an opportune time for a resurgence of populist anger, and it helped reinvigorate the push for reform, but after worrying for months that Dodd-Frank would be weakened by concessions to the right, we now started to worry it could get torqued too far left.

On May 10, for example, Senator Levin and fellow progressive Jeff Merkley of Oregon released an amendment they described as a tougher version of the Volcker Rule, along with a supportive statement from Paul Volcker himself. This proved to be a much shinier object than our version, and it became a new litmus test for the left. And our discomfort with Merkley-Levin's approach to proprietary trading became the latest evidence that we were soft on Wall Street.

Merkley-Levin did broaden the definition of proprietary trading beyond what we had proposed, but we didn't think it was better or in fact tougher than our approach. Its sweeping restrictions would be offset by all kinds of loopholes, making the amendment vastly more complicated than Volcker's one-page synopsis and much more difficult to implement. With admirable candor, Merkley told me he wanted to support a tough Volcker Rule, but to do that he needed to exempt insurance companies and real estate investments because those industries were vital to his state, and to many other pro-reform senators. In an email, Barr said Dodd also wanted to accommodate Scott Brown, fellow Republican Judd Gregg, and Democrats Mark Warner, Evan Bayh, and John Kerry "by carving out trusts, sweep accounts, a broader set of insurance companies & affiliates, feeder funds, hedge funds with seed capital, and most firms in Massachusetts." The amendment ended up looking like Swiss cheese.

Dealing with Congress, to put it mildly, did not feel like a careful, deliberative journey in search of the best public policy. I remember going to meet the personable Senator Brown, who had recently arrived in Washington after a campaign spent attacking the "Cornhusker Kickback" that Ben Nelson had procured for Nebraska in the health care bill. We talked about our kids and about triathlons. When the conversation finally turned to substance, he said he liked the idea of financial reform and expected to be with us. But without any irony or self-consciousness, he said he needed to protect two financial institutions in Massachusetts from the Volcker Rule's restrictions.

Then he furrowed his brow and turned to his aide.

"Which ones are they, again?" he asked.

In a circuitous effort to protect those two companies—the aide identified them as Fidelity and State Street—Brown would later propose a broader weakening of the entire Volcker Rule, allowing banks to invest up to 3 percent of their capital in hedge funds and private equity funds. My staff didn't like this, and neither did Volcker, but there wasn't much we could do about it. We needed sixty votes for reform. We didn't have many Republican options, and a few Democrats were threatening to vote no. These concessions weren't going to ruin the legislation, but Barr fretted about death by a thousand cuts.

"Nothing tragic, but signs of fraying similar to House," he warned me, as the grueling negotiations pressed on. "Need to close this off soon."

Despite their impasse on the overall bill, Dodd cut a deal with Shelby that actually improved the House's language on resolution authority, eliminating the mandatory haircuts for failing banks as well as the pre-financed FDIC "bailout fund." But they also reached an agreement to scrap the broad FDIC guarantee authority that had helped calm the crisis, a serious problem. As a concession to anti-bailout anger, we had agreed to eliminate the Fed's ability to engineer firm-specific rescues as it had done with Bear Stearns and AIG, because we thought the combination of effective resolution authority plus FDIC guarantees (as well as the Fed's general authority to support the system in "unusual and exigent circumstances") would make one-off rescues, never appealing, less necessary. But I told Dodd that curtailing the guarantees without restoring the Fed's ability to intervene to save a failing firm would leave the system more vulnerable than ever in a panic.

Dodd told me not to worry. It was too late to fix the Senate bill, which would pass May 20. But the House and Senate still had to reconcile their different versions.

"We'll fix it in conference," Dodd told me.

I was worried anyway, and I said so to the President. But we both knew he couldn't veto reform on the grounds that it would make bailouts too difficult.

WE HAD a big meeting on the Hill in June to go over our priorities for the House-Senate conference. But by that time, Dodd and Frank didn't want to hear about anything that would complicate the endgame. My only memory of that session was that the Los Angeles Lakers were playing in the NBA finals on a television behind me, and everyone's eyes kept straying to the game. At one point Rahm interrupted to point out his brother, a Hollywood agent, sitting in the front row.

We still hoped that Dodd would restore those FDIC guarantees he said he would fix in conference. But a few days later, our banking lawyer, Laurie Schaffer, attended a follow-up meeting with Dodd's counsel, who reported the guarantees were off the table.

"She said we will have to come back in a year or two and fix," Schaffer wrote. "She said that hopefully there will not be a financial crisis in the interim."

Yes, hopefully. On the bright side, the conference adopted the Senate's version of resolution authority. The Lincoln amendment made it into the final bill, but in a narrower form that only required banks to move a few types of derivatives into affiliates. The consumer agency was technically housed inside the Fed—it became the Consumer Financial Protection Bureau, or CFPB—but the final language fully protected its independence.

The final piece of real drama took place just after the conference finally wrapped up at 5:30 a.m. on June 25. The Congressional Budget Office had "scored" the cost of Dodd-Frank at about $20 billion, so the conference had approved an equivalent amount in fees on big banks and hedge funds to pay for it. Scott Brown, who had ridden the Tea Party wave into the Senate, suddenly announced he could no longer support the legislation, because it would violate a pledge he had signed not to raise taxes. Democratic Senator Robert Byrd of West Virginia was gravely ill, and his fellow Democrat Russell Feingold of Wisconsin was refusing to support the bill from the left, so Brown was our sixtieth vote.

"Brown statement—did he leave himself room?" I emailed Barr.

"Brown left himself room, but I'm worried about him," Barr replied.

Wolin and Barr suggested the alternative "pay-fors" that lured Brown back on board. The most fitting was a provision eliminating our authority to spend $225 billion in TARP money that we had never touched. At the same time the U.S. government was taking action to reduce the risk of future crises, it was declaring the last crisis over.

The House approved the Wall Street Reform and Consumer

Protection Act on June 30 by a 237–192 vote, with three Republicans switching to yes on final passage. The Senate followed suit in mid-July, 60–39, also with just three Republican votes. GOP leaders blasted the bill as big-government liberalism run amok, an assault on free enterprise, a continuation of the bailout mentality. Meanwhile, many liberals dismissed it as fake reform, a triumph for too-big-to-fail Wall Street banks. Dodd-Frank was messy and complicated. It occupied that shrinking pragmatic center of the American political system. It certainly wasn't perfect; it's impossible to get that kind of ship to shore without picking up some barnacles. But it was a major substantive achievement. President Obama had promised to make our Wild West financial system much safer, and he kept his promise.

ONE REASON this progress has been overlooked is that our top priority for reform was strengthening the system's shock absorbers, and that was not a primary focus of the legislative fights over Dodd-Frank. I testified that financial stability would depend on capital, capital, capital, but we didn't set those requirements in Dodd-Frank. That was by design. We gave the responsibility for new restrictions on capital, liquidity, and leverage to the Fed and the other bank supervisors, and pushed for a new international agreement to give them global force. And we succeeded.

The new Basel III standards required banks to hold much more capital and much higher-quality capital. The final requirement for common equity was about three times higher than the existing standard and effectively four times higher for the largest banks. We pushed to force the biggest banks to hold extra capital to offset the extra danger they pose to the global system; this "systemic surcharge" is like a tax on pollution, forcing firms to internalize costs they impose on the world. And the Fed's new standards for the United States were even tougher than the new international standards. From 2009 through 2012, as a result of the new rules as well as our strategy to recapitalize the system through TARP and the stress test, the eighteen largest U.S.

Stronger New Global Shock Absorbers

Capital Requirements Under Basel III

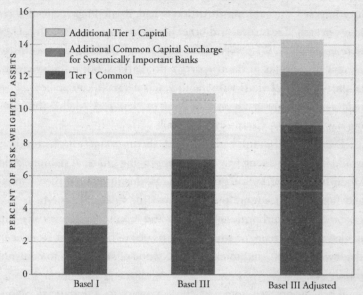

The Basel III reforms dramatically increased the quantity and the quality of capital that banks have to hold, with even stronger requirements for systemically important banks. The reforms also redefined risk-weighted assets, so the full impact of the rules (right bar) effectively requires the biggest banks to hold more than twice as much Tier 1 capital and four times as much of the highest-quality common equity as they were required to hold before the crisis.

Sources: Bank for International Settlements, Bloomberg, Federal Reserve Board, and company estimates.

banking institutions doubled their common capital, from $400 billion to $800 billion.

Basel III also introduced the first international leverage restrictions, another way of limiting risk-taking, and U.S. regulators have proposed even stricter limits for the biggest banks. At the same time, Basel III created new liquidity standards that have swiftly helped reduce the banking system's reliance on short-term funding that can run when confidence withers. Before the crisis, U.S. banks had

$1.38 in runnable short-term funding for every dollar in stable retail deposits; by 2012, that figure was down to $0.64. Before the crisis, the fifty largest U.S. banking institutions had about 14 percent of their assets in cash, Treasuries, and other liquid instruments; by 2012, they were up to about 23 percent. The Fed is still working on reforms to prevent disruptions in the tri-party repo markets, but intraday credit, tri-party's most obvious vulnerability, has decreased 90 percent. This reduces the danger of a reprise of Bank of New York Mellon threatening not to unwind Countrywide's book.

Even if Dodd-Frank hadn't passed, those stronger shock absorbers would have gone a long way toward improving financial stability. And Dodd-Frank gave U.S. regulators the power to enforce their capital and liquidity rules more broadly across the financial system. It also gave them new authorities to identify and monitor systemic risks—in banks, tri-party repo, or whatever turns out to be the next frontier in shadow banking—and to expand the scope of safeguards to confront those risks.

The law granted some of those powers to a Financial Stability Oversight Council, rather than the Fed, which was a setback for accountability. Treasury chairs the council, but it has little power to compel independent regulators to take coordinated actions for the good of the broader system. Still, Dodd-Frank did ensure that the Fed would have a dominant role supervising the systemically important firms designated by the council, and would take the lead setting capital and liquidity standards in the United States. And I believe the council has served a valuable coordination function, providing a forum for regulators to work together, even though it was partly designed to protect their independent fiefdoms.

Dodd-Frank also mandated rigorous annual stress tests, making one of our crisis innovations a standing feature of U.S. banking supervision. It will require systemically important firms to prove they have enough capital to survive a severe crisis in order to get approval for dividend payouts, stock buybacks, and other actions that could erode their capital buffers in good times. The Fed's stress tests are now more exacting and conservative than the original exercise that helped calm the crisis. Its 2013 scenario included loss estimates based on a recession with unemployment rising above 12 percent and GDP plunging at a 6 percent annual rate.

The bulk of our derivatives reforms also made it into Dodd-Frank. Standardized derivatives must now be submitted to central counterparties, or "clearinghouses," and traded on open platforms or "exchanges." Derivatives dealers will face capital requirements, and will have to collect and post mandated margin on derivative transactions. The scaled-back Lincoln amendment prohibits banks from using some non-standardized derivatives, but they can still use derivatives to hedge their risks and their customers' risks.

The Consumer Financial Protection Bureau, the most important new U.S. regulatory body since the Environmental Protection Agency, ended up much as we had proposed it, with an even stronger and broader mandate than Elizabeth Warren had envisioned in her original essay. It got the authority to write and enforce consumer rules for much of the financial system, including debt collectors, payday lenders, credit reporting firms, mortgage originators, student loan servicers, and other operators who used to evade scrutiny. Its budget comes from a Fed funding stream that isn't subject to congressional appropriations, so lawmakers won't be able to neuter it if they don't like how it treats their favorite payday lender. The only major disappointment was the carve-out for auto dealers, an unavoidable cost of doing business on Capitol Hill. Otherwise, the CFPB was a tremendous victory for the President over powerful interests who wanted to kill it or weaken it.

Dodd-Frank became a bit of a Christmas tree, as is typical of major legislation, but most of the ornaments were fine with us. There were quite a few reforms addressing problems that we didn't think were central to the crisis, but they were mostly sensible reforms. For example, even though the Volcker Rule didn't end up the way we drew it up, it's already prompted institutions such as Citi and Bank of America to close their proprietary trading desks and divest of their hedge fund and private equity holdings, a good thing for stability. The law also expanded disclosure of executive compensation at public companies, gave shareholders more "say on pay," and opened the door to clawing back compensation at firms that have to restate their financials—modest but positive steps toward limiting the Wall Street excesses that infuriated Volcker and so many Americans.

Several reform proposals that were a bit unwieldy in initial design made it into the bill in more practical form. Minnesota Senator Al Franken's proposal to have rating agencies randomly assigned to evaluate companies and securities regardless of their capabilities—we called it the *Wheel of Fortune* plan—was consigned to a study. Instead, Congress took steps to increase transparency and reduce conflicts of interest at the rating agencies; these moves made sense, although they obviously wouldn't ensure foresight or competence in credit ratings, as we would learn firsthand in 2011.

We did not support Delaware Senator Ted Kaufman's effort to impose a limit on the precise size of American banks, but we embraced a House alternative that gave regulators authority to break up banks if they become a grave threat to financial stability. The bill also included our proposal for new limits on bank concentration, which would prevent mergers that concentrate more than 10 percent of the system's liabilities in any single bank. Today, our largest banks are somewhat larger than they were in 2007, a natural consequence of all the shotgun marriages that took place during the eHarmony stage of the crisis. But they're still much smaller than foreign banks relative to the size of our economy, and much less concentrated. U.S. banking assets are roughly equivalent to our GDP, while German banks are about three times their GDP, French and Swiss banks are closer to four times GDP, and British banks are about eight times GDP.

On the firefighting side, Dodd-Frank was more of a mixed bag. We were pleased with the final version of resolution authority, which gave the FDIC the power to place failing systemic firms into receivership and wind them down in an orderly fashion. The cost to the Treasury would be fully repaid by assessments on the industry, making taxpayers whole. The legislation didn't mandate haircuts for senior creditors, which would have been disastrous, and it didn't create the much-lampooned "bailout fund." Larger firms were also required to submit "living wills" to their supervisors, emergency protocols proposing how they could be safely dismembered. It's like leaving a floor plan on file with the fire department, or as we used to say at Treasury, planning your own funeral. More than one hundred financial firms now have blueprints for their breakup in case they run into trouble.

These changes—along with the new limits on concentration, the stronger shock absorbers across the system, and the "systemic surcharge" imposing higher capital requirements on the largest banks—are quietly reducing the risks of too-big-to-fail. As the FDIC has formalized its rules for resolution authority, the rating agencies have reduced their "ratings uplift" for the unsecured debt of larger banks; they're no longer considered negligible default risks regardless of their financial condition, because markets are less confident the government would step in to save them if they fail. Today, many small and midsize institutions pay less to borrow than the supposedly too-big-to-fail banks.

On a less positive note, Dodd-Frank's elimination of the broader FDIC guarantee authority, together with the loss of the Fed's power to lend to individual nonbanks, leaves the financial system weaker and more exposed to future panics. Letting systemic firms collapse during a crisis without the ability to prevent the panic from spreading can be devastating. That's why the fall of Lehman was so horrible. And that's why Sheila's willingness to extend the FDIC's guarantee authority to senior bank debt over Columbus Day 2008 was so important, reducing the flight incentives of nervous creditors. But Sheila was not willing to fight to preserve that authority for her successors amid the anti-bailout fever of the legislative process, and we couldn't persuade Congress to restore an unpopular power for an agency that didn't want it.

The U.S. Banking System Is Small Relative to Our Economy
Assets of Deposit-Taking Institutions by Country (end-2012)

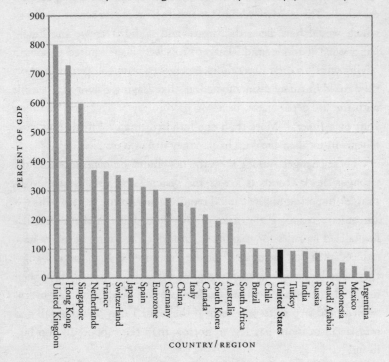

U.S. banks have assets equivalent to about 100 percent of U.S. economic output, much lower than advanced nations in Europe and Asia. Among other things, this means that we are much more able to withstand the potential damage caused by the failure of large banks.

Source: Financial Stability Board.

Taking away the fire department's equipment certainly ensures that the equipment won't be used, but it isn't much of a strategy for reducing fire damage. When it comes to financial crises, taking away the tools of first responders is a good way to ensure that the next crisis will burn out of control, with greater damage to the economy and greater cost to taxpayers. The more power the government has, the

U.S. Banks Provide a Relatively Small Share of Credit

Banking System as a Share of Financial Assets (end-2012)

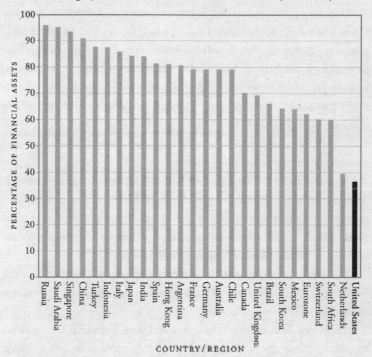

Other advanced countries rely on banks to fund a larger share of their financial assets than the U.S. does. This means our financial system is less dependent on banks, and the U.S. economy can generally benefit from alternative sources of credit if the banking system is under pressure. However, in the crisis this became a substantial source of risk, because nonbanks without access to the traditional bank safety net were much more vulnerable to panic.

Source: Financial Stability Board.

more credibly it can commit to avert catastrophic outcomes; that makes it less likely that it will need to use its power and less likely that catastrophes will occur. Strong firefighting authorities actually make it easier to let firms fail; when you know you have the ability to prevent fires from spreading out of control, you can afford to let them burn for a while.

It almost goes without saying that Congress did not, as Senator Dodd's aide suggested, "come back in a year or two and fix" the FDIC guarantee authority. But it will have to eventually, in the heat of the next crisis if not before. Even in an emergency, Congress is likely to be slow to restore it, which is why its loss is so dangerous. We saw in 2008 that even after the panic induced by Lehman and the falling dominos that followed, the House rejected TARP and crashed the markets before coming to its senses. Politicians don't like taking votes that can be caricatured as pro-bailout.

When I left the Treasury in 2013, I discussed this particular conundrum with one of Larry's classes at Harvard. He pointed out that the prevailing narrative, on the left and the right, has been that Dodd-Frank has increased moral hazard, ratifying the too-big-to-fail status quo, making future bailouts more likely.

"Let me get this straight," Larry said with a grin. "You feel like the biggest problem with Dodd-Frank is not enough emergency bailout authority?"

Yes, I do. The president is entrusted with extraordinary powers to protect the country from threats to our national security. These powers come with carefully designed constraints, but they allow the president to act quickly in extremis. Congress should give the president and the financial first responders the powers necessary to protect the country from the devastation of financial crises.

DODD-FRANK LEFT a few other serious problems unaddressed.

The legislation punted money market fund reforms to the SEC, which has so far failed to produce reforms that could prevent future runs. In 2012, after the SEC's Mary Schapiro announced that her fellow commissioners had refused to support her reform proposals, I wrote a letter as chairman of the new Financial Stability Oversight Council proposing options for the council to pursue. "Four years after the instability of money market funds contributed to the worst financial crisis since the Great Depression, with the failure of the SEC to act, the Council should now move forward," I wrote. Mary welcomed the letter to help her push for action at the SEC, which soon began a process to consider reforms. But more than five years after the Reserve Primary Fund broke the buck, money market funds have so far been able to block significant changes to the status quo. This is a glaring vulnerability, and it would be unforgivable to fail to address it before post-crisis amnesia sets in completely.

We also decided early in the financial reform process that trying to overhaul housing finance in Dodd-Frank would be too heavy a political lift. There was no immediate rush; we knew Fannie and Freddie would be in conservatorship for a while, and that private mortgage lending was too deeply damaged to come back soon. The Consumer Financial Protection Bureau would go on to write some powerful rules to combat mortgage lending abuses, banning incentives that encourage lenders to steer borrowers into unsafe loans, reining in "teaser rates," "no-doc loans," and other sketchy underwriting practices, and promoting a fairer foreclosure process. But for now, the U.S. government—through Fannie, Freddie, and the Federal Housing Administration—remains the dominant force in mortgage finance.

Eventually, Congress will have to make some tough choices about the mortgage market—not just how to reduce the government's dominant role, but how to balance the trade-off between safety and accessibility. We should require substantial down payments for borrowers, which would make it harder for some families to become homeowners but would help reduce the risk of the terrible collapses we saw in this crisis. Higher down payment requirements would help serve as shock absorbers for the system—much like capital requirements for financial firms or margin requirements for derivatives investors—limiting the risk of excessive booms by limiting highly leveraged borrowing. And while I believe some kind of government guarantee for mortgage finance is necessary to support lending when the private market retreats during severe recessions, the guarantee should be explicit, more limited in scope, and more expensive, with private actors assuming larger losses to reduce the risks for taxpayers. Powerful real estate and financial interests tend to align with progressive consumer advocates to fight measures that could make mortgage lending more conservative and mortgage credit less affordable, so change will be a challenge, but it can't wait forever.

Other than the creation of the consumer bureau and the elimination of the OTS, our reforms largely left in place our stunningly fragmented regulatory structure, with three federal bank supervisors, two market regulators, five agencies responsible for the Volcker Rule, and ten voting members on the council monitoring systemic risks. This level of bureaucratic balkanization is better than what we had in 2007, but it is not good enough. It is the largest source of complexity and delay in the rulemaking for Dodd-Frank. It limits accountability for outcomes. It will slow the regulatory system's ability to evolve in response to future market innovations. The President and I considered coming back to this in 2011 and 2012, launching a new fight for a much simpler, more consolidated system, but the politics seemed insurmountable.

The financial system is safer, but it certainly isn't perfectly safe. We will have future booms in credit. Markets will find ways around constraints on risk-taking, the way rivers flow around stones. Financial interests will try to use their political clout to weaken constraints over time. Financial innovations tend to outpace financial regulations. Banking is an inherently risky business. And unless Congress can find a way to restore the FDIC's guarantee authority, the financial system's first responders will show up to the next crisis with their hands tied.

In general, though, I thought the President, the regulatory community, and Congress—congressional Democrats, mostly—were remarkably effective in addressing a very complicated problem. I saw plenty of appalling political behavior, and it was kind of stunning to watch members of Congress juggle appeals to populism with the imperatives of fund-raising. There was a lot of preening in public about the evils of finance, with a lot of accommodation in private to financial interests. The dominant advocacy groups on the wings of each party, what Robert Gibbs referred to as "the professional left" and its even more intransigent equivalent on the right, had a remarkably strong grip on the process. But that's politics. Legislating is the art of the possible. And I didn't think purism or neatness at the expense of reform was a virtue. A bill that couldn't pass Congress wouldn't help fix the system, so we accommodated some cringe-worthy requests.

Many financial executives, facing a much more stable but somewhat less profitable future, see Dodd-Frank as a radical assault on capitalism, and they still resent the administration's role in their post-crisis vilification. Many liberal activists, appalled by our financial rescues and the rapid recovery of the financial industry, have ignored the objective safety improvements to the banking system while continuing to portray us as defenders of big banking interests. Even the President's steadfast support for a consumer protection bureau, a progressive victory for the ages, was overshadowed by controversy over who would lead it.

THE LEFT wanted Elizabeth Warren.

She was a thoughtful and passionate consumer advocate, and the bureau grew out of her idea. As soon as Dodd-Frank passed, labor leaders and liberal activists began circulating petitions and lobbying the administration, arguing that naming Warren to lead the new agency would prove we cared about protecting the public in the financial marketplace.

I had a complicated relationship with Warren. Her criticisms of the financial rescue, if well intentioned, were mostly unjustified, and her TARP oversight hearings often felt more like made-for-YouTube inquisitions than serious inquiries. She was worried about the right things, but she was better at impugning our choices—as well as our integrity and our competence—than identifying any feasible alternatives. On the other hand, she really was smart and innovative about consumer protection, with sophisticated ideas about reform. She had a gift for explanation, which would be important as we created the agency and tried to help the public understand its mission. When we met for dinner in downtown Washington that summer shortly after Dodd-Frank passed, her proposals for redesigning consumer protection were thoughtful—and more market-oriented, incentive-based, and practical than her detractors realized.

There was a lot to be said for making Warren the first CFPB director, but one consideration trumped all others: The Senate leadership told the White House there was no chance she could be confirmed. Republicans were vowing to block anyone we tried to appoint to run the bureau, to try to strangle it in its crib. We couldn't afford divisions on our own side, and some moderate Democrats opposed Warren as well. They didn't want to vote for a controversial liberal at a conservative moment. They were also worried about the intense opposition in the business community. Senate Democrats, even her supporters, were not confident she would get a majority, much less the necessary sixty votes.

Mark Patterson and I thought about options, and after a few discussions with Rahm and Pete Rouse, I proposed that we make Warren the acting director, with responsibility for building the new bureau, while we continued to look for alternative candidates. This would give her a chance to be the public face of consumer protection, which she was exceptionally good at, and the ability to recruit a team of people to the new bureau right away, which she wouldn't have been allowed to do if she had been in confirmation limbo. Over time, maybe her prospects for confirmation by the Senate would improve. Rouse had another idea: Maybe she could run for the Senate herself, taking on Scott Brown in Massachusetts.

The temporary position seemed like a reasonable solution, but it took an enormous amount of time and energy to get there. We had endless discussions about whether to bring Warren in, whether to mount a futile confirmation battle that would leave no one in place to set up the agency, whether the President should give her a recess appointment, what kind of role and responsibilities she might accept. "We have a lot more pressing issues," Rahm wrote in an email. "We are all spending a lot of time on one person."

The President was torn. Progressives were turning Warren into another whose-side-are-you-on litmus test. The head of the National Organization for Women publicly accused me of blocking Warren, calling me a classic Wall Street sexist. Valerie Jarrett, the President's confidante from Chicago, was pushing hard for Warren, too, and she was worried I would stand in the way. At a meeting with Rahm and Valerie, I told the group that if the President wanted to appoint Warren to run the CFPB, I wouldn't try to talk him out of it, but everyone in the room knew she had no chance of being confirmed. The President, who almost never called me at home, made an exception on this issue. It was really eating away at him. He had a huge amount of respect for Warren, but he didn't want an endless confirmation fight, and he was hesitant to nominate someone so divisive that it would undermine the agency's ability to get up and running, as well as its ability to build broader legitimacy beyond the left.

Eventually, the option Patterson and I had floated prevailed. We would ask Warren to come in on an interim basis, reporting to me as well as the President. She was skeptical that I'd let her have a substantive role after our conflicts over TARP; I had to call and assure her I really wanted her involved. The President announced her appointment with huge fanfare at a Rose Garden ceremony. On her first day of work, I gave her a police hat to signify the new cop on the beat.

We were initially amused, and eventually a bit annoyed, when Warren, who had spent so much time bemoaning Treasury's nefarious work against the public interest, quickly began trying to hire away a bunch of our staffers. She was unapologetic when my team finally confronted her about it, and you had to respect her determination to get things done. We ended up having a productive working relationship, and she did an excellent job getting the bureau off the ground. And Rouse, in his deft and mysterious way, helped persuade her to run for Senate, which delighted the left while avoiding an unwinnable confirmation war.

Instead, the President nominated former Ohio Attorney General Richard Cordray, another impressive lawyer with credibility on the left, to be the CFPB's first director. When Senate Republicans blocked his nomination, the President gave him a recess appointment so he could start work right away, and he moved quickly to try to build support among moderate Republicans. He wouldn't be officially confirmed until 2013, but he has helped make the CFPB a prominent new force in the American economy. The bureau has already secured more than $3 billion in relief for ten million wronged consumers. It has created disclosure requirements, standardized documents, and online tools that are helping Americans comparison shop for mortgages, credit cards, and financial aid for college. Rouse's plan worked out well for Warren, too. She's now a U.S. senator, still watchdogging the financial industry, still occasionally attacking the administration from the left.

The U.S. financial crisis was over, and we had done what we could to prevent it from happening again. But we still had to deal with its aftermath—a European crisis, a deeply wounded Main Street economy, swollen fiscal deficits, and a political nightmare.

ELEVEN

Aftershocks

In August 2010, two weeks after the President signed financial reform into law, I wrote a *New York Times* op-ed summing up our economic progress to date. The U.S. economy had been growing for a year, and adding jobs since March. Banks were much stronger, and our bank rescues were on track to make money for taxpayers. The slimmed-down auto industry was generating profits again.

"We suffered a terrible blow," I concluded, "but we are coming back."

I was careful not to strike a celebratory tone when so many families were still suffering: "We all understand and appreciate that these signs of strength in parts of the economy are cold comfort to those Americans still looking for work." I noted that the share of workers who had been unemployed for at least six months was at a record high; that small businesses were struggling; that recoveries after financial crises are always slow and painful. "The process of repair means economic growth will come slower than we would like," I wrote.

No one would remember any of that. What people would remember was the snarky headline the *New York Times* editor chose for my column: "Welcome to the Recovery." It made me look like I was de-claring mission accomplished.

In fact, private-sector job growth was faltering again, casting a shadow over what the White House had touted as a "Recovery Sum-mer." Economic analysts thought we might be stumbling toward a double-dip recession. Political analysts knew we were stumbling toward a disastrous midterm election. House Minority Leader John Boehner, campaigning to become Speaker, called on Larry and me to resign, calling us the public faces of "the President's job-killing agenda."

Some of the swoon resulted from a natural and necessary de-leveraging after a credit boom and bust. Americans were reducing their debts rather than buying new stuff. Banks weren't lending to marginal borrowers. Residential construction, the economy's jet fuel for so long, was now sugar in its tank, dropping from two million new homes a year during the bubble to just half a million after it popped. The after-math of a financial crisis is always brutal, and this was an exceptionally brutal crisis. Americans had emerged with less wealth, less disposable income, and less confidence about the future.

But there were two additional anchors dragging down our recov-ery, and I would spend the rest of my time at Treasury dealing with their consequences.

The first was fiscal austerity. The Recovery Act was still pumping hundreds of billions of dollars into the economy, but state and local governments were offsetting the federal stimulus with spending cuts and tax hikes that sucked cash out of the economy. We were at risk of repeating the mistake of 1937, when President Franklin D. Roosevelt hit the fiscal brakes before a recovery could sustain itself; despite the Recovery Act, the United States had shed more than three hundred thousand government jobs since President Obama took office. And the politics of stimulus had turned toxic. The $1.3 trillion federal deficit sounded gigantic and indefensible to Americans who were cut-ting their own spending to make ends meet. Republicans were clam-oring for austerity, and many Democrats were unwilling to push back, wary of being tarred as big spenders. Congress had no appetite for additional stimulus.

The second drag on our recovery was Europe, which was in financial and economic disarray. The eurozone was America's largest trading partner, and our financial systems were also inextricably linked, so the European mess was a serious threat to us. Greece was in the midst of a devastating sovereign debt crisis. Ireland and Portugal were heading for similar trouble for different reasons. Markets were also running from Italy and Spain, the world's seventh-largest and ninth-largest economies. The statistics were staggering. Spain had 20 percent unemployment; Ireland poured more than 20 percent of its GDP into rescues for its troubled banks; Greece's national debt was approaching 150 percent of its GDP. Confidence was dwindling that these countries could avoid default, and that the entire eurozone—the monetary union launched just a decade earlier—could avoid collapse.

We were feeling their pain. Europeans had less money to buy U.S. goods, which hurt our economy. As global fears of a European meltdown sent investment capital scurrying into safe Treasuries, the dollar got stronger and U.S. goods got more expensive, which further hurt our economy. And in the same way the fall of Lehman had pounded European banks, the renewed turmoil in Europe threatened the U.S. financial system; even the *possibility* of contagion was shaking confidence, tightening credit, and depressing growth in the United States.

The fever for austerity and the mess in Europe were both sizable aftershocks from the financial crisis, and they would be the central economic dramas of the rest of President Obama's first term. The dominant domestic narrative would revolve around a series of intense fiscal negotiations with Republican leaders, who would threaten to shut down the government and even force the Treasury to default on the nation's debts if we didn't agree to deep cuts in the safety net. The dominant international narrative would revolve around our efforts to prevent European leaders from reigniting the financial crisis and pushing the global economy back into the abyss.

America's stimulus-versus-austerity fiscal wars had been raging since President Obama took office, but the chaos in Europe took me by surprise. I couldn't believe that Europe's governments would set themselves on fire and risk another worldwide inferno so soon after we put out the flames of the initial crisis.

I remember when I first got very worried, because I was in an unusual place.

• • •

THERE'S NEVER been a G-7 meeting in a less likely location than Iqaluit, the tiny Canadian outpost just south of the Arctic Circle where we convened in early February 2010. Temperatures routinely dipped to 25 degrees below zero that time of year, so the central bankers and finance ministers in attendance dressed more casually than I had ever seen them. Japan's finance minister wore a bright orange sweater over a turtleneck; Canada's wore one of those snowflake sweaters your aunt gives you for Christmas; my ragged gray pullover was no less fashionable. There were opportunities for us to tour igloos, ride dogsleds, and eat seal blubber in Iqaluit, though I left those particular diversions to the others.

Just before the opening dinner, I checked the market report on my BlackBerry. Europe was imploding. European bank stocks had plunged, mainly because Greece looked like it might be heading toward default. A newly formed Greek government had announced that its 2009 budget deficit had been three times as large as the previous government had claimed. Now the cost of insuring against a Greek default had soared 60 percent in just a month, approaching the levels faced by the largest U.S. banks in the weeks after Lehman fell.

The sudden panic in Europe was shocking. And the discussion over dinner was not reassuring. The Europeans spent most of the meal complaining about Greek profligacy and mendacity. There were strident calls for austerity and Old Testament justice, determined vows to avoid moral hazard, confident assertions that the crisis could be contained to Greece. The outrage about Greece's fiscal irresponsibility was justified, but we had just witnessed the dangers of big messy defaults, especially when other borrowers appeared to be in similar positions. If it began to look like the eurozone wouldn't stand behind one of its members, investors would run from other weak countries. Countries on the "periphery"—Portugal, Ireland, Italy, and Spain, which along with Greece were being derided as "the PIIGS"—were already seeing higher borrowing costs, a troubling sign of contagion.

I told the Europeans that if they were planning to keep their boots on Greece's neck, they also needed to assure the markets they wouldn't allow defaults by sovereign countries or the collapse of entire banking systems.

"Just don't overdo it," I said. "If you don't take out the risk of catastrophic failure, you have no chance of solving this."

They didn't seem to agree. I had known several of them for more than a decade, and after hearing me advocate for so many financial rescues, they surely thought of me as the walking embodiment of moral hazard. Germany and France didn't want lectures from the United States, anyway; they still blamed our Wild West financial system for the meltdown of 2008. They weren't going to be swayed by suggestions from the reckless Americans that they should take it easy on the reckless Greeks. In reality, Europe had enjoyed a wild credit boom of its own, with much of the risky borrowing in the periphery funded by risky lending by banks in the German and French "core." After the bust, the Fed's swap lines for European banks and loans to U.S. operations of European banks had helped prevent the collapse of the European banking system, which had borrowed way too many dollars—no favor to us—in order to invest in U.S. mortgage assets during the boom.

Now Europe was burning again, and it did not seem to have the tools or the desire to contain the fire. The eurozone was sixteen nations with sixteen fiscal policies and sixteen banking systems, all joined together under a common monetary policy. A default by one would affect them all, but they all had different priorities, and it wasn't clear how the stronger and weaker nations could coordinate a response that could be approved by sixteen parliaments. When I wrote my first paper at Treasury on European economic integration twenty years earlier, I had noted that it was at heart a political project, designed to bind disparate nations together to avoid another world war. For all the flaws of the U.S. system, our fragmented regulatory agencies were at least part of the same nation, with a common language and traditions, and we routinely transferred resources to economically weak regions through our national budget. The Germans felt no obligation to help the Greeks—and their politicians knew that excessive generosity could get them booted out of office.

It was perhaps fitting that our military plane out of Iqaluit couldn't get us home—not because of weather in the Arctic, but because of weather in Washington, which was in the throes of the historic "Snowmageddon" blizzard. I once again had a terrible sense of foreboding, a feeling that the world was relapsing. This time, it wasn't all on me; in fact, it was largely out of my hands. In some ways, that felt worse. Europe needed overwhelming force but didn't seem willing to apply it.

Two weeks later, the Europeans floated an absurdly stingy package of bilateral loans for Greece—at most 25 billion euros, which wouldn't even cover its borrowing needs through the spring—combined with harsh demands for tax increases, spending cuts, wage freezes, and other austerity measures. The proposed conditions sparked strikes and riots in Athens. Some German politicians suggested Greece should auction the Acropolis to pay its bills, which did not calm the furor. Clearly, Greece needed to rein in a budget deficit that had exceeded 15 percent of its GDP in 2009. But imposing too much austerity too quickly would be counterproductive, further depressing its economy, shrinking its tax revenues, and actually increasing its deficit.

By the spring, European leaders had made some concessions to reality, committing alongside the IMF to a rescue of 110 billion euros. That at least seemed like enough for Greece to meet its obligations for a couple of years. But they were still insisting on draconian budget cuts, and their harsh Old Testament rhetoric was roiling the markets, undermining the power of their aid. On April 25, our new undersecretary of the Treasury for international affairs, Lael Brainard, a former Clinton White House economist who had just been confirmed after a maddening yearlong wait, sent me a wire story headlined "Germany, France Signal Hard Line with Greece." The German finance minister, Wolfgang Schäuble, had warned that severe fiscal austerity would be "unavoidable and an absolute prerequisite" for aid. His French counterpart, Christine Lagarde, warned that if Greece defaulted, "we will immediately put the foot on the brake." Lael was particularly unhappy about the reference to default, the kind of talk that makes bondholders panic.

"Extremely unhelpful and ill-considered," she wrote.

The desire to impose losses on reckless borrowers and lenders is completely understandable, but it's terribly counterproductive in a financial crisis. In the United States, the FDIC's insistence on haircutting WaMu's creditors instantly panicked other creditors and raised borrowing costs for everyone else. In Europe, the talk of inflicting pain on Greece was having a similar effect on confidence and borrowing costs across the continent. The logic is inescapable: When lenders think a loan to WaMu or the Greek government will be worth pennies on the dollar, they get very cautious about extending new loans to anything that looks like WaMu or Greece, and very aggressive about calling in loans they have already extended. That rapid contraction of credit is what deeper recessions are made of, and that's why talk about haircuts and default in Berlin was so damaging.

Greece's credit default swaps implied a 50 percent probability that it would default within five years; its two-year bond yields rose into double digits, while Germany's remained below 1 percent. Italy came under severe pressure, and banks throughout the eurozone struggled to borrow dollars. We had a chilling scare on May 6, during a general market swoon triggered by concerns about Europe, when U.S. stocks suddenly plunged an additional 5 percent in a few minutes. The cause of this "flash crash" turned out to be a malfunctioning trading algorithm, but as it was happening we thought the fear in Europe might be spiraling out of control.

"This sucks," Rahm declared in a typically succinct email.

On a G-7 conference call the next day, I told the Europeans they needed a much broader and more aggressive strategy to contain the crisis. The first and most important element would be a massive firewall to prevent the Greek inferno from spreading, a demonstration that Europe had the capacity and the will to prevent contagion. I also suggested that stronger European countries needed to start supporting growth across the continent, rather than adopting a generalized strategy of austerity, which would only lead to worse recessions, higher deficits, and a deeper crisis. Because of the monetary union, the weaker countries couldn't devalue their currencies to ease their pain and boost their relative competitiveness; I thought the stronger countries at least ought to refrain from inflicting more pain.

The Europeans said they actually were thinking about a firewall, a rescue fund of about 50 billion euros financed out of existing European Union funds. I was stunned. How would a pool of cash less than half the size of the loan to Greece reassure markets that the Europeans were willing to stand behind other countries? I interrupted before they could finish explaining their concept.

"If you announce that, you'll be laughed at," I said. "You'll be pouring gasoline on the fire. You should be thinking more like *five hundred* billion euros."

After huddling over the weekend, the Europeans announced a 500 billion euro rescue fund. The IMF indicated it would put up another 250 billion euros. And Jean-Claude Trichet announced that the European Central Bank would start buying the sovereign debt of Greece and other weaker European countries that private investors, spooked by the default fears and all the moral hazard rhetoric, had been abandoning in droves. Trichet, who had chastised me after the fall of Lehman destroyed confidence in U.S. financial firms, understood the danger of a similar run on European countries. He was a forceful advocate for escalation, complaining privately to me that Europe's political leaders had no real understanding of markets and no idea how precarious the situation was.

But the ECB couldn't solve this itself. The most powerful country in Europe, Germany, was deeply committed to a strategy of austerity, and skeptical of forceful financial rescues. I had met Schäuble, a survivor of an assassination attempt that left him in a wheelchair, for the first time in Iqaluit, and I had found him compelling—direct, smart, strong. On substance, though, we were often far apart. He had a clear view: Greece had binged, so it needed to go on a strict diet. Other nations with unsustainable deficits had to do the same, even though it would cause pain for their citizens, even though many of them had been fiscally responsible before the crisis. Schäuble said Germany would slash its own budget in solidarity with the rest of the continent, to show that it wouldn't ask for sacrifices it wouldn't make itself. I thought that would just make the problem worse; in the near term, the German government and German citizens needed to do more spending and less saving.

"You know, you sound a bit like Herbert Hoover in the 1930s," I said. "You need to be thinking about growth."

The loan for Greece, the rescue fund for Europe, the ECB's bond-buying program, and a Fed decision to reinstate its central bank swap lines did buy some calm. Markets came back a bit. European leaders also agreed to launch a round of stress tests for their banks, just as we had done. At times, they signaled a desire to take catastrophic risk off the table. German Chancellor Angela Merkel told President Obama and me that "we won't do a Lehman," which we took to mean that Europe wouldn't allow a disorderly default of Greece. I thought Chancellor Merkel was smart and impressive, although I'm not sure the feeling was mutual; she turned to me in that meeting with the President and said Paul Volcker had told her I was "very close to the markets," which I don't think she meant as a compliment.

Unfortunately, after building some credibility with the markets, the Europeans quickly squandered it, a pattern that would recur over time. They made a point of emphasizing that the Greek rescue was a one-off, reigniting fears about the rest of the continent. Their austerity targets for Greece seemed wildly unrealistic. They squabbled over the design of their new firewall, ultimately limiting its power. Investors again lost confidence in Europe's ability to defuse the crisis.

"It sort of feels like people are waiting for a rabbit to be pulled out of a hat," Meg McConnell, my former New York Fed colleague, wrote to me on May 25, 2010. "Even the guy with the hat keeps peering in hopefully."

The initial European bank stress tests also inspired widespread scorn. They were virtually stress-free, concluding that eighty-four of Europe's ninety-one largest banks already had enough capital, and that the other seven only needed another 3.5 billion euros. Two of those supposedly well-capitalized banks, Allied Irish and the Bank of Ireland, had to be rescued by the Irish government a few months after receiving their clean bills of health; their rescues would require twice as much capital as the stress tests had prescribed for the entire European banking system.

The early fires of the European crisis contributed to the disappointment of our Recovery Summer. And Europe continued to burn in the fall. Ireland's support for its failing banks was on the verge of bankrupting its government. Germany was pushing to make rescues from the new European fund conditional on haircuts for creditors— the euphemism was "private-sector involvement"—which further unnerved the markets.

Meanwhile, austerity fever was spreading; Greece was the only country that had been exceptionally profligate in the lead-up to the crisis, but the bad economy was driving up deficits throughout the European periphery, which prompted some counterproductive anti-Keynesian efforts to tighten belts during a downturn. Spain and Portugal slashed spending in fruitless attempts to avoid ratings downgrades. The United Kingdom pivoted to austerity after David Cameron and the Tories ousted Gordon Brown, and would soon lapse back into recession. Meanwhile, Germany was pushing for a European fiscal union with the power to restrain the borrowing and spending of its members.

French President Nicolas Sarkozy was understandably cool to the idea of giving Germany power over the budgetary decisions of other countries. Unfortunately, he defused this threat to French sovereignty by persuading Merkel to back off the fiscal union in exchange for his support for the German mandatory haircut policy. In other words, a European government would have to restructure its debt to be eligible for assistance from the European rescue fund. Not only was Europe failing to make a credible commitment that it wouldn't allow a Lehman, it looked like it was committing to regular WaMus. It was also increasingly evident that Greece's initial rescue wasn't going to be enough, and it wasn't clear what would come next. Investors sprinted away from Ireland and Portugal, which looked like the nations most likely to need help. Their borrowing costs skyrocketed, which made it even more likely that they would need help, a frightening doom loop.

By Thanksgiving 2010, Ireland's government and banks clearly needed a rescue package. And Europeans were openly debating how deeply to haircut creditors. On another G-7 call, I told them that was crazy.

"You're going to accelerate the run," I said. "Nobody's going to lend to a European government or bank that's showing weakness if they think you're going to impose haircuts as a condition for your rescues. You're undermining your defenses, and it's going to cost you a lot more money in the long run."

Trichet was deeply concerned as well, as animated as I had ever heard him. We argued that the Europeans couldn't force countries to restructure their debts until they had a credible plan to protect the rest of the system from contagion. The Lehman failure and the WaMu haircuts had been so disastrous in part because we didn't have a firewall in place to protect other financial firms; Europe was similarly naked. I told them that at some point they might be able to safely restructure the debts of the weaker governments and banks, but right now they shouldn't even be discussing it publicly. And making haircuts a necessary condition of all rescues would be like announcing that no loans to the weaker European banks or governments were safe.

"You just cannot afford all this loose talk about haircuts," I said.

That weekend, the Europeans approved an 85 billion euro rescue for Ireland, and changed the proposed design of the permanent firewall. While they didn't rule out haircuts, they agreed not to make haircuts mandatory. The markets rallied again, especially after Trichet suggested that "pundits are underestimating the determination of European governments" to end the crisis.

I hoped that was true. But I suspected the pundits were right.

● ● ●

BACK HOME, Republicans spent the fall of 2010 running a disingenuous Tea Party campaign against Big Government. They blamed President Obama for the budget deficit he inherited; they blamed the stimulus for the jobs problem it helped ease; they raged against the bank bailouts that saved the global financial system and the auto bailouts that saved the U.S. auto industry. They portrayed the President's push for universal health insurance as the death of American liberty. With unemployment still hovering near 10 percent, the strategy worked. The midterm elections, as the President put it, were a "shellacking." The Republicans reclaimed the majority in the House and gained six seats in the Senate. They pledged to slash spending, shrink the deficit, and force the federal leviathan to live within its means. They sounded more committed to austerity than the Germans.

The national media were also caught up in the austerity fever, inspired by the Simpson-Bowles fiscal commission the President had created. On December 1, 2010, Alan Simpson and Erskine Bowles released a deficit reduction plan that mesmerized the Beltway. It called for $4 trillion in savings over ten years, including deep cuts in military spending, reductions in Social Security benefits, and an overhaul of the tax code that would raise $2 trillion in revenues. The plan would have been dead on arrival on Capitol Hill, but it never even arrived; the eighteen-member commission voted against sending it to Congress, with House Budget Committee Chairman Paul Ryan, the lead Republican on fiscal issues, among the no votes.

There was a lot of good policy in Simpson-Bowles, including cuts in wasteful farm subsidies and increased infrastructure spending to boost growth, but the benefit cuts and tax reforms were pretty regressive and the health care savings very modest. Nevertheless, the plan would attain mythic status among Washington elites as a symbol of noble bipartisan seriousness. Our critics—including Ryan and other Republicans who wouldn't accept any tax hikes under any circumstances, much less the $2 trillion in Simpson-Bowles—would cite the President's failure to embrace it as proof of his irresponsibility. Larry had been wary of creating a commission we couldn't control—he warned of "McChrystal risk," a reference to the former U.S. commander in Afghanistan who ran a review of U.S. strategy that the White House thought boxed in the President—and, in retrospect, Larry was prescient about that, too.

We were at the start of a big fight about how to get the government to live within its means—a fight worth having, but a little premature when unemployment was still above 9 percent and growth was still modest. We also faced a more immediate risk to the recovery.

President Bush's tax cuts were scheduled to expire on January 1, 2011, triggering a $3 trillion tax increase. For all their rhetoric about excessive debt, Republicans were still united in their allergy to taxes, especially taxes on the wealthiest Americans. They talked about reducing the deficit, but what they really wanted to reduce was spending, or at least nonmilitary spending. And while Democrats did want to let the Bush tax cuts expire for the top income brackets, the President wanted to preserve them for families earning less than $250,000 a year. He had vowed not to raise taxes on America's cash-strapped middle class, and we were afraid that across-the-board tax hikes could push us back into recession.

Republicans wouldn't assume control of the House until January 2011, so the President and the lame-duck Democratic Congress—along with the Republican minority in the Senate, which could still filibuster legislation it didn't like—would have to work together in December to avoid raising America's taxes. Minority Leader McConnell made it clear that Senate Republicans would block any deal—and even any unrelated legislation—that did not extend all the Bush tax cuts, including the upper-income tax cuts.

I thought the Bush tax cuts for the wealthy were unaffordable, unfair, and inefficient; extending them would provide windfalls for the Americans least likely to spend the extra money and stimulate the economy. In August, when Democrats were avoiding the tax issue during the campaign season, I had given a speech at the Center for American Progress making the economic case for letting top rates return to Clinton-era levels. "Borrowing to finance tax cuts for the top two percent would be a seven-hundred-billion-dollar fiscal mistake," I said. I didn't think it was too much to ask for the wealthiest beneficiaries of American freedoms to pay the rates they had paid in the 1990s to help their country pay for defense, health care, and other public investments that help give all Americans a chance to succeed. But my desire to restore slightly higher tax rates for the top 2 percent was not as strong as my desire to avoid a large tax increase on the bottom 98 percent. I also thought it was crucial to extend unemployment benefits and a slew of Recovery Act tax cuts that were about to expire. We couldn't afford to dent the fragile recovery.

Vice President Biden handled the negotiations, and at an Oval

Office meeting on December 4, he outlined McConnell's proposal: a two-year extension of all the Bush tax cuts, as well as a sharp reduction in estate taxes for a few thousand wealthy Americans. In return, Senate Republicans would be willing to extend unemployment benefits and some of the expiring Recovery Act tax cuts, but only if they were not "refundable," which meant low-income taxpayers would no longer benefit.

"We can't accept that," I said. "If they want to argue that we can't raise taxes in a weak economy, then nobody's taxes should go up."

I thought we should be willing to swallow two more years of the Bush tax cuts for the wealthy, but not if we had to add to the burden of the middle class and the working poor. After the meeting, Axelrod thanked me for saying what others were thinking.

Over the next couple of days, McConnell agreed to most of what we wanted, although he insisted on keeping the egregious estate tax cuts for multimillionaires. We also engineered a clever switch conjured up by Gene Sperling, replacing the Making Work Pay tax cut for most of the American workforce—which Republicans hated because it was part of President Obama's stimulus—with a one-year payroll tax cut. Not only was the payroll tax cut twice as large as Making Work Pay, but Gene (correctly) suspected that Republicans would agree to extend it again in 2011 rather than risk being portrayed as payroll tax hikers.

On December 6, the President announced an $857 billion bipartisan deal. It was essentially another stimulus, although naturally we didn't use that eight-letter word; despite all the austerity talk, we would avoid massive tax hikes and continue to give the economy some needed support. The upper-end Bush tax cuts and estate tax cuts were the weakest kind of stimulus, and they were anathema to many congressional Democrats. But they amounted to less than one-seventh of the package. The rest of the deal would benefit low-income and middle-class Americans, and private forecasts suggested that it would create more than a million jobs.

Once the deal was done, McConnell kept his word to let the Senate resume its business, enabling a final flurry of legislative activity before the Republican takeover of the House. Before the lame-duck session was over, the Senate would ratify the START Treaty, a landmark nuclear arms reduction agreement with Russia; Congress would repeal "don't ask, don't tell," a major civil rights victory that allowed gays to serve openly in the military; and Republicans would stop blocking health benefits for first responders to the September 11 attacks. I attended the signing ceremony for the "don't ask, don't tell" repeal, the most moving event I had witnessed in public life. It was such a refreshing contrast to the ugly politics of the Hill, and such a noble achievement for the President, allowing men and women who protect our country to live and love honestly and openly. As much as the President would have liked to let the upper-end tax cuts expire, he got to accomplish a lot in return for extending them.

Some critics would later complain that we should have insisted on increasing the federal debt limit as part of the lame-duck deal, so that we wouldn't run out of borrowing authority in 2011, but neither party's leadership on Capitol Hill had any interest in doing that after the Republican landslide. I thought it was still a good deal, and the White House asked me to help brief Hill Democrats about it and defend it on the Sunday TV shows.

Instead, I got to spend some quality time at the hospital getting a kidney stone removed. Pete Rouse sent Mark Patterson a note with his condolences: "Ask Tim which is more painful—the kidney stone or the tax deal briefings." My ever-protective daughter, Elise, visiting me in the hospital from Stanford, tried to fend off my constant work-related interruptions so I could get some rest. At one point, my lead Secret Service agent poked his head through the door to inform me that POTUS was on the line.

"Who the fuck is POTUS?" Elise asked with exasperation.

She agreed to let me take the call after we explained the acronym of the President of the United States.

• • •

PETER ORSZAG and Christy Romer left the White House in mid-2010, and Larry would return to Harvard at the end of the year. That fall, while waiting for a meeting with the Chinese during a session of the UN General Assembly, President Obama and I discussed their possible successors. I said he should think about a successor for me as well. We had defused the financial crisis and passed financial reform, my overriding priorities at Treasury. Now we were heading into a fiscal moment, and I thought he could use a secretary who knew the politics of the budget and the Hill better than I did. I also felt burned out and ready to leave.

I wanted a normal life again, without a Secret Service detail, with fewer strangers telling me I looked taller on TV. It was weird being a public figure; once while I was on vacation waiting to catch a wave, a fellow surfer asked if I thought he should buy yen at eighty. Carole was uneasy with people staring at us when we went grocery shopping. She hated the Beltway game, the constant criticism, the politicization of everything. She deeply admired the President and was fine about attending the occasional White House event—especially if there was music—but that was never going to be her scene. She was so offended by the thought of getting treated differently because of my position that after she finished her young-adult novel, *If Only,* she considered publishing it under her maiden name. Ben and Elise also had mixed feelings about my job; they had learned to be wary of classmates who seemed too interested in their father's fame. Carole and I had told Ben he could go back to Larchmont for his senior year if he wanted, and I didn't want to break another promise to Carole that we wouldn't do the long-distance commuting thing again.

I gave the President a long list of potential replacements for me. Jack Lew, who had just replaced Orszag as budget director, was an experienced fiscal negotiator. Erskine Bowles would have credibility with many Republicans, which would be important with a divided government. I even suggested asking Hillary Clinton to take her star power from State to Treasury; among her many strengths, she had an underappreciated ability to reach across the aisle. But the President said he still needed my financial crisis experience. He was worried about Europe and the risk of the unexpected; I'm sure he also wanted to avoid a protracted confirmation fight.

I kept pushing Rahm to start vetting candidates, knowing the process would take time, but Rahm left the White House that fall to run for mayor of Chicago. In my first meeting with his successor, Bill Daley, I told him he needed to start looking for my replacement right away.

"They told me my top priority was to get you to stay," Daley said.

As we entered 2011, I continued to remind the President he needed a new secretary, but my reminders never seemed to spur action. Daley used to joke about making me wear an ankle bracelet. To the surprise of the pundits who had pegged me as a short-timer after my rocky start, I was now the only remaining principal from the President's original economic team. I was glad to see my indefatigable counselor, Gene Sperling, take over at the National Economic Council, but I knew I'd miss my daily debates with Larry. We had our differences during the crisis, and nothing was ever easy when he was around, but he was the most talented policy thinker I knew. I felt bad that the Fed chairmanship hadn't worked out for him. The job would open up again in 2014, but when the President, on my recommendation, nominated my excellent former Fed colleague Janet Yellen to be vice chair in April 2010, Larry mused that she was certain to be the next Fed chair, because she would be too compelling a choice to pass over—another correct prediction.

The White House would be a very different place without Rahm, whose energy and drive had set the rhythm of our first two years; Larry, who had enlivened every economic meeting; and Axelrod, who was returning to Chicago to oversee the President's reelection campaign. My press aides started sending me clips about my newfound influence, but I felt like I had enjoyed a remarkable degree of influence and deference from the beginning.

I wasn't a close friend of the President's, but he seemed to trust and value my judgment. He had stuck with my financial crisis strategy despite its political costs. I think he appreciated that I was careful not to overstate my conviction or overstep my boundaries. We had a standing meeting every week, but I gave up my slot when I had nothing important to discuss, which was apparently rare in a city where presidential face time is a measure of your worth. He seemed to want to know what I thought, even when he knew that what I thought would mean trouble. He subjected my judgments to withering debate, but he gave me a lot of latitude; some might say too much.

For all the personnel shifts inside the administration, the big change in Washington would be the new balance of political power on Capitol Hill. If it had been tough moving the President's agenda without a filibuster-proof majority in the Senate, it would be nearly impossible without control of the House. Republicans now believed they had a mandate to roll back the Obama presidency, starting with the $100 billion in immediate spending cuts they had promised in their campaign "Pledge to America." And they had some leverage we couldn't just wish away. We would need their cooperation in the spring to pass a budget, or else the federal government would shut down. We would also need their cooperation in the summer to raise the debt ceiling, or else the federal government would default on its obligations, ravaging the full faith and credit of the United States. These would be real challenges, because many new House Republicans were Tea Party champions who had promised to fight the President on everything. Some saw default not as an epic catastrophe that would destroy global confidence in the United States, but as a desirable wake-up call for a nation that had lost its way. And Republicans who weren't true believers had to worry that insufficient hostility to the President would earn them a Tea Party primary challenger.

A week after the midterms, the President and I endured a dismal

G-20 summit in Seoul; the press coverage was all about waning American influence. In the car between meetings, we discussed the dark political landscape at home. He was somber and reflective, chastened but not discouraged. I urged him not to limit his agenda to fit the constraints of divided government, to lay out a broad vision for our long-term economic challenges, to push back against the deflating sense that they were beyond our ability to solve. We couldn't cede the initiative to the Republicans. I didn't know if we could negotiate a bipartisan long-term budget deal that would get the nation on a sustainable fiscal path while advancing his agenda of public investments and equal opportunity. But I thought it was worth a shot, and I didn't see how it could happen unless he laid out his priorities on tax reform, entitlement reform, and growth. Yet again, plan beat no plan.

"You're still in charge," I said. "We've got to have a view."

The President listened, but politically, he had a very tough needle to thread. He would need Republican support to pass a budget, but Speaker Boehner would need the support of the ascendant Tea Party wing of his caucus to do just about anything, and Democrats would be unlikely to support anything remotely attractive to the Tea Party. The leaders of both parties were saying they didn't want a government shutdown or a default, but it wasn't clear how we would find common ground to avoid them.

At a meeting early in 2011 in Daley's office to discuss fiscal strategy, we debated how to respond to the Republican push for cuts in domestic spending. David Plouffe, who had just replaced David Axelrod as the President's top political adviser, made the case that we couldn't ignore the public clamor for fiscal discipline, and, politics aside, the President believed in fiscal discipline. "We didn't run on a platform of permanently increasing the size of government," said Plouffe, who had managed the President's 2008 campaign. Plouffe wasn't suggesting that we lurch into austerity, just that we couldn't afford to be against *all* cuts. In our fiscal strategy discussions, Dan Pfeiffer, the President's communications director and another 2008 campaign veteran, often took the other side of the debate, saying we couldn't afford to alienate our base and split a weakened Democratic Party in pursuit of an imaginary compromise with Republicans who didn't want to compromise.

At another meeting in the Roosevelt Room, I told the President I thought there was a chance that he could break at least some Republicans away from their no-new-taxes mantra and forge a deal to stabilize our long-term debt. It wouldn't be a deal that his base would like, but if he wanted to get anything through the House, he couldn't be bound by the demands of Democrats.

"You have a chance to split the Republicans," I said. "But only if you're willing to split the Democrats."

OUR NEGOTIATIONS with Senator McConnell over the Bush tax cuts had gone surprisingly well. Our initial negotiations with Speaker Boehner over the 2011 budget would go well, too. In retrospect, they probably went too well.

I kind of liked Boehner. He had an easygoing manner, and he seemed lonely in his new position as a pragmatic conservative surrounded by extremists. He had been in the House leadership when Speaker Gingrich shut down the government in 1995, a political disaster that helped ensure President Clinton's reelection, and he didn't want to replay that movie in 2011. But the House Republican caucus was dominated by right-wing bomb-throwers who craved a confrontation; they saw Boehner as an overly accommodating establishment figure. Boehner sometimes warned us his caucus didn't believe in compromising with the President, and might turn on him if he cut a deal. I'm sure he emphasized these pressures as a negotiating stance, pushing us to make concessions to get the Tea Party insurgents off his back. But the pressures were real. House conservatives blasted his initial demand for $32 billion in spending cuts as grossly inadequate, and many in Washington believed that House Majority Leader Eric Cantor wanted his job.

That March, we twice approached the brink of a government shutdown, which would have furloughed hundreds of thousands of public employees. Both times, Congress passed last-minute budget extensions of a couple weeks, after House Republicans attached modest spending cuts as a kind of "toll." But Boehner was losing control of the process. House conservatives started demanding extraneous ideological add-ons to defund Planned Parenthood and bar the Environmental Protection Agency from regulating carbon, ensuring that another short-term extension couldn't pass the Senate. By early April, it was choosing time: either a budget deal with Boehner for the last six months of the fiscal year or else a shutdown.

I told Daley and Lew several times that we should seriously consider refusing the Republican demands for spending cuts and let them shut down the government. It would be an unpleasant and costly outcome, but what really scared me was the prospect of Republicans forcing the United States into default that summer, an unthinkable outcome. I thought a shutdown might let the Tea Party vent some of its fury, while giving Boehner some obstructionist credibility with his caucus so he could behave responsibly over the debt limit. But there was concern inside the White House that a high-profile standoff over spending after the Tea Party landslide could backfire politically, making the President look like he didn't get it. And after a few rounds of negotiations, the funding gap between Boehner and the administration was remarkably small. It would have been tough to justify a shutdown over a few billion dollars in spending. A political confrontation could have been helpful if it had exposed the Tea Party's unreasonable demands, but in this case, the Tea Party wasn't getting its way.

Late at night on April 9, the White House and Republican leaders reached a last-minute deal to cut $38 billion out of the 2011 budget. President Obama and Speaker Boehner both hailed the agreement as the largest spending cuts in U.S. history. Liberals accused us of getting rolled and selling out, complaining that we had cut more than

Boehner's initial request. But in reality, the cuts were very gentle, and many of them looked like accounting fictions; my team called them "air sandwiches." A few days later, the nonpartisan referees at the Congressional Budget Office concluded that the deal would reduce actual 2011 spending by only $352 million, hardly a revolutionary reduction in the size of government.

House conservatives went ballistic. Boehner had delivered less than 1 percent of the cuts they promised in their Pledge to America. He would now have to be much more aggressive to prove his right-wing bona fides to his caucus, which was not what we wanted as we approached the much higher stakes of the debt limit negotiations. We failed to break the Republican fever in the spring, so Boehner would face even more pressure to drag us to the edge of Armageddon that summer.

Now it was time for the President to lay out a more comprehensive long-term economic plan, as we had discussed on and off since Seoul. He planned to announce his fiscal framework in a speech on April 13. I liked the draft that went to the President—except for one structural problem. The speech would include a detailed critique of the Republican fiscal vision enshrined in Paul Ryan's House budget, describing its combination of upper-income tax cuts with deep spending cuts to vital programs as virtually un-American. Only after that would the President propose his own much more balanced plan. I told the President I thought he should reverse the order.

"You should say what you're for first," I said. But he liked the order as it was.

The President did begin his speech at George Washington University with a summary of his we're-in-this-together philosophy: free markets as our engine of prosperity, plus government investments to do as a nation what we can't do individually—defend and educate our people, build and repair roads and bridges, finance programs such as Medicare and unemployment insurance that protect us all from hard times or bad luck. He also recounted how the surpluses of 2000 became trillion-dollar deficits in 2009, thanks to President Bush's tax cuts, two wars, and a prescription drug benefit that were never paid for, followed by the Great Recession.

He then pivoted to a withering attack on the Ryan budget—not its goal of $4 trillion in savings over ten years, the same as Simpson-Bowles, but its path to get there, including a 70 percent cut in clean energy funding, a 30 percent cut in transportation, and a 25 percent cut in education: "These aren't the kind of cuts you make when you're trying to get rid of some waste," the President said. "These are the kind of cuts that tell us we can't afford the America that I believe in and I think you believe in." He denounced Ryan's effort to transform Medicare from a guaranteed entitlement into a voucher program, while slashing Medicaid for low-income families and kids with autism and Down syndrome. "These are the Americans we'd be telling to fend for themselves," he said. The President saved his harshest criticism for the $1 trillion in new tax breaks, which had been conveniently omitted in press stories that lionized Ryan's plan as "serious" and "courageous."

"There's nothing serious about a plan that claims to reduce the deficit by spending a trillion dollars on tax cuts for millionaires and billionaires," the President said. "I don't think there's anything courageous about asking for sacrifice from those who can least afford it and don't have any clout on Capitol Hill."

Ryan was sitting in the front row, so the press focused on the President's attacks, suggesting he had been partisan and rude. It barely noticed the President's plan.

But it was a sensible plan. It adopted the Simpson-Bowles goal of $4 trillion in savings while back-loading its deficit reduction to protect the recovery. It called for a balance of tax increases as well as defense and nondefense spending cuts, in contrast to the Republican insistence on nondefense spending cuts alone. It aimed to save $500 billion through Medicare and Medicaid reforms designed to rein in health care costs, but the President vowed to protect seniors and other vulnerable citizens from sharp benefits cuts. He also pledged to invest in research, infrastructure, education, and other areas important to America's competitiveness.

The President acknowledged the widespread skepticism that Democrats and Republicans could work out a long-term deficit reduction deal. "After a few years on this job, I have some sympathy for this view," he joked. But he announced that Vice President Biden would host a series of negotiating sessions with leaders of both parties to try to hash something out. "Americans deserve and will demand that we all make an effort to bridge our differences and find common ground," he said.

That's what we wanted. The question was: What did Republicans want?

FROM THE start of negotiations in early May, it was clear a grand bargain would be tough. The Republicans were combining their traditional orthodoxy of tax cuts skewed toward the rich with radical new ambitions for cutting government spending—slashing the safety net for the poor, shifting Medicare costs to retirees, and dramatically reducing "nondefense discretionary spending," the roughly 15 percent of the budget that funds everything from the FBI to the National Institutes of Health. At the same time, they wanted to increase Pentagon spending.

"I'm a whatever-it-takes kind of guy on defense," Senator Jon Kyl, the Arizona Republican who had championed the expensive estate tax cut, said during one session.

"That's a fine position to take, but you need to be willing to pay for it," I replied. "You can't be a responsible national security hawk if you're never willing to raise taxes, and you're only willing to borrow or cut the safety net."

The age-old Republican hostility to new tax revenues was obviously going to be a problem. Even more troubling, Republicans were already suggesting they wouldn't raise the federal debt limit unless we caved to their demands. Raising the debt limit would not authorize any new spending; it would merely allow the Treasury to pay for spending that Congress had previously authorized. Republican leaders knew the limit had to be raised to avoid a global financial meltdown. But they also recognized its value as a hostage. They could strap a financial bomb to their chests and try to extort a ransom in exchange for agreeing not to blow up the economy.

"What are you going to give us for the debt limit?" Eric Cantor asked.

"We're not going to give you anything," I said. "It's your responsibility to raise the debt limit. It's not a gift to us."

By that point, however, the White House had already signaled that we were willing to negotiate over the debt limit. Mark Patterson and I had argued that we should refuse to concede anything in exchange for a debt limit increase, but the White House did not believe that was a realistic position. In an austerity moment, even our Democratic allies were afraid to vote for a bill that would make them vulnerable to charges they were pro-debt.

Still, I was appalled when the Speaker announced "the Boehner Rule" on May 11, declaring that Republicans would demand a dollar of spending cuts for every dollar of additional borrowing authority. I thought he was painting himself and the country into a dangerous corner. After all the agony caused by the most damaging financial crisis in generations, he and his party were threatening a completely unnecessary reprise in pursuit of a policy agenda that would make the economy worse.

Historically, the debt limit had served mostly as a grandstanding opportunity for the minority party. Even President Obama, as a senator, had once voted against raising the debt limit, a symbolic gesture to protest the Bush deficits; that had been irresponsible, as he now admitted, but not consequential, because there had been no danger that the debt limit wouldn't be raised. But what the Republicans were doing, using the debt limit as a tool of extortion to impose their political agenda, was without precedent. It jeopardized the full faith and credit of the United States, the good name and trust we had earned over more than two centuries. The assumption that the United States would always pay its debts underpinned the stability of global finance.

I didn't understand why Boehner would give so much leverage to the extremists in his caucus. He was raising their expectations that they could use a routine piece of legislative housekeeping to achieve their wildest policy dreams. Many of them truly seemed to believe that default could cleanse the sins of the U.S. economy, which was insane. Boehner knew perfectly well that default would have destroyed the U.S. economy. By creating mass uncertainty about the historically risk-free Treasury debt that was the foundation of global finance, it would have created an economic Armageddon. And the constitutional precedent was awful. Conceding to the demands of a party that controlled just one house of Congress would alter the balance of power between the executive and legislative branches in ways that Republicans would surely regret when they next occupied the White House. But Boehner was unwilling, at that point, to correct the delusions of much of his caucus.

It was hard to believe that while Greece and Ireland and Portugal were desperately trying to avoid default, we were discussing voluntary default. I liked to remind people what President Reagan had said when confronting a considerably milder brushfire over the debt limit decades earlier: "The full consequences of a default—or even the serious prospect of default—by the United States are impossible to predict and awesome to contemplate."

THERE WERE plenty of twists and turns in the debt-limit talks, but the basic narrative didn't change much. House Republicans wouldn't accept new tax revenues, and neither the President nor the Democratic leadership in the Senate would accept deep cuts in entitlements as part of a $4 trillion "grand bargain" without new tax revenues. For all their soliloquies about the tragic debt we were leaving our grandkids, Republicans didn't consider it tragic enough to justify the elimination of a single tax break. They weren't prepared to break their no-new-taxes pledges to cut a deal with a president their supporters loathed. Plenty of ink would be spilled on tick-tocks investigating who moved which goalposts, trying to unravel the mystery of who killed the bargain. At the time, though, it didn't feel mysterious.

There was a weird dynamic to the talks, because Boehner truly seemed to want a deal, while Cantor and his colleagues seemed to be watching Boehner to make sure he didn't cut a deal. I found the Speaker's obvious discomfort with the far right wing of his caucus sort of appealing; it was too visceral to be entirely tactical. He always warned that their intransigence might scuttle any compromise, that they would consider any deal he cut with the President inherently suspect.

"I'm out in front of them," Boehner once said in the Oval Office. "I don't know if I can bring them along."

In our initial talks, we put the most controversial questions—taxes and potential reforms of Medicare, Medicaid, and Social Security—to the side. We focused on how to limit growth in other domestic spending, from civil service benefits to medical education subsidies to Pentagon programs. We did find some common ground on potential savings, and we hoped they could be a down payment on a larger deal. But on June 23, Cantor suddenly announced he was dropping out of the talks. He blamed our demand for new tax revenues, even though we had barely discussed tax revenues. "There is not support in the House for a tax increase," he said. "Regardless of the progress that has been made, the tax issue must be resolved before discussions can continue."

Around that time, Boehner opened up a back-channel negotiation with the President. Initially, he signaled he was willing to accept tax reforms that would raise $800 billion in new revenues. But he then publicly withdrew from those talks as well, explaining that House Republicans couldn't accept tax increases. "Despite good-faith efforts to find common ground, the White House will not pursue a bigger debt reduction agreement without tax hikes," he said on July 9.

Jack Lew had been the main White House liaison to the Hill, but a few days later, Boehner summoned Daley and me to his office to try yet again. "Most of my caucus thinks it's crazy to do a deal with you guys, but we should keep talking," he told us. The President and the Speaker met the next day, and things seemed to be back on track, with Boehner again suggesting he could accept $800 billion in new revenues through tax reforms that lowered overall rates while eliminating tax breaks, if we could accept reforms to Medicare, Medicaid, and Social Security.

Of course, nothing could be agreed to until everything was agreed to, and we had no evidence Boehner had the support of his caucus. The Speaker and his staff kept insisting they needed a scalp for the right; at one point, he proposed we scrap Obamacare's individual mandate for health insurance, an obvious nonstarter. We were getting a bit nervous about our side, too. Harry Reid and Nancy Pelosi had told the President they could support a grand bargain, but the outlines of the deal made the Democratic leaders uncomfortable. It would raise substantially less revenue than Simpson-Bowles or a draft proposal by a bipartisan Senate group known as the Gang of Six. And the entitlement reforms were going to be a tough vote for Democrats, especially with Republicans still insisting on some kind of Obamacare scalp. I remember during one Roosevelt Room prep session before I appeared on the Sunday shows, I objected when Dan Pfeiffer wanted me to say Social Security didn't contribute to the deficit. It wasn't a main driver of our future deficits, but it did contribute. Pfeiffer said the line was a "dog whistle" to the left, a phrase I had never heard before. He had to explain that the phrase was code to the Democratic base, signaling that we intended to protect Social Security.

On July 21, Boehner, remarkably, stopped returning the President's calls. He soon announced he was abandoning the grand bargain. This time, his rationale was that the President had moved the goalposts by asking for an extra $400 billion in revenues. But that was just a pretext; the negotiations were fluid. We had raised the revenue target, and their drafts still were calling for unacceptable political scalps, but the President hadn't drawn a line in the sand. The problem was that most of Boehner's caucus was unwilling to accept any new revenues, and many had pledged never to vote to raise the debt ceiling; he once told us that he was more interested in doing big things than being Speaker, but ultimately he was unwilling to split his caucus and risk his job. The President, by contrast, was willing to alienate some of his Democratic allies to pass an agreement he believed would be good for the country.

For months, I had been urging the markets to ignore the political theater, assuring the world it was inconceivable the United States would decide not to pay its bills. But it was starting to look conceivable. Our deadline to raise the debt limit was August 2, and the "fear index" measuring market volatility shot up 40 percent the week before. Analysts questioned the dollar's status as the world's reserve currency. Some commentators wanted us to sell gold from Fort Knox to pay our bills, or unilaterally invoke the Fourteenth Amendment's assurance that U.S. debt "shall not be questioned," or use a loophole in a law authorizing commemorative coins to mint a trillion-dollar platinum coin to circumvent the debt ceiling. But none of those options were viable. We were not a banana republic. We needed a deal through the democratic process.

Behind the scenes, Vice President Biden was making progress with McConnell on a deal with more modest spending cuts, drawing on the negotiations earlier in the summer, as well as the President's budget. We had the outlines of an agreement on Sunday morning, July 31, 2011, but Boehner was holding out for more Pentagon spending, saying his caucus was balking. Whoa. That afternoon, two days before the deadline, we met in the Oval Office to discuss whether I should make a statement preparing the world for the gruesome spectacle of the United States defaulting on its obligations for the first time in history. Even at my lowest points after Lehman and in early

2009, I had never felt this kind of dread. One reason we had been able to resolve our financial crisis was the exceptional faith that prevailed around the world in the credit of the United States of America. If House Republicans couldn't bring themselves to support anything that could pass, we could destroy that faith and create a much worse crisis—this time, a voluntary crisis.

But by nightfall, we had a deal. And on August 2, Congress barely made its deadline to pass the Budget Control Act, which would initially save $900 billion over ten years by capping growth in discretionary spending. The new law also created a bipartisan "supercommittee" that would try to agree on more savings; otherwise, starting in January 2013, a "sequester" would automatically trigger another $1.2 trillion in across-the-board spending cuts over the next nine years, half of them from defense. Republicans would later try to blame the President for the "Obamaquester," which was kind of amazing; they were the ones who threatened to force a default if we didn't agree to spending cuts equivalent to any debt-ceiling increase.

We didn't like inflexible across-the-board cuts—some programs are more important than others—or the focus on discretionary non-defense spending that was already low by historical standards. But the hope was the sequester would be so unpalatable to both parties that there would be motivation to compromise to avoid it. And we were relieved the deal delayed most of the cuts until 2013. With the unemployment rate still at 9 percent, and with Recovery Act spending tapering off, we feared that drastic short-term austerity could have killed the recovery. The deal also suspended the debt ceiling until after the 2012 election, which was an important substantive victory, not just a political one. Another hostage drama in the heat of a campaign could have ended in disaster, with Republicans under even more pressure to avoid compromise with the President.

Still, this was no way to run a superpower.

The drop in consumer confidence during the debt limit debate was larger than the drop during any U.S. recession since World War II.

And growth had already slowed considerably in the second quarter. This was partly because of continued dysfunction in Europe, higher gas prices driven by unrest in the Middle East, auto supply chain slow-downs caused by the devastating tsunami in Japan, and continued state and local budget cuts. We had a lot of economic headwinds, and a brutal drought that summer would create more. But our fiscal wars and political dysfunction were self-inflicted problems.

DESPITE ALL my efforts to escape Washington, those problems would continue to be my problems. Rumors had been flying that I would leave Treasury once the debt ceiling mess was resolved, but the President was adamant that I stay.

Carole was eager for us to return to a life with more privacy. She had been my anchor of stability and reality throughout the darkness of the crisis, always supportive, always having faith in me, though never caught up in the glamour or power of the office. She was justifiably hard on me at times, usually about my failure to be there for her and the kids. Now she and our son, Ben, were moving back to Larchmont for the start of his senior year. I'd have to commute again.

On August 4, two days after the deficit deal, we were sitting in the Rose Garden for the President's fiftieth birthday party. While the military band was playing, the President took Carole by the hand and asked her to take a walk.

"Usually, I'm good about people's family priorities," the President said to Carole. "But I can't let Tim go. I need him. Other countries need him. Things are so fragile now." I had told the President how Carole hates to see me attacked, especially by liberal columnists she often agreed with. "I know you don't like the criticism," he told her. "Michelle hates it, too. These jobs are incredibly difficult." Carole listened but didn't really respond; she's tough about standing up to pressure, even from the commander-in-chief. She later told me his tone shifted a bit at that point.

"As President, I just can't let him go," he said. He ended the conversation by walking over and introducing Carole to Tom Hanks and his wife, Rita Wilson, who the President said knew something about the challenges of living apart for long periods of time. Carole wasn't exactly appeased, and she didn't feel any better when Michelle's toast mentioned how nice it was that the President came home for dinner every night at 6:30 p.m. The next day, though, she wrote the President a gracious note thanking him for the personal explanation.

"It was hard for me, but I got your message," she wrote. "Even when I am most anxious for Tim's liberation, I am in complete support of you."

The President was generous to me; for my own fiftieth birthday two weeks later, he gave me a framed nineteenth-century patent for a tennis racket, with a funny inscription about how it might remind me of the equipment of my youth. While it was great to have the support of my boss, I was eager for my liberation from Washington, too. And while Carole was writing her conciliatory note, the United States was absorbing yet another blow to its financial reputation.

ON FRIDAY, August 5, three days after we avoided Armageddon, Standard & Poor's called the Treasury around 1 p.m. to let us know it planned to downgrade the AAA credit rating of the U.S. government. In April, S&P had warned that we had two years to demonstrate our commitment to deficit reduction to avoid a downgrade; now that we had passed a deficit reduction package, a rating agency that had given AAA seals of approval to all kinds of toxic mortgage securities suddenly planned to declare the world's safest investment a credit risk. It was a stunning act of folly. Even during the crisis, Treasuries had been the favored refuge from risk for global investors. Our deficits were falling as a share of our economy, and our new fiscal agreement had locked in significant additional savings. But as I said to my team: "It is what it is."

Except it wasn't. John Bellows, a twenty-nine-year-old economist on my team, quickly realized that S&P's numbers were way off. They had used the wrong baseline to evaluate the Budget Control Act, so they had overstated our projected deficits by an astounding $2 trillion over ten years. In their draft press release, S&P justified the downgrade by projecting a rapid rise in the U.S. debt-to-GDP ratio; without the $2 trillion error, the ratio would be much less scary, in line with plenty of AAA-rated countries with less productive economies than ours. My team called S&P's analysts to explain the problem and, a few hours later, they admitted their mistake.

That evening, S&P decided to go ahead with the downgrade anyway. It simply corrected its math error and rewrote its press release to suggest that its main rationale was political dysfunction—that the debt limit standoff had reduced their confidence that the American political system would be able to agree on more substantial fiscal reforms any time soon.

"I think S&P has shown really terrible judgment," I said on CNBC that Sunday. "They've handled themselves very poorly, and they've shown a stunning lack of knowledge about basic U.S. fiscal budget math."

On Monday, the stock market dropped 6.7 percent, the worst day since the height of the financial crisis. And the first-ever downgrade of the U.S. government was not even the worst problem in the global financial markets. Europe was burning again. I remember calling Trichet to commiserate from a chair outside Daley's office.

"I know we're about 75 percent of what's going on in the markets," Trichet said. "But you're making it worse."

* * *

EUROPE HAD spent most of 2011 flailing. Portugal got emergency help from the rescue fund to avoid default. Spain and Italy kept deteriorating. And Greece was a wreck. Austerity was further eroding its economy, so it was having trouble meeting its fiscal targets, sparking calls for deeper austerity. Its credit default swaps implied a three-in-four chance of default within five years. Increasing expectations of haircuts continued to drag down markets, as did rumors that Greece could leave the monetary union entirely, the so-called Grexit option.

On July 21, the same day Boehner announced the end of our grand-bargain talks, the eurozone restructured its aid to Greece, doubling the size of the loan but including conditions that implied a 20 percent haircut for some bondholders. Europe announced some new flexibility for the rescue fund, and Trichet expanded the ECB's bond-buying program to help prop up Spain and Italy. But Europe was not persuading investors that it had a credible strategy to fix its broken economies or contain the risk of a run on its weaker governments and banks.

Europe needed a larger and more credible firewall. With Greece's needs expanding, an internal Treasury report concluded that the 500 billion euro rescue fund would need to be doubled or possibly tripled to provide an effective backstop for the rest of the eurozone. But Chancellor Merkel, facing an anti-bailout backlash at home, was insisting that Germany's checkbook was closed. She did not like the way recipients of European assistance—Spain and Italy as well as Greece—were backsliding on promises of reform, and she didn't think giving them more of Germany's hard-earned money would improve their behavior. I saw her point—I sometimes told the Germans that I was more German than they realized—but the lines she was drawing in the sand were limiting Europe's options.

Our preferred solution was for Europe to expand the firepower of its rescue fund by using it to leverage the ECB's balance sheet. The central bank could provide much more aggressive financing, with the government fund protecting it against potential losses. We had done something similar with the Term Asset-Backed Securities Lending Facility during our crisis, jump-starting U.S. consumer credit markets by using a little government money to leverage a lot of Fed financing. The central bankers for Canada and Switzerland, Mark Carney and Philipp Hildebrand, pitched the idea of a TALF for Europe, but the German government and especially its central bank, the Bundesbank, still didn't like the idea. At one point, the Europeans began reaching out to Asian governments for financing they could use to augment their rescue fund, a pretty amazing spectacle. Unsurprisingly, Japan and China weren't eager to write checks to save the European project that the Europeans weren't willing to write themselves. The request just made them look more desperate.

That September, the Europeans invited me to speak at an Ecofin meeting of European financial ministers and central bank governors in Poland. It was a scary time in Europe. Spreads on Italian bonds were blowing up, and even France's credit default swaps had more than doubled in three months. I knew it would be sensitive and unorthodox for an American Treasury secretary to attend a European strategy session, so I checked with some of my European counterparts to make sure they really wanted me there, and that my presence wouldn't be counterproductive. They said I should definitely come.

In Poland, I gave a carefully phrased, polite set of remarks about crisis doctrine—speaking with the knowledge of our mistakes, as an American who bore the scars of our own crisis. "This is your crisis," I said. "You have to decide how to fix it." I acknowledged that the United States had our own formidable challenges. "You've watched us struggle with them," I said. "Our politics are terrible, maybe worse than in many parts of Europe. We're not in a particularly strong position to provide advice to all of you, so I come with humility."

Still, I was emphatic about some things Europe needed to do, starting with strengthening its firewall. Europe's most important responsibility, I said, was to take catastrophic risk—of cascading sovereign defaults, bank runs, and the breakup of the eurozone—off the table.

"Nothing is possible unless you do that," I said. "The firewall you build has to be perceived as larger than the scale of the problem. You can't succeed by shrinking the problem to fit your current level of financial commitments."

I told them they needed to put money behind their banking system as well as struggling governments, not one or the other. And I said the crisis had to be solved by governments as well as the European

Central Bank, working together. We would support more financing from the IMF, but not as a substitute for a more substantial European commitment. I also repeated my warnings against overdoing it with reforms designed to punish the profligate, along with my usual push for the healthier countries to promote growth. My main message, familiar to those who knew me, was that the crisis wouldn't end until Europe demonstrated the will to end it.

"It's more dangerous to escalate gradually and incrementally than with massive preemptive force," I said. "If you can show you're willing to do what needs to be done, you're more likely to have the private markets bear the burden of the financing, and you'll reduce the risk that taxpayers take on too much."

I thought that was basic and obvious advice, but a few European officials complained to the press that I had read them the riot act, asking who I thought I was to harangue them to spend more on bailouts and stimulus. They had invited me to share my views, but those views were clearly unwelcome to many in Europe. Austria's finance minister said it was "peculiar" that I would try to tell Europeans what to do after our own credit downgrade; Belgium's finance minister suggested I should listen rather than talk. The *New York Times* ran a front-page story about declining U.S. influence on global finance, with the requisite photo of me looking grim. The headline was "Advice on Debt? Europe Suggests U.S. Can Keep It." In fact, the Europeans were continuing their pattern of publicly castigating any American proposal, before eventually adopting a renamed and often mangled version of it.

We were less concerned about Europe's resentment of our influence than we were about Europe's unwillingness to leverage its rescue fund, protect its creditors, and fix its economies. "Momentum faltering again," Lael wrote me in early October. "ECB has put down a hard line on leverage. Continued squabbling about Greece [haircuts]. No leadership." On October 26, European leaders announced another revision to their deal for restructuring the Greek debt, this time with 50 percent haircuts. They did announce a modest plan to try to leverage the rescue fund using private money, but it was poorly designed and more than anything else seemed to signal the limits on what Europe was willing to do. It certainly didn't calm the markets; bond spreads throughout the periphery continued to deteriorate.

The President talked to European leaders regularly that fall, and Lael and I were in constant touch with our European counterparts. Some of them seemed to resent our intrusions at the same time they were inviting them. They often asked us to intervene to pressure Chancellor Merkel to be less stingy, or the Italians and the Spanish to be more responsible. At one point that fall, a few European officials approached us with a scheme to try to force Italian Prime Minister Silvio Berlusconi out of power; they wanted us to refuse to support IMF loans to Italy until he was gone. We told the President about this surprising invitation, but as helpful as it would have been to have better leadership in Europe, we couldn't get involved in a scheme like that.

"We can't have his blood on our hands," I said.

The President spent much of a G-20 meeting in early November in Cannes hosting backroom negotiating sessions, trying to help save Europe from itself. Most of the meeting was about pressure on Berlusconi, but we kept coming back to the need for a stronger firewall, and there was plenty of pressure on Merkel as well. Merkel felt isolated and under attack; I have never seen her so upset. At one point, the President and I stood quietly on a terrace overlooking the Mediterranean.

"You know, this would be really interesting if it wasn't so consequential," he said.

In Cannes, we didn't make much headway on the European firewall or reform on the periphery. But I did have some promising talks about the use of overwhelming force with Mario Draghi, who had just replaced Trichet as the head of the ECB. Draghi was an Italian who had run his country's central bank and served in its finance ministry, yet he was appointed with the support of the Germans, so he was in a rare position to help bridge the gaps in Europe. And just after

Cannes, Greek Prime Minister George Papandreou resigned to make way for a unity government; a week later, Berlusconi was replaced by Mario Monti, an economist who exuded technocratic competence; a week after that, Spain elected an impressive new prime minister, Mariano Rajoy, who had campaigned for fiscal reform. All these changes seemed promising, in part because they helped break down Germany's resistance to more aggressive measures to attack the crisis.

In early December, Draghi announced a massive blast of long-term financing for the European banking system, a more expansive version of the TAF lending facility the Fed had launched to address U.S. liquidity shortages back in December 2007. Basically, the ECB agreed to lend banks unlimited amounts of money for three years against a broad range of collateral. This had an instant stabilizing effect. The ECB provided about 1 trillion euros in financing to its banks over the next several months; more important, Europe had shown some force and some will.

By February 2012, when the G-20 finance ministers and central bankers met in Mexico City, the mood was more upbeat than I had seen it in a while. The Europeans were relieved, with many declaring that the crisis was over.

I didn't think so. This felt more like a lull than a resolution.

THE UNITED States was in a lull, too, economically and politically.

Growth was steady but unimpressive. Unemployment had declined to 8.3 percent, better than double digits but still way too high. The Fed and other forecasters kept predicting that the recovery was about to take off, but Europe, our fiscal drag, and our other economic headwinds kept holding it back.

Inside the administration, we had countless meetings to discuss ways to boost jobs and growth. But with Republicans now in charge of the House—and focusing mainly on symbolic votes repealing Obamacare, financial reform, and other Obama achievements—there weren't many realistic legislative options. It felt a bit like we were hockey goalies, just blocking bad stuff, all defense, no offense, with limited mobility. With Republicans pinning their hopes on a new president in 2013, it wasn't clear how we could pass good stuff.

Still, we figured we might as well say what we were for. We thought there was an outside chance that public pressure could move Republicans into supporting policies that might help strengthen growth. Even if it didn't, Plouffe, Pfeiffer, and the rest of the White House political team were eager to contrast our agenda with the Republican agenda. We began in the fall of 2011 with the American Jobs Act, a $447 billion stimulus bill the President proposed at a joint session of Congress. It was full of measures that were popular as long as they weren't described as "stimulus"—a massive public works program, a massive school modernization program, aid to states to protect jobs of teachers and first responders, a "Returning Heroes" tax credit for firms that hire unemployed veterans, and so on. The President barnstormed the country campaigning for his jobs plan, but aside from extending the payroll tax cuts and unemployment benefits from the lame-duck deal, Republicans were unmoved, and most of the plan died in Congress.

In early 2012, we proposed "the Buffett Rule," a set of measures to ensure that high earners would pay an effective tax rate of at least 30 percent, inspired by Warren Buffett's observation that he paid a lower tax rate than his secretary. Larry let me know he thought this was a gimmicky appeal to populism and soak-the-rich class warfare. He also thought it was bad politics, letting Republicans portray the President as an anti-success tax hiker. I thought the Buffett Rule was perfectly sensible, especially as an illustration of the need for broader tax reforms. It had the modest aim of limiting the extent to which better-off Americans could take advantage of tax breaks and lower rates on capital gains and dividends to lower their tax burden. The Republicans opposed it, of course, but many Democrats were uneasy, too, and it went nowhere.

That February, after months of internal debate, we proposed a framework for growth-oriented corporate tax reform that would lower overall rates for businesses while eliminating some of the pork that riddled the tax code. Many of the President's political advisers argued that it would split the Democratic Party over another plan with no hope of passing, but I thought we had to keep proposing reforms that were good for the economy, even if the likelihood of Republican support was low. To limit the political blowback, we put out a framework rather than comprehensive legislation. But parts of the Democratic base were still furious; the next time Richard Trumka, the head of the AFL-CIO, was in my office, he looked like he wanted to take a bat to my head. Once again, we had angered the left, without getting Republicans to play.

The election-year gridlock was frustrating, but in some ways oddly freeing. That February, when I testified about our budget before Paul Ryan's committee—my sixteenth and final budget hearing—I decided not to sit back and be a prop for the usual theater and abuse.

"We know defending this budget is no easy task, so we really do appreciate your time," Ryan quipped in his welcoming remarks.

"Not as hard as your job on your budget," I shot back.

Ryan laughed. "It's going to be a fun day," he said.

I laughed, too. "You have my sympathy," I said.

The hearing went on like that. I told Tim Huelskamp, a Tea Party Republican from Kansas, that his grand theory of White House failure reflected "an adolescent perspective on how to think about the impact of economic policy." When another Tea Party Republican, Jason Chaffetz of Utah, tried to get me to blame the Senate for partisan gridlock in Washington, I told him he was using his time poorly, since I wasn't part of the Senate. He complained that I was smirking.

I usually loathed Capitol Hill theater, but I did enjoy that last Budget Committee hearing with the fundamentalists. When Ryan tried to wrap up, I asked if we could keep going. Afterward, Ryan told me I had riled up the Tea Party types on his committee. "You just get under their skin," he said. That weekend, my communications director, Jenni LeCompte, told me someone had tweeted that I was the "Honey Badger of the Obama administration." I had no idea what that meant, so she sent me a viral YouTube video of "the Crazy Nastyass Honey Badger" devouring snakes and diving into beehives, as a narrator explained that the honey badger doesn't give a shit what other animals think. A Treasury secretary is supposed to exist above the political fray; I took my honey-badger moment as another indication that I had stayed in Washington too long.

In 2012, though, almost everything was political; when I was asked about silly Republican economic critiques, I said they were silly. That April, I got asked about a flawed claim by Mitt Romney, the Republican presidential nominee, that women were losing a disproportionate amount of jobs under President Obama. In fact, the economy had regained four million of the private-sector jobs lost in the Great Recession. The public sector was still losing jobs, and women were bearing the brunt of the layoffs of teachers and other government workers, but Republicans were blocking our efforts to reverse those cuts. "It's a ridiculous way to look at the problem," I said on ABC's *This Week*. "To borrow a line from Mario Cuomo, you're going to see a lot of politicians campaign in fiction. But we have to govern in *fact*."

I let myself get dragged into the fray again when CNBC asked me about an op-ed by Romney's economic adviser, Glenn Hubbard, who had claimed that the President's plan implied an 11 percent tax hike on families earning less than $200,000 a year. In fact, the plan included no tax hikes on those families, but Hubbard argued that since the President wasn't cutting entitlements enough—an ironic argument, since Romney was attacking the President for cutting Medicare—he would eventually have to raise taxes on everyone. "That's a completely made-up, remarkably hackish observation for an economist," I said. This caused some consternation on the right; Senator Tom Coburn of Oklahoma called me the most partisan Treasury secretary in history, which was amusing for me, a registered independent, especially given how many Democrats had called for my head.

Interestingly, a month earlier, at a dinner where I was speaking to the Economic Club of New York, Hubbard had complained to me about our unwillingness to endorse the Simpson-Bowles plan.

"Really, Glenn?" I asked. "There's a two-trillion-dollar tax increase in there. When you guys are willing to raise taxes, we can talk about Simpson-Bowles."

"Well, of course we have to raise taxes," Hubbard told me. "We just can't say that now."

BY JUNE 2012, the European crisis was burning hotter than ever.

Austerity measures were prompting riots and strikes on the periphery while depressing growth across the continent. Spain, with its jobless rate approaching 25 percent, needed a 100 billion euro credit line for its bank rescues. The debt-to-GDP ratios of Italy, Portugal, and Ireland all topped 110 percent, while Greece's neared 150 percent even after it haircut its bonds. Bank deposits were fleeing those countries as well, and their governments were too deep in debt to do anything about it.

Europe had failed to persuade the world that it would not allow a catastrophe. Its firewall still looked flimsy. Its politics were still a mess. Every time its leaders announced new measures to try to control the crisis, they undercut their message with bad execution, strict conditions, and moral hazard rhetoric emphasizing their limited ability and desire to rescue their neighbors. Its loan packages were often more stigmatizing than stabilizing. And the markets still thought there was a meaningful possibility of a cascade of defaults by countries or banks, or a devastating breakup of the eurozone.

I had a long history and a good relationship with Mario Draghi, and I kept encouraging him to use the power of the ECB to ease those tail risks. "I fear Europe and the world will again look to you for another dose of smart, creative central bank force," I wrote to him in June. Draghi knew he had to do more, but he needed the support of the Germans to do it, and the Bundesbank representatives on the

ECB kept fighting him. They didn't have a plan to save Europe, but they knew what they were against. They took a strict interpretation of the limits of the ECB's legal authority, and they opposed anything that could create moral hazard, which included just about any strategy that had a chance of calming the crisis.

That July, Draghi and I had several conversations reminiscent of my talks with Ben Bernanke in January 2008, when Ben decided he would rather be hung for his own judgments than the judgments of the Fed's inflation hawks. I told Draghi that there was no way any plan that could actually work would get Bundesbank support. He had to decide whether he was willing to let Europe collapse.

"You're going to have to leave them behind," I said.

Draghi knew that. Credit spreads were blowing up again. The world was no longer confident the eurozone was viable. Germany was threatening to cut off the Greeks, who had failed to meet their austerity commitments—partly because of foot-dragging, but mostly because it's hard to reduce your debt-to-GDP ratio when your GDP is crashing at a 7 percent annual rate. On July 26, 2012, a Citigroup report concluded there was a 90 percent chance that Greece would leave the euro within eighteen months. And other weak countries in Europe seemed likely to follow.

That day, toward the end of a speech at a London investment conference, Draghi uttered twenty-three words that would prove to be a turning point. "Within our mandate, the ECB is ready to do whatever it takes to preserve the euro," he said. "And believe me, it will be enough." Draghi had not planned to say this, but he was so alarmed by the darkness expressed by hedge funds and bankers at the conference that he ad-libbed an unequivocal commitment to defend Europe. Markets were delighted. At the time, though, I was worried that Europe would again undercut a commitment to action with caveats and Old Testament backsliding. The words were welcome, but the ECB didn't have a specific plan to back up Draghi's statement.

A few days later, I flew to meet Wolfgang Schäuble for lunch during his vacation at a resort in Sylt, a North Sea island known as Germany's Martha's Vineyard. Schäuble was engaging, but I left Sylt feeling more worried than ever. He told me there were many in Europe who still thought kicking the Greeks out of the eurozone was a plausible—even desirable—strategy. The idea was that with Greece out, Germany would be more likely to provide the financial support the eurozone needed, because the German people would no longer perceive aid to Europe as a bailout for the Greeks. At the same time, a Grexit would be traumatic enough that it would help scare the rest of Europe into giving up more sovereignty to a stronger banking and fiscal union. The argument was that letting Greece burn would make it easier to build a stronger Europe with a more credible firewall.

I found the argument terrifying. Letting Greece go could create a spectacular crisis of confidence, regardless of what Europeans committed to do afterward. It wasn't clear why a German electorate that hated the Greek bailouts would feel much better about rescuing Spain or Portugal or anyone else. And the flight from Europe, once it got momentum, might be impossible to reverse.

After Sylt, I stopped in Frankfurt to see Draghi. He was reassuring, in the sense that he recognized how bad the situation was and knew the ECB would have to deliver. But it wasn't clear yet what they were actually prepared to do. When I got back to Washington, I told the President I was deeply worried, and he was, too. The U.S. economy was still growing steadily but modestly; a European implosion could have knocked us back into recession, or even another financial crisis. As countless pundits noted, we didn't want that to happen in an election year, but we wouldn't have wanted that to happen in any year.

Two days after I saw Draghi, the ECB laid the groundwork for a program it announced in early September called "Outright Monetary Transactions," where it committed to buy the sovereign bonds of eurozone countries in secondary markets. The program was essentially a

"Draghi Put," a promise to put a floor under bond prices in European countries, lowering their borrowing costs and making it clear they would not be allowed to default. Draghi did not consult Merkel and Schäuble in advance, but they supported him publicly, even though the Bundesbank's ECB representative voted no.

The announcement of the new bond-buying program—and Merkel's vital support—persuaded the markets that the Europeans were serious about keeping the eurozone intact. The risk indicators that had been deteriorating that summer all started moving in the right direction. The mere existence of the program soothed doubts about the European firewall, building confidence that troubled countries would avoid default; so far, it has never been used. When central banks and governments take catastrophic risk off the table, markets become investable again.

But Europe's commitments were still messy and incomplete. They had no real plans to build a common European deposit insurance system. They could not agree to pool together their resources to support a substantial Europe-wide program to directly recapitalize their financial system like TARP. Any assistance from the European rescue fund or the ECB's new bond-buying program would come with politically perilous conditions. A chaotic bailout of Cyprus in 2013, and new European bank resolution plans announced later, would remind creditors that haircuts were still very much on the table.

By the end of 2013, unemployment in Spain would be 26 percent, and over 50 percent among young people. Greece's budget would be back in balance, but its unemployment rate would be 28 percent. Overall, unemployment throughout the eurozone was 12 percent, far worse than in the United States, and growth was stagnant, a testament to the dangers of financial turmoil and misplaced austerity. There was a lot of needless suffering behind those numbers. The mistakes by the Europeans—and their belated and often ineffectual attempts to imitate us—provided a pretty good advertisement for our crisis response. But they had a harder challenge. A currency union without unified fiscal policies, banking policies, or political representation was not ideally situated to handle a monumental emergency. It was more proof that the American system, for all its faults, had a lot of strengths we took for granted.

CAROLE AND I went to an Election Night party at Neal Wolin's house, but we went home early so we could watch the results in private. We could tell from the gloomy anchors and frequent commercial breaks on Fox News that it was going to be an excellent night, a gratifying validation of the President's work. My liberation from Washington was imminent either way, but a Romney victory would have been a depressing coda to four tough years.

Romney had framed the election as a simple question: Are you better off than you were four years ago? For most Americans, the answer was yes. While 2 percent growth was disappointing, it was a lot better than –8 percent growth. Adding fewer than 200,000 jobs a month was better than losing more than 750,000. The budget deficit was shrinking at the fastest rate since World War II—actually too fast, when we still needed stimulus—and the stock market was up 75 percent since Inauguration Day 2009. Romney had vowed to repeal health care reform and financial reform, and embraced his running mate Paul Ryan's approach to slashing government spending. A majority of voters were not moved by that vision.

We didn't have much time to celebrate, because we had more fiscal deadlines looming, which meant more negotiations on Capitol Hill. The first huge deadline was the "fiscal cliff" of January 1, 2013, when our two-year extension of the Bush tax cuts would expire, and the "sequester" from our 2011 budget deal would start slashing federal spending across the board. Then a few weeks after the cliff, Treasury would again bump up against the debt limit, raising the specter that Republicans would again try to use the full faith and credit of the United States as a bargaining chip. And I was worried about expectations in Congress. Democrats were in no mood to make concessions

Reviving Private-Sector Job Creation
Monthly Change in Total Private Nonfarm Payrolls

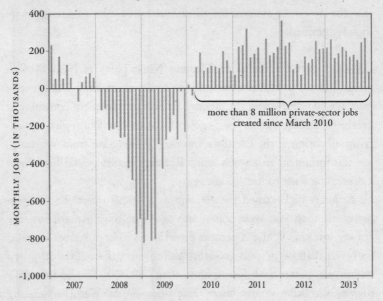

When President Obama took office, we were losing more than 750,000 jobs per month. The Recovery Act, our financial stability efforts, and our other support for the economy stopped the free-fall in 2009, and job growth began again in March 2010. Over the past four years, the United States economy has created more than 8 million private-sector jobs.

Source: Bureau of Labor Statistics (seasonally adjusted).

after President Obama's decisive victory, which they saw as a powerful electoral mandate for Democratic policies. But Republicans still controlled the House, and they saw their own reelections as vindication of their own policies. It was frustrating that we still had to negotiate over demands that a majority of the American people had rejected, but congressional elections had consequences, too.

We definitely did not want a stalemate to send the country over the cliff. The Congressional Budget Office estimated that the resulting tax hikes and spending cuts would push the economy back into recession in 2013, killing about 1.5 million to 2 million jobs. President Obama had vowed not to extend the upper-income Bush tax cuts again, but we wanted to keep the tax cuts in place for household income below $250,000 a year. We also wanted to avoid the sequester, which took a meat-axe approach to budget cuts, but we made it clear we were willing to use a scalpel, proposing about $400 billion in health care savings over ten years and even a modest reduction in Social Security benefits. At the same time, we proposed more short-term stimulus to protect the recovery, including another extension of the payroll tax cuts and additional infrastructure investments.

For a while, Speaker Boehner wouldn't engage, except to say that all the Bush tax cuts should be extended, and that our proposals were "job killing." One problem for Boehner was that many House Republicans still believed we should just capitulate to their demands; another problem was that they couldn't agree on their demands. Theoretically, they wanted entitlement cuts, but Medicare and Social Security are popular, so they wanted us to be the ones to propose the entitlement cuts. When we did, they just demanded more, without saying exactly what they wanted. And on taxes, we had the same problem we had before. There was no way to do a bipartisan deal without tax hikes as well as spending cuts, but Boehner couldn't get his caucus to support tax hikes, even though inaction would produce enormous tax hikes.

As the cliff approached, we moved a bit toward Boehner, but he couldn't move toward us. He walked out of the talks in mid-December, then announced that House Republicans would pass his "Plan B," extending the Bush tax cuts on all income up to $1 million a year, but with no spending reforms. But his caucus wouldn't even agree to raise taxes on only the top 0.2 percent, so he had to withdraw the legislation on December 20. It was now clear to everyone that Boehner couldn't get a majority of his caucus to support anything; he famously recited the Serenity Prayer during the backbench revolt against Plan B.

We spent the next eleven days negotiating an alternative to the cliff with Senate leaders. While far from optimal, the deal did some good things and avoided disaster. We preserved the Bush tax cuts for families earning up to $450,000 a year but restored the higher Clinton-era rates above that, raising about $600 billion in new revenue and making the tax code more progressive. We also extended unemployment benefits, along with many of the Recovery Act's tax credits, including relief for the working poor and college students. Senate Republicans would not agree to any additional stimulus, and the deal only delayed the dreaded sequester for two months; it did not even address the debt limit. But it was a truly bipartisan agreement, and at 2 a.m. on January 1, the Senate overwhelmingly approved it, 89–8. Eric Cantor immediately announced he would oppose the deal, and two-thirds of the House Republican caucus followed his lead. But to his credit, Boehner voted yes, as did almost all of the Democratic caucus, keeping the country from plunging over the cliff and into recession.

Now the President needed to figure out a way to raise the debt limit and avoid the sequester, but it looked like he would get to enjoy those challenges without me. The President was about to nominate Jack Lew, his chief of staff at the time, to be his next secretary of the Treasury.

"Congrats on avoiding the cliff—and triple if you manage to get out before debt limit," Larry wrote to me. "I will be impressed if you pull that off."

In fact, we started dealing with the debt limit while I was still at Treasury. And our way of dealing was to make it clear there would be no more deals, so a congressional faction could never again extort concessions by threatening to force the U.S. government into default. On January 14, 2013, the President laid down the gauntlet, saying he wouldn't negotiate over the debt limit. The Republicans had to choose whether they would let America pay its bills or whether they preferred to crash the global economy.

They backed down a few days later. Boehner announced that the House would pass a clean three-month extension of the debt limit, postponing the next fight over the country's full faith and credit. The Republicans would focus on the fight over the sequester, which was still two months away. My last day would be January 25, so those fights would no longer be my fights.

In his congratulatory note about the cliff, Larry added a gracious valedictory about my "very successful run," neatly summing up the previous four years in a very Larry way.

"We are back to worrying about bubbles rather than panics and inflation as much as deflation," he wrote. "Treasury remains a juggernaut. Europe is pretty under control. Regulators can't blame the lack of statutory authority for their next fuckup. Unemployment more than halfway back from peak to normal. Some predicate for tax reform. And lots of yahoo nonsense avoided."

MY STAFF made a funny video for my departure from Treasury, starring my son Ben as me. The first scene had a faux President-elect Obama trying to persuade me to take the job, as I argued that I was unqualified, that I cursed too much, that I wouldn't be able to sell my house because of my ugly bathroom tiles, and so on.

"People will say all kinds of crazy things," I protested. "After the bailouts we did, they'll probably think I'm in the pocket of Goldman Sachs!"

"That's ridiculous, Tim," a Treasury staffer playing the President replied. "Nobody would say that about you."

The next scene featured a typical meeting in the secretary's small conference room, with various members of my team reporting in deadly serious tones that markets were crashing, unemployment was rising, the eurozone was dissolving, we were defaulting on our debt, there were nine new requests for me to testify before Congress, and the latest draft of our housing white paper was up to 914 pages. Jenni LeCompte then explained that she had been managing the various exit profiles the media were writing about me.

"The common theme that seems to be emerging is that you are a very bad person who loves banks and hates America," she said. "We're pushing back on that."

Scene three was mostly an accumulation of my stock phrases: *I don't think that's the right way to think about it. Plan beats no plan. Life is about alternatives. I'd choose pain now over pain later. Un-fucking-believable. He's got an excess of conviction relative to knowledge. Hope is not a strategy. No fucking way.* The film concluded with President Hillary Clinton—well, another Treasury staffer playing her—in the Oval Office on January 21, 2017, saying she needed me to stay at Treasury for just six more months. Or possibly a year.

"With Europe still in trouble and another debt ceiling standoff coming, how can you leave?" she asked.

But no, I was really leaving. After twenty-five rewarding years of public service, after four exhausting years as Treasury secretary, it was time, to use another of my stock phrases, for someone else to have that privilege. I was proud of what we had achieved in the President's first term. Things were not perfect but things were much better. I did a bunch of farewells, including one at the New York Fed, because we had been way too busy to do one when I left in January 2009. My successor, Bill Dudley, said I would finally have time to sit for my official portrait.

"The good news is that Tim is a little bit older, so now his portrait will look more appropriately central-banker-like, rather than the somewhat more boyish version that we all remember when he was here," Dudley said.

Departures are times for taking stock, and for all my concern about our uneven recovery, the contrast with the terrifying free fall the President inherited four years earlier could not have been starker. The economy was growing, house prices were rising, and credit was flowing through the repaired pipes of the financial system. The Fed in Washington had done a farewell for me in January 2009; that was the event where Jeff Lacker joked about giving me the New York Fed's Maiden Lane vehicles, since they wouldn't exceed our $25 gift limit. By the time Ben Bernanke hosted another farewell for me in January 2013, taxpayers had already made a $23 billion profit on our investments in AIG, and were projected to make more than $2 billion on Bear Stearns—definitely above the gift limit.

Overall, after widespread predictions of trillions in losses, the U.S. government's financial interventions were in the black. Every major program turned a profit except the auto rescue and, of course, our foreclosure prevention programs, which were never supposed to be recouped. Taxpayers would end up making $24 billion on TARP's bank investments alone. At the Fed dinner for me, I asked Rubin, who had been very dark about the economy throughout my time in office, how he felt about having bought so much insurance against the risk that we might fail.

"That must have been expensive for you, Bob," I teased him.

"Yes," he laughed. "Very expensive."

The President gave me a pretty remarkable parting gift: engraving plates for the ten dollar bill, featuring Alexander Hamilton on the front and the Treasury building on the back. His inscription was gracious: "Thanks for navigating us through a terrible storm; Hamilton would be proud!" He and the vice president came to my official farewell ceremony, as did former secretaries Rubin and Paulson, Ben Bernanke, and a lot of Treasury's civil servants and political appointees.

I used the occasion to rehash some of the rules I had adopted since I first arrived at Treasury in 1988, from *Be for stuff, not just against stuff* to *No peacocks, jerks, or whiners.* And I tried to express my appreciation for the awesome colleagues who had fought the crisis by my side. It really had been a terrible storm. The world had looked to us for leadership, and despite some stumbles and setbacks and conflicts, we had gotten the job done, even if the world didn't think so.

"It was not easy work," I said. "There was no risk of public affirmation or affection. You were subjected to a lot of second-guessing, but you persevered, and because of your resolve and your creativity and your ingenuity, our economy is stronger, even with all the challenges we still face."

"I walked into this building in 1988 a younger man, eager to work on issues that matter," I continued. "And I leave Treasury so thankful for this opportunity to have worked with such an amazing group of people, so grateful to have been part of something consequential, something larger than ourselves."

EPILOGUE

Reflections on Financial Crises

In November 2008, when I told then President-elect Obama that his most important achievement would be preventing a depression, he said he intended to do a lot more than that. And he has. He ended the war in Iraq, is winding down the war in Afghanistan, and eliminated Osama bin Laden. His health care reforms are not only expanding insurance protections for millions of Americans, they are contributing to a dramatic slowdown in the medical cost growth that threatens our fiscal future. He has made tremendous strides on issues like gay rights, clean energy, and education reform. History will recognize him as a remarkable and consequential president.

But his success in preventing a major depression is still at the heart of his broader legacy. It made most of his other achievements possible, because a depression would have been an unimaginable catastrophe, substantially worse than anything we experienced in terms of unemployment, foreclosures, and poverty. When President Obama took office, we were heading that way. The U.S. economy was on a path to lose nine million jobs in 2009. The housing market and auto industry were collapsing. The financial system, despite

The U.S. Recovery Has Outperformed the Developed World
GDP Levels in Major Advanced Economies

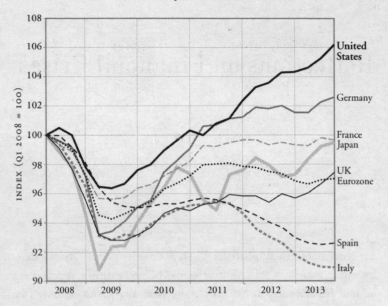

Because of the aggressive fiscal, monetary, and financial force we deployed, the U.S. economy has grown faster than other major advanced economies since the financial crisis.

Source: Organisation for Economic Co-operation and Development (Q1 2008 = 100).

all our government interventions and guarantees, was still fragile and broken. The five bombs—Fannie, Freddie, AIG, Citi, and Bank of America—were all serious threats to explode, and they were all much larger than Lehman Brothers.

They did not explode. And the U.S. economy escaped its death spiral. It started growing again within six months. By the end of 2013, our GDP was 6 percent higher than before the crisis; Japan, the U.K., and the eurozone were still below their pre-crisis output levels. After declining by $15 trillion, U.S. household wealth was also higher than the pre-crisis peak. As I write this in March 2014, we have enjoyed

Worse Initial Shock, but No Great Depression
Comparison of Market and Economic Indicators

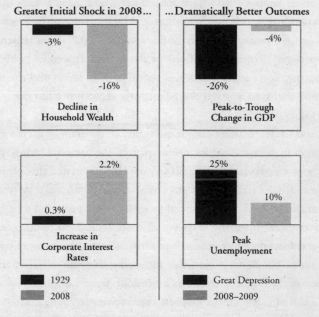

Greater Initial Shock in 2008...   ...Dramatically Better Outcomes

Decline in Household Wealth: -3%, -16%

Peak-to-Trough Change in GDP: -4%, -26%

Increase in Corporate Interest Rates: 0.3%, 2.2%

Peak Unemployment: 25%, 10%

1929 / 2008

Great Depression / 2008–2009

The shock that preceded our crisis in 2008 was larger than the initial shock that precipitated the Great Depression in 1929, but our outcomes were dramatically better.

Sources: Federal Reserve Board, Bureau of Economic Analysis, Bureau of Labor Statistics, Council of Economic Advisors, and Historical Statistics of the United States, Millennial Edition.

forty-eight consecutive months of private-sector job growth, with 8.7 million private-sector jobs created. Our 6.7 percent unemployment rate is still high, but it is a lot lower than our peak of 10 percent, or the current eurozone rate of 12 percent.

By contrast, six years after the start of the Great Depression, U.S. employment was still 10 percent below its pre-crisis peak. Our shock in 2008 was even worse than the shock of 1929, but our outcomes have been much better. If our economy had followed the trajectory of the 1930s, it would be $2.5 trillion smaller today—the equivalent of losing the entire output of both Texas and New York—and 13 million fewer people would have jobs. That would have been a disaster for Main Street, not just Wall Street. The recovery of the stock market—up 175 percent from its bottom in early 2009—has replenished the personal savings of millions of Americans as well as public and private pension funds. The stabilization of Wall Street and the rest of the financial system saved the Main Street economy from the trauma of another depression.

And while we didn't design our financial programs with the expectation of making money for the taxpayers, the financial industry paid for the rescue. As late as April 2009, the IMF estimated that we would incur nearly $2 trillion in direct costs saving the financial system, but at the end of 2013, our financial programs were projected to generate a positive return for the taxpayer of more than $150 billion, enough to fund federal cancer research at current levels for the next twenty-five years. But many Americans just remember the initial characterization of the financial rescue as a handout. Jenni LeCompte once sent me a clip of CNN's Erin Burnett interviewing a young activist from Occupy Wall Street, asking him if he knew that the Wall Street bailouts had been profitable for taxpayers.

"I was unaware of that," he told Burnett.

Would that make him feel differently about TARP?

"Oh, sure," he replied.

That earnest protester also might have been interested to learn about all the money President Obama poured directly into the Main Street economy. In his first term, the Recovery Act and other stimulus initiatives included about $1.4 trillion worth of tax cuts, government investments that boosted employment, and direct aid to low-income and middle-class families. That total does not include the President's rescue of the auto industry, which resuscitated dying manufacturers and helped prevent a regional depression in the Midwest, or his lifelines for Fannie and Freddie, which kept mortgage rates low and

Projected Taxpayer Returns from the Crisis Response

Projected Returns and Losses from Government Investments (end-2013)

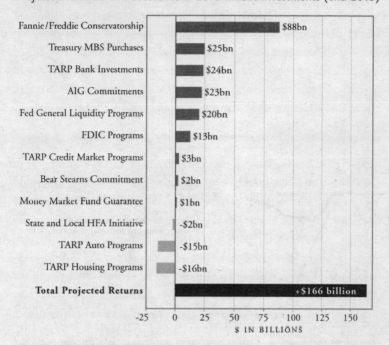

Fannie/Freddie Conservatorship	$88bn
Treasury MBS Purchases	$25bn
TARP Bank Investments	$24bn
AIG Commitments	$23bn
Fed General Liquidity Programs	$20bn
FDIC Programs	$13bn
TARP Credit Market Programs	$3bn
Bear Stearns Commitment	$2bn
Money Market Fund Guarantee	$1bn
State and Local HFA Initiative	-$2bn
TARP Auto Programs	-$15bn
TARP Housing Programs	-$16bn
Total Projected Returns	**+$166 billion**

-25   0   25   50   75   100   125   150
$ IN BILLIONS

In early 2009, the IMF estimated that the U.S. government would end up spending nearly $2 trillion rescuing the financial system. In fact, the U.S. government's crisis response not only prevented the collapse of the financial system and helped revive the broader economy, but as of the end of 2013 it was projected to generate about $166 billion in positive returns for taxpayers.

Sources: Compiled from Congressional Budget Office, Federal Deposit Insurance Corporation, Federal Reserve Board, Office of Management and Budget, and U.S. Treasury Department.

helped revive the real estate market. Jon Stewart used to make the case on *The Daily Show* that we should have written checks to the American people instead of writing checks to the banks. We wrote a lot of checks to the American people.

Still, the financial crisis left tragic pain and suffering in its wake. Financial crises always do. The economists Carmen Reinhart and Ken

The U.S. Recovery Has Also Outperformed
Historical Comparisons
Total Civilian Employment

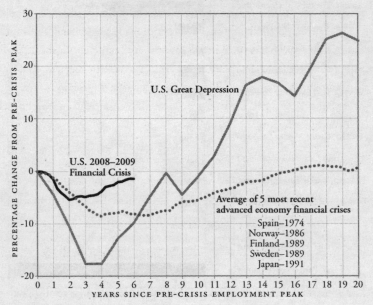

Recoveries that follow severe financial crises are always slow, but our post-crisis employment growth has been much stronger than other advanced economies that have experienced severe banking crises since World War II.

Sources: Census Department, Organisation for Economic Co-operation and Development, and U.S. Treasury Department.

Rogoff, my former IMF colleague who played chess in his head during meetings, have calculated that it takes the average country eight years after a financial crisis to reach its pre-crisis income levels. Even though we did much better than the average, and our crisis was much worse than the average, Americans absorbed a terrible blow. Long-term unemployment is still at alarming levels, with a devastating effect on workers as well as the economy at large. Poverty is still shockingly high. Income growth for most households is still stagnant. Our housing programs could not prevent millions of foreclosures. And despite the President's insistence on raising taxes on the wealthy, lowering taxes for the poor and the middle class, and expanding the federal safety net, inequality is still rising, continuing a decades-long trend.

The juxtaposition of the slow economic recovery and the rapid financial recovery has fueled the sense that we cared more about Wall Street than Main Street. That is simply not true. But it is true that the U.S. economic recovery, while strong compared to previous crises or other countries in this crisis, has been weak compared to normal post-recession recoveries.

WHY IS that?

It's mainly the reality of deleveraging after a financial crisis. After a long period of too much borrowing, too much home-building, and too much financial leverage, Americans have been saving more, paying down debts, and working through the excess inventory in the real estate market, while banks have been reining in risk. This is all part of the healing process, but it has slowed our rate of growth. We also had some bad luck with shocks beyond our control, like unrest in the Middle East, the tsunami in Japan, the lingering mess in Europe, and drought in parts of the United States.

But we also had a serious and frustrating self-inflicted wound: our prematurely tight fiscal policy. The President has been a strong advocate for fiscal stimulus, starting with the Recovery Act, the largest stimulus in history, continuing with several modest stimulus bills and more substantial stimulus proposals even after "stimulus" became a dirty political word. But since 2010, government cutbacks at the federal, state, and local levels have sliced about one percentage point off GDP each year—the difference between the tepid growth we had and the solid growth we could have had. And in March 2013, the blunt across-the-board spending cuts of the so-called "sequester" took effect, chopping another half point off GDP. We didn't quite repeat the 1937 mistakes to the extent that Europe did, so premature

The Economy Started Growing Again Remarkably Quickly
Quarterly Real GDP Growth

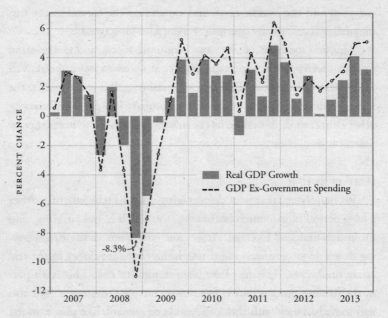

The overwhelming force of the policies we deployed in early 2009 turned an economy contracting at an annual rate of more than 8 percent into a growing economy within six months. Since the end of the Great Recession, the economy has expanded at an average annual rate of 2.4 percent, despite headwinds from the European financial crisis, state and local government cutbacks, and a more recent shift to austerity at the federal level. Excluding government spending, GDP has grown at an average rate of 3.5 percent since 2010.

Source: Bureau of Economic Analysis (chained 2009 dollars, quarterly, seasonally adjusted annual rate).

austerity didn't kill our recovery; but insufficient stimulus definitely sapped its strength.

The right has continued to caricature President Obama as an irresponsible big spender who doesn't care about deficits, which is bizarre given the actual numbers. The $1.2 trillion budget deficit he inherited in 2009 shrank to $680 billion by 2013, the fastest reduction since the demobilization after World War II. On the President's watch, the deficit will fall from a scary 10 percent of GDP to about 3 percent in just over five years—partly because of responsible policies like the end of the Bush tax cuts for the most affluent Americans, partly because of premature austerity like the sequester, partly because of the stronger economy. Discretionary spending relative to GDP is projected to fall to the lowest it's been since the Eisenhower administration. Health-care-cost growth since 2010 has been the lowest on record, and a significant part of that seems to be due to the President's reforms. With interest rates still remarkably low by historical standards, we ought to take advantage of our vastly improved fiscal outlook to increase our long-term investments in education, research, and especially infrastructure, ideally in the context of more fiscal reforms that would make our long-term commitments more sustainable.

In general, political dysfunction—and the fear that Washington gridlock could lead to disastrous outcomes for the economy—has been a drag on growth. The debt-limit showdown that brought the United States to the brink of default in the summer of 2011 was brutal for business and consumer confidence. Republicans continued to play chicken with the economy in the fall of 2013, refusing to pass a budget unless the President agreed to repeal Obamacare, which obviously wasn't going to happen; their leaders finally backed down after a pointless two-week government shutdown. Superpowers really aren't supposed to bumble around like that. But the President again refused to negotiate with Republicans over the debt limit in 2013, and Republicans agreed to extend it into 2015 after failing to extract any concessions. I strongly believe Congress should abolish the debt limit, so political extortionists can never again use the full faith and credit of the United States as a bargaining chip.

Today, the U.S. economy is still growing modestly. It's strong enough to create jobs but not to quell the concern that Main Street has been left behind. The Fed has begun to "taper" its monetary stimulus, reducing its bond-buying by $10 billion every month, and there is no additional fiscal stimulus on the horizon. But we are getting stronger. After several years of deleveraging, the average U.S. household is in a healthier financial position, with about 20 percent less debt relative to income. We still have the world's most innovative, resilient, and diverse economy, and it's considerably more productive than it was before the crisis. Our divisive and adolescent political culture is still a problem—unable to deliver many policy reforms that could help ordinary Americans, always a threat to make things worse—but most other countries face even more daunting political challenges.

THE UNDERSTANDABLE sense of disappointment and unease that so many Americans feel about their economic future has been accentuated by an acute sense of resentment and outrage about the rising fortunes of the wealthiest few. The success of our financial rescues and the speed of the stock market's recovery look like evidence that we sided with the arsonists who burned down the economy, bailing them out of bad bets, protecting their crazy compensation. Even though the prevailing view on Wall Street is that our financial reforms are a tyrannical assault on free enterprise, many Americans believe we helped Wall Street get away with the heist of the century.

Some of this anger reflects a misunderstanding of what we did during the crisis. For example, our interventions did not shield Wall Street from all financial pain. We let the weakest parts of the financial system fail, and forced many of the survivors to shrink in size or scope. Bear Stearns ceased to exist as an independent firm after its "bailout." Investors in Fannie, Freddie, and AIG were so upset about the losses they absorbed during their "rescues" that they actually sued the federal government. After all the public furor over our supposed generosity, after all the outrage from moral hazard fundamentalists about the green light we supposedly gave to the excessive risk-takers of tomorrow, it's been odd to also stand accused of being overly harsh to failing financial giants.

Through TARP and the stress test, major banks were diluted in proportion to the risks they took: The more capital they needed, the more their shareholders saw their stakes in those firms reduced. An investor or an executive who owned 1 percent of Citigroup's stock before the crisis would have owned 0.16 percent of the firm by the end of the crisis. That was certainly better than getting totally wiped out through failure, but it was much less generous than our critics suggest. And the CEOs of the troubled institutions that required a majority government stake (Fannie, Freddie, AIG) or a merger with a stronger partner (Bear, WaMu, Countrywide, Merrill, Wachovia) all lost their jobs. That ought to help strengthen the incentives of future bank investors and executives to temper their risk-taking. Our financial reforms will tie future compensation packages more closely to long-term performance, with legal authority for clawbacks when firms run into trouble. And because the tax system is now more progressive, a larger share of financial-industry bonuses are helping to finance education, the safety net for the poor, stronger enforcement of new financial rules, and other critical functions of government.

The perception that Wall Street paid no price for its misbehavior is also inaccurate. By early 2014, the big banks had paid more than $100 billion in fines related to the crisis. Overall, there has been a substantial increase in enforcement penalties for U.S. financial firms, and the new Consumer Financial Protection Bureau and the stronger authorities and resources granted to the other financial regulators will create an even more credible deterrent in the future—much stronger, I believe, than in any other major economy.

It's also true that individual Wall Street CEOs haven't been marched off to jail en masse, as many Americans thought they should be. But this was not a conspiracy of public corruption or ineptitude. Federal prosecutors and state attorneys general had all the right incentives to go after high-profile financial scalps, and they have brought down some insider traders and Ponzi schemers. For the most part, they have simply concluded that the financial activities most responsible for the crisis weren't illegal, however unethical or dumb they may have been. There was an appalling amount of mortgage fraud during the credit boom; it caused a lot of pain, and it deserved a more forceful enforcement response than the government delivered. But the bulk of the huge boom in borrowing that caused the crisis was between consenting adults who took risks they believed would pay off, risks that did pay off for a long time, risks fueled by genuine but imprudent beliefs that rising real estate values would make future defaults extremely unlikely. When Elizabeth Warren explained her theory of consumer protection to me over that dinner after we passed Dodd-Frank, she made the correct observation that banks did not and could not make money on loans that consumers had no hope of repaying. In any case, federal laws do not prohibit greed or ignorance or excessive optimism or even excessive risk-taking.

The lack of financial prosecutions combined with the revival of financial profits have contributed to the belief that nothing has changed, that if anything the system is even more dangerous. We still do have big banks, some even bigger than they were before the crisis, and the banking system overall is somewhat more concentrated. This in part reflects a long-term industry trend, and in part reflects all the emergency mergers during the crisis. But the U.S. banking system is much smaller relative to the size of our economy, and our economy is much less dependent on banks, than in the other major economies.

And our reforms have made the entire financial system much safer. Capital and liquidity requirements are much tougher. There is less dependence on runnable short-term funding. Much of the derivatives market has been brought out of the shadows, with margin requirements to reduce the danger of panicked sell-offs. By some measures, the so-called "shadow banking system" has been cut in half since 2007, and much of that Wild West is now subject to stronger oversight. The government also has the authority to wind down systemic firms, so markets are now much less confident the government will save them from future mistakes. The new consumer bureau is already a robust force protecting Americans from financial predation.

Reform is a "forever war," to borrow the title of the Dexter Filkins book on Afghanistan. It is an endless process, and we left some unfinished business. We still need stricter rules for money market funds, a new approach to the government's role in housing finance, a reorganization of our fragmented regulatory system, and stronger emergency authorities, such as a restoration of the FDIC's ability to provide broader guarantees. There was a lot of messiness in the initial wave of regulations that will have to be refined over time. But the notion that the financial status quo prevailed is absurd. Banking has become more conservative and less profitable. Before the crisis, the largest six banks earned 21 cents for every dollar of common equity; these days it's less than half that.

This is not to suggest that public perceptions of our generosity to the financial industry are unfounded. We provided extraordinary support to the financial system in general and some very poorly managed financial firms in particular. We didn't do it to help their executives buy fancier mansions and sleeker jets. We did it because there was no other way to prevent a financial calamity from crushing the broader economy. When the financial system stops working, credit freezes, savings evaporate, and demand for goods and services disappears, which leads to layoffs and poverty and pain. When investors and creditors start to panic, consumers and businesses follow suit. And to solve a major financial crisis, you have to do things you would never do in normal times or even in a modest crisis.

This is the central paradox of financial crises: What feels just and fair is often the opposite of what's required for a just and fair outcome. It's why policymakers generally tend to make crises worse, and why the politics of crisis management are always untenable.

The intuitive response after the busting of a credit boom fueled by reckless risk-taking and excessive leverage is to try to rein in credit

Financial Activity Is Moving Out of the Shadows
Bank vs. Market Funding

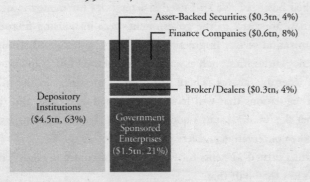

1990 — $7.1 TRILLION

Asset-Backed Securities ($0.3tn, 4%)

Finance Companies ($0.6tn, 8%)

Broker/Dealers ($0.3tn, 4%)

Depository
Institutions
($4.5tn, 63%)

Government
Sponsored
Enterprises
($1.5tn, 21%)

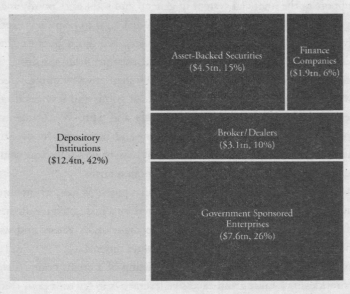

2007 — $29.5 TRILLION

Asset-Backed Securities
($4.5tn, 15%)

Finance
Companies
($1.9tn, 6%)

Broker/Dealers
($3.1tn, 10%)

Depository
Institutions
($12.4tn, 42%)

Government Sponsored
Enterprises
($7.6tn, 26%)

2012 — $28.1 TRILLION

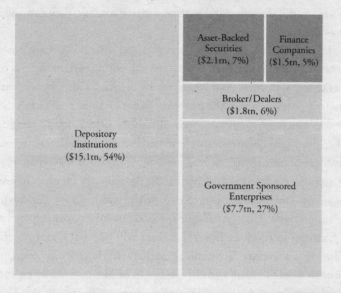

The decades-long expansion of financial activity in the "shadow banking system" began to reverse itself after the financial crisis and the Dodd-Frank financial reforms of 2010. A smaller percentage of overall financial activity is happening outside traditional banks, and that activity is now subject to additional regulation, as indicated by the lighter shading.

Sources: Federal Reserve Board and Financial Stability Oversight Council.

and risk-taking and leverage. When you're in a hole, the first thing you're expected to do is stop digging. The instinctive reaction of the policy wonk as well as the politician to an epic financial crisis is to punish the perpetrators and impose losses on their creditors while limiting taxpayer exposure to catastrophic risk. It seems obvious that government should discourage the risky behavior that created the mess, and certainly shouldn't reward it. On the fiscal side, it seems just as obvious to many that exploding budget deficits should prompt fiscal restraint, that when families and businesses have to tighten their belts, the government should tighten its belt as well.

All that sounds right. It usually is right. But in a severe crisis, it's wrong. And if those natural instincts infect strategy, they can cause a lot of damage.

In a crisis, when confidence vanishes and risk-taking stops, government measures that further discourage risk-taking further depress confidence and spur runs. And when private demand withers, government austerity only intensifies the problem. What's needed to avoid a vicious cycle in which the financial system and the broader economy drag each other down are counterintuitive remedies: more private credit, more government borrowing, more confidence even if the mess was created by excessive confidence. Unfortunately, the only way for crisis responders to stop a financial panic is to remove the incentives for panic, which means preventing messy collapses of systemic firms, assuring creditors of financial institutions that their loans will be repaid, and generally reducing uncertainty in financial markets. In these severe cases, government needs to lean against the forces of gloom, borrowing more, spending more, and exposing taxpayers to more short-term risk—even if it looks profligate and immoral, even if it seems to reward incompetence and venality, even if it fuels perceptions of an out-of-control, money-spewing, bailout-crazed Big Government.

That's why we stood behind so many mismanaged firms. That's why we provided support for institutions and financial markets with more than $30 trillion in financial liabilities. And that's the main reason that people think we cared more about Wall Street than Main Street. The narrative of good-versus-evil was irresistible: We were saving irresponsible bankers while they continued to pay themselves huge bonuses. The conventional wisdom hardened quickly, and with a few honorable exceptions, the media rarely tried to explain that the situation was not so black-and-white.

We didn't do a good job of communicating the gray, either. That's partly because I wasn't a natural communicator. I remember that when I read Chief Justice John Roberts's decision upholding Obamacare, I felt envious of the clarity of his argument, whatever the quality of the legal reasoning. Nobody ever accused us of that kind of clarity. We were kind of busy, of course, and we faced a different kind of challenge. We didn't emphasize how awful things were in early 2009, because we didn't want to depress confidence further, and we didn't emphasize how much better things were getting later, because we didn't want to look like we were celebrating when so many Americans were still hurting. But I wasn't very eloquent—and rescuing banks from failure, protecting creditors from haircuts, and spending borrowed money after a borrowing boom were always going to be hard to explain.

Herein lies the paradox. In a brutal financial crisis like ours, actions that seem reasonable—letting banks fail, forcing their creditors to absorb losses, balancing government budgets, avoiding moral hazard—only make the crisis worse. And the actions necessary to ease the crisis seem inexplicable and unfair.

One benefit of our latest brush with catastrophe is that it illuminated as clearly as ever which kind of strategies are helpful in a crisis and which are not. We got to see the effect of our decisions in real time, and I hope the policymakers who have to confront the next crisis can learn from our successes as well as our mistakes. Because there will be a next crisis, despite all we did to improve the resilience of the system. Perhaps my experience can help future policymakers prepare for it, react to it, and try to defuse it before it does too much damage.

• • •

Y. V. REDDY, India's central banker, gave me a book during the crisis called *Complications: Notes from the Life of a Young Surgeon,* by Atul Gawande. He told me it was the best book I would ever read about central banking, and the parallels with financial crisis management really are striking. It's about making life-or-death decisions in a fog of uncertainty, dealing with the constant risk of catastrophic failure. It's not a coincidence that after the crisis wound down and I started watching some TV again, I got into *House M.D.,* the series about a misanthropic doctor who leads a team focusing on mysterious medical cases. I could relate—not to the misanthropy, but to the complex problem-solving, the inevitable complications, the team sitting around a table debating diagnosis and treatment.

That's financial crisis management, more or less. It's diagnosis and treatment, prevention and cure, triage and surgery. The stakes are high and the outcomes are uncertain. Every case is different, but some protocols can be applied broadly. Here, then, is a general framework for thinking about the craft of financial crisis management, along with some thoughts about how we applied it. I'll start with what policymakers need to do in advance to try to prevent and prepare for crises.

REINHART AND Rogoff titled their history of financial crises *This Time Is Different,* because experts always have clever reasons why the boom they're enjoying will avoid the disastrous patterns of the past— until it doesn't. We actually know what to look out for, especially a sustained rise in private borrowing relative to GDP, the phenomenon captured by the "Mount Fuji" chart that Lee Sachs showed me at the New York Fed. The other big danger sign is a sustained rise in uninsured short-term liabilities issued by the financial sector, the kind of money that can quickly run when good times stop rolling. This is scary when it builds up in highly leveraged banks; it can be even scarier when the risk and leverage migrate outside the traditional banking system to institutions and markets with less supervision and less access to the bank safety net.

Regulators can discern these warning signs, but they will never be omniscient or omnipotent. There's no way to be sure exactly when a bubble will pop, no certain way to prevent a mania from becoming a panic. Manias are inherently unpredictable, and regulators are not immune to them. Long periods of success in avoiding financial collapses can actually increase vulnerability to catastrophe, because stability can breed instability. At the New York Fed, I got to see how much power the belief in the "Great Moderation" had over smart people, and to witness its expression in the credit boom. Even though we leaned against the prevailing winds, warning about the growth of leverage and the risks of the shadow banking system, taking some useful steps to encourage stress-testing and limit the danger of derivatives, we were not forceful or creative enough, and we didn't have the tools necessary to avert disaster.

Financial crises can't be reliably anticipated or preempted, because human interactions are inherently unpredictable. But there is a lot that can be done in advance to make crises less damaging. These can be divided into *safeguards* that help reduce the likelihood and severity of crises, and *emergency authorities* that help policymakers limit the damage when crises erupt. The goal should not be to prevent the failure of firms that take on too much risk, but to make the system safe for their failure, to prevent their failures from unleashing panics that lead to crashes, to avoid the extreme crises that can lead to depressions when they spiral out of control.

The most important safeguards are the constraints on risk-taking that I've described as "shock absorbers," starting with strict capital requirements that restrict leverage and ensure that institutions can absorb losses in a downturn. Other shock absorbers include liquidity requirements that limit financial institutions' reliance on runnable short-term financing, deposit insurance and discount window access for depository institutions, margin requirements for derivatives and other financial instruments, and mortgage down-payment requirements that restrict leverage for ordinary borrowers. Making the risks in banks more transparent, as we did in the stress test, can also help limit the tendency of investors in a panic to run from everyone. To be effective, these safeguards must be applied broadly across the financial system, not just to the legal entities known as "banks" but to any large firm that behaves like a bank, borrowing money short-term in order to lend or invest it in longer-term assets. Otherwise, risk will just migrate to the unconstrained firms, fueling the growth of a parallel system with more leverage and more vulnerability to runs.

There are some economic costs to shock absorbers that require firms to operate with more conservative funding and thicker cushions of loss-absorbing capital, and the financial industry will always complain about them. But those costs are small compared to the economic benefits of less frequent and severe crises. Strong shock absorbers not only reduce the probability that any bank will fail, they reduce the risk that the failure of a bank—or a stock market crash, a real estate slump, or a recession—will create a panic that could threaten the rest of the system. They also reduce the danger that if a crisis does erupt, banks will have to rein in their lending to conserve capital, depriving the economy of financial oxygen and offsetting the power of crisis-fighting tools like fiscal and monetary stimulus.

Shock absorbers for borrowers are helpful, too. Higher down-payment requirements for homeowners provide a cushion in case of job losses, medical emergencies, or housing downturns, protecting the market as well as the individual borrowers. Initial margin requirements for investors not only limit their leverage and potential losses if prices fall, they limit the risk of forced fire sales to meet margin calls, and the vicious dynamics of margin spirals. Those kinds of tools can take some of the momentum out of a mania, reining in excessive risk-taking.

When firms and investors and ordinary families have strong appetites for risk, money tends to find its way around all those safeguards, the way water in a river flows over and around stones, the way risk migrated into the shadow banking system before our crisis. Regulators should try to expand the scope of those safeguards over time, to capture the changing sources of financial and economic risk, even though they will always lag behind the markets. Financial regulation will never keep up with financial innovation, but regulators should regard it as a constant challenge, and keep at it.

DURING THE boom before our crisis, U.S. capital and liquidity requirements were too weak, but they were strong enough to fuel a huge buildup of risk outside our traditional banking system—in Fannie and

Freddie, in investment banks like Bear and Lehman, in other non-banks like AIG and GMAC. The problem with our rules was not just that they were insufficiently conservative, but that they were too narrowly applied. At the New York Fed, I was worried that the major banks we helped supervise didn't have enough capital—as it turned out, some of them didn't—but I was even more worried about the thinly capitalized nonbanks outside our purview. I tried to raise awareness about these problems through my speeches and our horizontal risk reviews, pushing for more rigorous stress-testing and more conservative risk management. We managed to fix some of the plumbing problems in the derivatives market through our work with the Fourteen Families. And we did push to limit leverage in unregulated hedge funds through the "indirect channel" of our supervision of the banks that lent them money.

With the knowledge we have today, it's clear we didn't do enough. Before the crisis, I didn't push for the Fed in Washington to strengthen the safeguards for banks, nor did I push for legislation in Congress to extend the safeguards to nonbanks. I also could have tried to use the indirect channel of supervision more aggressively to rein in other parts of the shadow banking system that were connected to traditional banks, like tri-party repo, asset backed commercial paper, and the off-balance-sheet vehicles that ended up doing so much damage.

Our financial reforms have dramatically improved the safeguards in the system, forcing banks to hold more capital and rely less on short-term funding. The requirements are even tougher for larger banks, whose failure can cause even more damage. And the new financial stability council is now responsible for monitoring risks throughout the system, with the power to extend enhanced regulation where it's needed. Our oversight system is still flawed, but it now has more authority to respond to threats in the shadows. The Fed is also subjecting the largest banks to genuinely stressful stress tests, forcing them to imagine the unimaginable and maintain enough capital to survive it.

Our crisis, after all, was largely a failure of imagination. Every crisis is. For all my talk about tail risk, for all our concern about "froth," we didn't foresee how a nationwide decline in home prices could induce panic in the financial system sufficient to drag down the broader economy. But good crisis prevention does not depend on imagining the precise form of the unimaginable. You can't expect to preempt surprises. You just have to recognize that surprises will come, and force the system to build stronger defenses that can help it withstand the extreme ones.

THERE'S NO foolproof strategy to prevent financial fires, so policymakers also need to make sure they have adequate firefighting tools before fires start. If they don't have the authority to act, their crisis-management skills won't matter.

Two of the most vital tools, fiscal stimulus and monetary stimulus, don't require emergency authorities, but their effectiveness can still be enhanced or diminished in advance. A government in a strong fiscal position—with a modest budget deficit, if not a surplus, and a sustainable ratio of debt to GDP—will be in a better position to borrow at low rates to finance a massive temporary stimulus and maintain the stimulus as long as is necessary to cushion the effects of deleveraging. Similarly, on the monetary side, a central bank with a strong record of maintaining low inflation in the past will have more room to expand the money supply dramatically during a crisis without inviting too much fear of inflation in the future.

The deterioration of the U.S. fiscal position before the crisis, the product of the Bush administration's deficit-financed tax cuts and spending increases, helped limit the political appetite for a more aggressive and sustained fiscal response to the crisis. We could have afforded to do more than we did for a longer period of time, and the world would have financed it at low interest rates, but with the deficit already projected to be over $1 trillion before President Obama took office, there was significant opposition in Congress and among the public to additional doses of stimulus. Profligacy in good times can painfully constrain a government's ability to respond to crises, substantively and politically. By contrast, the Fed came into the crisis with a strong reputation for keeping inflation low, which helped Chairman Bernanke pursue such aggressive monetary policy actions without a damaging increase in inflation expectations, and helped make those actions more effective than they would have been without market credibility.

But no matter how responsibly governments and central banks act before a crisis, they need emergency authority that can be deployed quickly on a massive scale when a crisis hits, just as heads of state have the power to respond to a military attack. This authority should be reserved for the most dangerous situations, and there should be some uncertainty about its deployment to reduce the risk of moral hazard, but it should come with a lot of discretion and a lot of force.

What should be in the toolbox? The vital tools are: an ability to extend the lender-of-last-resort authority to provide liquidity where it's needed in the financial system; resolution authority to allow the orderly wind-down of failing financial firms; and, along with deposit insurance to prevent It's a Wonderful Life–style bank runs, broader emergency authority to guarantee other financial liabilities.

We went into our crisis with a toolbox that wasn't exactly empty, but also wasn't remotely adequate for our complicated and sprawling modern financial system. At times it felt like we were fighting World War III with General Washington's army. The Fed did use its authorities to provide liquidity throughout the shadow banking system, while supporting markets like tri-party repo and commercial paper. The FDIC had an excellent emergency room for banks of modest size, but the government did not have resolution authority for complex giants like Bear or Lehman or AIG, so we had no way to wind them down through an orderly process. The U.S. government as a whole fell too far behind the curve of the panic, lurching from emergency to emergency, averting disasters with duct tape and string and ad hoc authorities, failing to persuade the markets we had the ability to stop the run.

It was only after Hank Paulson and Ben Bernanke persuaded a reluctant and angry Congress to give us the authority to inject capital into troubled firms, and the FDIC agreed to guarantee bank debts, that we were able to break the momentum of the panic. We eventually put out the fire, and Congress ultimately provided resolution authority in Dodd-Frank, but we would have put out the fire a lot faster if we had had all those tools from the start, and that would have limited the damage suffered by millions of Americans.

While Dodd-Frank's resolution authority will help firefighters in the future, its elimination of the FDIC guarantee authority will hinder the response to the next crisis. And the final legislation took away the Fed's ability to intervene with specific firms, as it did with Bear, AIG, Citi, and Bank of America; that power wouldn't be as necessary if the FDIC still had broad guarantee authority, but losing both could be disastrous.

These firefighting authorities do create some moral hazard, just as the existence of smoke alarms and firehouses make smoking in bed feel somewhat less risky. But it's a lot better to have the power to put out the fire. The potential benefits of avoiding a depression far outweigh the potential costs of saving people who don't deserve to be saved. And when you have the ability to provide guarantees and other emergency assistance that can prevent a financial fire from spreading, you can afford to let the fire burn for a while.

In fact, once the time for prevention and preparation is over, letting the fire burn for a while is the right opening move.

In the early stages of a financial fire, there's no way to be sure if it's systemic, if the problems of a few firms reflect pervasive problems that will lead to a broader panic. Substantial increases in private credit, financial leverage, and short-term financing can all indicate a system's vulnerability to a severe crisis, but there are no clear thresholds that determine the boundary between the modest and catastrophic shock, the five-year and hundred-year flood. You have to feel your way.

This fog of diagnosis is among the toughest problems for a crisis manager. If you treat every shock as a catastrophe and ride to the rescue too quickly, you can create too much moral hazard and plant the seeds of a future catastrophe. Protecting private investors from the consequences of their risk-taking encourages risk-taking in the same way generous flood insurance can encourage excessive development in floodplains. But if you assume every shock will be benign and escalate too slowly, you risk letting a panic gain too much momentum. Once you fall behind the curve of a crisis, it can be hard to catch up.

There's nothing wrong with starting out tentative, as long as you're prepared to get aggressive if circumstances change. Letting the fire burn can help determine the severity of the crisis. It can also wipe out the weakest firms and the riskiest financing mechanisms, laying the groundwork for a restructuring of the financial system the way a natural wildfire can clear out the underbrush and improve the health of a forest.

But you don't want to let it burn too long or too hot. You don't want the fire to gain enough force to create a general panic that can consume relatively strong firms along with the hopelessly insolvent. And the line between containable and uncontainable is not always easy to discern. You can afford to start slow only if your government and central bank have the authority and the will to accelerate quickly into something approaching overwhelming force. Ideally, you want to provide just enough liquidity and other support for the system to prevent it from falling apart, but not so much that you sustain unsalvageable firms or unsustainable asset prices. The goal is to let the system start to adjust and deleverage without tipping into panic and collapse, which sounds a lot easier in theory than it is in practice.

In any case, once the fire burns too hot, once the mania turns to panic, once the diagnosis is complete and dire, the time for tentative is over.

• • •

THE INCONVENIENT truth of financial-crisis response is that the actions that feel right are often wrong. The natural instinct is to wait as long as possible before intervening, to escalate as gradually as possible, to minimize taxpayer exposure to losses, to impose stringent conditions on assistance, to teach the arsonists a lesson, to address the root causes of the crisis. Let failing firms fail. Let the creditors who financed their binges pay the price. But that is a recipe for making a systemic crisis worse. The public will want Old Testament justice, punishment for the venal. The moral hazard fundamentalists will want to send a message that irresponsible behavior will not be rewarded. If policymakers listen, they will court disaster.

The principles of effective crisis response are mostly counterintuitive. The more you commit to do, the less you'll have to do. If you take the extreme risk out of the market, you'll assume less risk of extreme losses, and you'll attract more private capital to provide stability that would otherwise require government capital. You should err on the side of doing too much rather than too little; you'll make mistakes no matter what, but you should try to make the mistakes that are cheaper to correct. It's easier to arrest a financial panic than to clean up after an economic disaster.

Eventually, you'll want to address the root causes of the crisis, to reform the financial system, to rein in excessive leverage. But as Saint Augustine said, not yet. In an emergency, you need to lean against the forces of panic, to restore confidence, to reduce uncertainty, to make the system investable again. That means no messy failures of systemic firms and no haircuts that would encourage runs. The goal is to make it irrational to run. There will be intense pressure to let major firms fail, avoid moral hazard, minimize government intervention. But that's a formula for a larger crisis that will ultimately require greater government intervention and create more moral hazard.

When the government does intervene, it will be tempting to try to maximize the immediate losses absorbed by the private sector, as the FDIC tried to do when it haircut WaMu's senior creditors. But in a severe crisis following a boom, the private sector is already by definition overextended and in retreat. It doesn't have the financial capacity to overwhelm the forces of panic, and shifting more risk its way will only amplify the panic, the way the WaMu haircuts prompted Wachovia's creditors to run. In general, the more the government commits to do up front, the less it will end up doing. The more risk taxpayers take up front, the less they end up paying.

The original Powell Doctrine emphasizes that military policymakers should go to war only as a last resort, and that is true of financial policymakers as well. But it's also true for financial policymakers that once war is unavoidable, you need to commit to overwhelming force—a combination of fiscal policy, monetary policy, and financial firefighting. None of those instruments will be powerful enough alone, and weakness in any of them will undermine the effectiveness of the others.

You should also plan for a long war. Long credit booms can produce a lot of damage that can require years of sustained government support for the economy to heal. The deleveraging process makes post-crisis recoveries slow and fragile. Governments tend to step on the brakes too early, weakening the recovery, adding to the economic costs as well as the fiscal costs of the war.

The playbook for monetary and fiscal policy is fairly simple. You want to be as expansive as possible, providing substantial stimulus for the economy for as long as necessary. After a major shock that depresses demand and creates a risk of deflation, central bankers should ease monetary policy, aggressively lowering interest rates. Once the overnight rate approaches zero, they should find new ways to stay on the accelerator, as Ben did through quantitative easing. They need to signal that they'll eventually hit the brakes, and that they'll remain vigilant about inflation going forward, but the threat of future inflation is much less worrisome than the threat of imminent deflation and depression. Loose monetary policy can have limited power in a crisis, because low interest rates don't help that much when borrowers don't want to borrow and lenders don't want to lend, but as the central bankers of the 1930s demonstrated, tight monetary policy can be disastrous.

On the fiscal side, the government should do as much as it can to reduce taxes and increase spending in order to offset the loss of wealth, the tightening of credit, and the collapse in private demand. It's important to make credible commitments to unwind this emergency stimulus down the road, especially if you go into the crisis with large deficits or unsustainable debt, but an emergency is no time to be preoccupied with immediate spending restraint or a quick path to balanced budgets. The composition of fiscal stimulus is important, too, and should ideally combine speed and power. Tax cuts tend to be fast but weak; infrastructure investments tend to be powerful but slow; aid to low-income families is fast as well as powerful. But in a crisis, you can't worry too much about optimal design. Politics will ultimately determine what gets done, and you can't afford to get bogged down in a protracted fight.

The financial rescue protocol is more complex. You want to conduct a form of triage that distinguishes between the insolvent and the merely illiquid, between firms that will never be viable and firms that just need protection from being caught in the stampede. You have to decide where to set the boundaries of your firewall, your defense against the run. If you set these too narrowly and leave too much undefended, you can get overwhelmed and allow too much damage, but if you set them too broadly, to try to save everyone, you can end up spending trillions of dollars, propping up zombie banks, and laying the groundwork for the next crisis.

There is no automatic formula for success. The inherent complexity and unpredictability of markets and human behavior require flexibility. Policymakers need authority, they need discretion to use their authority as the situation demands, and they should be accountable for having used that authority effectively and responsibly. In using that discretion, they should consider a few basic guidelines.

• • •

THE FIRST step in crisis management is classic Bagehot. A lender of last resort should make funding available to the banking system, starting with short-term loans backed by safe collateral, going longer and broader if needed. A central bank should lend freely, at a penalty rate, and the "freely" part is important. Ideally, you want to make the loans expensive, so that banks will replace them with private funds when the panic recedes, but you don't want them so expensive that borrowing becomes a signal of desperation. If the rate is too high, the stigma associated with borrowing will cause banks to sell assets and reduce lending instead, adding to the destructive pressures on the financial system and the economy. In general, crisis managers have to be careful about tying too many strings to emergency assistance, to avoid undermining its effectiveness.

If the financial system relies heavily on nonbank financing, you might need to backstop those markets and institutions as well, to protect them against runs. We extended Fed lending to investment banks before we brought the largest of them under the constraints of the banking system. We backstopped Fannie and Freddie by placing them into conservatorship. We also supported commercial paper and other highly-rated securities backed by mortgages, auto loans, credit cards, and student loans. If you allow runs outside the traditional bank safety net, they can cause a lot of damage in a hurry.

These funding facilities can be very powerful, but there is only so much risk that central banks can take. In a severe crisis, governments ultimately will need to take catastrophic risk off the table by guaranteeing a broader range of financial liabilities. They should charge a fee for the guarantees to help reduce reliance on them as conditions improve. They should cover catastrophic risk, not all risk. But there's no way to break a true panic without guarantees. While they're often attacked on moral hazard grounds, because they're seen as indulgence for the weak, they can actually reduce moral hazard, because you can let the weak fall only when you have the power to protect everyone else. And there's no way to attract private capital to a financial system in crisis without credible guarantees.

In our crisis, we expanded FDIC deposit insurance and guaranteed business transaction accounts at banks. The Treasury guaranteed money market funds, which were behaving like banks and experienced runs reminiscent of banks before there was deposit insurance. And once Sheila Bair agreed to use the FDIC's authority to guarantee new bank debt, we were able to remove some of the uncertainty that had hovered over creditors since the Lehman collapse and the WaMu haircuts. Unfortunately, our successors will have to go back to Congress and ask for the restoration of that authority when they need to put out a future financial fire.

Central bank lending and government guarantees are both essential. But crisis managers should also insist on forcing capital into the financial system quickly, to make sure it can eventually stand on its own and provide credit to the broader economy without support from the government. The financial community will always prefer naked guarantees—the more widely available and generously structured, the better—in part because they don't want shareholders to be diluted. But while guarantees are a vital short-term palliative, more capital is a long-term cure, preparing the financial system to support an economic recovery and absorb losses in the future. Naked guarantees can preserve the status quo, helping weak firms limp along in a dependent state, but that's not the goal of crisis management.

The goal is to stabilize and restructure the financial system so that it can lend again to families and productive businesses. Insolvent firms should be allowed to fail, but not to tear down the entire system in the process. Viable firms should be protected from the hysteria of the moment, but also required to thicken their capital buffers in order to survive a long and severe downturn. This kind of triage would be simple if policymakers had a perfect way to distinguish merely illiquid banks from insolvent ones during a crisis, along with unlimited resources they could use to provide guarantees to stop runs and inject capital to repair banks. But the real world doesn't work like that, so triage in a crisis is exquisitely hard. And if a country's financial system has been allowed to grow very large relative to its economy—as was the case in Ireland, Iceland, Switzerland, the United Kingdom, and other parts of Europe—it dramatically narrows the options available in extremis and makes triage even harder.

We conducted a lot of triage during our crisis, not all of it intentional. We allowed a lot of failure, and we pushed a lot of doomed firms into the arms of healthier competitors—not just out of deference to the Darwinian imperative, but also because we didn't have the authority to guarantee liabilities or inject capital into the system's weaker links. We got that authority after the horrific fall of Lehman, when Congress passed TARP and Sheila Bair agreed to put the FDIC's guarantee authority behind many bank liabilities. That quelled the panic for a few months. But the TARP capital and the FDIC guarantees were not unlimited. And as the broader economy deteriorated, ratcheting up the expected losses facing financial firms, markets once again lost confidence that we had the capacity to protect bank creditors and repair the financial system.

We designed the stress test to solve these problems for us, letting the private sector conduct our triage while committing government resources to avoid chaotic failures of systemic firms. By disclosing the losses the firms could face in a horrible downturn and forcing them to raise enough capital to survive that scenario, we let the market decide which ones could survive with private capital and how much government help the others would need. The objective of the stress test was to maximize the likelihood that private investors would recapitalize the system, minimize the eventual burden to the taxpayers, and ensure that the worst-capitalized firms would face the worst dilution. We hoped to limit the government's long-term involvement in the financial system and accelerate the restructuring necessary for the financial system to support growth.

It worked. The stress test was rigorous, its results were reassuring, and because the test was also transparent, those results were credible. We forced the system to raise enough capital so that it could survive a depression, and that made the depression less likely. Most of the banks that did need more capital had little trouble raising it from private investors; confidence returned so quickly that most of the TARP money invested in banks was paid back by the end of 2009.

We were certainly relieved that the stress test did not reveal massive capital shortfalls throughout the financial system, but it wasn't just a matter of luck that the banks proved healthier than the markets' worst fears. The combined force of the stimulus in the Recovery Act, the Fed's monetary policy actions, and our various programs to strengthen the guarantees behind the financial system, together with our commitment to recapitalize the financial system, convinced the world we weren't going to fall off the cliff. The stress test worked in part because these efforts began to get traction.

We used as much force as we could; in an epic crisis, caution is a much riskier strategy. And even though my maiden speech as Treasury secretary was a disaster, and the markets doubted the seriousness and the efficacy of our pledges to stabilize the system, we kept following through on our commitments, and the markets began to believe. We restored confidence in the financial system and the economy, even though the public lost confidence in their government.

DURING MY years as Treasury secretary, when my friends would ask me about Washington, my stock response was: "It's even worse than you think."

I would describe in vivid detail the challenges of dealing with the "hyenas" among the press corps—their shrill recitations of conventional wisdom about our latest outrages, their unwillingness to challenge simplistic black-and-white narratives, their refusal to correct the record when events proved them wrong. I would tell stories about the peacocks and jerks in Congress, showboating at hearings where very little hearing was ever done, kowtowing to donors and lobbyists and ideological advocacy groups, putting partisanship and popularity over the fate of the country. It was deeply discouraging to watch so many Republicans refuse to back President Bush on TARP or President Obama on anything when the fate of the entire economy was at stake, to hear them blame us for the deficits they created, to see how comfortable they were dragging the United States to the brink of default. And I was often frustrated with the populist left, which never seemed to recognize the very real constraints the President was facing or the progressive legacy he was compiling.

I despaired at the backbiting and posturing and political gamesmanship in Washington. It put all kinds of unnecessary obstacles in the way of good policy. I can't say I enjoyed my confirmation hearing, or the derisive reviews of my initial speech and the plan it promised, or the early demands for my resignation from liberals and conservatives alike. It wasn't fun for me, and it was especially hard on the people I love. But looking back at that period in our history with the benefit of some distance, I offer a revision: *It's better than you think.*

The financial crisis was a true stress test for the United States, a full-blown financial panic that obliterated $15 trillion in household wealth and triggered the worst recession in generations. It demanded the kind of response that democratic governments aren't built for—swift, consistent, coordinated action that prioritized the desperate needs of the nation over the immediate demands of the public. The crisis certainly exposed rot in our system. At times, our response was neither swift, nor consistent, nor coordinated. Some of the brutal costs of the crisis could have been prevented if we had adopted our eventual strategy earlier, more forcefully, and with more support across the government—and if we had continued the fiscal support longer.

But as dysfunctional as it seemed, Washington turned out to work better than people thought. A Republican president and a Democratic president both stood behind good policy at a time when the politics could not have been worse. Key financial policymakers—including intrepid Republicans like Hank Paulson and Ben Bernanke as well as impressive Democrats like Larry Summers and President Obama's other advisers—grappled with the crisis with a relentless focus on efficacy, not always agreeing but genuinely trying to figure out the right answers. We had incredible support from hundreds of public servants who worked insane hours without recognition or reward to help their country and the world.

And despite the steady stream of absurdity emanating from Capitol Hill, Congress did not ultimately block us from doing what needed to be done to save the financial system and the economy. In fact, at moments of extreme peril, enough of the nation's lawmakers—mostly Democrats, occasionally joined by a few brave Republicans—were willing to do the right thing to prevent an already tragic situation from metastasizing into a second Great Depression. It wasn't easy to fix the financial rules of the road to prevent similar disasters in the future, either, but again, a mostly Democratic coalition rose to the occasion, largely defying the power of financial interests, enacting comprehensive reforms that were not a panacea but were a tremendous improvement over the status quo.

I HAVE plenty of regrets about my time in public service, starting with all the pain I caused my family, through my absences as well as my public notoriety. I wish I had pushed harder to improve the financial system's ability to withstand a crisis of confidence when I was at the New York Fed. I wish I had figured out a way to respond more aggressively to the initial panic, and to sustain the initial power of our fiscal stimulus. I wish we had expanded our housing programs earlier, to relieve more pain for homeowners. I wish I had persuaded Congress to create more authority for the Fed and the Treasury in the financial reform legislation, and to make sure policymakers have the tools they need to engineer unpopular financial rescues in the future. And I wish I had done a better job of explaining our strategy, so that more Americans would have understood that we were working on their behalf, and wouldn't have lost so much faith in their government. I remember one of the times I offered to resign during the spring of 2009, when "embattled" seemed to be part of my official title, Rahm said I wouldn't be allowed to escape that quickly—but that when I did escape, I should probably expect my official Treasury portrait to be done in crayon.

I don't think the public ever really got to know me. Barbra Streisand said when we met at that state dinner that I must be all right because I was a Brooklyn Jew, which was kind of her, except that I'm not Jewish and I've never lived in Brooklyn. The broader misperception that I was a Wall Street lifer on loan to the government was damaging not just to me but to the President, and at times the country; even Angela Merkel seemed to think I spoke for the markets. I always tried to be a happy warrior, sometimes joking about my reputed past as a bankster, but these myths served to undermine people's faith in my motives and intentions and cast a shadow over everything we did. Now that I finally have escaped, and have chosen to learn a new craft in the investment world, I know I may reinforce those perceptions. I loved my work in government, and I'm proud of what I did in public life, but I couldn't do it forever.

I hope this book will help cast a brighter light on what we did and why we did it, because that's really important—not just for me and my colleagues, but for the country. The lingering public revulsion for what we did, for bailouts and stimulus and government intervention to resolve financial crises, is a serious problem for the policymakers who will stand in my shoes in the future. Because this time really was different. As bad as it was, it was better than it could have been, much better than the pattern of history.

I also hope this crisis encourages Americans to reconsider the value of strong public institutions and capable public servants. When we were successful in limiting the damage, it was with the force available only to governments and central banks. And there is no viable strategy for reducing the damage of future crises that does not depend on strong government rules and oversight, and the ability to attract talented people to oversee the system. The success of our financial rescue did not solve the many problems we still face as a nation, from high levels of poverty to global warming to appalling inequality in access to quality education and health care. These challenges will require better government—not necessarily more government, but smarter policies, designed on the merits, less distorted by politics and money. It would be good for the country if we could bring a similar level of creativity and ambition and force to these challenges, along with the quintessentially American pragmatism that helped keep us out of the financial abyss.

There are lessons for the world in our mistakes as well as our successes. My hope is that they won't have to be rediscovered in the fires of the next crisis.

TRIBUTE TO THE CRISIS TEAM

THE TEAM

There was a lot that was remarkable about this financial crisis—the force of the panic, the extent of the economic damage, the size and novelty of the financial programs, the degree of international cooperation, and the sting of the political backlash. Also exceptional were the people involved in the response and their spirit of cooperation. I wanted to recognize them and give you a sense of their contributions, since I could not do them justice in the book.

I am enormously grateful to President Obama, for asking me to work for him, pushing for an aggressive strategy, and sticking with it. And despite my efforts to escape, I am glad he compelled me to stay for his full first term. It was a great privilege to spend four years serving with him. Nothing we achieved would have been possible without his leadership and support.

The four main architects of the strategy—Hank Paulson, Ben Bernanke, Don Kohn, and I—worked together with a degree of mutual respect and confidence in one another that is exceptionally rare in Washington and that I had never seen in other countries faced with a crisis. We had our debates, and we made our mistakes, but we kept searching for what would work, trying to honor President Franklin D. Roosevelt's phrase that the country needed a period of bold, persistent experimentation.

We were very complementary in our backgrounds, with a fortunate combination of experience in markets, monetary policy, and financial crises as well as knowledge of the economics of depressions. And we were willing to take risks and adjust course and change our minds. We didn't peacock at one another's expense, and we didn't let our staffs do it in the press.

Larry Summers, with his uniquely high ratio of thrill to torture, pushed and pushed to get us closer to the frontier of the possible. I valued and relied on his counsel, even when it was most uncomfortable.

Hank Paulson brought together a very strong group of financial talent to the Treasury. Dan Jester and Steve Shafran helped design some of the largest and most complicated financial interventions and programs in history, including the GSE conservatorship, the money market guarantee program, and the TARP capital injections of 2008. They had a lot of help within Paulson's Treasury from Bob Hoyt, Neel Kashkari, David Nason, and Ken Wilson, among many others.

Ben Bernanke and Don Kohn directed the vast resources of the Federal Reserve toward solving the crisis during its most active period in history. Janet Yellen, as president of the San Francisco Fed and then as vice chairman of the Board was a thoughtful and consistent advocate of more aggressive policy at those dangerous moments when it was most vital for the central bank to act; the Fed will be in good hands with her as its chair. Kevin Warsh was a great resource to Ben, present on virtually every crisis conference call, providing his valuable mix of financial market and political advice. The governors of the Federal Reserve Board and the other members of the FOMC gave the chairman the votes he needed to act, even when many were deeply uncomfortable.

The barons of the Federal Reserve Board staff—Scott Alvarez, Brian Madigan, David Stockton, and David Wilcox—helped Ben and Don expand the frontiers of central banking, not just in the design of the emergency liquidity and credit programs, but in finding ways to help monetary policy continue to help the economy after short-term interest rates were brought to zero. Michelle Smith did a masterful job improving the transparency of Fed decisions, and she was a valuable source of guidance on many of the toughest policy questions we faced.

Also on the staff of the Federal Reserve Board, Tim Clark, Mike

Foley, Andreas Lehnert, Nellie Liang, and Coryann Stefansson—working closely with Bev Hirtle, Kevin Stiroh, and others from the New York Fed—led the design of the stress test and guided teams of analysts and supervisors from across the regulatory community in its execution. These individuals deserve enormous credit for its success.

I have particular admiration for the work of Pat Parkinson, who was a great partner to my New York Fed colleagues in the design of many of the liquidity and credit programs. Pat and Mark Van Der Weide, another exceptionally knowledgeable Fed staffer, came to work at Treasury in early 2009 and were central in helping to design the financial reforms.

At the New York Fed, I had the privilege of working with a very talented group of classic central bankers. Tom Baxter, Terry Checki, Bill Dudley, Sandy Krieger, Chris McCurdy, Bill Rutledge, Joe Tracy, Simon Potter, and Jamie McAndrews, along with Chris Cumming, carried most of the burden of educating and advising me, first as we were trying to lean against the wind of the financial boom, and then as we were trying to contain the fire.

Meg McConnell, as my adviser, played a critical role in all we did—sharp and funny, amazingly hardworking, always seeing the cloud in any silver lining, always searching for a deeper understanding of every problem, always pushing for a smarter response.

Mike Silva was my able chief of staff, often pushing me to action, always providing balance and stability during a period when both were rare. Michael Held, the corporate secretary, graciously shared many of Silva's responsibilities during the most intense periods of the crisis and provided me with critical support as I transitioned from the New York Fed to the Treasury.

The unique amalgam of talent and expertise that is the New York Fed—economists; analysts; bank supervisors; traders; experts in payment, clearing, and settlement infrastructures; and many others—coalesced into a relentlessly innovative crisis fighting team. They worked together to diagnose and solve problems the Fed had never before confronted. Their insights and actions were central to the development and execution of the arsenal of Fed credit and liquidity facilities—with the confusing acronyms of TAF, TSLF, PDCF, CPFF, AMLF, TALF; to the special facilities of the Bear Stearns and AIG interventions; and to the overall strategy for recapitalizing the financial system. They worked in complete obscurity, never seeking credit, with months and months of endless days and nights, remaining focused and calm as the world was burning around them. They were brave and careful, taking exceptional risks and working diligently to manage those risks despite the turmoil and uncertainty.

As a measure of the extent of their teamwork and their non-peacock tendencies, when I would later ask any one of them to remind me who deserved most credit for one thing or another, the common response was, "It was a mix of us." That mix included Art Angulo, Adam Ashcraft, Sarah Dahlgren, Jeanmarie Davis, Richard Dzina, Ken Garbade, Joyce Hansen, Spence Hilton, Bev Hirtle, Michael Holscher, Lori Logan, Theo Lubke, Jamie McAndrews, Meg McConnell, Susan McLaughlin, Helen Mucciolo, Simon Potter, Marc Saidenberg, Mike Schetzel, Til Schuermann, Kevin Stiroh, and legions of others.

Tanshel Pointer and Marlene Williams ran the Office of the President, during the most exacting moments of the crisis, managing a blizzard of conference calls and meetings while working terrible hours. And Tanshel gave me the most generous gift of moving to Washington to work at the Treasury for the first few months of the new administration.

Under Nick Proto's guidance, the FRBNY's security force took very good care of me. I am particularly indebted to officers Eric Brisbon, Charles Henderson, Joseph Mitchell, Cary Newberry, Joe Sclafani, and Jorge Vasquez.

I am very grateful to the directors of the Board of the Federal Reserve Bank of New York. They gave me a lot of advice and support. With the demands of the crisis, it was a bit more than they bargained for. Pete Peterson and John Sexton were serving as chairman and deputy chairman when I started. John Sexton became chairman in 2004 and was succeeded by Jerry Speyer, then Steve Friedman. Jerry Speyer also served ably as deputy chairman prior to becoming chairman and was succeeded by Denis Hughes.

The FDIC, led by Sheila Bair, oversaw the delicate, complicated process of taking over and resolving hundreds of failed banks with a system that is the envy of countries around the world. And then under her successor, Marty Gruenberg, the FDIC designed an innovative framework for dealing with the failure of large complex financial institutions in the future.

John Dugan's OCC played a valuable role in the messy triage of the crisis and in the design of our strategy to recapitalize the banking system.

At Treasury, I was privileged to work with an incredibly talented, hardworking, ethical group of career civil servants and political appointees. The team of senior political appointees that came to Treasury to work for the President took on a crushing burden of policy challenges with grace and poise, never complaining, full of humor, proud to be working for their country. They gave me all sorts of ideas, and executed them with skill. They were quick to challenge me, and never too deferential.

I am recognizing here the individuals most central to the design of the financial rescue and the reforms, but we also had a superb group of colleagues managing the complexity of tax policy, our financial sanctions regime, the government's payments system, the Treasury borrowing strategy, and a great deal of other important work. They are too numerous to mention, but I am grateful to them all and proud to have been their colleague.

Richard Gregg, a thirty-five-year Treasury veteran and the most senior career official, who agreed to return from retirement as fiscal assistant secretary, once stopped in my office to tell me that this was the most impressive team at Treasury he had ever seen. What he found remarkable was not just their competence, but how effectively they worked together.

As President Obama took office, in the eerie quiet of those empty hallways on the third floor of the Treasury building, twenty-two Obama appointees came to work at Treasury that first day, when I was still awaiting confirmation: Marti Adams, Sarah Apsel, Sara Aviel, Stephanie Cutter, Al Fitzpayne, Paige Gebhardt, Amias Gerety, Mary Goodman, Michelle Greene, Julie Herr, Matt Kabaker, Jenni LeCompte, Jacob Leibenluft, Pat Maloney, Andrew Mayock, Brian Osias, Mark Patterson, Lee Sachs, Ian Solomon, Gene Sperling, David Vandivier, and Kim Wallace.

Six of them stayed at Treasury until the end of President Obama's first term—Al Fitzpayne, Amias Gerety, Julie Herr, Jenni LeCompte, Pat Maloney, and Mark Patterson—and several have stayed into the second term.

Steve Shafran, Neel Kashkari, and Seth Wheeler, who had all worked for Hank Paulson, did me and their country a great favor by agreeing to stay on for a time and continue the work they had begun in the fall of 2008.

Lee Sachs left his work and family in New York to come to Washington in November 2008 and oversee the transition from the Bush to the Obama Treasury. He introduced me to Matt Kabaker, and together they formed the core of the group formulating that next stage of the financial strategy.

Lee ran the coordinating process with the Fed and other regulators. He also managed the diplomacy with the rest of the economic team, so that they had the right sense of involvement without ceding too much influence. He oversaw the design of the full slate of new programs we deployed in 2009 to get the financial system working again. Careful and unassuming, always worried about what might go wrong, Lee was the decisive factor in the success of those programs.

Mary Goodman, who worked for Larry Summers during the

transition and then at the White House, was a great source of ideas and judgment.

Lew Alexander, formerly of the Fed's international staff, served as the economic conscience of the Treasury financial team.

Jeffrey Goldstein and Mary Miller served successively as undersecretaries for Domestic Finance, and backing them up were Michael Barr, Matthew Rutherford, Cyrus Amir-Mokri, and Richard Gregg, the "dean" of the Office of Domestic Finance. I could not have had a better team of market experts as we dealt with so many difficult challenges, including the insanity of multiple debt-ceiling impasses.

Also in Domestic Finance, Herb Allison ran the TARP programs in the first two years and was succeeded by Tim Massad; together they and their team earned four clean audits. They ably managed our investments, recovering every dollar and even generating billions of dollars of returns for the taxpayer.

Sam Hanson, David Scharfstein, Jeremy Stein, and Adi Sunderam took leave from Harvard to advise Larry and me and were an enormously valuable source of ideas.

George Madison and then Chris Meade led a very strong group of lawyers, including Peter Bieger, Bernie Knight, Laurie Shaffer, and Chris Weideman.

The housing team, which over those four years included Michael Barr, Tim Bowler, Phyllis Caldwell, Darius Kingsley, Michael Stegman, and Seth Wheeler, designed and implemented a creative mix of programs that helped millions of struggling homeowners, despite the terribly frustrating constraints they faced.

The auto team, led by Steve Rattner and Ron Bloom, with a lot of help from Brian Deese at the National Economic Council, conceived and executed a very successful restructuring of General Motors and Chrysler, saving hundreds of thousands of jobs and restoring both firms to profitability.

Neal Wolin, who parachuted in at a fraught time as deputy secretary, was my closest adviser on the most important challenges we faced, all while helping to manage the vast Treasury empire. He ably represented Treasury around the world and across the street in the White House situation room, where the National Security Council met constantly.

Neal led the financial reform negotiations on the Hill, with Michael Barr and Diana Farrell, aided by the extremely capable Amias Gerety as well as Laurie Schaffer's excellent team of lawyers. And Neal oversaw the tortured, complicated Dodd-Frank implementation process, including building the new Financial Stability Oversight Council and the Office of Financial Research.

Jim Millstein, Treasury's chief restructuring officer, took on the seemingly impossible task of recovering the taxpayers' investments in AIG. With his help, and that of the NY Fed team led by Sarah Dahlgren, the taxpayers ultimately made a $23 billion profit on those investments.

Two distinguished economists, Alan Krueger from Princeton and Jan Eberly from Northwestern, served ably as assistant secretaries for economic policy. John Bellows, who had lent his economic genius to the 2008 Obama campaign, was a great source of advice on the fiscal wars.

Lael Brainard, with her signature mix of toughness and skill, led Treasury's international team, and in particular our policy toward the European financial crisis and China. Charles Collyns and Marisa Lago were her top lieutenants. Ted Truman and Mark Sobel came up with much of the G-20 strategy in the financial crisis and laid the groundwork for international coordination on regulatory reform. Christopher Smart and Brad Setser carried much of the burden of the European crisis.

The relentless and amazing Gene Sperling was incredibly valuable to me, first as counselor at the Treasury for two years, and then after the President asked him to succeed Larry Summers as head of the NEC.

After the fierce and talented Stephanie Cutter ascended to the

White House, Jenni Engebretsen LeCompte led Treasury's communications staff, with her wonderful combination of calm and skill, working under great duress to explain and defend our strategy to a skeptical public.

Jake Siewert, who served as President Clinton's last press secretary at the age of twenty-eight, lent us his remarkable talent as a counselor for twenty-six months, providing his exceptional candle power and creativity, and his wry humor, to everything consequential.

Michael Mundaca served as my assistant secretary for tax policy, followed by Emily McMahon and Mark Mazur. They capably handled a vast and complex array of tax issues during the crisis and the fiscal debates, and in development of proposals for tax reform.

Kim Wallace, later succeeded by Al Fitzpayne, served as assistant secretary for legislative affairs. They guided me around the dangers, toils, and snares of the Hill and absorbed nonstop incoming fire, yet in keeping with the Treasury way, they were always magnanimous and never let the stress show.

Sara Aviel was my invaluable adviser for the most grueling part of the President's first term. Self-appointed progressive conscience of the Treasury, she worked the longest hours, traveled on every trip, and brought her exceptionally high standards to helping to run the Treasury. After becoming deputy chief of staff, Wally Adeyemo later took on much of the travel burden with his characteristic cool efficiency.

Shirley Gathers and Cheryl Matera ran my office, always present and thoughtful, extremely capable, with seventy years of combined history at Treasury. They took care of me, looked out for me, during endless days and weekends, with their special style of smiling, reassuring competence.

Julie Herr, who had been a colleague in the Clinton Treasury Department, returned to run the busy scheduling and advance office. Her judgment, unflappability, mastery of logistics, and knowledge of protocol ensured that every foreign trip and every event we hosted at Treasury went off without a hitch. She was ably assisted by Daniel Balke, Bhumi

Shah, Elizabeth Ashwell, and a team of terrific advance people whose work was unseen and unglamorous but deeply appreciated.

Mark Patterson served as chief of staff—enforcer of the "no jerks, no peacocks, no whiners" regime, vital counselor on every issue, master of strategy on the debt limit and the fiscal wars, patient adviser and protector to me.

I am particularly grateful to the men and women of the Secret Service who protected the employees of the Treasury during my tenure, and to those who served on my Secret Service detail. Sean McCarthy, Curtis Nelson, and Dan Connolly led the teams that stood with me twenty-four hours a day, in cities around the world, during those four years. Jim Gorman, Greg Ligouri, Chris Emery, Jay Nasworthy, Todd Rassas, and Chris Gaskell were all part of that capable team of protectors. George Morgenthaler, a former sniper, was at the helm of the armored Suburban most of my Treasury time. We had some fun together. I am deeply honored by their service to me and my family.

A final thanks to some friends who offered me shelter and food during my first year away from home. Dan Zelikow and Marcelo Sanguinetti let me stay in their beautiful home for most of nine months. Merna and Joe Guttentag also lent me their apartment for several weeks. Blair Downing, who was the first person I met in my first job at the Treasury in 1988, brought me multiple dinners without ever being asked.

Public service is filled with opportunities to make a positive difference, but it comes with challenges. I did it for twenty-five years because I believed in the cause and loved the craft of economic policy. But that would not have been true without the people around me who chose to devote some or all of their careers to serving their country. The commitment and the public spiritedness of my colleagues in government are, for me, what made it truly rewarding and worthwhile. I will always be grateful to them for their dedication and their friendship.

ACKNOWLEDGMENTS

Charlie Rose asked me once when I was Treasury secretary if I was planning to write a book. I was thinking about it, but I was reluctant, and I told him then that I wasn't the kind of person who liked to sit in a room alone and write. I also didn't like the idea of writing in the first person about a set of decisions that so many others were involved with. I was concerned about the frailty of memory, the temptation to rely on the wisdom of hindsight, to reimagine events in a more favorable light. I did not think I had the patience to sit still long enough to do it. And I am not a natural writer.

But I thought about it more and decided I should try to write something useful. I was fortunate to have a lot of help.

Richard Haass gave me the great gift of an office at the Council on Foreign Relations and generous support for me and two colleagues. This was the second time I was able to benefit from the Council's graces; the first time was in early 2001, when I left the Treasury after the end of President Clinton's administration.

Bhumi Shah—always calm and cheerful—agreed to come with me from Treasury and continue to apply her remarkable mix of management and organizational skills to my complicated life.

Robert Barnett did me the favor of guiding me through the process of presenting a book to the publishing world and advising me on a range of other challenges, with his famous and rare mix of practical wisdom.

I am grateful to Molly Stern and Vanessa Mobley at Crown for agreeing to take on this book and to Vanessa for her support and guidance, and for her many valuable contributions as editor.

Michael Grunwald agreed to join me as a collaborator, taking leave from *Time,* and worked valiantly to make the dark and complex mess of financial crises compelling and accessible. We didn't know each other, and he had not covered the financial crisis from beginning to end, but I had read and admired his work. He was smart and wonderfully well-prepared, and brought a fresh and interesting perspective that was exceptionally valuable. He was relentless in pushing me to explain better the choices we made and the nature of our debates, and to add some life and color to our failures and our successes.

Charlie Anderson, who had worked closely with me at Treasury, did extensive analysis and research on the economics and the politics of this financial crisis, and helped make sure we were grounded in fact, unpeeling the layers of myth and misperception. He ran the exacting, complicated process of producing a book with grace and skill.

Charlie convinced two other talented former Treasury colleagues, Mike Schmidt and Ian Samuels, to join us. They provided excellent research support, with Schmidt delivering especially thoughtful insights on financial reform and Samuels bringing his oracular knowledge of financial markets to bear on disentangling the story of the crisis.

Sam Hanson and Adi Sunderam, both professors at Harvard Business School, who had each spent a year in the administration working for Larry Summers and me, reviewed the book as we wrote it, assessing the economics of our explanations, helping to point out the weaknesses in my framework of lessons and ideas for better crisis prevention and response.

A wide range of my former colleagues at the Fed and Treasury spent time with Charlie, Mike, and me, going over the history of our key decisions, reviewing what we missed, reflecting on the paths we did not take. They did this generously and patiently, and with great care and reflection. They demonstrated—as they so often had in the crisis—that they were more than willing to push back at me, to disagree, and to challenge, a service that is invaluable to anyone who has had to make complicated decisions. Those long dinners and meetings made me appreciate anew how incredibly fortunate I was in the quality of people I got to serve with at the Fed and at Treasury.

This group of participants in our effort to revisit history included Tom Baxter, Terry Checki, Bill Dudley, Meg McConnell, Helen Mucciolo, Marc Saidenberg, Mike Schetzel, Mike Silva, and Kevin Stiroh from the New York Fed; Tim Clark, Don Kohn, Sandy Krieger, Pat Parkinson, and Mark Van Der Weide from the Federal Reserve Board; and Michael Barr, Matt Kabaker, Jenni LeCompte, Mark Patterson, Lee Sachs, Laurie Schaffer, Jake Siewert, Mark Sobel, and Ted Truman from Treasury.

In addition to my editor Vanessa Mobley, a number of former colleagues reviewed and commented on the chapters. Tom Baxter, Matt Kabaker, Jenni LeCompte, Meg McConnell, Chris Meade, Mark Patterson, Laurie Richardson, Lee Sachs, Jake Siewert, Josh Steiner, and Neal Wolin reviewed the entire book. Brad Setser and Ted Truman reviewed the international pieces. Michael Barr, Laurie Shaffer, and Mark Van Der Weide read the sections on financial reform. I am incredibly grateful for the time they spent and for the quality of their suggestions.

My wife, Carole Geithner, stood with me, read every word, patiently commented on every chapter. I have always envied and admired her skill as a writer, and I am so lucky to be able to benefit from it in this book. She helped me remember many things I had forgotten or blocked out, and she pushed me to be more open and candid about the worst things, the fear and the anger and the doubt.

She did not want me to be secretary of the Treasury, and she had the worst part of the deal, carrying the sense of responsibility and obligation I felt, and the loss of privacy and loss of time together as a family. I am so grateful for her love and support, for being willing to let me do work that I found so deeply interesting, consequential, and satisfying, and for helping me do it with more maturity and care and wisdom, however limited, than I ever could have done on my own.

I am grateful to my spirited and creative children, Elise and Ben, for being patient with me, putting up with the burdens of a father in public life with grace and humor, and welcoming me back into their lives after my long absences.

My sister, Sarah Adam, and my brothers, Jonathan and David Geithner, after relentlessly teasing me when we were kids, were protective and loyal when it meant the most to me.

And I am so grateful to my parents, Deborah and Peter, who gave me the horizon-expanding experience of a childhood living in other countries, their shining example of generosity and humility, and the invaluable gifts of love and confidence.

AUTHOR'S NOTE

In writing this book, I relied on my memory of events, aided by the recollections of my colleagues and the documentary record at the Federal Reserve Bank of New York and the Treasury. This documentary record was extensive and very valuable, though it did not include comprehensive contemporaneous notes by participants of the innumerable meetings and phone calls where the consequential decisions were made.

I did not take notes of meetings, and I wrote little of substance in email, mostly because of the extraordinary pace and burden of the events of that time. I try to describe what I was thinking, to the best of my recollection. As a check, however imperfect, against the limitations of memory, I tested my recollections against the memories of those men and women who thought through those decisions with me.

I tried to write the bulk of this book without having read any of the existing histories that covered portions of this crisis, so that my memory was not altered by those reports. But as I got further along, I checked my account against those of other participants, most importantly Hank Paulson's excellent book, *On the Brink*, and those based on extensive reporting at the time by journalists, most notably David Wessel's *In Fed We Trust* and Andrew Ross Sorkin's *Too Big to Fail*.

Where I quote directly from meetings or conversations, I do so only when I am confident that I was able to capture the essence of what was said. A few of the quotes have appeared in other accounts of the crisis; I included those where I provided the quote to those authors during their reporting, or I was a witness to the conversation recounted.

Our decisions were quite naturally the subject of extensive internal and external debate. I have tried to describe those debates and to represent fairly the beliefs of those who opposed or were uncomfortable with my choices.

This manuscript was carefully reviewed for accuracy by a wide range of my former colleagues at the Treasury and the Fed. But I alone am responsible for any failures to accurately portray these events.

NOTES

Introduction: The Bombs

14 have averaged more than 10 percent of GDP: Studies of the direct fiscal costs of the financial crisis have found that financial crisis responses are typically very expensive for taxpayers. For instance, in 2008, Luc Laeven and Fabian Valencia, both IMF researchers, published a study of forty-two financial crises between 1970 and 2007 that estimated that the direct fiscal costs, net of recoveries, averaged about 13.3 percent of GDP. In early 2009, the IMF estimated that the cost of U.S. financial crisis response would be 12.7 percent of GDP. These estimates do not take into account broader losses imposed on the economy, for instance, through lower GDP and higher unemployment.

Two: An Education in Crisis

48 had a fixed exchange rate: Technically, Mexico had a "crawling" exchange rate peg, meaning the government would allow the rate to move slowly over time. This was a distinction without much of a difference: The Mexican government intervened aggressively enough that the exchange rate moved far more slowly than if it had been determined by market forces, and that left it overvalued.

48 short-term bonds called *tesobonos*: *Tesobonos* were structured so that Mexico would pay back the borrowers in however many pesos it took to produce the dollar amount of the bond. So if a dollar was worth 3 pesos, a *tesobono* holder owed $100 would receive 300 pesos. But if Mexico broke the peg and a dollar became worth 6 pesos, the same bondholder would receive 600 pesos. So for Mexico, borrowing in *tesobonos* carried some of the same currency risks as borrowing in dollars directly.

48 But it had an immediate *liquidity* problem: The distinction between illiquidity and insolvency is not black-and-white, and it's hard to apply to governments, who, after all, have the ability to tax. An insolvent firm is fundamentally unable to repay its debts in the long run, while an illiquid firm doesn't have enough cash on hand to pay its bills coming due in the near term. If an illiquid but solvent institution is lent sufficient funds to address its near-term problems, it will be able to sustain itself over time. Lending to an insolvent institution, by contrast, risks throwing good money after bad. We thought Mexico was experiencing a "sovereign liquidity crisis"; its overall debt load was manageable, but the burden of its short-term obligations was too great.

Three: Leaning Against the Wind

81 "sufficient cushion against adversity": Remarks Before the New York Bankers Association's Annual Financial Services Forum, "Change and Challenges Facing the U.S. Financial System," March 25, 2004.

81 it could go to the Fed's discount window: The "discount window" is the facility through which the Fed provides collateralized loans to depository institutions that are judged to be in sound financial condition, at a discount to the value of the collateral. This discount provides additional protection to the Fed; if the borrower were to default, the Fed would own collateral with a higher value than the amount it lent to the borrower. The name survives from the days when depository institutions would actually send a representative to a Fed bank teller window in order to access the facility.

81 "shadow banks": *Shadow banking* is a term often used to describe entities with bank-like risk that are not regulated as banks. There is no precise definition of shadow banking, and some use it very broadly to include financial instruments as well as a wide range of financial firms, from investment banks to insurance companies to money market funds. One qualification to this popular descriptor is that many of the largest firms and markets described as "shadow" activity were operating in broad daylight, as public companies or subject to the public disclosure requirements of securities laws.

82 Chart, The Rise of "Shadow Banking": Methodology based on "Financial Stability Monitoring: Federal Reserve Bank of New York Staff Report no. 601" (2013), Tobias Adrian, Daniel Covitz, and Nellie Liang. "Shadow banks" derived from flow of funds data: commercial paper (L.208), federal funds and security repurchase agreements (L.207), GSE liabilities and agency- and GSE-backed mortgage pools (L.123 & L.124), asset-backed securities (L.125), and money market funds (L.120), net of GSE repo (L.207), GSE holdings of GSE debt and GSE-backed mortgage pools (L.123), ABS holdings of GSE-backed mortgage pools (L.125), money market fund holdings of repos (L.120), commercial paper (L.208), and GSE-backed securities (L.120). This does not include hedge funds and other investment funds, which some also include in definitions of "shadow banking."

85 exploiting their implicit federal backstop: Prior to the crisis, markets expected that the government would step in to prevent the failure of Fannie and Freddie if they ran into trouble, in part because they were "government sponsored." There was no explicit legal requirement for the government to bail them out, and government officials would loudly deny that any "implicit guarantee" existed. But

Fannie and Freddie were able borrow at cheap interest rates, reflecting the expectation of government support.

92 "risk-weighted assets": A bank's capital level is generally expressed as a ratio relative to its assets, adjusted for their riskiness. These "risk weightings" mean that the bank has to hold less capital against safe assets like Treasuries as compared to riskier assets like corporate loans. However, risk-weightings before the crisis were crude and did a poor job of fully differentiating between the riskiness of assets.

92 leverage dramatically increases "wipeout risk": Under the regulations that applied at the time, a bank had to have about $8 of "capital" for every $100 of risk-weighted assets, and about $3 of capital for every $100 of total assets, without adjusting for risk. But, in addition to common equity, banks were allowed to count as capital a variety of hybrid debt-like instruments, such as trust-preferred securities (TruPS) and cumulative perpetual preferred securities, which were less able to absorb losses in a downturn. Investment banks and other nonbanks had no comparable constraints on leverage during the boom, and the markets enabled some of those institutions to take on significantly more leverage than banks were allowed to under the prevailing regulations.

94 "even at the most sophisticated institutions": Remarks at the Institute of International Bankers Luncheon in New York City, "Challenges in Risk Management," October 18, 2005.

94 "could be more acute": Remarks at the Institute of International Finance, Inc.'s Annual Membership Meeting in Washington, D.C., September 25, 2005.

94 "future stresses to the financial system": Remarks Before the Economic Club of New York, "Perspectives on the U.S. Financial System," May 27, 2004.

94 "prepare for war or instability": Remarks Before the Conference on Systemic Financial Crises at the Federal Reserve Bank of Chicago, "Changes in the Structure of the U.S. Financial System and Implications for Systemic Risk," October 1, 2004. This is an adaptation of a common maxim among military analysts.

94 "How do we generate . . . the immediate future looks strong?": Remarks Before the Economic Club of Washington, D.C., February 9, 2005.

96 just 3 percent of assets . . . barely 1 percent of the assets: These capital ratios are measures of common equity relative to total assets. Because the investment banks and Fannie and Freddie were not regulated like banks, there were not good comparative measures of capital relative to risk-weighted assets for investment banks or GSEs in the pre-crisis period.

98 imposed few constraints on leverage: The SEC created the Consolidated Supervised Entity (CSE) program in 2004 to supervise the investment banks on a consolidated basis, meaning that the SEC would be responsible for supervising all of their subsidiaries. The program was developed in response to requirements that financial firms operating in Europe have a consolidated supervisor—and the threat that if we didn't figure out a way to supervise our investment banks the Europeans would do it for us. But the investment banks participated in this program voluntarily; the SEC did not have the legal authority available to bank supervisors to impose bank-like limits on leverage and liquidity risks, and systemic risk was not their mandate or their expertise.

102   crises that do erupt more damaging and harder to contain: Remarks at the New York University Stern School of Business Third Credit Risk Conference, New York City, "Implications of Growth in Credit Derivatives for Financial Stability," May 16, 2006; Remarks at the Distinguished Lecture 2006, sponsored by the Hong Kong Monetary Authority and Hong Kong Association of Banks, Hong Kong, "Hedge Funds and Derivatives and Their Implications for the Financial System," September 15, 2006.

102   Trades remained unconfirmed for months: Post-trade confirmation is an important part of the process of completing a derivatives transaction. Leaving a trade unconfirmed can result in large amounts of legal uncertainty, accelerating fear if the validity of a trade is called into question during periods of increased market stress. The back office plumbing for derivatives was so primitive that often trade information would be exchanged by phone or fax, scribbled on paper, and stuffed in desk drawers or filing cabinets.

108   adjusting the "federal funds rate": To raise or lower interest rates, the Federal Open Market Committee (FOMC) traditionally establishes a "target" rate for short-term lending between banks. It then executes this monetary policy by buying and selling securities through "open market operations," so that the effective federal funds rate (the rate actually paid for banks to borrow from one another) stays close to the target rate.

108   that the "Greenspan Put": A "put" is a derivatives transaction in which one party insures the other against a decline in the value of a particular asset. When central banks adopt accommodating monetary policies in response to market distress, critics often condemn them as giving investors an implied, broad-based put—in the form of protection from the risk of further declines in prices.

109   a situation Greenspan dubbed "the conundrum": Ordinarily, the Fed can influence the rates on mortgages and other long-term debt by adjusting short-term rates. But this relationship broke down during my time at the New York Fed; as Alan Greenspan noted in his crisis postmortem, the correlation between long-term and short-term rates dropped from 0.86 in the twenty years that preceded the pre-crisis bubble to 0.10 in the period from 2002 to 2005.

111   "adverse tail, or the negative extreme": Remarks at the 2007 Credit Markets Symposium hosted by the Federal Reserve Bank of Richmond, Charlotte, North Carolina, "Credit Markets Innovations and Their Implications," March 23, 2007.

Four: Letting It Burn

123 "commercial paper": Commercial paper is short-term debt that matures within 270 days. Broadly speaking, it comes in two forms. "Unsecured" commercial paper represents a general obligation of the company that issues it; its riskiness depends on the creditworthiness of the issuer (that is, the borrower). "Asset-backed" commercial paper (often referred to as "ABCP") is secured by collateral, such as mortgage-backed securities; its riskiness depends on both the quality of the underlying assets and any financial support promised, or perceived to be promised, by the company arranging for the issuance of the ABCP. Countrywide funded its business with both unsecured commercial paper and ABCP.

124 BoNY's role in tri-party repo: Under a repurchase agreement (or a "repo"), one party agrees to sell securities to another party, while agreeing to repurchase them at a pre-specified price and date, often as soon as the next day—in effect a short-term, secured loan. This allows the "borrower" of a repo to borrow cash from the "lender," using the underlying securities as collateral. In the "tri-party" repo market, a "clearing bank" functions as a third party facilitating this transaction, matching lenders and borrowers and managing the flows of cash and securities. This market peaked at $2.7 trillion in 2008. But the two clearing banks (JPMorgan and BoNY Mellon) were themselves taking poorly understood risks, exposing themselves to possible loss if borrowers defaulted during the day. Despite the fact that the vast majority of underlying collateral was very high quality (such as Treasuries and agencies), the tri-party repo market became increasingly focused on the risk that a borrower would default. If an anxious clearing bank decided that it didn't want this exposure to a particular firm, it could immediately threaten the viability of that firm—and the stability of the entire tri-party repo market.

124 Money market funds need to remain liquid: Money market funds are mutual funds that—because of a special regulatory exemption devised in the 1980s after intense industry lobbying—behave in many ways like banks, but without any of the safeguards of banking. They were some of the most active lenders in commercial paper and tri-party repo markets, financing companies like Countrywide. However, because of SEC restrictions on the types of securities they could hold, a default by a major counterparty would require them to quickly liquidate the mortgage securities that might collateralize those repos. This meant that if Countrywide defaulted and the money funds got stuck with the collateral, they would be forced to sell it—at the worst possible time, pushing down prices and further destabilizing markets, potentially in fire-sale conditions.

129 "discount rate": The discount rate is the rate at which the Fed lends to banks in its capacity as lender of last resort. A bank that is considering borrowing at the discount window's "penalty rate" might worry that doing so signals to markets that it is unable to secure funding on reasonable terms from private sources. While the Fed would not announce the banks that borrowed from the discount window in real time, the disappearance of a bank from interbank lending markets could spark rumors that it was relying on the Fed for funding, calling into question its health. By cutting the discount rate, we tried to signal that use of the discount window should be viewed more as an economic decision, rather than an act of desperation.

129 find some way to use the discount window: The Federal Open Market Committee, which includes presidents of the regional Fed banks, sets the federal funds rate that is regularly adjusted to conduct monetary policy. But the decision to change the discount rate is made by the Federal Reserve Board in Washington, a separate body. Generally, changes to the discount rate are made simultaneously with changes to the Fed funds rate, which means that the FOMC is involved in the decision as a matter of practice. But in the heat of the crisis, when we were making decisions that involved new uses of the discount window, there was often not much advance consultation with or warning to the other Reserve Bank presidents.

136 "structured investment vehicles": SIVs were off-balance-sheet entities—generally "sponsored" by big banks—that issued debt and used the proceeds to buy assets, such as CDOs or MBS, which in turn served as the collateral for the debt SIVs would issue. Typically, the SIVs would buy assets that were widely traded but did not mature for years, and finance themselves with short-term funding. Their assets were more liquid than those of banks in normal times, but in some ways they had risks similar to a bank's—but without bank-like safeguards. Banks didn't always have a legal obligation to pay off the debts of the SIVs with which they were affiliated, but for reputational or other reasons, they often ended up assuming these obligations even when they were not contractually bound to do so. SIVs were often structured to circumvent accounting rules, allowing banks to avoid reflecting them in their financial statements. The result was that investors, regulators, and even the banks themselves underappreciated the amount of risk that banks were exposed to as a result of their SIV-sponsoring activities.

138 count lower-quality capital: One goal of capital is to allow firms to absorb losses without having to file for bankruptcy, but low-quality capital lacked this feature. For example, firms still have to make interest and principal payments on subordinated debt to avoid default, even in periods of distress. At this time, the only way for such investors to take losses was for the bank to file for bankruptcy. Common equity can absorb losses pre-bankruptcy, meaning it is the first line of defense to keep a bank alive.

141 foreign exchange swap lines: Under these swap arrangements, the Fed and the European Central Bank (for example) would exchange dollars and euros at the prevailing market exchange rate, while promising to reverse the transaction at the same exchange rate on a specified future date, plus interest. The ECB could then use these dollars to provide liquidity to European banks in need of dollar funding.

160 haircuts for bondholders and other creditors: A bondholder "haircut" occurs when lenders receive less than they are owed from borrowers. For example, if company A owes $100 to company B and after going into bankruptcy repays only $80 of that loan, company B is said to have received a "haircut" of 20 percent.

Five: The Fall

194 "TED spread": The three-month Treasury-Eurodollar, or TED, spread measures the difference in borrowing costs on three-month Treasury bills and the cost that banks pay to borrow from each other for three months, as reflected in the London Interbank Offered Rate (LIBOR).

195 prime money market funds: There are three primary types of money market funds: Treasury and government funds that buy Treasury and agency securities; tax-exempt funds, which invest in short-term municipal securities; and prime funds, which typically pay higher rates of interest by investing in a broader range of riskier securities, including unsecured commercial paper and asset-backed commercial paper. Institutional investors use money market funds for cash-management purposes and are often more likely to move their money at the first sign of stress than individuals or retail investors. The $300 billion outflow was primarily shifted out of riskier prime funds into the other, safer types of money market funds.

196 a four-fifths stake: This equity stake was delivered to a trust that existed independently of the government and operated for the benefit of the taxpayer.

Six: "We're Going to Fix This"

225 the government could buy $500 billion of its assets: Technically, the bank that sells $500 billion in mortgage assets to the government would get $500 billion in cash, another asset, so its leverage ratio would still be 40:1 immediately after the transaction. But either by netting out cash, a risk-free asset, or paying down $500 billion in liabilities, the bank's leverage ratio would be reduced to 20:1.

226 capital alone wouldn't stop a run already in progress: We had no way of determining then how much capital would be enough, but we knew we wouldn't have unlimited amounts of capital to deploy. That meant that guarantees were needed alongside capital to credibly backstop the system.

227 "fear index": The Chicago Board Options Exchange Market Volatility Index, or VIX, is a measure of market volatility popularly referred to as the "fear index." The measure is based on the implied volatility of options on the S&P 500 index of stocks. The VIX captures investor expectations of near-term stock market volatility—how uncertain investors are about whether and how far the S&P will rise or fall.

246 two complex new Maiden Lane vehicles: Among AIG's major liquidity needs were their securities lending operations and the credit default swaps written by AIG Financial Products on collateralized debt obligations. Maiden Lane II and III addressed these issues, respectively, by purchasing the underlying collateral from AIG and its counterparties and canceling the CDS contracts that AIG owed against them. This eliminated the risk that these contracts would continue to result in additional margin calls that would further drain AIG's cash.

Seven: Into the Fire

265 hardworking homeowners who were underwater: A home is "underwater" or has "negative equity" when the mortgage debt on the home exceeds its value. Thus, a $100,000 home with a $120,000 mortgage would have negative equity of $20,000.

282 Bank shareholders had no idea whether they would face substantial dilution: When a firm increases its number of shares of common stock, existing shareholders are "diluted," meaning they own a smaller percentage of the future profits of the company. For example, if a firm with one million shares outstanding needs to raise $1 million at $1 per share, it would issue one million additional shares. Its existing shareholders would then own half the company instead of the entire company. Of course, the firm would also have $1 million of additional cash, but if the new shares were issued at a discounted value, the value of existing shareholders' holdings would have been correspondingly diminished. So, if a bank might be forced to raise capital or receive a big government capital injection at a low price in the future, investors might be scared away, causing a downward spiral in the stock price.

284 the problem of having the government set prices . . . seemed insurmountable: Similar challenges applied to ring fencing: The complexity of determining which distressed assets to guarantee and how the government would share losses with the banks made a ring fencing approach very difficult, too. The previous Citi and BofA ring fences demonstrated that complexity: The announcement of the Citi ring fence, though critical at the time, was followed by months of haggling over which assets would be backstopped, and the BofA ring fence was actually never finalized.

302 mortgage servicers: Most homeowners don't pay mortgage payments directly to their lenders. Instead, their payments go to "mortgage servicers," companies that process payments and perform other services tied to mortgages and mortgage securities. Our efforts to keep Americans in their homes would require the competence and cooperation of the mortgage-servicing industry, but these firms were not prepared for the complexity of the challenge.

Nine: Getting Better, Feeling Worse

367 by year's end, we had recouped about two-thirds of the federal outlays for bank rescues: Following the release of the stress test results in May 2009, a number of participating banks requested to repay their TARP funds. Treasury and the bank regulators allowed this under two conditions: first, that banks had already met the capital need identified by the stress test; and second, that they demonstrated their ability to raise private capital and issue long-term debt without the support of an FDIC guarantee. Under these conditions, nine of the nineteen institutions repaid $67 billion in TARP funds in June 2009, while raising nearly $30 billion in additional common stock. After extended discussions between Treasury and bank regulators, banks were issued guidance in November 2009 allowing them to repay $2 of TARP preferred equity for each dollar of new common equity they raised. Bank of America, Wells Fargo, and Citigroup all repaid TARP funds before the end of 2009 on the heels of this guidance. By the end of December we had gotten nearly $180 billion of cash back from the bank-rescue programs out of a total maximum outstanding of about $245 billion, or about two-thirds of the total bank rescues.

369 Chart, Extraordinary Commitments, but Not for Long: *Federal Reserve* includes Discount Window, Term Auction Facility (TAF), Primary Dealer Credit Facility (PDCF), ABCP MMMF Liquidity Facility (AMLF), AIG, Term Asset-Backed Securities Loan Facility (TALF), Commercial Paper Funding Facility (CPFF), Maiden Lane, Maiden Lane II, Maiden Lane III, Asset Guarantee Program (AGP), Term Securities Lending Facility (TSLF), and central bank swap lines. Excludes all Federal Reserve purchases under the quantitative easing programs. *Federal Deposit Insurance Corporation (FDIC)* includes temporary increase in deposit insurance from $100,000 to $250,000 (pre-Dodd-Frank Act), Transaction Account Guarantee (TAG) through December 2010 (does not include Temporary Unlimited Coverage for Noninterest-Bearing Transaction Accounts under the Dodd-Frank Act), Temporary Liquidity Guarantee Program (TLGP), and Asset Guarantee Program (AGP). *U.S. Treasury Department (Treasury)* includes TARP, temporary guarantee program for money market funds, agency MBS purchase program, and gross draws under GSE preferred stock purchase agreements.

380 changed the trajectory of the recovery: 11 million households—22 percent of mortgage borrowers—were underwater, of which three quarters were current on their mortgage payments. A large share of the money spent to eliminate negative equity would have been directed to current borrowers, and as a result the overall economic impact of that would be very small. My economics team figured that increases to wealth from the reduction of negative equity would result in only an annual three- to five-cent increase in GDP for every dollar spent on debt reduction; by contrast, a dollar of stimulus used to increase income would have at least ten times that effect in the year it was received.

Ten: The Fight for Reform

390 This was a necessary condition, though not a sufficient condition: As discussed in chapter 3, low interest rates were only partly a function of monetary policy. The Fed increased short-term rates by over 4 percentage points between 2004 and 2006, but a huge amount of foreign money was flooding the country's capital markets, pushing down interest rates for longer-term products like mortgages.

390 the crisis became a kind of Rorschach test: A Boston Fed paper by three economists—Christopher Foote, Kristopher Gerardi, and Paul Willen—called "Why Did So Many People Make So Many Ex Post Bad Decisions?: The Causes of the Foreclosure Crisis" explored the data behind the causes of the housing bubble and foreclosure crisis. Instead of fraud, misplaced incentives, or new products, the twelve facts they present about the crisis make a compelling case that distorted beliefs about home price appreciation drove lenders and borrowers to make overly optimistic decisions about investments in housing.

390 repeal of . . . Glass-Steagall limits on bank activities: While much attention has been given to Congress's formal repeal of Glass-Steagall in 1999 through the Gramm-Leach-Bliley Act, in practice many of the law's original restrictions had already been lifted through regulatory changes during the 1980s and 1990s.

409 a surefire panic accelerant: Secured creditors are protected by the collateral underlying their loans in the event that a borrower defaults, which substantially reduces the risk that they will lose money. But imposing haircuts on secured creditors would mean that they could no longer count on the full value of their collateral to backstop their loan, making them far more likely to run for the exits during times of financial distress.

425 Chart, Stronger New Global Shock Absorbers: *Basel I:* Tier 1 Common requirement extrapolated from regulatory guidance that common equity should be the "dominant component" of the 6 percent Tier 1 Capital "well capitalized" standard. *Basel III:* 7 percent Tier 1 Common includes a 4.5 percent minimum and a 2.5 percent capital conservation buffer. Common capital surcharge reflects the 2.5 percent maximum surcharge currently applied to the largest global banks. The only U.S. bank currently in the 2.5 percent bucket is JPMorgan. In total, eight U.S. banks are subject to a common capital surcharge as of November 2013 under BIS standards, which will be phased in through 2019. *Basel III Adjustments:* In addition to increasing capital requirements, Basel III substantially increased the risk weights on certain types of assets and limited the extent to which various factors could count to the common equity requirement.

Eleven: Aftershocks

441 eurozone: "Eurozone" denotes the subset of sixteen European nations—later seventeen when Estonia joined at the beginning of 2011, then eighteen when Latvia joined at the beginning of 2014—that comprise the economic and monetary union using the euro as its currency, not to be confused with the "European Union," which is a broader set of twenty-eight countries that collectively function more like a trading bloc.

464 "the Boehner Rule": Under any plausible budget plan, the Boehner Rule would require massive spending cuts. In May 2011, Treasury put out a fact sheet that explained: "Even if the House Republican Budget were made law immediately, the debt limit would still have to be increased within the next several weeks. Additionally, according to Congressional Budget Office and House Budget Committee estimates, the spending included in the House Republican Budget Resolution would necessitate a nearly $2 trillion increase in the debt limit by the end of Fiscal Year 2012. Moreover, it would require trillions of dollars in additional debt limit increases beyond that amount for the next several decades." The Boehner Rule would have required trillions of dollars of additional spending cuts beyond the extreme cuts in the Republican budget proposals, which would have hurt the economy as it was trying to recover.

Epilogue: Reflections on Financial Crises

496 projected to generate a positive return for the taxpayer of more than $150 billion: We will earn well over a hundred billion dollars on our crisis response programs. The FDIC now estimates it will "lose" $88 billion on the small bank failures; however, by law it has to recoup these costs through higher deposit insurance fund assessments on all banks, so taxpayers have no exposure to those potential losses. By making the deposit insurance fund assessment based on total assets rather than total insured deposits, Dodd-Frank shifted the burden of higher deposit insurance fees toward large banks.

497 Chart, Projected Taxpayer Returns from the Crisis Response: All estimates reflect the conventions adopted by OMB and CBO for the respective programs for budget purposes, including both realized gains to date and projected future returns unless otherwise noted. These estimates may change due to future market conditions. Some estimates include financing costs (when required by law or budgetary conventions for the particular program), while others are projected on a cash-in/cash-out basis. Charts include income and costs for the financial stability programs only. They do not include figures related to the Recovery Act or tax revenues lost from the financial crisis. Unless otherwise noted, data come from Treasury Department, "The Financial Crisis Five Years Later," or relevant financial disclosures from the Federal Deposit Insurance Corporation, Federal Reserve Board, and U.S. Treasury Department.

Federal Reserve Board

Federal Reserve General Liquidity Programs. Reflects gross income and fees from each program on a cash-in/cash-out basis. For more information, see "Federal Reserve Liquidity Facilities Gross $22 Billion for U.S. Taxpayers" (http://liberty streeteconomics.newyorkfed.org/2012/11/federal-reserve-liquidity-facilities-gross -22-billion-for-us-taxpayers.html).

Bear Stearns Commitment. Reflects net realized gain/income of $765 million of accrued interest and $1.5 billion mark-to-market value of remaining assets in Maiden Lane LLC. Source: November 2013 Quarterly Report on Federal Reserve Balance Sheet Developments.

U.S. Treasury Department

TARP Bank, Credit and Auto Programs. Estimates of the impact of TARP programs and investments on the Federal budget. Includes financing costs and a market risk-adjusted discount rate. Includes Treasury portion of $425 million termination fee from Bank of America that was apportioned between the Treasury, Federal Reserve, and FDIC, and proceeds from Citigroup TruPS provided in consideration for ring fence. Source: Treasury Department, "The Financial Crisis Five Years Later," TARP Monthly 105(a) Report to Congress.

AIG Commitments. Represents realized gains on a cash-in/cash-out basis (not including financing or administrative costs). Includes repayments, other income, and canceled commitments in excess of disbursements and commitments over the life of the programs from September 2008 to December 2012. On a cash basis, Treasury realized a gain of $5.0 billion overall, while the FRBNY realized a gain of $17.7 billion. Note that Treasury's holdings of AIG common shares consisted of shares acquired in exchange for preferred stock purchased with TARP funds (TARP shares) and shares received from the trust created by the FRBNY for the benefit of Treasury as a result of the FRBNY loan to AIG (non-TARP shares). Treasury managed the TARP shares and non-TARP shares together, and disposed of them pro-rata in proportion to its holdings. In addition, as noted above, the official TARP estimates include financing costs (Treasury borrowing). A cash-in/cash-out basis (without financing or administrative costs) is used here in order to present the results of the Treasury and Federal Reserve assistance to AIG on a combined basis.

Source: U.S. Treasury Department AIG Wrap-Up and New York Federal Reserve Bank of New York AIG Financial Information.

TARP Housing Programs. The CBO May 2013 figure is an estimate of total amount disbursed over the programs' lifetimes. OMB currently estimates a $38 billion cost, assuming that all funds currently allocated to the programs are disbursed. Source: Congressional Budget Office.

Fannie/Freddie Conservatorship. $188 billion gross preferred stock purchase agreement disbursements net of $55 billion of dividends through December 31, 2012, and projected dividends through FY2023 of $220 billion, adjusted for FY2014 Mid-Session Review. Source: Office of Management and Budget FY2014 Budget and Mid-Session Review.

Money Market Fund Guarantee and State and Local HFA Initiative. Reflects Treasury estimates of income/costs.

Treasury MBS purchases. Represents taxpayers' total cash returns of $250 billion from MBS portfolio through sales, principal, and interest, which exceeds initial investment by $25 billion. The program generated a negative subsidy of $12 billion on a Federal Credit Reform Act basis. Source: U.S. Treasury Press Release "Treasury Completes Wind Down of Mortgage-Backed Securities Investment, Generates $25 Billion Positive Return for Taxpayers," March 19, 2012.

FDIC

Transaction Account Guarantee. The FDIC collected $1.2 billion in fees, net of estimated TAG losses on failures of $2.1 billion as of December 31, 2012. Does not include Temporary Unlimited Coverage for Noninterest-Bearing Transaction Accounts under the Dodd-Frank Act.

Temporary Liquidity Guarantee Program. FDIC collected $10.4 billion in fees, net of estimated TLGP losses on failures of $153 million as of December 31, 2012. Includes FDIC portion of $425 million termination fee from Bank of America, and proceeds from Citigroup TruPS provided in consideration for ring fence.

515 Chairman Bernanke pursue such aggressive monetary policy actions: A central objective of post-crisis monetary policy is to get the nominal interest rate below the nominal rate of GDP growth, which will help facilitate a softer deleveraging, or what the hedge fund manager Ray Dalio describes as a "beautiful deleveraging." The Fed was able to deploy monetary policy that helped accomplish that objective.

515 resolution authority to allow the orderly wind-down of failing financial firms: Though it is a significant enhancement to our pre-crisis toolkit, the new statutory resolution authority will not make the system invulnerable to damaging runs and contagion. While resolution authority may be effective in the case of an idiosyncratic failure, it may be less effective in addressing a panic. For instance, if resolution is triggered by a run on a systemically important firm, many other firms are likely to be experiencing at least some liquidity problems; the act of putting one firm into resolution may cause the creditors and counterparties of other firms to accelerate the rate at which they are pulling back. Committing to protect short-term debt will help slow the run, but it may not solve the problem—and will create the incentive for creditors to shorten the maturity of their exposure to banks as risk increases, thus making the broader system more vulnerable. That's why an array of firefighting tools in addition to resolution authority, such as liquidity facilities and broad-based guarantees, are needed to stem broad-based, systemic panics when they occur.

518 The principles of effective crisis response: There are lots of different types of financial crises. The principles described here are most relevant in financial crises that follow long booms in private credit in developed economies that retain the ability to borrow in their own currency and have banking systems of a manageable size relative to GDP. Emerging economies, or countries such as Greece and Ireland with unsustainable fiscal positions or banking systems many times the size of their economies, face a different set of challenges that may require a different set of policy responses, as well as a different mix of financing and restructuring.

518 tempting to try to maximize the immediate losses: Guarantees can be designed lots of different ways, and many have argued that it would be better to extend them only to short-term borrowing and never to long-term senior debt. The risk in this approach is that it strengthens the incentives for banks to fund themselves with short-term debt in the future, increasing their vulnerability to runs.

INDEX

Page numbers in *italics* refer to charts.